The Age of Revolution and Reaction
1789–1850

SECOND EDITION

THE NORTON HISTORY OF MODERN EUROPE

General Editor: FELIX GILBERT, Institute for Advanced Study

The Foundations of Early Modern Europe, 1460–1559

EUGENE F. RICE, JR.

The Age of Religious Wars, 1559–1689, *2nd edition*

RICHARD S. DUNN

Kings and Philosophers, 1689–1789

LEONARD KRIEGER

Eighteenth-Century Europe: Tradition and Progress, 1715–1789

ISSER WOLOCH

The Age of Revolution and Reaction, 1789–1850, 2nd edition

CHARLES BREUNIG

The Age of Nationalism and Reform, 1850–1890, 2nd edition

NORMAN RICH

The End of the European Era, 1890 to the Present, *3rd edition*

FELIX GILBERT

The Age of
Revolution and Reaction
1789–1850

SECOND EDITION

CHARLES BREUNIG
Lawrence University

W · W · NORTON & COMPANY
New York · London

For L.L.B.

W. W. Norton & Company, Inc., 500 Fifth Avenue, New York, N.Y. 10110

Copyright © 1977, 1970 by W. W. Norton & Company, Inc.

Cartography by Harold K. Faye
Picture research by Liesel Bennett

Library of Congress Cataloging in Publication Data
Breunig, Charles, 1920-
The age of revolution and reaction, 1789-1850.

(The Norton history of modern Europe)
Bibliography: p.
Includes index.
1. Europe—History—1789-1815.   2. Europe—History—
1815-1848.   I. Title.
D308.B795   1977   940.2'7   77-24695

Contents

Introduction   xiii

CHAPTER 1   *The French Revolution and Its Impact on Europe*   1

THE GENESIS OF THE REVOLUTION   1
THE OUTBREAK OF THE REVOLUTION   7
THE COURSE OF THE REVOLUTION, 1789–1799   16
ACHIEVEMENTS OF THE CONSTITUTIONAL MONARCHY, 1789–1792   18
DECLINE OF THE CONSTITUTIONAL MONARCHY   23
EUROPE AND THE FRENCH REVOLUTION, 1789–1792   28
ESTABLISHMENT OF THE REPUBLIC, SEPTEMBER, 1792   31
PRELUDE TO THE TERROR   36
THE REIGN OF TERROR, 1793–1794   41
THE DIRECTORY, 1795–1799   51
FRANCE AND EUROPE   57
THE WAR OF THE SECOND COALITION, 1798–1802   57
REACTION OUTSIDE FRANCE, 1792–1799   60
A FINAL APPRAISAL   63

CHAPTER 2   *Napoleon*   65

THE CONSULATE, 1799–1804   69
NAPOLEON'S ADMINISTRATION   70
THE NAPOLEONIC REGIME AS A POLICE STATE   74
PEACE WITH THE CHURCH: THE CONCORDAT   76
INTERNATIONAL DEVELOPMENTS   79
THE END OF THE SECOND COALITION: PEACE WITH AUSTRIA AND BRITAIN   79
THE REORGANIZATION OF GERMANY, 1803   81
THE EMPIRE, 1804–1814   82
THE PROCLAMATION OF THE EMPIRE, 1804   82
WAR WITH BRITAIN AND THE THIRD COALITION   86
DEFEAT OF PRUSSIA AND RUSSIA: THE TREATIES OF TILSIT, 1807   91
NAPOLEON'S GRAND EMPIRE   95
THE CONTINENTAL SYSTEM, 1806   100
THE PENINSULAR WAR, 1808–1813   101

THE SHORT WAR WITH AUSTRIA, 1809 — 103
THE EMPIRE IN 1810 — 104
THE INVASION OF RUSSIA, 1812 — 109
THE WAR OF LIBERATION, 1813–1814 — 113
THE BOURBON RESTORATION AND THE HUNDRED DAYS — 115
THE ACHIEVEMENT AND THE LEGACY OF NAPOLEON — 118

CHAPTER 3 *The Concert of Europe, 1815–1848* — 121

THE SETTLEMENT OF 1815 — 121
THE TREATY OF CHAUMONT AND THE FIRST TREATY OF PARIS — 122
THE CONGRESS OF VIENNA — 123
THE SECOND TREATY OF PARIS AND THE HOLY ALLIANCE — 131
THE SETTLEMENT OF 1815 APPRAISED — 135
THE FATE OF THE CONFERENCE SYSTEM — 136
THE CONGRESS OF AIX-LA-CHAPELLE — 137
THE REVOLUTIONS IN SOUTHERN EUROPE, 1820–1823 — 138
THE GREEK REVOLT, 1821–1832 — 142
THE BELGIAN REVOLT, 1830–1831 — 146
THE "EASTERN QUESTION," 1832–1841 — 150

CHAPTER 4 *The Industrial Revolution and Its Impact on European Society* — 155

POPULATION GROWTH — 156
BEGINNINGS OF THE INDUSTRIAL REVOLUTION IN GREAT BRITAIN — 158
THE SOCIAL IMPACT OF THE INDUSTRIAL REVOLUTION — 163
THE CONDITION OF THE WORKING CLASSES — 168
EXPANSION OF THE MIDDLE CLASS — 170
ECONOMIC LIBERALISM — 173
THE EMERGENCE OF SOCIALISM — 175

CHAPTER 5 *Restoration and Romanticism* — 180

CONSERVATISM — 180
OPPOSITION TO THE RESTORATION — 185
EARLY NINETEENTH-CENTURY LIBERALISM — 188
EARLY NINETEENTH-CENTURY NATIONALISM — 191
ROMANTICISM — 196

CHAPTER 6 *The Transformation of the European States during the Restoration Era* — 205

REACTION AND REFORM IN GREAT BRITAIN — 205
TORY RULE, 1815–1830 — 205
PARLIAMENTARY REFORM, FREE TRADE, AND CHARTISM, 1830–1848 — 210
THE RESTORATION AND THE JULY MONARCHY IN FRANCE — 216
THE BOURBON RESTORATION AND THE REVOLUTION OF 1830 — 216
LOUIS PHILIPPE AND THE JULY MONARCHY, 1830–1848 — 221
METTERNICH'S REPRESSION IN CENTRAL EUROPE — 228

Contents / vii

THE GERMANIC CONFEDERATION, 1815–1832   229
GERMANY IN THE VORMÄRZ ERA: ECONOMIC DEVELOPMENT PRIOR TO 1848   233
THE AUSTRIAN EMPIRE, 1815–1848   236
ITALY: THE BEGINNINGS OF THE RISORGIMENTO, 1815–1848   239
RUSSIA   243
   ALEXANDER I AND THE DECEMBRIST REVOLT OF 1825   243
   RUSSIA UNDER NICHOLAS I, 1825–1855   248

CHAPTER 7   *The Revolutions of 1848*   252

   THE FEBRUARY REVOLUTION IN FRANCE   254
   THE REVOLUTIONS OF 1848 IN THE GERMAN STATES   260
     PRUSSIA   260
     THE FRANKFURT PARLIAMENT   262
     THE AUSTRIAN EMPIRE   267
   THE REVOLUTIONS OF 1848 IN ITALY   272
   CONSEQUENCES OF THE REVOLUTIONS OF 1848   276

Suggestions for Further Reading   279
Index   289

Illustrations

Callet, *Louis XVI* (Photographie Bulloz) 4
David, *Emmanuel Joseph Sieyès* (Photographie Bulloz) 9
David, *The Tennis Court Oath* (Bibliothèque Nationale) 11
The taking of the Bastille (Bibliothèque Nationale) 12
Assignat (Photographie Bulloz) 23
Departure of the Heroines of Paris for Versailles (Photographie Bulloz) 24
The royal family is brought back to Paris (Bibliothèque Nationale, Cabinet des Estampes) 27
Georges Jacques Danton (Photographie Bulloz) 32
Execution of Louis XVI (Photographie Bulloz) 35
A National Guardsman (Bildarchiv Preussischer Kulturbesitz) 38
A Revolutionary committee in debate (Bibliothèque Nationale) 39
Maximilien de Robespierre (Photographie Bulloz) 43
"Only the title of 'citizen' is employed here" (Photographie Bulloz) 45
David, *Marie Antoinette* (The Louvre) 45
Swebach-Desfontaines, *Inauguration of Robespierre's "Cult of the Supreme Being"* (Musée Carnavalet) 48
The Insurrection against the Convention (Bibliothèque Nationale, Cabinet des Estampes) 50
Napoleon Bonaparte (Bibliothèque Thiers, Paris) 57
David, *Bonaparte, the Consul* (The Louvre) 66
Jean Guérin, *Josephine de Beauharnais* (Collection Girod de l'Ain) 67
Coronation of Napoleon (Bibliothèque Nationale, Cabinet des Estampes) 84
David, *Napoleon Crowns Himself* (The Louvre) 85
Turner, *The Battle of Trafalgar* (Tate Gallery) 89
Tsar Alexander I and Napoleon on the Niemen River (Musée de l'Armée, Paris) 94
"The Plumb-Pudding in Danger" (The Mansell Collection) 97
Gillray, *The Handwriting on the Wall* (Bibliothèque Nationale) 108
Debucourt, *The Café Frascati* (Bibliothèque Nationale) 108
David, *Charles Maurice de Talleyrand* (Musée Carnavalet) 109
Faber du Faur, *The Last Remnants of the Grand Army en Route to Smolensk* (Formerly in the Bavarian Army Museum, Munich) 111
The rout of Napoleon's army at the Berezina River (Musée de l'Armée, Paris) 112
Wounded soldiers brought back to Paris before the city capitulated (Musée historique de Versailles) 116

Martinet, *Napoleon's Arrival in Paris after His Escape from Elba* (Musée de la Marine, Cap d'Antibes)   117
The Congress of Vienna (Historisches Museum der Stadt Wien)   124
A masked ball in the Hofburg (Historisches Museum der Stadt Wien)   125
Lawrence, *Klemens von Metternich* (Oesterreichische Nationalbibliothek)   126
"Dividing the Cake" (Formerly in the private library of the Habsburg royal family)   130
Delacroix, *Massacre at Chios* (The Mansell Collection)   144
Battle of Navarino (Courtesy of the Académie Française)   147
Lord Palmerston (Radio Times Hulton Picture Library)   149
Mehemet Ali (John R. Freeman)   151
Doré, View of a London slum (Radio Times Hulton Picture Library)   157
Sheffield (From the Museum's Department of the City of Sheffield)   159
Manchester (Radio Times Hulton Picture Library)   160
Hargreaves' Spinning Jenny (The Mansell Collection)   161
Weaving machines in a German textile mill (Bildarchiv Preussischer Kulturbesitz)162
The Rocket (The Mansell Collection)   163
Entrance to the railway at Edge Hill, Liverpool (Radio Times Hulton Picture Library)   164
View of Bute Docks at Cardiff (The National Library of Wales)   165
Children sent to work (The Mansell Collection)   167
Refuge for the Destitute: The Male Ward (Radio Times Hulton Picture Library)171
Louis Blanc (The Warder Collection)   177
Edmund Burke (The Bettmann Archive)   182
An upper-class drawing room in Vienna (Historisches Museum der Stadt Wien) 186
Living and sleeping quarters of a factory worker in Vienna (Historisches Museum der Stadt Wien)   186
Giuseppe Mazzini (The Bettmann Archive)   192
Hegel with his students (Deutsches Literaturarchiv, Schiller Nationalmuseum) 193
Friedrich, *Ruins of a Monastery and Its Graveyard ("Abtei im Eichwald")* (Schloss Charlottenburg, Berlin)   196
Delacroix, *Liberty Leading the People* (The Louvre)   198
Cornelius, illustration to Goethe's *Faust* (Städelsches Kunstinstitut, Frankfurt am Main)   200
Peterloo Massacre (The Manchester and Cheshire Library)   207
A Chartist procession in London (The Bettman Archive)   215
Scene from the July Revolution of 1830, Paris. From *L'Histoire de Paris.* (Courtesy of the Académie Française)   220
Deputies calling the duke of Orléans to the throne (Photographie Bulloz)   221
Anonymous drawing of the Parisian restaurant *Boeuf à la mode.* From *L'Histoire de Paris*, Editions Litteraires et Artistiques. (Courtesy of the Académie Française) 222
Philipon, *Louis Philippe* (M. Paul Philipon Collection)   225
Silk weavers of Lyons (City Archives of Lyons)   226
Daumier, *Massacre in the rue Transnonain* (Collection Viollet)   227
The festival of the Burschenschaften at the Wartburg Castle (Ullstein Bilderdienst)   231
View of a factory near Munich (Bildarchiv Preussischer Kulturbesitz)   234

View of Moscow from a terrace in the Kremlin (Ullstein Bilderdienst)   243

Parade in St. Petersburg (Ullstein Bilderdienst)   247

Tsar Nicholas I (The Bettmann Archive)   248

Blindfolded Polish rebels are interrogated by Russian officers (Courtesy of MYSL, Moscow)   250

The February Days in Paris. From *L'Histoire de Paris* (Courtesy of the Académie Française)   256

Revolution of 1848 in Berlin (Bildarchiv Preussischer Kulturbesitz)   261

View of the Paulskirche in Frankfurt (Bildarchiv Preussischer Kulturbesitz)   263

Student guards at the old university of Vienna (Historisches Museum der Stadt Wien)   268

Title page of the Communist Manifesto (German Information Office)   277

Maps

France: The Governments before 1789   20
Revolutionary Departments after 1789   20
Napoleon's Military Campaigns   77
Europe in 1812   106
Europe in 1815   132
Redistribution under the Reform Bill of 1832   211

Introduction

Two REVOLUTIONS profoundly transformed the lives of Europeans in the years from 1789 to 1850: the great French Revolution and the Industrial Revolution. Any attempt to comprehend the history of Europe in this period requires an analysis of the subtle and complex ways in which they worked themselves out in the material existence, the institutions, and the ideas of Europeans. Some individuals and groups tried to resist or contain the revolutions; others accepted their consequences and tried to exploit them; no European was unaffected by them.

The French Revolution has traditionally been viewed as a major dividing line in modern Europe's history, an event which destroyed that complex of political, social, legal, and juridical institutions known as the "old regime" and inaugurated a new era characterized by a greater emphasis upon individual rights, the spread of representative government, and the emergence of a new kind of loyalty to the nation. These generalizations about the French Revolution still retain much of their validity as long as they are qualified in some significant ways.

The break with the past was not nearly as sharp as has often been contended. Some of the traditional institutions and conceptions associated with the old regime had already been challenged earlier in the eighteenth century. A series of lesser revolts and disturbances in Europe and her colonial possessions beginning about 1760 preceded and, in some respects, contributed to the major upheaval of 1789. After 1789, many traditional institutions and ideas persisted through the revolutionary and Napoleonic eras into the age of the Restoration, from 1815 to 1848. Indeed, in most parts of Europe the Restoration was dominated by rulers who reacted against the revolutionary doctrines and who, if they could not turn the clock back to the old regime, did their best to maintain the status quo against growing pressures for reform and change.

Not surprisingly, the French Revolution had its greatest initial impact upon France itself, where the revolutionaries proceeded to sweep aside the complex set of administrative institutions inherited from the old regime and to substitute for them a new, more efficient organizational structure that would at the same time be more responsive to the needs of the entire

nation. This structure, further refined or altered by Napoleon, has endured substantially to the present day. In class terms, the revolution also wrought significant changes in France; the ultimate beneficiaries were the bourgeoisie, who, having eliminated the traditional privileges of the aristocracy, made certain that political power remained in the hands of the possessors of property.

Outside of France the French Revolution and the Napoleonic regime which succeeded it had results that were both creative and destructive. During almost a quarter century of intermittent conflict between the French armies and the powers that resisted them, Europeans suffered disruption of their lives and established institutions. Old states went out of existence; new ones came into being. Territories conquered and occupied by the French underwent significant changes. In the last analysis, however, the revolutionary ideals of the French may have had more profound and lasting effects upon Europe than did their armies. In the powerful revolutionary slogan "Liberty! Equality! Fraternity!," in the fundamental political rights enunciated in the Declaration of the Rights of Man, and in the successive constitutions drawn up by the revolutionary assemblies, nineteenth-century liberals found their political programs and their source of inspiration. Even more important, France had shown during the revolution what powerful forces could be released when a people is galvanized by loyalty to a national ideal. Many of the fundamental characteristics of modern nationalism emerged for the first time during the revolution, and France provided models that were widely imitated in the century that followed.

In the long run, the Industrial Revolution undoubtedly transformed the lives of Europeans even more thoroughly than did the French Revolution, but its principal impact in the first half of the nineteenth century was restricted to Great Britain and the states lying in the northwestern tier of the European continent. Central, southern, and eastern Europe underwent similar changes only in the second half of the century. In countries affected by industrialization, long-established patterns of life were shattered as production was mechanized and moved into factories. The need to situate factories near the sources of power led to massive shifts of population and to the phenomenal growth of towns and cities. Wherever industrialization occurred, it dramatically increased the size and strength of the older bourgeoisie and brought into existence a new social class, the industrial proletariat. That these changes in class structure would have a significant effect upon the political life of the European states was inevitable. One of the main themes of the period from 1789 to 1850 was the struggle of the new manufacturing interests for political power and influence commensurate with their rising economic status.

The revolutions of 1848 provide a striking finale to the period. In the series of uprisings that swept across Europe in that year can be discerned

the combined effects of the French revolutionary legacy and the Industrial Revolution. The demands of the revolutionaries still tended most often to be couched in the political terminology of the French Revolution — constitutions, representative assemblies, and the extension of political rights — but the movements of 1848 brought into focus underlying social discontents and grievances that stemmed from the Industrial Revolution.

CHAPTER 1

The French Revolution and Its Impact on Europe

THE GENESIS OF THE REVOLUTION

WHAT FEATURES of French society under the Old Regime help explain the outbreak of the revolution in 1789? What grievances or injustices, what aspirations or ideals, contributed to the overthrow of a political system that had lasted for centuries?

One historical view that has gained currency within the last generation is that it is impossible to answer questions such as those just posed by looking at France alone. Supporters of this view charge that historians have been too inclined to regard the late eighteenth-century revolutions in Europe and America from an exclusively national perspective. Instead, they argue, the revolution in France as well as the earlier revolution of the thirteen American colonies must be seen as part of a supranational European or even Atlantic revolution that began about 1760 and continued until at least 1800. In addition to the American and French revolts, they cite disturbances in the city-state of Geneva in the 1760's and 1780's, unrest in Ireland and England in 1780, and a revolutionary disturbance in the Netherlands as evidence of a general ferment working in the period prior to 1789. One of the leading exponents of this view, Robert R. Palmer, further maintains that these disturbances, together with revolts in America and France, had a democratic character that constituted the common denominator of them all.[1] By the term "democratic" he does not mean to imply that the goal of the revolutionaries was universal suffrage or some of the other features associated with twentieth-century democracy, but rather that there emerged in this era "a new feeling for a kind of equality, or at least

[1] Professor Palmer develops his thesis in *The Age of the Democratic Revolution: A Political History of Europe and America, 1760–1800,* 2 vols. (Princeton, N.J., 1959–1964).

a discomfort with older forms of social stratification and formal rank." In political terms, the revolutionaries challenged the continued control of government by "established, privileged, closed or self-recruiting groups of men," but the positive alternatives they favored varied greatly from one country to another. ·

The argument for a European-wide or Atlantic revolution just described is supported by a considerable body of evidence and has resulted in a broadening of the perspective of historians of the late eighteenth-century revolutions. However, some critics, acknowledging that the revolutions can no longer be viewed in isolation, contend that the similarities among the revolts have been exaggerated. Can one compare meaningfully, they ask, municipal strife in Geneva with the entire complex of grievances that precipitated the war for American independence? Were not the economic and religious circumstances that provoked the Gordon Riots in London in 1780 of a quite different character from the deep-seated social and political tensions that culminated in the great upheaval of 1789 in France? Others challenge the use of the term "democratic" to describe the variety of revolutions and revolutionary movements, arguing that at least in some cases those groups initially most active against their rulers were aristocratic.

One of the most common misconceptions about revolutions is that they occur in societies that are economically depressed and on the verge of collapse. Never has this view been more clearly disproved than it was by the state of affairs in prerevolutionary France, which, during the half century before 1789, enjoyed a period of steady economic growth indicated by rising industrial production, an expansion of the volume of foreign trade, and the increasing prosperity of the merchant class. But there were certain important flaws in this generally favorable situation. First, the wealth of the country was unevenly distributed. The prosperity of the merchant class was shared, though to a less striking degree, by the nobility and the clergy who, as landowners, benefited from the rising prices of foodstuffs during the eighteenth century. This price rise was largely attributable to the increased demand for foodstuffs resulting from a rapid growth of population after 1750. But prosperity did not invariably reach all elements of the population. Because wages failed to keep pace with rising prices, artisans and wage earners in the cities suffered from a decline in purchasing power. Nor do the peasants as a group appear to have profited from the rise in food prices during the prerevolutionary decades despite the fact that they owned an estimated 30 to 40 per cent of the land in France. Their problem was an inability to produce on their relatively meager landholdings crops large enough so that a surplus remained to be sold on the market after their families had been fed and their church and feudal dues and taxes had been paid. The French peasants were undoubtedly much better off in many respects than their counterparts in central and eastern Europe, but they were still far from satisfied with their lot.

Second, the general expansion of the French economy from 1730 to the 1780's was interrupted by periodic economic crises, which brought suffering to the unprivileged groups. During the 1770's and 1780's a gradual decline in grain prices and a temporary drop in wine prices resulting from over-production worked particular hardship upon the peasantry. Landlords, trying to compensate for declining revenues, acted rigorously to collect the traditional dues owed them by peasants. Poor harvests in both 1787 and 1788 provoked a new crisis and further suffering. Acute shortages—particularly of grain—led to a marked rise in price of bread and other foodstuffs. At the same time, increased competition from British manufacturers contributed to a decline in textile production and widespread unemployment in the cities. The resulting misery among city dwellers of the lower classes helps explain why they supported the revolution of 1789 by joining in food riots and challenging their municipal governments as well as storming the Bastille and, in October, marching on Versailles.

Finally, in qualifying our generalization concerning the soundness of the French economy, we must note the desperate financial condition of the government, which contrasted strikingly with the condition of the country as a whole. The volume of trade was growing and the upper classes were prosperous, but the monarchy—which had been in financial straits ever since the reign of Louis XIV (1643–1715)—found itself unable to tap this wealth in order to meet its obligations. Faced with repeated refusals on the part of the privileged orders to abandon their traditional exemption from certain taxes, the king continued to borrow, until by 1788 the interest on the debt consumed more than half of the royal government's expenditures. Such a condition could not endure forever, yet attempts on the part of a succession of finance ministers during the decade prior to the revolution to discover ways out of the financial impasse met with such resistance that their proposed reforms had to be dropped. The crisis reached its climax in 1788 when the king, unable to secure either fiscal reform or further loans, reluctantly agreed to summon the Estates-General, a body which had the traditional right to institute taxes, but which had not met for 175 years. The convening of this body in the spring of 1789 and the subsequent secession of the Third Estate from the other two in order to form the "National Assembly" marked the first stage of the French Revolution.

Little needs to be said concerning the political weaknesses of the Old Regime. A government which could not raise adequate revenues clearly revealed its lack of political effectiveness. General confusion and inefficiency prevailed in the royal administration, which consisted of successive layers of offices, bureaus, and agencies that had piled up over many centuries, with jurisdictions that were now ill defined and sometimes contradictory. Dealing with this rigid bureaucracy—frustrating for everyone—was particularly exasperating for the enterprising merchant or landowner. Finally, in a regime which was still absolutist in theory, if not in fact, the character

King Louis XVI. *Portrait by Callet. Petit Trianon, Versailles.*

of the ruler was a matter of considerable importance. Here the Bourbon dynasty was particularly unfortunate. The times called for a ruler of intelligence and resolution—and France in 1774 got Louis XVI, honest and well intentioned, but lacking in will and unable to comprehend the dangers of the situation. Fat, dull, and slow-witted, he was the laughing stock of his own courtiers. A leading historian of the revolution, speaking of Louis XVI, concludes, "It is scarcely doubtful that events would have taken a different turn if the throne had been occupied by a Henry IV or even a Louis XIV."[2]

In a France suffering from economic and political weaknesses, what were the existing attitudes toward the regime? Crane Brinton, in his *Anatomy of Revolution*, notes a phenomenon which he labels the "desertion of the intellectuals." Analyzing four prerevolutionary societies, he argues that in each the intellectuals (defined roughly as the "writers, artists, musicians, actors, teachers and preachers") were close to unanimous in their opposition to the established regime, ". . . bitterly attacking existing institutions and desirous of a considerable alteration in society, business, and government."[3] Eighteenth-century France is the classic example of a country

[2] Georges Lefebvre, *The Coming of the French Revolution*, trans. by R. R. Palmer (Princeton, N.J., 1947), p. 25.
[3] Crane Brinton, *Anatomy of Revolution* (New York, 1957), pp. 44, 45.

where almost all intellectuals were critical of existing social and political institutions. Voltaire, Rousseau, Diderot, and Condorcet were simply the most prominent of a vast company of *philosophes* intent upon remaking society in accordance with the laws of nature. Their proposals for reform varied greatly, but they all were highly critical of existing institutions. Yet even it it can be established that the intellectuals were alienated from the regime to an unusual degree, one may still ask whether their discontent reflected that of the population as a whole. Such a question is impossible to answer with certainty. But it is a matter of record that many works critical of existing political and social institutions, such as Rousseau's *Social Contract* (1762), went through numerous editions in the years before the revolution and were apparently widely read by the educated. The ideals and aspirations of the *philosophes* also found an echo in the *cahiers de doléances*, the celebrated lists of grievances drawn up by the assemblies summoned to elect representatives to the Estates-General in 1789. Although the peasants' complaints tended to be quite specific and concrete, the *cahiers*, taken as a whole, embodied abstract demands for some kind of constitution, for the limitation of the authority of the monarchy, and for the guarantee of individual rights—all reflections of eighteenth century political philosophy. A further indication of the degree to which the *philosophes* struck a responsive chord among their contemporaries may be found in the public declarations of revolutionary leaders, who frequently echoed the sentiments of a Voltaire in their attacks upon the clergy or the views of a Condorcet in their expressions of faith in man's capacity for unlimited progress.

Finally, class antagonisms were mounting steadily during the last years of the Old Regime, and played a role in the outbreak of revolution. French society was officially divided, as it had been for centuries, into three estates. The clergy constituted the First Estate, and the nobility, the Second. The Third Estate included all the rest of the population but had traditionally been represented in the medieval assembly, the Estates-General, by members of the bourgeoisie, commonly town dwellers. To be sure, French society did not consist of neatly separated, coherent, self-conscious social groups, each pursuing its own interest. But among individuals of similar social or professional status certain common sentiments did exist; hostility was often strong toward those who were higher on the social scale and possessed greater privileges. Paradoxically, those complaining the loudest were often those best off financially—that is, the upper bourgeoisie. It was precisely because wealthy merchants and manufacturers had improved their economic position so markedly during the eighteenth century that they resented the remaining restrictions—social and political—upon their activity. For an individual of this class, two courses of action with respect to the traditional aristocracy were possible. He could try to become a noble himself, or perhaps marry his daughter to a noble, or he could set out to eliminate the privileges of the noble caste. Up to a decade or two before the revolution, many members of the bourgeoisie chose the first alternative, since it was still possible to gain entrance into the nobility, either by royal appointment or by the purchase of offices carrying noble status. Indeed, the royal courts of law and the more important administrative offices were staffed by the newer "nobility of the robe," which in contrast to the more traditional "nobility of the sword" was composed of former commoners, who were quick to forget their bourgeois origins once they received noble status. But because of an "aristocratic resurgence," it was increasingly difficult after 1760 to secure such appointments. Jealous of the centralizing and despotic tendencies of the monarchy on the one hand and of the threat to their position from the newer moneyed classes on the other, members of the French nobility did their best to defend their position and make their privileges more exclusive. Specifically, the nobles sought to regain a monopoly over appointments to high positions in the army, the church, and the government and to discourage the mingling of the aristocracy with those less wellborn. Such a campaign naturally provoked the resentment of the ambitious bourgeois hoping to improve his social status, and increased his readiness to accept affirmations of "natural rights," civil equality, equality of opportunity, and so on. The sense of frustration was perhaps greatest among wealthy financiers and merchants, because in economic position and in mode of life they were so like the nobility, but the resentment against aristocratic privilege and discrimination based on birth was shared as well by the lesser bourgeoisie—the shopkeepers, artisans, and petty bureaucrats.

The conditions of life among the peasants, who formed the great mass of the Third Estate and an estimated 80 per cent of the total population, varied widely from one region of France to another. It is particularly difficult to generalize about the sentiments of this class on the eve of the revolution. Although serfdom was rare in France by the end of the eighteenth century, many feudal or manorial obligations remained to plague the peasants—fees, dues, payments in kind to the landlords who retained ultimate jurisdiction over the peasants' holdings. To the clergy was owed the tithe, as well as a levy on grain and other farm products which was particularly resented. And a more recent burden superimposed on these traditional obligations was royal taxation, which fell most heavily upon the peasant class—direct taxes such as the *taille* (head tax) and indirect taxes like the *gabelle*, the government monopoly on salt which kept the price of this product artificially high in a good part of France. The question remains of whether peasant resentment over these obligations was any greater in the decade or so before the revolution than it had been before. Certainly France had seen peasant discontent, and even revolts, long before the eighteenth century. Yet two circumstances, in particular, appear to have sharpened the antagonism after 1750. One was a marked increase in the peasant population, which made it more difficult for peasants to support their families on the land available; the other was a tendency on the part of the landowning aristocrats to reaffirm their rights over the peasants and to make sure that they were exacting all that was due them in the way of fees and other obligations. A particular grievance in this connection was the encroachment of the landlords on various kinds of "common land," where the peasants had traditionally grazed livestock, gathered dead wood, and cut trees. Since the lords held the ultimate rights over such lands, they were permitted by the courts to break them up and put them under cultivation for their own profit. Inevitably, the result was an increase in the bitterness of the peasants toward their landlords, as the lists of peasant grievances drawn up in 1789 make clear.

To summarize, then, fairly strong class tensions had developed in France by the end of the eighteenth century. Some of the grievances of the Third Estate were long-standing, but they were sharpened after 1750 by rising food prices, by a marked growth in the peasant population, which taxed their available land resources, and finally by a reassertion of privileges and a growing exclusiveness on the part of the nobility. These ills alone were perhaps not sufficient to provoke a revolution; but they built up a sense of frustration in the unprivileged groups, and, once the revolution had begun, they caused it to turn into a mass movement of incomparable fury.

The Outbreak of the Revolution

One of the great ironies of the French Revolution is that it was most directly provoked by the class whose privileges it did much to destroy—the nobility. By their repeated refusals to submit to new taxation, the nobles finally forced the king to adopt their own proposal—that is, to summon the Estates-General, the only body they regarded as competent to levy new taxes. The nobles were convinced that they would be able to dominate this assembly and use it as an instrument for strengthening their own position at the expense of the monarchy. But the outcome was not what they had anticipated. For the election and convocation of the Estates-General in 1789 provided representatives of the Third Estate with an opportunity to assert their claim to equal status with those of the other two orders, and ultimately, when this was denied, to proclaim themselves the true representatives of the "nation."

Because the Estates-General had not met since 1614, considerable research was necessary to determine precisely how representatives should be elected to the assembly and how voting within the assembly should be conducted. The second of these questions was the more controversial. Traditionally, each estate, or order, voted as a unit. But spokesmen for the

Third Estate—particularly a group known as the Patriots, who espoused the cause of constitutional reform—realizing that the Third Estate would be outvoted on questions involving the privileges of the other two orders, came up with alternative proposals. Their plan called for double representation for the Third Estate, so that the commoners would elect as many representatives as the other two orders combined; and for voting by head rather than by order, so that each individual vote would be counted. In this way they felt they could secure a majority for their reforms, since they could count on some defections from the clergy and on the support of a few liberal noblemen. At the end of 1788 the king accepted the first part of this plan, announcing that the Third Estate could have twice as many representatives as each of the other two estates, but the question of whether the voting would be by order or by head had still not been settled when the Estates-General assembled at Versailles on May 1, 1789.

Delegates to the Estates-General had been named by voters who met in the chief town of each district. Members of the clergy and nobility had voted directly for their representatives, but voters from the Third Estate— that is, almost all male citizens over twenty-five—had named their delegates through an indirect system which had the effect of eliminating as candidates all but an educated elite drawn from the middle and upper bourgeoisie. Most representatives of the Third Estate were lawyers or career bureaucrats rather than peasants or wage earners. Indeed, some of the most prominent representatives of the Third Estate were maverick aristocrats or clergymen who could not have been named by their own orders. One such, for example, was Honoré Gabriel Riqueti, count of Mirabeau (1749–1791), who became one of the most prominent statesmen during the first phase of the revolution. Born of an aristocratic family of Provence, Mirabeau as a young man estranged himself from his family by his excesses, which more than once caused him to be thrown into prison. By 1789 he had already achieved a reputation as a violent opponent of the privileges of his own class and as a critic of the Old Regime. Despite his ugly, pockmarked countenance he had a commanding presence and soon distinguished himself as an orator. Elected a representative of the Third Estate by the voters of Aix-en-Provence in 1789, he soon manifested shrewd qualities as a tactician and emerged as the principal spokesman of the Third Estate.

Emmanuel Joseph Sieyès (1748–1836) was another important representative of the Third Estate drawn from the ranks of a different order. An indifferent clergyman in the years before the revolution, Abbé Sieyès won national renown in January, 1789, through the publication of his pamphlet *What Is the Third Estate?* This spirited attack upon the privileges of the nobility and clergy began:

The plan of this pamphlet is very simple. We have three questions to ask:

Emmanuel Joseph Sieyès. *Portrait by David. Painted in 1817 when Sieyès was sixty-nine years old. Private collection, Paris.*

1st. What is the third estate? Everything.
2nd. What has it been heretofore in the political order? Nothing.
3rd. What does it demand? To become something therein.[4]

Not surprisingly, he failed to win election to the Estates-General by his fellow clergymen, but he was named by the electors of Paris a delegate of the Third Estate. In this capacity he played an important role in the initial stages of the revolution, participating in the drafting of the Declaration of the Rights of Man and the Constitution of 1791. Abbé Sieyès demonstrated remarkable powers of survival during the revolutionary and Napoleonic eras. Serving in successive revolutionary assemblies, he voted for the execution of the king, lived through the Reign of Terror, reemerged as an important figure in the reaction that followed, and later helped engineer the *coup d'état* which brought Napoleon to power in 1799.

On the momentous occasion of the assembling of the Estates-General, the optimism of the commoners was tempered by the treatment they received from the king. The somber black costumes that the king required the representatives of the Third Estate to wear contrasted sharply with the rich and colorful attire of the nobility and the clergy. At a formal reception given for the delegates on May 2, Louis XVI kept the commoners waiting for hours and then received them coldly while representatives of the other two estates looked on.

[4] Stewart, *A Documentary Survey of the French Revolution*, ed. by John Hall Stewart (New York, 1951), p. 42.

At this point, the king had still announced no decision on the crucial problem of how votes would be counted, although a speech delivered by Jacques Necker (1732–1804), the king's finance minister, had intimated strongly that on certain questions the vote would be by order. In protest, the representatives of the Third Estate refused to present their credentials for verification; the resulting deadlock between the king and the Third Estate lasted for five weeks and was broken only when the commoners announced that they were presenting their credentials not as delegates of the Third Estate, but as representatives of the nation. After a number of parish priests who were delegates for the clergy had joined them, the commoners issued a statement proclaiming themselves the "National Assembly" of France, representing the entire nation. This declaration, dated June 17, has been termed the first genuinely revolutionary act of 1789; it was followed three days later by the more famous Tennis Court Oath. On June 20, the commoners found their regular meeting place barred to them, ostensibly for repairs. They adjourned therefore to a nearby indoor tennis court, and amid great enthusiasm, swore "not to separate, and to reassemble wherever circumstances require, until the constitution of the kingdom is established and consolidated upon firm foundations." Faced with this open act of defiance, the king wavered. At first he announced his intention of maintaining the distinction among the three orders, and declared the actions of the Third Estate on June 17 and June 20 invalid, but the continued resistance of the commoners, coupled with the desertion from their own assemblies of more representatives of the clergy and a minority of the nobles, forced him to recognize a *fait accompli*. On June 27 he ordered the remaining delegates of the first two estates to take their places in the National Assembly alongside the representatives of the Third Estate. The National Assembly set about its self-appointed task of giving France a new constitution.

Within two weeks, however, the deliberations of the Assembly were interrupted by popular demonstrations in Paris which gave events a more violent turn and also provided Frenchmen with that great symbolic act which has been associated with the revolution ever since—the storming of the Bastille. The origins of these riots are obscure; apparently they were in part a reaction to what appeared to be an alarming concentration of royal troops around Paris and Versailles. The dismissal by the king on July 11 of his chief minister, Necker, who had a popular reputation as an advocate of reform and conciliation, and the appointment of several ministers of a more conservative outlook, seemed to give substance to the rumor that the king was planning a military *coup d'état* against the National Assembly. Whether this rumor was correct or whether the king had brought in the troops to protect the Assembly, as he contended, has never been settled; in any event, the view of many Parisians seems to have been that the Assembly

The Tennis Court Oath, June 20, 1789 *by David. Members of the Third Estate raise their arms to take the oath as spectators peer through the caged windows far above.*

was in danger. Inspired by a number of agitators, some of whom were undoubtedly in the pay of Louis Philippe Joseph, duke of Orléans (1747–1793), the popular cousin of the king, crowds paraded through the streets of Paris, carrying busts of the duke and of Necker. Among those whipping up the enthusiasm of the mob was Camille Desmoulins (1760–1794), a radical journalist, whose pamphlets and speeches were at least partially responsible for the violence that subsequently occurred. The electors of Paris (who had earlier named delegates to the Estates-General and now reconstituted themselves as an active group), were alarmed, on the one hand, by the threat of a royal attack and disturbed, on the other, by the mounting unrest of the Paris mob; they therefore improvised a provisional municipal government and organized a militia of bourgeois volunteers, later christened the National Guard.

On July 14 a search for arms and gunpowder led these bourgeois volunteers to the Bastille, the celebrated old feudal fortress on the eastern side of Paris, which had served as a prison for many years. The Bastille was a symbol of royal despotism; stories were rife about the alleged mistreatment and torture of political prisoners supposed to be confined in its deep dungeons. The fortress, with ten-foot-thick walls, ninety-foot towers, and a moat, would have been easy to defend against the relatively unarmed crowd if De Launay, the governor of the prison, had not mishandled the situation. A deputation sent by the provisional municipal government of Paris from the Hôtel de Ville (city hall) to negotiate with the governor for the surrender of gunpowder was assured by him that he would not turn his cannon upon the demonstrators unless the Bastille were attacked. A short time afterward two men succeeded in lowering a drawbridge leading from the outer to the inner courtyard surrounding the prison. Although the drawbridge at the main gate into the prison was still closed and defended, De Launay, thinking that a frontal attack was imminent, gave the order to fire on the crowd. When the volley was over, some ninety-eight of the besiegers lay dead and seventy-three had been wounded. The governor's apparent betrayal of his promise provoked the mob, which had now been joined by two detachments of French guards, to fight its way into the inner courtyard and to train five cannon against the main gate. De Launay decided to surrender and ordered the main drawbridge lowered. The crowd swarmed into the prison and slaughtered six or seven of the 110 guards defending it. De Launay himself was decapitated. Ironically, the Bastille yielded only seven prisoners—five ordinary criminals and two madmen.

The fall of the Bastille, insignificant in terms of its immediate results, was

The taking of the Bastille, July 14, 1789. *The governor of the prison, De Launay, was seized by the insurgents and was later beheaded.*

an event of great symbolic importance; it marked a deepening of the revolution. Disregarding the advice of those urging him to flee the country, the king decided to attempt a reconciliation. Only a day or two after the fall of the Bastille, Louis XVI announced that the royal troops would leave Versailles and that Necker would return to his post in the ministry. He also recognized the new municipal government of Paris and the newly established citizens' militia, the National Guard. In a final gesture, he agreed during a visit to Paris to wear the tricolor cockade, which combined the white of the Bourbons with the red and blue of the city of Paris. The Paris mob had intervened successfully, as it would on many subsequent occasions during the revolution.

Careful studies have exploded some popular myths concerning the social composition of the crowd of eight or nine hundred that took the Bastille. Far from being vagabonds or criminals drawn from the lowest elements of Paris society, the attackers appear to have been primarily small tradesmen, artisans, and wage earners, people with established occupations. Their revolutionary temper can be explained in part by their discontent over rising living costs in Paris, but also by their fear that the Assembly and the hopes they placed in it were endangered by some kind of aristocratic plot. It also appears that the storming of the Bastille was a less spontaneous affair than has been generally supposed. As has been mentioned, the crowd consisted largely of formally enrolled members of the recently organized bourgeois militia, and their actions on July 14 were guided to some degree by the provisional municipal government.

Paris was not the only site of popular disturbances in the summer of 1789. At about the same time that the Bastille fell, new municipal governments were established in a number of other major cities, a development that suggests some degree of coordination in the activities of the revolutionaries. More alarming to the large landowners was the series of disturbances in the country districts which began before July 14 and mounted steadily through the summer. These riots, which came to be known as the Great Fear, arose in part from rumors that the feudal aristocracy, the *aristos*, as they were called by the peasantry, were sending hired brigands to attack peasants and pillage their land. Actually, there is no evidence of any large-scale brigandage or of a counterrevolutionary plot, and the origin of these rumors is uncertain. But they did create a near panic—particularly in the eastern and some of the western provinces—that ultimately resulted in violence against local lords and their stewards and in the burning of châteaux and of records of feudal obligations. Local police were helpless to stop this anarchy and the king did not dare employ regular troops because he feared they might join the rebels. As the violence increased, alarm spread in the National Assembly, not only among the noble deputies but also among those members of the Third Estate whose income included feudal rents from their estates. A committee appointed by the Assembly to consider the situation recommended measures of repression, but a different solution was found during the famous night session of August 4: first the viscount of Noailles and then the duke of Aiguillon, another liberal noble, voluntarily abandoned their feudal privileges and revenues; then, one by one, other deputies followed suit, renouncing privileges and rights of various sorts. The clergy relinquished their tithes, the wealthy bourgeois their individual exemptions from taxation, the cities and provinces their ancient customs and privileges, Before that dramatic night was over the feudal regime in France had been abolished and all Frenchmen were, at least in principle, subject to the same laws and the same taxes and eligible for the same offices. What provoked this apparently spontaneous sacrifice and mass renunciation of privileges? Disinterested self-sacrifice may have been the motive of some; others may have acted on impulse. But a great many deputies probably felt that their privileges were doomed anyway and that a gesture of this sort might calm the peasantry. When the formal decrees which embodied these decisions were issued, the terms were somewhat less generous than the promises of August 4. Feudal dues were not renounced outright; such a renunciation would have been too strong a threat to the principle of private property. Rather, the peasants were to compensate their landlords through a series of direct payments for the obligations from which they had supposedly been freed. In this instance, as in others during the next two years, members of the National Assembly made revolutionary gestures but remained essentially moderates, bent on safeguarding the right of private property. After all, even the delegates elected to represent the Third Estate, though they talked of equality and natural rights, were men of the bourgeoisie, hardly ready to turn the country over to the masses.

Members of the National Assembly (also referred to as the Constituent Assembly) viewed as one of their principal tasks the drafting of a constitution which would substitute a new, rational set of political institutions for the antiquated forms of the Old Regime. Before settling down to work out the details of political organization, the Assembly, following the precedent of both English and American revolutionaries, issued the Declaration of the Rights of Man and of the Citizen, a statement of the general principles on which the new order was to rest. This historic document, approved on August 27, 1789, in a sense links the eighteenth and nineteenth centuries: it is a remarkable distillation of those political ideals of the eighteenth-century Enlightenment which became, during the first half of the nineteenth-century, the gospel of European liberals.

Central to the declaration, as its title suggests, is the concept that there exist certain "natural rights" which should be enjoyed equally by all citizens. The aim of every political association, the declaration maintains, must be to preserve the natural and inalienable rights of man—"liberty, property, security, and resistance to oppression." Five of its seventeen articles deal specifically with these rights, an enumeration which recalls the Bill of

Rights of the American Constitution and the seventeenth-century English documents which inspired it: included are freedom from arbitrary arrest, trial by established laws, the presumption that a man is innocent until proven guilty, freedom of speech and of the press, and so on. In Article 6, the declaration explicitly emphasizes the equality of all men before the law.

Popular sovereignty is the second general principle asserted in the document; or, as Article 2 puts it, "The source of all sovereignty resides essentially in the nation; no group, no individual, may exercise authority not emanating expressly therefrom." Precisely how this power was to be exercised is not specified in detail, although Article 7 contains a statement concerning the law-making powers that is strongly reminiscent of the political philosophy of Rousseau: "Law is the expression of the general will; all citizens have the right to concur personally, or through their representatives, in its formation . . . ." The declaration implies the general right to vote, or universal suffrage, but we shall see that the constitution drawn up by the National Assembly interpreted the term "citizen" rather narrowly and made the right to vote dependent upon property ownership.

Indeed, the importance of property rights is reiterated in the declaration itself. It appears as one of the "natural and inalienable rights" of man, and it reappears in the final article of the declaration, "Since property is a sacred and inviolable right, no one may be deprived thereof unless a legally established public necessity obviously requires it, and upon condition of a just and previous indemnity."

Many historians, particularly Marxists, have branded the revolution of 1789 as "bourgeois," asserting that it merely substituted the rule of one privileged class for that of another. The emphasis on the "sacred" right of property found in the Declaration of the Rights of Man, the restrictions upon voting contained in the Constitution of 1791, and the actual workings of the new revolutionary regime tend to confirm the view that the regime produced by the revolution was intended to preserve the interests of the propertied classes. Yet this fact should not obscure the more radical aspects of the upheaval. Mid-twentieth-century democrats take for granted many of the rights proclaimed in 1789, but these rights had been denied to most Frenchmen for centuries. Before the revolution the mere fact that a man was born into a noble family gave him the right to receive special treatment before the law courts, to occupy certain official positions closed to others, to obtain exemption from certain taxes, and to exercise numerous other privileges. In 1789 distinctions based on birth alone were abolished forever. It is quite true that the old aristocracy of birth was replaced, in time, by a new aristocracy of wealth and that the possession of a specified minimum of property became the prerequisite for voting as well as for holding public office, but wealth and property were, in theory at least, accessible to every man. On these grounds it can be argued that this was a genuinely democratic revolution.

THE COURSE OF THE REVOLUTION, 1789–1799

After issuing the Declaration of the Rights of Man, the Assembly settled down to the more routine business of writing a constitution for France. During the two years it took to complete this task, the Assembly also acted as a legislative body, sharing with the king the responsibility for ruling the country. Before examining the problems confronting the constitutional monarchy, let us look for a moment at the subsequent development of the revolution and survey the successive phases through which it passed. Whether one should speak of a single French Revolution lasting for a decade or of several separate revolutions is a matter of interpretation, but most historians agree that the convoking of the Estates-General and the proclamation of the National Assembly in 1789 marked the beginning of the revolution and that the assumption of power by Napoleon Bonaparte in the *coup d'état* of Brumaire in 1799 marked its end.

It is easier to name France's successive governments in this crowded decade than to discern a general trend and classify the regimes accordingly. The government between 1789 and 1792 is regarded as a limited or constitutional monarchy even though the constitution was not formally completed until 1791. After issuing the Constitution of 1791 the Assembly resigned and was replaced by a Legislative Assembly elected under the provisions of the constitution. When this body had served for about a year, a "second" revolution, in August and September of 1792 resulted in the overthrow of the monarchy and the proclamation of a republic. (The French state was formally known as a republic for the remainder of the revolutionary era.) The Legislative Assembly now gave way to a newly elected National Convention, which officially ruled France until 1795 and produced a new instrument of government, the Constitution of 1793, which was never put into effect. During the period of rule by the Convention, France underwent the celebrated Reign of Terror, when power was concentrated for about a year (from the summer of 1793 to the summer of 1794) in the hands of a few men acting in the Committee of Public Safety, responsible, in theory, to the Convention. The third and final phase of the revolution, from 1795 to 1799, saw the establishment of the Directory, a regime provided for by the Constitution of 1795 (drawn up by members of the outgoing Convention), which assigned the executive power to five "directors" and the legislative power to a bicameral assembly. This was the regime which Napoleon overthrew in 1799.

In following the revolution through these successive regimes one may find it useful to keep in mind some of the interpretations of its course. One standard interpretation sees a political trend toward the left in the regimes which succeeded one another from 1789 to 1794, and a steady development back to the right from 1794 to 1799. In this connection, it is noteworthy that the political terms "right" and "left" originated during this era. It became the custom in the revolutionary assemblies for the more conservative deputies to take their places to the right of the speaker's rostrum, in the horseshoe-shaped banks of seats, while the others ranged themselves according to their political inclinations in the center or to the left of the speaker. A shift in the composition of successive assemblies did in fact occur. As the more conservative deputies of one assembly failed to be re-elected to the next, those in the center moved to the right to take their places. At the same time, the leftist members of one legislative body were forced to move to the center in the next to make room for newly elected deputies of even more radical views. This trend continued up to the end of the Terror in 1794; then it was reversed and a movement in the opposite direction set in. The question to be kept in mind is whether one can legitimately refer to the government in power during the Terror as the furthest to the left because of the composition of its assembly, or whether factors other than the political complexion of the legislators must be taken into account in evaluating the nature of the several revolutionary regimes.

According to another interpretation, strongly deterministic in character, the French Revolution followed a dynamic inherent in all revolutionary disturbances: power is inevitably transferred by a series of successive shocks to ever more radical groups until the initial momentum of the revolution is finally exhausted and a turning point is reached; then the more moderate elements may begin to regain control, or a dictator, claiming to embody the will of the people, may seize power.

A third view is presented by Crane Brinton, who borrows his terms from pathology and compares a revolution to a fever or a disease. The revolutionary fever begins with the appearance of certain symptoms; it proceeds by advances and retreats to a crisis stage, or delirium. The crisis ends when the fever breaks; a period of convalescence follows, interrupted perhaps by a relapse or two before the recovery is complete. Applying his metaphor to the French Revolution, Brinton sees the revolutionary fever rising steadily after the outbreak of the illness in 1789 until a crisis is reached in the years 1793–1794, during the Reign of Terror. The end of the Terror in July, 1794, marks the breaking of the fever and the beginning of a long period of convalescence, punctuated by brief relapses during the years of the Directory, 1795–1799. Whether Napoleon's seizure of power in 1799 should be viewed as an indication of France's "recovery" is debatable, but unquestionably the country had achieved by that year a measure of the equilibrium that had been lost during the successive crises of the revolutionary decade.

Much of the work of recent historians of the revolution has focused upon social history and class analysis, but no consensus has been reached (or probably will be reached) on an interpretation of the revolution in strictly class terms. An attempt to break down French society in the revolutionary era into cohesive economic or social groups whose members were conscious of their class identity is bound to run into a reality that was much more complex. For example, the view that the revolution witnessed the triumph of the bourgeoisie over the older aristocracy has been challenged by those who maintain that the principal beneficiaries of the revolution were not capitalists in any Marxist sense of the term but rather lawyers and bureaucrats whose ambitions had been frustrated under the Old Regime. Likewise, an analysis of the most radical element in Paris in 1793–1794, the so-called *sans-culottes*, reveals that they were not class-conscious proletarians but rather small shopkeepers, tradesmen, and artisans who shared many of the ideals of their middle-class representatives in government though they may have pressed for more active means of implementing these ideals.

One additional feature of the revolution must be mentioned before we proceed with the account of its events. This is the crucial role played by the people of Paris. We have already noted the impact upon the king of the attack upon the Bastille by a Paris mob. In the October Days of 1789, as we shall see, a Paris mob was responsible for the transfer of the court and the seat of government from Versailles to Paris. But the influence of Paris upon the course of the revolution became really evident beginning in the summer of 1792, with the advent of the "second" revolution. Had the fate of the monarchy been left to the rural population of France, it might well have survived, but an increasingly radical minority of Parisians, acting through political organizations such as the Jacobin clubs and spreading their propaganda through popular pamphlets and newspapers, provided the impetus for the overthrow of the monarchy and the establishment of the republic. In these events the elected assembly, including representatives from all over France, capitulated to the revolutionary Commune, a committee of Paris radicals who seized power from the legal government of the city on August 10, 1792. From this point on, the Commune played a leading role in the government of France, frequently dictating policy to the elected representatives of the nation. The weapon of the Paris radicals was force and the threat of force. Over and over again, carefully organized demonstrations staged outside the meeting place of the deputies succeeded in swaying the hesitant to a course of action desired by this or that faction of Paris radicals. In this way the will of a determined minority, sure of its goals, was imposed upon the more or less passive majority of Frenchmen. How this minority gained control of the government and its bureaucracy, how it enforced its decrees throughout the country, forms an important part of the story of the revolution.

Achievements of the Constitutional Monarchy, 1789–1792

After the violence of the summer and fall of 1789, a calmer period ensued; indeed, no serious disturbances erupted until the summer of 1792. The National Assembly took advantage of this interlude of relative tranquillity to initiate some of the most significant measures of the revolutionary era. Most important in terms of their long-range impact were the Constitution of 1791, the new administrative system, and the confiscation of Church lands and the promulgation of the Civil Constitution of the Clergy.

Having proclaimed in the Declaration of the Rights of Man that "men are born and remain free and equal in rights," the National Assembly immediately denied this principle in the constitution by dividing Frenchmen into "active" and "passive" citizens, a distinction based upon the amount of direct taxes one paid. Only "active" citizens—those who paid direct taxes equal in value to at least three days of labor in their particular region—had the right to vote. This arrangement denied the franchise to about a third of the adult males in France. Domestic servants were also excluded from "active" citizenship. To those who had taken the promises of the Assembly literally, this provision of the constitution naturally came as a bitter disappointment. The method of election to the Assembly further emphasized the importance of property. Citizens were denied the privilege of voting directly for their representatives. Instead they met in primary assemblies to choose "electors," for whom the property qualification was considerably higher than for the voters, and these in turn named the deputies to the Assembly. The makers of the constitution were clearly determined that the country should not be turned over to the mob.

The constitution included a system of checks and balances designed to prevent undue concentration of power in the hands of a single individual or governmental body. Still, the Legislative Assembly was clearly intended to be the most powerful political institution in the state. It had the exclusive right to initiate and enact legislation, fix tax assessments, and control public expenditures. No declaration of war or ratification of a treaty could be made without its consent, and it supervised the ministry and directed diplomacy. The King was given a veto over legislation, but it was merely suspensive since it could be overridden by the approval in three successive assemblies of the proposal in question.

France's administrative system was thoroughly overhauled by the National Assembly, and this revision reveals most clearly the impulse of the revolutionaries toward the kind of rationalization and systematization advocated by the *philosophes*. In place of the overlapping and confusing divisions, districts, and bureaus of the Old Regime, the revolutionary deputies established a new uniform administrative organization. France was divided into eighty-three *départements*, or departments; each department into *arrondissements*, or districts; each district into cantons; and each canton into communes. Each department was kept small enough so that its citizens could reach the *chef-lieu*, or capital, in no more than a day's journey by horse-drawn vehicle. Time-honored provinces like Normandy, Brittany, and Champagne were deprived of official status. The new departments were named after rivers, mountains, and other natural features of their respective regions. Such a measure was bound to offend many Frenchmen whose

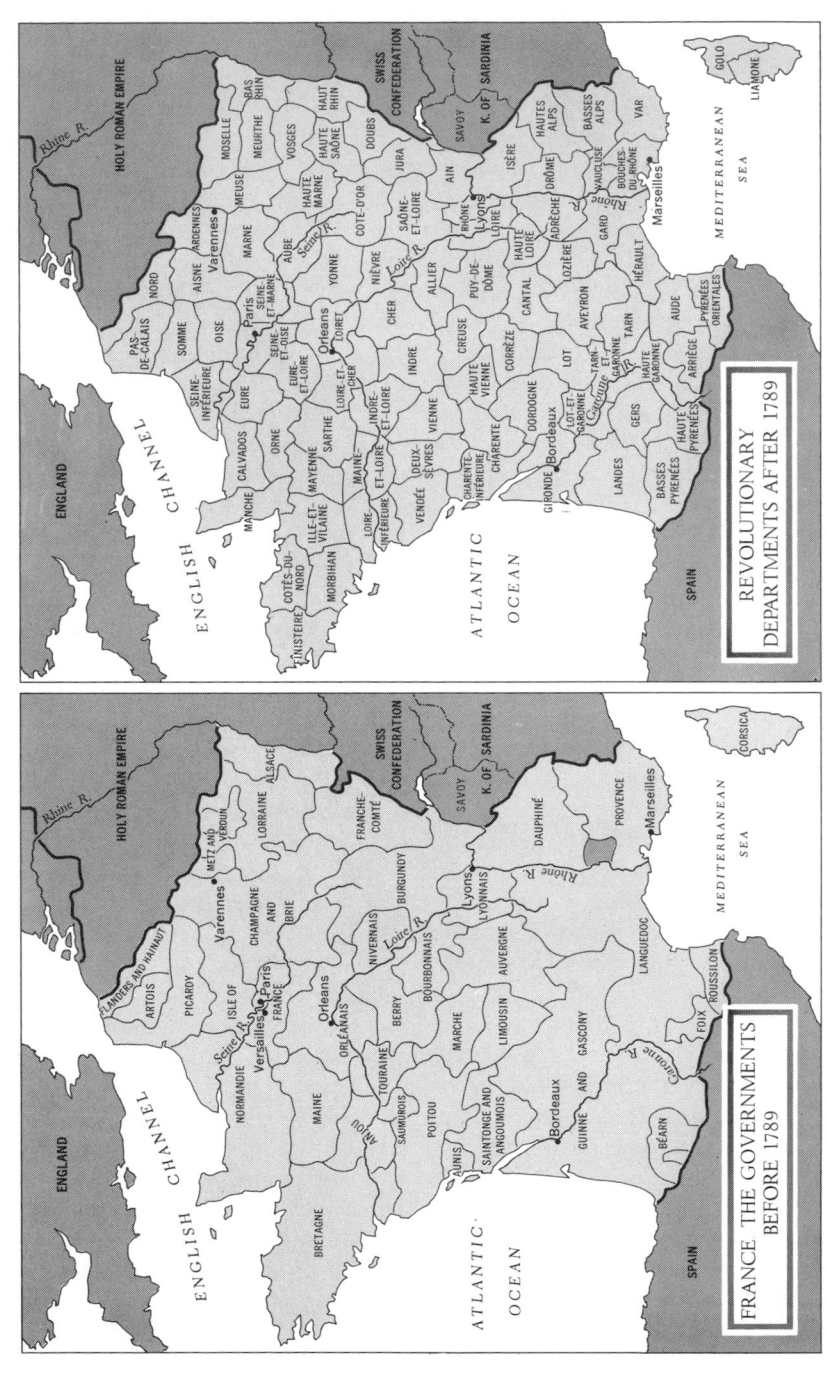

REVOLUTIONARY DEPARTMENTS AFTER 1789

FRANCE THE GOVERNMENTS BEFORE 1789

attachment to their particular regions was strong, but the revolutionaries hoped precisely to eliminate differences among their countrymen, to create unity of feeling and loyalty to the new regime.

At the same time, a substantial decentralization of government was introduced. Local and regional officials were elected (again only "active" citizens had the right to vote); at each level of government, an elected council served as both the deliberative body and the permanent executive bureau. Lacking training and experience, these officials had difficulty in carrying out all the tasks with which the royal bureaucracy had formerly been charged. The result was considerable confusion and inefficiency, particularly at the local level. Subsequently, Napoleon replaced the elected officials of the revolutionary era with a corps of appointed functionaries, carefully supervised from the capital by the minister of the interior; however, the departments and districts established in 1789–1790 survived the revolution and have persisted through numerous changes of regime to this day.

The most critical question facing the National Assembly in 1789 was how to finance the government; it was, after all, Louis XVI's failure to solve this problem that had brought on the revolution. The easiest, and in some ways the most obvious, solution would have been to repudiate the national debt, but this option was never seriously considered by the men of property who composed the Assembly, and who in many instances were themselves creditors of the government. Other alternatives were considered and some were tried. First, the Assembly imposed direct taxes upon income from land and other sources, but it failed to raise the anticipated revenue. The Assembly then instituted a "patriotic tax," a kind of voluntary capital levy, with the individual expected to give a quarter of a year's income to the government, in payments spread over three years. Since this tax was not compulsory, the results were naturally disappointing. Meanwhile the deficit in the national treasury continued to mount; the government had to find money somewhere.

The solution ultimately adopted—the confiscation of the land of the Catholic Church—was full of consequences for successive revolutionary governments and constitutes one of the most controversial decisions of the whole era. Among the most frequently voiced arguments used to justify the seizure of the Church's land was the claim that this land was not private property in the sense implied in the Declaration of the Rights of Man. Rather, the Church was a "corporation" which existed to perform certain services and which therefore had a special status under the law. If the state assumed the obligation for guaranteeing these services, it could "take back" the land from the Church. Defenders of the Church challenged such reasoning, arguing that a corporation as well as an individual had certain rights and that one could no more legitimately be deprived of its property than the other. By November, 1789, the decision had been reached. The

Assembly voted to place the ecclesiastical land at the disposal of the state, which assumed the obligation of paying the clergy, meeting the expenses of worship, and relieving the poor.

The confiscation of Church lands did not solve the financial problem of the government immediately. Land could not, after all, be used to pay the state's debts. The government planned to sell the lands; in the meantime, it issued to its creditors interest-bearing notes (known as *assignats*) which had the former Church lands as security. Whoever acquired *assignats* was entitled to certain privileges in the purchase of Church lands. The state was to retire the notes as the lands were sold. But not long after the *assignats* had been issued, they began to circulate as paper currency, and the government yielded to the temptation to put more and more of them into circulation. So began the inflation that formed an important part of the history of the revolution. During the later stages of the revolution, as the government printed more and more *assignats* to meet its obligations, they lost over 99 per cent of their face value. Yet the inflation of these years was not without its benefits: it enabled successive revolutionary regimes to liquidate much of the national debt by paying off their creditors in cheap money, and it spurred the growth of a class of enterprising businessmen who acquired the *assignats* at their depreciated value and used them at their face value to purchase Church lands.

Perhaps more significant than the purely economic consequences of the confiscation of Church lands was the new relationship established between the French state and the Catholic Church. Among the obligations the National Assembly agreed to assume were payment of the clergy and maintenance of the churches. Details of this arrangement were spelled out in the Civil Constitution of the Clergy, completed by July, 1790, which not only set salary scales for the various ranks of the clergy but also reorganized the Church. Old dioceses were abolished and new ones were created to coincide with the newly formed administrative departments. Parish priests were to be elected by the district assemblies and bishops were to be named by the department assemblies, the same bodies that functioned as local and departmental governments. The pope had no voice in the appointment of the clergy; he was simply to be notified of the choices.

This arrangement was clearly unacceptable to the pope, particularly since it had been drawn up by the National Assembly without any consultation with Roman authorities. And when the Assembly decided in November, 1790, to require an oath in support of the constitution and the Civil Constitution of the Clergy from all public servants, the stage was set for a bitter struggle between Pius VI, pope between 1775 and 1799, and the revolutionary government. Those priests who agreed to take the oath became a part of the new "constitutional" church; the others, a little more than half the clergy, were branded "refractory" priests by the Assembly and were subjected to intense persecution. Perhaps no single action of the

Assignat. *One of the interest-bearing notes issued by the revolutionary government using nationalized church lands as security.*

revolutionary governments caused greater resentment among Frenchmen than the policy toward the Church. Though Napoleon was later to reach a compromise with the pope which resulted in improved relations, the bitterness of many French Catholics toward the revolution and toward those who carried on the revolutionary heritage dates from this era.

Decline of the Constitutional Monarchy

Despite certain errors and despite the animosity it aroused among the clergy and some other groups, the government of the National Assembly did come to grips with a number of France's fundamental problems and was responsible for most of the constructive reforms of the revolutionary era. Why did this regime survive only until 1792? Who was responsible for the failure of France's first experiment in constitutional monarchy?

Exponents of a deterministic interpretation of the revolution argue that nothing the king or his ministers might have done could have saved the constitutional monarchy from the fate it suffered in 1792, that it was only natural for control of the revolutionary government to pass from moderate to more radical leaders.

Without rejecting entirely this view, one may still single out certain mistakes made by Louis XVI and his advisers, certain actions by his opponents, and certain initiatives taken by foreign powers, which contributed to the ultimate downfall of the monarchy.

Louis XVI could hardly be expected to collaborate wholeheartedly with an assembly which had deprived him of powers traditionally held by French rulers. Moreover, as early as October, 1789, he and the members of his family were subjected to indignities, an experience which increased his hostility to the revolution. During that fall, mounting unemployment combined with a shortage of bread created renewed unrest among Parisians. Alarmed by the threat, the king summoned troops to Versailles, contending that he must protect the National Assembly from the Paris mob. But his action gave rise once more to rumors that he intended to use the troops against the Assembly and the revolutionary cause. In these circumstances a more or less spontaneous demonstration of Parisian women for bread on October 5 was transformed by popular agitators into a "march on Versailles." Along the twelve-mile route the women were joined by adventurers and curiosity seekers. The climax of the October Days came early the following morning, when some of the angry mob invaded the palace and were fired upon by troops. Entering the inner rooms, they forced the queen, Marie Antoinette, to flee for her life to the king's apartments. Only by appearing on a balcony with his family was the king able to appease the crowd. Even so, he was forced to agree to leave Versailles, where he was thought to be surrounded by evil advisers, and move to Paris. Accordingly, the royal family departed the same day, in a carriage escorted by the cheering mob. The king took up residence in the Tuileries palace, in the heart of Paris, and the National Assembly followed him to the new seat of government.

Departure of the Heroines of Paris for Versailles, October 5, 1789. *A variety of weapons was assembled for the march on Versailles.*

Though the king outwardly collaborated with the revolutionary government in the months that followed, he had serious reservations about the regime and his position in it. He was particularly offended by the measures taken against the Church, and clearly sympathized with members of the clergy who refused to take the oath in support of the constitution. Among his advisers were many who counseled resistance to the Assembly and its decrees. And even if the king had wanted to accept his responsibilities under the constitution, such a course would have been difficult because of the activities of the *émigrés*, those who had left France in the early stages of the revolution in the hope of stirring up a counterrevolutionary crusade to restore the Old Regime. As early as July, 1789, many members of the court had fled to seek the support of the Holy Roman emperor (whose power stemmed from his rule of Austria), the king of Prussia, and other European monarchs in combating the revolution and restoring the king to his rightful position. Foremost among the *émigrés* were the count of Provence and the count of Artois, Louis' younger brothers, who were far more uncompromising than the king in their opposition to the revolution, and whose projects Louis was forced to disavow on more than one occasion. That Louis ultimately sought the aid of his brother-in-law Leopold II of Austria (ruled 1790–1792), and communicated through intermediaries with other European monarchs is beyond question, but the charges that he maintained close ties with the *émigrés* are without foundation; actually, their plotting more often than not proved a source of embarrassment to him. It has also been suggested that the failure of the constitutional monarchy was caused by the absence of outstanding leaders among the moderates. Had a truly skillful minister emerged, it is argued, he might have reconciled the king to his constitutional role and brought about the necessary collaboration between the king and the various factions in the Assembly. But no such individual appeared. Neither of the two most prominent statesmen in France during the constitutional monarchy, Mirabeau and the marquis de Lafayette (1757–1834), appears to have been of sufficient stature. Mirabeau, with his outstanding oratorical ability, was the unquestioned leader of the National Assembly for a time, but he was never wholly trusted by the more righteous members, who could not forgive him his dissolute past. And despite his conviction that the best regime for France would be one in which the monarch retained strong powers, he never enjoyed the full confidence of the king. His premature death at the age of forty-two in 1791 has been lamented by those who argue that he was the one statesman capable of saving France from the excesses that followed, but the consensus of modern historians is that Mirabeau's political position and prestige had so seriously deteriorated by 1791 that he could not have substantially altered the course of events.

Lafayette, despite his considerable prestige, was not a man of great intelligence or political shrewdness. He had won his reputation as a military leader in the American Revolution, and enjoyed substantial popularity during the initial phases of the French Revolution, first as a liberal noble who voted with the Third Estate, and later as commander of the National Guard of Paris. But he was a poor speaker and lacked influence in the Assembly. And despite his services to the royal family during the October Days, when he protected them from what might have been even greater violence, he was not popular with the king and queen.

The absence of effective leadership in the moderate camp was all the more important to the monarchy because of the steady growth in influence between 1789 and 1792 of radical "clubs," which ultimately came to favor a republican form of government. The most famous of these was, of course, the organization of Jacobin clubs, which after the downfall of the monarchy in 1792 became the most important political group in France and provided the revolution with some of its most celebrated leaders. The Jacobins had their origins among a group of radical deputies in the National Assembly who in 1789 formed the Society of Friends of the Constitution. This group became known as the Jacobin Club when it began to hold its meeting in the library of a former Jacobin monastery in Paris. At first it was merely a debating society, where deputies from the Assembly discussed radical policy, but it soon broadened its membership to include nondeputies as well, and established ties with similar clubs in other cities of France. Gradually, a vast network of clubs was built, with branches all over the country communicating with one another, holding district meetings, dispensing propaganda, and attempting to influence elections. The membership of the Jacobin clubs was overwhelmingly middle class, consisting primarily of professional men and educated businessmen, though a number of well-to-do artisans joined as the organization grew. With its centralized structure, its strict discipline, and its ties at the local level, the Jacobin machine resembled the single party of the twentieth-century totalitarian state. Mastery of the organization proved a considerable asset to radical leaders in undermining the monarchy, and it remained a valuable instrument of control after the establishment of the republic.

While Louis XVI's attitudes, the absence of effective moderate leaders, and the growth of the Jacobin clubs all contributed to the increasing alienation of the king from the revolutionary regime, the episode which probably sealed the fate of the monarchy was his attempt in June, 1791, to flee the country with his family. With the aid of the Swedish Count Hans Axel von Fersen, Marie Antoinette's lover, the royal family managed to escape from the heavily guarded Tuileries on the night of June 20, and the royal carriage made for a point on the border of Luxembourg. Royal troops were to ensure the safety of the king in his passage through France until he was met at the border by Austrian troops dispatched by the queen's brother, Emperor Leopold II. But the plan went awry when the royal family was recognized and their carriage was halted at Varennes, near the border. There they were detained until orders came from the Assembly to seize the king and bring

The royal family is brought back to Paris after its attempted escape from France, June 25, 1791.

the royal family back to Paris. What is perhaps most surprising about this episode is that it did not lead immediately to the dismissal of the monarch. Some radicals did indeed demand at this time that the king be declared to have abandoned his throne and that he be replaced by a new executive, but the Assembly was still moderate enough to reject this solution, recognizing that the radicals would probably gain control if the monarchy were abandoned. The moderate majority therefore adopted the fiction that the king had been abducted by enemies of France, and went ahead with plans to promulgate the Constitution of 1791, which retained the constitutional monarchy. However, after the flight to Varennes, Louis was little more than a prisoner of the Assembly.

How long the regime would have survived in peacetime it is impossible to say. The new Legislative Assembly, which met in October, 1791, was torn increasingly by factionalism. Disputes between local officials and the Assembly hampered the operation of government. But the major crisis which undermined the regime was the outbreak of war in April, 1792. The reasons for the war may be found partly in the reactions of the rest of Europe to the French Revolution. These will be discussed shortly, but first let us consider briefly those in France who desired war. Foremost among them was the king, who as early as 1790 considered asking for the intervention of foreign powers in the hope that a military demonstration by the Austrian and

Prussian rulers might strengthen his own hand and enable him to intimidate the revolutionaries. By the spring of 1792 he was convinced that his only salvation lay in a war between the revolutionary government and a coalition of European rulers, a war which—he thought—would end in defeat for the French armies. He would then act as mediator between the French people and the victorious powers. The several appeals for intervention which Louis accordingly directed to his fellow monarchs did indeed help to precipitate the conflict.

The most important group desiring war was the Girondins, members of a faction within the Legislative Assembly who were so named because a number of their mainstays came from Bordeaux, in the department of the Gironde. Since their most prominent spokesman at this stage was Brissot de Warville (1754–1793), they were also known to their contemporaries as the Brissotins. Brissot and some of his Girondin associates were at this time members of the Jacobin Club, but a division developed between Jacobins and Girondins in the final months of the Legislative Assembly and the two factions openly split after the National Convention was elected in September, 1792. In the spring of 1792 the Girondins hoped to precipitate war for two reasons. First of all, unlike the king they were convinced that the revolutionary armies would prevail over their enemies and that a war would make it possible to spread the benefits of the revolution beyond France. In short, a war would become a crusade in which the French armies would carry the torch of liberty to oppressed peoples still living under absolute rulers. In this goal they were encouraged by individuals who had come to France (in a kind of reverse emigration) hoping to enlist the support of the French for the cause of revolution in their own countries. Second, although this idealistic aim was most important to the Girondins, they also believed that a declaration of war would lead to the appointment of a Girondin ministry and a corresponding rise in their influence over the Assembly and the king.

In any event, both the king and the Girondins did what they could to heighten the tensions that existed between France and its potential enemies in the spring of 1792 and thus precipitate the conflict which they thought would serve their respective purposes. Both were mistaken in their expectations; the war which began on April 20 did much to hasten the downfall of the monarchy and to strengthen the extremist elements which ultimately won control from the Girondins.

Europe and the French Revolution, 1789–1792

To the first news of the revolution in France the response of many foreigners was ecstatic. William Wordsworth's rapturous cry is one of the most celebrated: "Bliss was it in that dawn to be alive. . . ." The Whig statesman, Charles James Fox, termed the fall of the Bastille "much the greatest event . . . that ever happened in the world! and how much the best!" In Germany the philosopher Johann Gottfried von Herder pronounced the revolution the most important movement in the life of mankind since the Reformation and saw it as a no less decisive step toward human freedom. Numerous associations sympathetic to the French cause sprang up in England; their members were primarily dissenters and radicals. Some of these likened the revolution of 1789 to England's own Glorious Revolution of 1688 and linked the struggle of the French for freedom with their own strivings for parliamentary reform. Certainly the educated classes throughout Europe followed the events of the revolution with the greatest interest and were familiar to a surprising degree with what was going on in France. One must remember that at this time, France was still the leading nation in Europe, the country whose literature, art, and manners were most admired.

But this initially enthusiastic response was followed by a less favorable reaction. In England, the celebrated Whig statesman, Edmund Burke (1729–1797), who was skeptical of the French Revolution from the start, in 1790 published his famous indictment, *Reflections on the Revolution in France*, in which he denounced the excesses of the revolutionaries and questioned the entire philosophy of "natural rights." Before long, others in England began to be disturbed by the effects of revolutionary propaganda at home and to call for measures curbing the radical associations. A similar change of heart occurred among admirers of the revolution in the German states, though their deepest disillusionment came only with the excesses associated with the Reign of Terror in 1793–1794.

The initial reactions of the rulers in Europe were complex and varied. In the light of what afterward occurred, it would be tempting to infer that all European monarchs "trembled on their thrones" at the news of the revolution and foresaw similar threats to their own positions. But this was not the case. Instead, events in France were viewed for the effect they might have on the complicated game of international politics. For the moment, France could be discounted as a major force in European diplomacy. In fact, Frederick William II, the ineffectual king of Prussia who succeeded Frederick the Great in 1786, saw the revolution at first as an opportunity for Prussia to detach France from its alliance with Austria (dating from the Seven Years' War) and to bring it into the existing alliance between Prussia, England, and the Dutch republic (Holland). Negotiations to this end proved fruitless, but they suggest that neither ideological considerations nor fear of revolution prevented the Prussian king from hoping for a tie with revolutionary France. Leopold II, the Austrian ruler, who came to the throne in 1790, sympathized with the plight of his brother-in-law and sister, the king and queen of France, but he did not undertake a crusade to rescue them from the revolutionaries. Indeed, Leopold was far more concerned at first with reestablishing order in his own Habsburg lands, which were in a state of turbulence after ten years of rule by Joseph II, his reforming predecessor. He was faced not only with demands from the Magyar nobility in Hungary for greater autonomy, and with awakening nationalist sentiment in the Bohemian part of the empire, but also with open revolt in the Austrian Netherlands (later Belgium). His principal effort, therefore, was to establish peace within the empire and to maintain peace abroad. Once he had subdued the revolt in the Netherlands, he was willing to make a gesture toward the French ruler. He joined the Prussian king, Frederick William, in the Declaration of Pillnitz (August 27, 1791), which stated that French affairs were the interest of all Europe and that the two sovereigns might intervene to protect Louis XVI if the other European powers would support them. Yet Leopold was well aware that since England would not consent to such an arrangement, he would not have to fulfill the obligation. As long as Leopold was on the Austrian throne, no war with France occurred. But his sudden death on March 1, 1792, and the succession to the throne of his less cautious young son Francis II, altered the Austrian position, bringing into prominence advisers who favored a more belligerent policy toward France.

War might still have been averted if the change in Austria had not coincided with the advent to power in France of a ministry dominated by the Girondins, who, as we have seen, were the leading advocates of a crusade of liberation. Charles François Dumouriez (1739–1823), a veteran soldier and adventurer, was minister of foreign affairs in the new government. Though not himself a Girondin, he strongly favored war, in which he hoped to play a leading role and thus achieve influence over the king. Pretexts for a conflict with Austria were not hard to find. The French government had repeatedly protested the activities of the French *émigrés* on Austrian soil and the leniency of the emperor toward them. Disagreement also existed concerning the claims of German princes who had been deprived of their feudal rights in the French province of Alsace by decrees passed on August 4, 1789. The princes had refused the indemnity offered by the French government, instead demanding the restoration of their rights and appealing for support to the Austrian emperor. Neither of these issues was important enough of itself to cause a rupture, but feeling had mounted so high in France that on April 20, 1792, the Assembly voted overwhelmingly to declare war on Austria. Almost immediately, the king of Prussia decided to join the Austrian ruler. Both were convinced that France, torn by factionalism and internal dissension, could be easily defeated.

Initially, their expectations proved correct. The French armies were ill prepared for the conflict. Half of the officer corps had emigrated, and many of the men had deserted; new recruits were enthusiastic but ill trained. Dumouriez's strategy was to invade the Austrian Netherlands, but in their first encounter, the French troops broke ranks and fled in disorder; a number of regiments even went over to the enemy. Had the Austrian and Prussian armies mounted a full-scale invasion at this point, France might have been defeated, but the German rulers were reluctant to devote all their resources to the war against France because of their concern over events in

Poland, which Russian armies had entered in April, 1792. Until an agreement was reached by the Austrian and Prussian rulers with Catherine the Great over the disposition of Polish territories, they hesitated to proceed against France.

Establishment of the Republic, September, 1792

Meanwhile, the initial reverses of the war produced an internal crisis in France that culminated during the late summer of 1792 in the overthrow of the monarchy and the establishment of a republic. As news of the first defeats reached Paris, and as the military situation grew steadily worse, popular discontent over the conduct of the war mounted. French officers were charged with betraying their troops. Aristocrats and refractory priests were suspected of being enemy agents acting in collusion with the hated *émigrés*. Finally, many were convinced that the king himself was engaged in treasonable negotiations with the monarchs who were opposing France. To this tension and fear resulting from the war was added an economic crisis that manifested itself in higher prices, marked depreciation of the *assignats*, and a food shortage caused in part by the requisition of supplies for the armies.

All these circumstances created a new revolutionary mood in the country. But the real impetus for the "second" revolution came from a determined minority of Paris radicals—many of them members of the Jacobin clubs—who were prepared to exploit the situation in order to seize power.

Their first step was to secure control over the administrative districts of Paris. For purposes of administration the capital was divided into forty-eight *sections*, each with its own assembly of "active" citizens who ruled the district and chose representatives to the city council. Because many eligible citizens took no interest in the government of their *sections*, radical politicians gradually managed to gain control of the assemblies and turn them into political action groups to be used for revolutionary purposes. These Jacobin-dominated bodies played a crucial role in the insurrection of August 10, 1792.

This uprising was triggered in part by the publication in Paris on August 3 of a manifesto that had been issued by the Prussian duke of Brunswick, commander in chief of the forces allied against France. With Prussian troops poised on the border of France, the duke declared the intention of the allies to restore Louis XVI to full sovereignty, and threatened to destroy the city of Paris if any harm should come to the royal family. The manifesto seemed to confirm popular suspicions concerning the king's treason. Representatives of the Paris *sections* reacted by presenting a petition to the Legislative Assembly demanding the deposition of Louis XVI. At the same time radical leaders completed their plans for an insurrection. They abolished the distinction between "active" and "passive" citizens in the *sections* and thus secured the support of the working classes in their districts. During

Georges Jacques Danton. *Anonymous portrait. Contemporaries commented on Danton's pockmarked visage and his brilliant eyes. Musée Carnavalet. Paris.*

the night of August 9–10 the tocsin was sounded, signaling the beginning of the uprising. Delegates of a majority of the *sections* succeeded in ousting the legal municipal government from the city hall and establishing a revolutionary Commune as the government of Paris. Meanwhile the mob, carefully organized by radical leaders, laid siege to the Tuileries, which was defended only by the king's Swiss Guard and a few loyal units of the National Guard. The king, losing heart, took refuge with the deputies of the Assembly in their meeting hall. As the attack on the Tuileries was intensified he gave orders to the Swiss Guard to lay down their arms, hoping that they would be spared. Instead, the mob invaded the palace, and enraged by their own losses, butchered the Swiss Guardsmen and the royal servants as well. The king was not pursued to his place of refuge, but the Assembly, yielding to pressure from the newly formed Commune, ordered him suspended from his functions and turned him and his family over to the Commune for imprisonment.

The removal of the monarch left the nature of the regime temporarily in doubt. The Legislative Assembly was unwilling to pass judgment upon the monarch, so it decided to summon a National Convention, to be elected by universal manhood suffrage, which would decide the fate of the king and draft a new constitution. In the meantime the Assembly named a provisional council of six ministers to hold executive power until the Convention could be named. In the weeks that followed, both the Assembly and the new ministers found their authority challenged and often usurped by the Paris Commune, which not only asserted its jurisdiction over the capital but sent delegates to the provinces to oversee and interfere with government officials. For six weeks these three bodies—the Assembly, the council of ministers, and the Commune—vied for control; more often than not, the will of the Commune prevailed.

Among the ministers named by the Assembly, the most prominent was unquestionably Jacques Danton (1759–1794), a lawyer and political organizer who had risen rapidly to leadership in the Jacobin Club because of his active involvement in almost every radical plot in Paris since the beginning of the revolution. Most recently he had distinguished himself as one of the principal organizers of the insurrection of August 10. Opinions differ as to Danton's real capabilities as a statesman, but he seems to have responded to the needs of the hour. He was an excellent orator, popular with the Parisians, and appeared to embody the patriotism required in the desperate situation in which France found herself. Prussian troops had continued their advance on French soil. With the enemy before Verdun, the last obstacle on the road to Paris, Danton called upon his countrymen to defend their country: "To triumph over the enemy . . . we must be bold, still more bold, ever bold, and France is saved." [5]

At this juncture, between the insurrection of August 10 and the assembling of the Convention on September 21, the celebrated September Massacres occurred. They must be viewed against the background of military defeats that appeared to spell imminent disaster for France. The prisons of Paris were overflowing with political prisoners—refractory priests, aristocrats, and royalist sympathizers arrested after August 10. All were suspected of treason. Somehow the rumor started that the prisoners were plotting to break out and attack from the rear the armies defending France, while the Prussians attacked from the front. To forestall this rumored conspiracy, patriotic mobs fell upon the prisoners, dragged them from their cells, and after summary trials, massacred them. More than a thousand were killed in this brutal fashion in a few days. Responsibility for the murders has never been determined, but the proceedings appear to have been carefully organized and no real attempt was made by the council of ministers or the Commune to halt them. Regardless of who was to blame, the gruesome September Massacres went far toward discrediting the revolution among its remaining sympathizers abroad.

Since the elections for the National Convention occurred at about the same time as the September Massacres, it is hardly surprising that royalist sympathizers stayed away from the polls; indeed, in Paris the Commune used terrorist methods to keep them from voting. Despite the provision for universal manhood suffrage, only 700,000 out of 7,000,000 qualified voters

[5] Quoted by Leo Gershoy, *The French Revolution and Napoleon* (New York, 1964), p. 221.

cast their ballots. Those whom they named to the Convention were overwhelmingly in favor of the republic. The first act of the newly assembled Convention on September 21, 1792, was the formal abolition of the monarchy in France. A supplementary decree passed the following day stated that henceforth all public documents would be dated according to a new revolutionary calendar in which September 22 became the first day of "the Year I of the French Republic."

The decrees just mentioned were passed unanimously. Before long, however, the differences which had split the left in the old Assembly reappeared among the members of the Convention. On the right now were the Girondins. On the left sat the group known as the Mountain, headed by Danton and some of the other leading Jacobins. Between these two groups, each of which held about 150 seats, lay the Plain (sometimes scornfully called the Marsh or the Belly), consisting of four hundred or more deputies who sometimes voted with the right, but usually ended by throwing their support to the Mountain. The history of the first eight months of the Convention is the story of the struggle between the Girondins and the Mountain for control, a struggle which the Mountain had won by the summer of 1793.

At first, both the Girondins and the Mountain numbered Jacobins among their members, but the leaders of the Mountain gradually forced the Girondins from the club, and eventually dominated it to such an extent that "Mountain" and "Jacobins" became almost synonymous.

To define the essential differences between the Girondins and the Jacobins is not easy. Deputies of both factions were bourgeois, not workers, though in general the Girondins may have come from somewhat higher social strata. Both voted for the republic. Both apparently favored continuation of the war against France's enemies. It has been said that the two may have differed in temperament rather than in class or doctrine. The Girondins, who would certainly have been considered dangerous radicals in any other country in Europe at this time, now occupied the moderate position in France, convinced that the revolution had gone far enough and opposed to any further social leveling. They tended to emphasize "liberty" in their speeches, advocating—among other kinds of freedom—the exemption of trade and industry from regulation by the state. Because many prominent Girondins came from the provinces, they distrusted Paris and the interference of the Commune in national politics. Though they had done nothing to prevent the September Massacres, they subsequently condemned those who were responsible for them.

The Jacobin leaders, though by no means all alike in temperament, were more inclined to emphasize "equality" in their public declarations. They favored the elimination of all civil and political distinctions, and although they were not prepared to abandon the principle of private property, they tended to be sympathetic toward the underprivileged, and to admit the right of the government in certain circumstances to intervene in the economy for the welfare of the society as a whole. Specifically, they inaugurated a system of government regulation of prices and wages in order to control the inflation from which France was suffering, and openly advocated confiscation of the wealth of *émigrés* as well as of priests. Whether they favored these measures as a matter of principle or because they appeared expedient is hard to determine. While not averse to adopting policies which would help them secure and maintain political power, the Jacobins were, it appears, genuinely convinced that they alone could save France.

Perhaps the most important reason for the victory of the Jacobins was that the Girondins had become moderates prepared to compromise or even vacillate in a situation that seemed to require bold, decisive measures. The position they took on the trial of the king is a good illustration of their weakness. The monarch and his family had remained prisoners in the tower of the Temple, a building formerly owned by the Knights Templars. The problem of what to do with the king was highly controversial. Some of the Girondins advocated clemency; others wanted to send him into exile; still others favored a popular referendum to determine his fate. In general, the Girondins were inclined to temporize, hoping to postpone a decision indefinitely. The position of the Mountain was clear: the king was a traitor; he should be brought to trial and suffer the penalty customary for such an offence—death.

The trial of the king was hastened by the discovery in a secret cupboard in the Tuileries of a cache of documents which proved conclusively Louis' knowledge and encouragement of foreign intervention. In December,

Execution of Louis XVI, January 21, 1793. *The executioner holds the king's head up for the crowd to see.*

1792, therefore, the Convention constituted itself a court to try "Louis Capet" (as he was then called) for treason. After prolonged debate, members of the Convention were asked in January, 1793, to vote publicly on the fate of the king. All agreed that he was guilty of treason, but there was sharp division on the nature of the penalty. The Mountain demanded Louis' death and won enough support from the Plain to carry the day. Even some Girondins at the last moment joined the majority in voting for the king's execution. The final vote was 387 to 334, with twenty-six of the majority favoring a delay in carrying out the sentence. On January 21, 1793, Louis was led under a tight security guard from the Temple to the Place de la Révolution (now the Place de la Concorde), where the guillotine had been placed. Showing courage to the end, he mounted the scaffold, and amidst the rolling of drums, was beheaded.

The vacillation of the Girondins throughout these proceedings discredited them with the minority who were shaping events in Paris. And because the Girondins were guilty of similar hesitation and disunity on other issues—the conduct of the war and the formulation of a constitution, for example—the Mountain seized the initiative and gradually consolidated its position. The climax of the struggle between the two factions did not come until June, 1793, when the Convention, under pressure from a carefully organized mob, voted the arrest of a group of Girondin deputies on charges of counterrevolution. This act paved the way for the dictatorship of the Mountain over the Convention, which began in July, 1793.

Prelude to the Terror

The celebrated era of the French Revolution known as the Reign of Terror lasted for a year, from the summer of 1793 to the summer of 1794. Because the leaders of the government justified their undemocratic procedures and harsh measures by claiming that France faced a desperate crisis, with the revolution threatened by enemies at home and abroad, we must briefly examine the nature of this crisis in the months preceding the establishment of the Terrorist regime to determine how serious it really was.

After the initial defeats of the spring and summer of 1792, the French armies enjoyed a temporary change of fortune, beginning at Valmy on September 20. At this point in northeastern France the advancing Prussian army was stopped by French forces under the leadership of General François Christophe Kellermann (1735–1820) and of Dumouriez, who had assumed command of the Army of the North after his resignation from the ministry in June. Though this victory was by no means striking, the fact that they had held against the Prussians and prevented their further advance provided a great boost in morale to French troops, whose feat was christened the "miracle" at Valmy. Encouraged, French forces took the offensive during the fall of 1792 and enjoyed a number of successes. The territory of Savoy, whose ruler had allied himself with Austria, was invaded in September and fell to the French along with the city of Nice. Farther to the north, General Adam Philippe de Custine (1740–1793) took the offensive against Austrian troops in the Rhineland and not only captured the cities of Speyer, Worms, and Mainz but crossed the Rhine and took Frankfurt. Finally, Dumouriez invaded the Austrian Netherlands and the revolutionary troops won their first great victory at Jemappes, on November 6. Brussels, Antwerp, and Liège subsequently fell, and the French occupied the whole of the Austrian Netherlands.

The response to French occupation and control varied. In general, the peasants and bourgeoisie at first welcomed the French, since their coming meant an end to the authority of reigning princes and a weakening of the position of the nobility. Before long, however, the armies of liberation began to seem more like armies of occupation as the French government took steps to annex the several territories to France and to impose upon the natives fiscal exactions designed to cover the costs of the occupying armies. This was the case, for example, in the Austrian Netherlands.

Another important consequence of the French conquests was that they provoked the opposition of certain European powers that had hitherto remained neutral. The most important of these was Great Britain. William Pitt the Younger (1759–1806), prime minister since 1783, had been determined to pursue a policy of neutrality when France went to war with Austria and Prussia in 1792, not so much because of the ideological divisions among Englishmen concerning the French Revolution, as because he saw no advantage to be gained by intervention. To be sure, British opinion was shocked by certain events in France: the insurrection of August 10, the imprisonment of the royal family, and the September Massacres. But not until the revolutionary armies took the offensive against the Low Countries in the fall of 1792 did Britain begin to see its strategic and commercial interests threatened. The capture of Antwerp, directly across the Channel, seemed to menace Britain's security. Moreover a decree of the Convention opening the Scheldt River to commercial navigation openly violated an earlier treaty which had guaranteed exclusive Dutch control over this river; a protest of the British government on this question was ignored. If the French could defy with impunity treaties affecting the maritime interests of other nations, they were, in Pitt's view, a real threat. Tension between Britain and France mounted steadily after November, 1792. The Convention's decision in January, 1793, to execute the king was used as a pretext by Pitt for expelling France's diplomatic representative. The Convention thereupon declared war upon Great Britain and its ally, Holland. Though the formal declaration of war on February 1 came from France, the British government had already decided that there was no alternative.

Britain and Holland were joined shortly by Spain and two of the Italian states, Sardinia and Naples, which came out openly against France only at this time. Along with the powers already at war with France, these came to

A National Guardsman. *Drawing made in 1793. On guard duty, the guardsman holds a gong with which to sound an alarm.*

constitute what is known as the First Coalition. During February and March, 1793, the allies began to assume the offensive against the French armies, forcing them to withdraw from some of the territories taken in the preceding year. In the Netherlands, for example, Dumouriez was confronted with a fresh Austrian offensive which resulted in two successive defeats of the French. Convinced that he had failed because of inadequate support from the war bureau and the government in Paris, Dumouriez entered into treasonable negotiations with the Austrian enemy. His plan was to evacuate the Low Countries and lead his troops on Paris, where he would seize power and restore the monarchy. When his army failed to support him in this venture, he was forced to flee across the border and join the enemy. The news of France's betrayal by one of its leading generals heightened the shock of the recent defeats in the Netherlands and in the Rhineland, where the Prussians had again taken the offensive. Dumouriez's treason also sharpened the division between Girondins and Jacobins, as each charged the other with complicity in his plots.

As if the stress of defending France against foreign invasion were not enough, the revolutionary government was faced in March with an open rebellion in the region known as the Vendée. (This included not only the department of La Vendée but also parts of the adjoining regions of Poitou,

Anjou, and Brittany.) The immediate pretext for the revolt was the government's attempt to conscript additional troops. Resentment against the revolutionary government's anticlerical policies was intense in this strongly Catholic region. Now the peasants, generally loyal to Church and king, refused to be drafted into the republican army and exploded into revolt. They were supported in their resistance by a group of Catholic noblemen in the region whose counterrevolutionary conspiracy had recently been discovered. By May the rebels had established a Royal Catholic Grand Army, which caused serious concern to the Convention.

To the problems caused by the steady deterioration at the front and the outbreak of civil war in the Vendée was added a new economic crisis in the late winter and spring of 1793. Requisitions for the armies had depleted stocks of grain and other foodstuffs, causing bread riots in Paris in February. War contractors and speculators in grain profited from the situation, thus contributing to a rise in prices. The government responded by issuing a new flood of *assignats*, with the result that their value depreciated even further. When popular resentment over these hardships culminated in antigovernment riots in Paris and other major cities, members of the Mountain in the Convention realized that they had to take drastic steps.

They found a ready-made program in the proposals of the *Enragés* ("Madmen"), groups of radicals led in Paris by a man named Varlet and a constitutional priest, Jacques Roux. The *Enragés*, claiming to speak for the

A revolutionary committee in debate, under the Reign of Terror, 1793–1794.

poor, demanded government regulation of food prices, subsidies for the poor, and a heavy graduated tax upon the wealthy to finance the costs of the war. Not all of their proposals were enacted immediately, but during the spring of 1793, the Convention passed legislation providing for public relief of the poor, imposed a war tax and a forced loan upon the rich, and on May 4 passed the First Law of the Maximum, which attempted to set maximum prices for grain and flour. The regulation proved to be unenforceable, but was a prelude to more stringent controls under the Terror.

The reluctance of the Girondin deputies in the Convention to adopt extreme measures of this sort, their earlier vacillation during the trial of the king, and their general moderation aroused suspicion among the more radical elements in Paris and elsewhere. Delegations from the Paris *sections* repeatedly petitioned for the expulsion of the Girondin deputies and hinted that the Commune was prepared to use force if the Convention failed to take action against them. The Girondins—recognizing that their principal support lay outside Paris—reacted by trying to stir up opposition to the capital among their sympathizers in the provinces. The tension reached a climax in early June. Unable to secure their demands by petitions, the Paris *sections* formed a revolutionary committee; this body, in turn, organized a mass demonstration around the Tuileries, where the Convention was meeting. Declaring that no deputy would be allowed to leave the building until the Girondin leaders had been handed over, the mob forced the Convention to vote the arrest of twenty-nine prominent Girondin deputies. The Mountain, backed by the Commune and the Paris populace, had apparently triumphed over the Girondin opposition.

Among the arrested deputies, some refused to submit without a fight. Instead of being imprisoned, they had just been detained in their homes, and twenty of the Girondin leaders escaped from Paris and sought to organize an insurrection against the capital. At first, it appeared that their "federalist revolt" might be successful. They were joined in their rebellion by other antigovernment groups, particularly the royalists, who were only too willing to exploit the situation. The Vendée was, of course, already in arms against the republic, and the revolt spread from there to all of Poitou, Anjou, and Brittany. Some of the major cities in France, including Lyons, Marseilles, and Toulon, fell to royalist forces. Only the departments around Paris, in central France, and on the eastern frontier appeared to remain loyal to the republic. As events subsequently showed, the strength of the rebels was illusory; their forces were scattered and lacked any sort of unified command, and their various members had radically different goals.

But in the summer of 1793, republican leaders could maintain with some justice that the country was in danger, that the revolution itself was threatened by its enemies. Only the most drastic measures, they argued, could save France in this hour of crisis. The situation of the republic was never quite so desperate as the government pretended, but the combined threat of foreign invasion and civil war did exist, and was exploited to justify the ruthless measures adopted during the Terror.

The Reign of Terror, 1793–1794

The precise nature of the political system by which France was ruled during the Terror must be explained before we turn to the activities of the regime. The Convention, elected in September, 1792, remained the official sovereign assembly throughout the Terror; indeed it remained in existence until October, 1795. But the Convention had been named in part to draft a constitution that would supplant the Constitution of 1791. Such a constitution was, in fact, completed by June, 1793, and sent for ratification to the primary assemblies of citizens in the departments, but it was never put into effect. It was easy for Jacobin leaders to argue in the midsummer crisis of 1793 that the country could ill afford the upheaval that the dissolution of the Convention and the election of a new assembly would cause. The Constitution of 1793 was therefore suspended for the duration of the war; as a matter of fact, it never was put into operation.

The stillborn Constitution of 1793 was in its provisions the most democratic of the constitutions formulated during the revolutionary era. It provided for universal manhood suffrage, without property qualifications for either voters or candidates. Gone was the distinction between "active" and "passive" citizens. Representatives to the legislative body were to be named directly by all citizens who voted in primary assemblies. The legislative body was to consist of one chamber, to which an executive council would be responsible. In order to allay the fears of the provinces, the constitution provided that the departments would name the candidates for the executive council, with the legislative body selecting the twenty-four officials from these candidates.

Paradoxically, the body which adopted this most democratic constitution also supported the most dictatorial regime of the revolutionary era. For the Convention continued to sit throughout the Terror, although its power was in fact vested in two executive committees which it had set up. The Committee of Public Safety, the more important of the two, was charged with general administration; it was composed at first of nine and later of twelve members. The Committee of General Security was given control over the revolutionary police. Members of both of these committees were chosen from the Convention and were theoretically responsible to it, but they became practically independent in their jurisdiction. After the autumn of 1793, their membership was automatically renewed by the Convention every month. They reported to the Convention occasionally on their activities, but their policies were never seriously challenged by that body until the summer of 1794, when the Terror ended.

The Terrorist regime has been called a dictatorship, but it was not a one-man dictatorship. Each of the members of the Committee of Public

Safety had particular interests or responsibilities and was relatively autonomous in his jurisdiction, though major policies had to be agreed upon by the group as a whole. All twelve members of the Committee were educated, middle-class radicals, members of the Mountain in the Convention, sincerely devoted to revolutionary ideals. Among them were six lawyers, two army officers, two men of letters, a civil servant, and a Protestant minister. Only gradually did Maximilien Robespierre (1758–1794), the thirty-five-year-old provincial lawyer with whose name the Terror is most closely associated, achieve a certain preeminence in the Committee, and his supremacy was frequently contested. Moreover, the power of the Committee of Public Safety was to some degree limited by the Committee of General Security, theoretically at least its equal, and by the Paris Commune, which continued to exercise considerable influence on government policies.

In regional and local administration the government of the Terror attempted to return to the tradition of centralization characteristic of the Old Regime. The administrative divisions established by the National Assembly—departments, districts, cantons, and communes—were retained, but the Terrorist government exercised its authority through appointed officials acting on behalf of the Convention. In the spring of 1793, "deputies on mission" were sent out by the Convention to the various regions of France to levy troops and stimulate revolutionary enthusiasm. When these officials threatened to become too independent, they were replaced by "national agents," one in each district or commune, directly responsible to the Committee of Public Safety. At the local level the national agents collaborated in some instances with "surveillance committees" (local revolutionary police) and with the Jacobin clubs, now termed "popular societies," but the clubs played a much less significant role than might have been expected.

This simple description of the machinery of the Terror does not begin to suggest the range of its activities or the messianic spirit of its leaders. The Terrorist regime had three basic goals: to win the war; to suppress the enemies of the republic at home; and to establish in France what Robespierre and others termed the "Republic of Virtue." A brief account of what was done to achieve each of these goals will illuminate some of the more important aspects of the Reign of Terror.

On August 23, 1793, the Convention, acting to meet the crisis caused by the war and the revolts in the provinces, issued a decree proclaiming a *levée en masse*, a plan for the universal conscription of French citizens to defend the republic:

Henceforth, until the enemies have been driven from the territory of the Republic, the French people are in permanent requisition for army service. The young men shall go to battle; the married men shall forge arms and

Maximilien de Robespierre. *Anonymous portrait. Musée Carnavalet, Paris.*

transport provisions; the women shall make tents and clothes, and shall serve in the hospitals; the children shall turn old linen into lint; the old men shall repair to the public places, to stimulate the courage of the warriors and preach the unity of the Republic and hatred of kings.[6]

This document, which constitutes the first appeal in modern times for the complete wartime mobilization of a people, suggests the kind of national loyalty which the revolutionary leaders hoped to inspire. They were not disappointed, for the *levée en masse* released a remarkable outburst of popular energy, characterized by Frenchmen of a later era as the "spirit of '93." Under its impetus the French armies halted the advance of the allied forces, and by the spring of 1794 recovered territories that France had conquered in the first months of the republic and later lost. By the end of the Terror, French armies once again occupied the Austrian Netherlands and the entire left, or west, bank of the Rhine.

Patriotism is certainly not a phenomenon that appeared for the first time during the French Revolution, but the attitude of the French citizen-soldier of 1793 toward his country differed considerably from that of the professional mercenary serving the Old Regime. Instead of fighting for a dynasty or a privileged caste, he was fighting for a nation in which he felt he had a personal stake. Nowhere else can one see quite so clearly the vital role of the doctrine of popular sovereignty in the emergence of an aggressive nationalist

[6] *A Documentary Survey of the French Revolution,* pp. 472–473.

spirit. The lesson was not lost on foreign observers. A few years later, after the French victory at Jena, the Prussian military leader Neithardt von Gneisenau remarked, "One cause above all has raised France to this pinnacle of greatness. The Revolution awakened all her powers and gave to each individual a suitable field for his activity." [7]

Part of the reason for French successes in the field lay in certain economic measures taken by the government, measures of the sort we have come to recognize as practically inevitable for a modern nation engaged in a total war. Among these were the celebrated Maximum, a law of September, 1793, which established maximum prices for certain basic commodities and also imposed controls on wages. These were essential to combat the continuing inflation which threatened the urban poor with starvation. Other measures included government requisitioning of supplies for military purposes at the maximum prices which had been set, the establishment of bread and meat rationing for civilians, and controls on foreign trade and exchange. Although these hastily improvised regulations proved hard to enforce, they worked well enough to fulfill some of the basic needs they were designed to meet; indeed, the value of the *assignat* was stabilized, and even rose, during the Terror, and the poorest classes were able to buy their own food instead of relying on charity. The armies were successfully provisioned, and as has been noted, they were generally victorious during this period.

To achieve its second goal—the suppression of the enemies of the republic at home—the Terrorist government used both its armies and a set of special revolutionary tribunals. Most of the revolts in the provinces had collapsed by the end of the summer of 1793, but opposition continued in certain key regions, notably in the Vendée and in the cities of Lyons and Toulon, both in the hands of the royalists. A concerted drive against Lyons reduced it to submission in October; Toulon, where the royalists had the help of the English, was recaptured in December. (One of the officers of the forces that took Toulon was a young artillery captain named Napoleon Bonaparte.) Bitter fighting continued in the Vendée until the end of 1793, and even after that republican troops continued to carry out bloody reprisals against the inhabitants. Responsibility for punishment of those who had participated in these revolts lay with the deputies on mission, who organized mass executions, or with special revolutionary tribunals set up for the purpose.

In the capital sat the highest court in the system of revolutionary justice, the Revolutionary Tribunal of Paris, which had been established in the spring of 1793 to deal with enemies of the revolution. At first its procedures were similar to those of a regular court of law, but as time went on its justice became increasingly summary. Its activities were stepped up in October, 1793, when the desire for vengeance against traitors to the republic

[7] Quoted by G. P. Gooch, *Studies in Modern History* (London, 1931), p. 197.

ON NE CONNOÎT ICI

QUE LA DÉNOMINATION

DE CITOYEN.

Placard posted during the French Revolution reads: "Only the title of 'citizen' is employed here."

Marie Antoinette. *Drawing by David. David made this sketch while watching from a window the procession taking the queen to her execution. The Louvre, Paris.*

seems to have reached a peak. Among the most prominent victims at this time were the queen, Marie Antoinette (known in her trial simply as "the widow Capet"), a number of the Girondin leaders who had been arrested in June, and several former generals who had not shown sufficient enthusiasm for the republic. All met their death on the guillotine which stood on the *Place de la Révolution.* The Revolutionary Tribunal of Paris was alone responsible for imposing death sentences upon 2,639 victims in the fifteen months of its existence.[8] Estimates of the total number of victims under the Reign of Terror run as high as 20,000.

A persistent myth concerning the Reign of Terror suggests that it was strictly class phenomenon. According to this old view, representatives of the middle and lower classes, having secured control of the government, relentlessly pursued the aristocrats and clergy over whom they had triumphed. But a careful analysis of the social origins of the victims of the Terror has led to the abandonment of this theory; only about 15 per cent of those sentenced to death by revolutionary tribunals belong to the nobility and clergy. The rest were members of the Third Estate, largely peasants and laborers. Surprising as this discovery appears at first glance, it is explained by the simple fact that the "enemies" of the republic were drawn from all social groups. In the Vendée, for example, the rank and file of the rebels (an estimated 90 per cent) were peasants loyal to king and Church, though some of their leaders were from the upper classes. Evidently, then, political necessity rather than class antagonism was the underlying motive for the mass executions of the Terror. The victims were those who had challenged

[8] Donald M. Greer, *The Incidence of the Terror During the French Revolution* (Cambridge, Mass., 1935), p. 135.

the republic, or who were thought to endanger it, regardless of their social origins.

A consideration of the ways in which Robespierre and his colleagues attempted to achieve their third goal, the Republic of Virtue, takes us to the heart of the Terror—its semireligious, messianic character. For at least some of the revolutionary leaders the founding of the republic marked the beginning of a new order on earth, the establishment of the Heavenly City of the eighteenth-century *philosophes*. More specifically, they drew their inspiration from Rousseau's vision of an ideal republic, founded on virtue, where the highest aim of the citizen would be to serve the general will. Only in such a community would men be truly free, living in harmony in accordance with the precepts of justice and reason and enjoying their "natural rights."

Not surprisingly, there were a variety of views on how this utopia could be attained. For some, the French nation was so closely identified with the ideal Republic of Virtue that patriotism became all-important. Any loyalty which could be regarded as detracting from allegiance to *la patrie* was immediately suspect. As a result of this sentiment, attempts were made to supplant Catholicism with a new state religion complete with martyrs, rituals, and civic festivals. One aspect of this campaign was the further elaboration in October, 1793, of the revolutionary calendar, which assigned new names to the months and did away with the sabbath and the saints' days of the old Christian calendar. Simultaneously more aggressive dechristianization activities were carried out in the provinces by some of the deputies on mission, who closed churches or converted them into "temples of reason," ordered the unfrocking of priests, and fostered anti-Catholic demonstrations.

Members of the Committee of Public Safety soon called a halt to these proceedings, feeling that they would alienate believing Christians from the republic. Nevertheless, Robespierre was convinced that Catholicism was fundamentally incompatible with the ideals of the republic, and set about devising an official religion which would serve the needs of the state. This emerged finally in the spring of 1794 as the Cult of the Supreme Being, which seemed to him to reconcile moral values with revolutionary principles and eliminate superstition and the corrupt influence of a priesthood; it retained only two positive articles of faith: belief in a Supreme Being and belief in the immortality of the soul. On 20 Prairial (June 8, 1794), Robespierre inaugurated the new religion in a ceremony in honor of the Supreme Being held in the Tuileries gardens. On this occasion he delivered an oration in which he denounced tyrants and exalted the Supreme Being, who had decreed the republic. At the end of the speech he declared, "French republicans, it is your task to purify the earth which they [tyrants] have defiled and to recall Justice which they have banished. Liberty and Virtue issued together from the Divinity: one cannot endure among men without the other." He then proceeded to demonstrate allegorically the triumph of Wisdom by setting fire to figures of Atheism, Vice, and Folly. From the ruins emerged a statue of Wisdom triumphant.

Another way to gain understanding of the Republic of Virtue is to examine the character and ideas of Robespierre, its chief exponent. One of the most controversial figures of the revolution, Robespierre has been denounced as a blood thirsty, power-hungry tyrant and praised as "the incorruptible," the man who best embodied the cause of the underprivileged during the revolution and who sought to bring about the equality envisioned by Rousseau. In the presence of these widely diverging opinions it is difficult to arrive at a true estimate of the man. Before the revolution he was an undistinguished but reasonably successful lawyer in Arras, in northern France, unmarried, chaste, and ascetic in his manner of living. Elected to the Estates-General in 1789 as a representative of the Third Estate, he remained relatively obscure in the National Assembly, but achieved a position of prominence in the Jacobin clubs because of his "sheer persistence, dogged consistency [and] fanatical conviction in the rightness of his own ideas." [9] Elected to the Convention, he soon emerged as the leader of the Mountain and after the elimination of successive opponents, became virtual dictator in the final stages of the Terror. Contemporaries described him as small and thin. During the revolutionary era, when most men adopted clothing that was informal or even careless, Robespierre continued to dress meticulously in the style of the Old Regime, wearing a light-blue coat and breeches, a clean frilled shirt, and carefully powdered hair. Portraits reveal a small face with eyes set far apart, a mouth with corners turned up in a slight smile; to some contemporaries his features were those of a cat or a tiger. Single-minded, fanatic devotion to a cause is perhaps the key to his personality, and to his success. In Crane Brinton's words, "Robespierre survived because the Terror was in large part a religious movement, and Robespierre had many of the qualities of a second-rate religious leader." [10] He regarded his opponents not simply as personal enemies, but as wicked men determined to prevent the salvation of mankind on earth.

One of the reasons for the success of the Terrorist regime was unquestionably the existence of a national emergency which demanded drastic measures. With the gradual removal of the threat of foreign invasion, and with the end of the civil war in the provinces, the sense of crisis abated. Just as a victorious coalition is apt to dissolve when war is over, so the victorious Jacobins began to be plagued with internal divisions and factionalism. It would be an exaggeration to refer to the several factions as political parties; rather they were loosely formed groups organized around particular individ-

[9] Gordon Wright, *France in Modern Times* (Chicago, 1960), pp. 69–70.
[10] Crane Brinton, *A Decade of Revolution, 1789–1799* (New York, 1934), p. 108.

June 8, 1794. *Robespierre inaugurates his new "Cult of the Supreme Being" before a large crowd in the Tuileries gardens. Note the two priests (on the extreme right) in attendance.*

uals. The Robespierrists were clearly the leading faction in the Committee of Public Safety by the beginning of 1794, but they were challenged by two other groups. One consisted of the Dantonists, or followers of Jacques Danton, the hero of the early days of the republic. Danton had remained one of the active leaders of the Mountain up to the fall of 1793, when he was outflanked by the more fanatic members of the Committee of Public Safety and forced into temporary retirement. But his belief that the revolution had proceeded far enough and that it was time for a return to a more moderate, conciliatory regime won him the support of a varied assortment of men—political adventurers, war profiteers, businessmen—at least some of whom hoped to benefit personally from a relaxation of the controls of the Terror. Danton's return to an active political role in the Convention early in 1794 appeared particularly menacing to Robespierrists. To the left of the Robespierrists emerged an even less coherent group around the Parisian demagogue Jacques Hébert (1755–1794); they called for an intensification of the Terror, further economic controls, a renewed attack on the Church, and concentration of greater power in the radical *sections* of Paris.

Aware of the threat to his position from these groups, Robespierre proceeded vigorously against them both by playing one off against the other.

The turn of the Hébertists came first, in March, 1794. Capitalizing on the anti-Parisian sentiment of provincial members of the Convention, Robespierre (with Dantonist support) secured from that body the indictment of the Hébertists before the Revolutionary Tribunal; the result was death by guillotine for the Hébertist leaders. A few weeks later he turned on the Dantonists. Charging Danton and his colleagues with criminal acts committed in office, Robespierre persuaded the frightened Convention to condemn them as well.

With both opposing factions eliminated, Robespierre appeared to have the situation in control, and could concentrate on creating the Republic of Virtue. But before long the dictator himself was in trouble. Many members of the Convention became fearful for their own safety after this double proscription. As if to confirm their fears, Robespierre convinced the Convention, in June, 1794, to pass a law speeding up the procedures of the Revolutionary Tribunal in Paris. With these new powers the tribunal sent some 1,300 victims to their death in the following six weeks. With the exception of the period following the suppression of the revolt in the Vendée, no stage of the Terror witnessed a greater number of executions than occurred in June and July of 1794. The result was the rallying of Robespierre's opponents to a plot conceived by Joseph Fouché (1763–1820), a former deputy on mission who had been dismissed because of his excessive brutality toward the people of Lyons. The climax came on July 27 (9 Thermidor in the revolutionary calendar). Appearing on the floor of the Convention to deliver a speech denouncing his enemies, Robespierre found himself howled down by the deputies. His last-minute attempt to rally the support of loyal Jacobins and the Paris Commune for an uprising against the hostile Convention failed. When troops of the Convention discovered him among the insurrectionists at the Hôtel de Ville, Robespierre apparently tried to shoot himself, but succeeded merely in shattering his lower jaw. The next day he was sent, along with twenty-one of his closest associates, to the guillotine.

Robespierre's death is generally viewed as a critical event in the history of the revolution, for it marked the beginning of the "Thermidorean reaction" against the extremes of the Terrorist regime. This development had not been anticipated by Fouché and his fellow conspirators, who were primarily concerned with saving their own lives, but the desire of most Frenchmen for a relaxation of tensions and an end to violence was strong enough to enable the moderates to regain control. Within the next few months the Convention, under the leadership of the moderate Thermidoreans, eliminated the Paris Commune, stripped the Committee of Public Safety of its powers, closed many of the Jacobin clubs, and removed the price and wage controls imposed by the Terrorist government. A similar reaction against the Terror appeared in the behavior of ordinary Frenchmen. For example, the Republic of Virtue had been characterized by a mode of dress that was austere and without frills. Patriotic Jacobin men—with the notable exception of Robespierre—had abandoned the *culottes,* or fancy knee breeches, of the aristocracy in favor of the simple, long trousers of the workingman. (Indeed, the term *sans-culottes* was used from 1792 to 1794 to describe the active, militant members of the Paris *sections* who played so important a role during the Terror.) Women had dressed in flowing white robes like those worn by females of the Roman republic. Both sexes had substituted for the wigs and powdered hair of the Old Regime hair styles that were simple and unaffected. During the Thermidorean reaction, fashions changed rapidly as men and women returned to more revealing and flamboyant clothing. At the same time, the French once again began to indulge in the pleasures that had been banned in the preceding months. Theaters, cafés, and ballrooms flourished in the freer atmosphere.

The Thermidorean era was not without its difficulties, however. With the relaxation of economic controls, inflation and its consequent hardships for the poorer classes returned. The spring of 1795 was marked by bread riots, and working-class agitation in Paris was exploited by the survivors of the Jacobin organization, who sought to direct it against the Convention. In the end, however, the only result of these demonstrations was the elimination of the remaining Jacobin leaders, who were shipped off to exile.

Despite the success of the Thermidoreans in ending the Jacobin threat, and despite the continued victories of the French armies, which led in 1795 to the conclusion of peace with both Prussia and Spain, the Convention was not generally popular. Its lack of support was dramatically illustrated by the reception accorded the Constitution of 1795, which was completed in

October 5, 1795. *The insurrection against the Convention failed. The Convention's defense was entrusted to the young and relatively unknown general, Bonaparte, whose troops dispersed the insurrectionists with a "whiff of grapeshot."*

August. Opponents of the new constitution objected not to its specific provisions, but to the condition that two thirds of the members of the new assembly were to be drawn from the rolls of the outgoing Convention. (These members came to be called "perpetuals.") The stipulation had been included to prevent extensive royalist victories in the forthcoming elections, but it was interpreted as merely an attempt by the members of the Convention to perpetuate their own power. Indeed, resentment against this proposal was so great that on October 4 (13 Vendémiaire) an insurrection against the Convention broke out in Paris. The uprising failed and would probably have been forgotten had it not been for the fact that the defense of the Convention was entrusted to young General Bonaparte, who dispersed the attackers with a "whiff of grapeshot." Bonaparte's success enabled the Convention to sit out its appointed term. Three weeks later the body dissolved itself and the Directory, the last government of the revolutionary era, came into being.

The Directory, 1795–1799

For the student of the revolution the years of the Directory, lasting from 1795 to 1799, have an anticlimactic quality. Following the excitement of the initial years of the revolution, the achievements of the National Assembly, and the extreme ruthlessness of the Reign of Terror, the Directory appears a prosaic interlude, finally brought to an end by the aggressive and dramatic dictatorship of Napoleon Bonaparte. Many French historians have termed the Directory incompetent in its handling of financial problems, inept in the conduct of foreign policy, and cynical in its manipulation of elections and electoral results. There is a measure of truth in each of these charges, but the tendency in recent years has been to take into account the magnitude of the problems facing the Directory, most of them inherited from the preceding regimes, and to be a little more charitable toward France's leaders during this era. And if the Directory was a government not distinguished for its positive achievements, it must be remembered that Frenchmen, after six years of revolution and three years of war, were looking more for order and stability than for innovation and excitement. Apologists for the regime have even pointed out that in a pragmatic way the Directory developed some of the techniques—administrative, electoral, and financial—which have been attributed to the Napoleonic government or which became standard in nineteenth-century bourgeois states. Finally, it should be noted that the regime collapsed in 1799 not as a result of its own inefficiency and corruption (as has often been suggested), but because a few determined individuals, with the support of the army, set out to destroy it.

In some respects the political institutions of the Directory were comparable to those of the constitutional monarchy. Power was shared by the executive and legislative branches, with the executive now consisting of five directors instead of a hereditary monarch. These five were to be chosen initially by the legislative body; after the first two years the legislative body was to replace one director annually. The legislative body, instead of being a unicameral assembly, was to consist of two councils, the Council of Ancients and the Council of Five Hundred. The latter was to initiate and discuss bills; the former could adopt or reject them. As in the Constitution of 1791, the suffrage was restricted, this time to those who paid a direct tax on wealth, landed or personal, and to soldiers who had fought for the republic. Such a restriction denied the vote to less than two million adult males out of a total of seven million, but because all top officials (including representatives to the legislative councils) were elected indirectly, the real power of franchise rested with a relatively limited group of wealthy men. In addition, it turned out that on more than one occasion the directors— dissatisfied with the results of an election—simply excluded legally elected deputies and named their opponents to the vacant seats. They defended such procedures on the grounds that the regime was threatened on the right by partisans of a royalist restoration and on the left by heirs of the Jacobins anxious to establish a democratic republic. That these threats were not wholly imaginary is proved by the sizable vote which went to opposition deputies in the elections to the legislative councils in 1797 and 1799, and by the several attempts to overthrow the regime.

One of these, not very significant at the time in terms of the number of people involved or of its chances for success, was the Conspiracy of the Equals, led in 1795–1796 by François Émile Babeuf (1760–1797), who, drawing his inspiration from the celebrated social reformers of the Roman republic, called himself "Gracchus." This episode, which ended in complete failure, has been singled out for considerable attention because some people detect in the egalitarian ideas of Babeuf the germs of modern socialist doctrine. He did, in fact, go considerably beyond the Jacobins, calling for the abolition of private property and the establishment of a communal society, but he did not spell out in detail the way in which these goals were to be achieved and he was content to proclaim as his immediate goal the restoration of the Constitution of 1793. In any event, the Conspiracy of the Equals was betrayed in advance by some of its members, and its leaders were arrested, tried, and condemned to death or exile.

Considerably more dangerous to the government was the recrudescence of the right in 1797, since the conservative camp included many who favored a restoration of the monarchy. Because the young son of Louis XVI had died in prison in 1795, royalists regarded one of the former king's brothers—Louis Xavier Stanislas, count of Provence (1755–1824)—as the legitimate heir to the throne. The prospect of a restoration was certainly unwelcome to those former members of the Convention who had voted for the death of Louis XVI and therefore feared reprisals against themselves as regicides. When elections to the legislative councils in 1797 returned a large bloc of conservative deputies, the moment seemed opportune for a rightist *coup d' état*. In order to forestall such an event, the three moderates among the directors—Jean François Rewbell, Louis Marie LaRévellière-Lépeaux, and the former viscount of Barras—called troops into the capital, claiming the existence of a royalist plot. Under their leadership the "loyal" members of the legislative councils nullified the elections of almost two hundred conservative deputies and condemned to deportation the two other directors, François de Barthélemy and Lazare Carnot. Barthélemy's secret royalist sympathies had been discovered, and Carnot had made the mistake of trying to heal the rift among the directors. This was the *coup d' état* of Fructidor (September 4, 1797); it ended, for the time being, the threat from the right.

When, in elections the following year, the left wing enjoyed a dramatic rise in its representation, the directors resorted to similar tactics and restored the balance by excluding from their seats many of those who had been elected. The legislative councils, resentful of the high-handed tactics of the directors and spurred on by the revived Jacobin clubs, retaliated in June, 1799, by arbitrarily replacing four of the directors with men whose outlook was more radical. The only director who survived all these changes was the pleasure-loving ex-noble Barras, who had been responsible, along with Bonaparte, for the defense of the Convention during the uprising of 1795. His colleagues now were Sieyès, who had served in the Convention and stayed on in the legislative body; Roger Ducos, a former Girondin; Louis Jérôme Gohier, a former minister of justice; and General Jean François Moulin. Although Sieyès had been named a director, he had nothing but contempt for the existing regime and was determined to strengthen the authority of the executive branch, by a change in the constitution if necessary. He found sympathy and support for his views among army leaders who were known to favor greater executive power, but because they had served the republic, feared the possibility of a restoration of the monarchy. Certainly these were the views of young General Bonaparte, who had made his reputation fighting in the defense of the republic, but scorned the parliamentary maneuvering that characterized the Directory.

Bonaparte, as we shall discover, had been absent from France for more than a year as commander of the celebrated Egyptian campaign, but had kept himself informed about political developments in Paris. Convinced that he could turn the disorders suffered by the Directory to his personal advantage, he slipped out of Egypt in the summer of 1799 and returned to France. Arriving unannounced on the Mediterranean coast, he established contact with the directors Sieyès and Ducos with a view to collaboration. Sieyès, as we have seen, had been contemplating a *coup d'état*, and he now determined to use Bonaparte to guarantee its success. Having reached an agreement, the two fixed 18 Brumaire (November 9, 1799) as the date for their seizure of power. A pretext for the *coup* was found in an alleged

Jacobin plot against the regime. The legislative councils were summoned to meet at Saint-Cloud, outside of Paris, ostensibly because they would not be subjected there to pressure from the Paris mob. Sieyès and Ducos resigned their posts in the Directory. Of the three remaining directors, Barras was prevailed upon to resign and the other two were arrested, so the government was without an executive. At this stage Napoleon appeared before the Council of Five Hundred to ask that he be given special powers to deal with the crisis confronting the country. Some of the deputies, seeing through the conspiracy, challenged him to produce evidence of a Jacobin plot. When he was unable to do so, they were on the verge of ordering his arrest. But quick action by his younger brother Lucien, who was president of the lower house, prevented the entire venture from collapsing. Lucien rallied the troops stationed outside the hall to Napoleon's cause, assuring them that he would plunge his sword through his brother's heart if Napoleon ever plotted against the liberty of the French people. Inspired by this declaration, the troops followed Napoleon's order to clear the hall of all deputies. A rump session of those sympathetic to the conspirators later voted full powers to Bonaparte, Sieyès, and Ducos, proclaiming them "temporary consuls." The *coup d'état* of Brumaire had succeeded; France had a military dictatorship. In this way the somewhat dreary political history of the Directory came to an end. It is perhaps worth pointing out, however, that the successive changes in the composition of the government under the Directory occurred with a minimum of violence and loss of life. In this respect, at least, the Directory was an improvement over the Terror, during which dissidents were normally sent to the guillotine. For a parallel in our own era one may compare the terrorist regime of Stalin with the more moderate administrations of his successors.

An evaluation of the Directory must take into account more than its political evolution. One of the government's acute problems was economic—a financial crisis of significant proportions inherited from the preceding regime. By 1796 the *assignats* had depreciated to less than 1 per cent of their face value. In an effort to establish the paper currency on a sounder foundation, the government stabilized the *assignats* at one thirtieth of their face value and announced that they could be exchanged on that basis for new paper money, the *mandats territoriaux*. Those who acquired the *mandats* could use them to buy the remaining nationalized lands at a price set by the government. In this way the *assignats* were withdrawn from circulation, but the measure was ultimately unsuccessful since the *mandats*, in turn, depreciated to about 10 per cent of their face value. In 1797 the Directory returned to a metal-backed currency, and although this step did not end the financial difficulties of the regime, it restored a measure of confidence among French businessmen. Other measures taken to improve the financial position of the government were the sharp curtailment of expenditures and the reorganization of the servicing of the national debt.

The latter step, though publicized as the "consolidation" of one third of the debt, constituted in fact a repudiation by the government of the other two thirds and temporarily undermined confidence in public credit. In the balance, however, the financial condition of the government and the country was better in 1799 than it had been in 1795. The Directory restored a measure of order to France's finances and laid the groundwork for Napoleon's subsequent fiscal reforms.

One major objective of the Directory was the conclusion of a general European peace which would at the same time guarantee France's security. This was never achieved. Prospects for peace were not bad in 1795. The Thermidorean regime had already ended the war with all of France's major enemies except Austria and Britain. In its first two years the Directory made more than one attempt to reach an agreement with Britain, but negotiations were complicated by France's determination to retain the lands that it had conquered in Belgium, Savoy, and Nice. Against Austria the Directory mounted a three-pronged attack in 1796. Two French armies were to invade the empire from the upper and lower Rhine. A third army, under the command of the twenty-seven-year-old General Bonaparte, was to drive the Austrians out of Italy and join the other two by way of the Tyrol. Although the northern armies were successful at first, they later ran into a counterattack led by the Austrian Archduke Charles Louis (1771–1847), who forced them to retreat. Bonaparte's Italian campaign was little short of phenomenal and established his reputation as France's most brilliant general. In a matter of months he advanced eastward along the Mediterranean coast, inflicted an initial defeat upon the Austrians, and managed to knock their Sardinian allies out of the war. Pursuing the Austrians farther, he ultimately gained control of most of northern Italy and then turned southward, toward Rome and the Papal States. The pope hastened to conclude a treaty with him, ceding the Romagna and the legations of Bologna and Ferrara to the French. In the spring of 1797 Bonaparte crossed the Alps to meet Archduke Charles advancing from Germany, and pushed the Austrian forces back to within seventy-five miles of the capital at Vienna. But because the Venetians had risen against French control and threatened his rear, Napoleon decided to negotiate a preliminary peace with the Austrians at Leoben. Some of the terms of his truce were incorporated six months later in the formal Treaty of Campoformio between Austria and France (October, 1797). Among the more important articles of this treaty were: first, the cession to France of Austria's Belgian provinces; second, the cession of Venice and the surrounding territory to Austria as compensation (Napoleon had crushed the revolt there and occupied the city); and third, the recognition by Austria of a new Cisalpine Republic, set up by the French, which included all of Napoleon's conquests in northern and central Italy. In secret clauses of the treaty Austria agreed to cede imperial territories on the left bank of the Rhine to France if France would support Austrian claims to

Salzburg and territories in Bavaria. The German princes, thus dispossessed of territories ceded to France, would receive compensation elsewhere in the Holy Roman Empire. Lastly, Austria agreed to a congress to discuss further the execution of this treaty in the empire and to consider the problems arising from the cession of the left bank of the Rhine to France. The Treaty of Campoformio provided a temporary respite in the struggle between France and Austria, but as we shall see before the territorial ramifications of the treaty in Germany could be settled, Austria, Russia, and Britain formed the Second Coalition against the French, and a general war resumed late in 1798.

Meanwhile, peace negotiations with the British had broken down toward the end of 1797, leaving Britain the lone power, except for its ally, Portugal, at war with the French. France had the support at this time of the Batavian Republic (Holland) and had concluded a naval and commercial pact with Spain in the summer of 1796. Although the French talked of an invasion of England and even gave Bonaparte the task of training troops for this purpose, the idea was abandoned as premature in 1798, and the Directory decided to attack Britain through its empire. Bonaparte was authorized to organize an expeditionary force of about thirty-five thousand troops for an invasion of Egypt. Apparently he had contemplated such an enterprise for a number of years as part of his dream for oriental conquest on the scale of Alexander the Great. He received support from the diplomat Talleyrand, who helped to persuade the Directory of the advantages of such a plan. The acquisition of Egypt, it was argued, would be the prelude to a march to India, where Tipu Sahib (ruled 1782–1799), a powerful native prince who had recently revolted against British rule, would join the French in driving the British from India. In the meantime, the acquisition of the Isthmus of Suez could be exploited by construction of a canal; this would give the French commercial supremacy over the British, who would be forced to continue their costly voyages around the Cape of Good Hope.

The expedition was organized in great secrecy. It sailed from Toulon in May, 1798. En route, Napoleon launched a surprise attack on the island fortress of Malta, which he took without difficulty. His forces landed at Abukir in June, captured Alexandria without firing a shot, and moved on to Cairo. Egypt, nominally a part of the Ottoman Empire, was defended only by a native military elite, the Mamelukes. Despite their excellent cavalry they were no match for a trained European army with artillery, and went down to defeat in the Battle of the Pyramids. So far, the expedition had been a complete success, but shortly afterward it met disaster at sea. The French fleet that had transported the expedition to Egypt, still anchored at Abukir Bay, was surprised and completely annihilated by a British fleet under the command of Admiral Horatio Nelson (1758–1805). Despite his initial victories Napoleon found himself a virtual prisoner in Egypt, cut off from his source of supplies and unable to carry out his ambitious plans for

Napoleon Bonaparte. *This portrait was done during his Egyptian campaign.*

the conquest of India. Refusing to admit defeat, he invaded Syria, another possession of the Ottoman Empire, but after early successes, his army suffered from an outbreak of the plague and was forced to retreat in haste to Egypt. Napoleon's forces were still strong enough to withstand an attack by Turkish forces at Abukir in July, 1799, but he realized that he could gain no further advantage for himself by remaining in the Near East, and he managed to slip back to France, where, as we have seen, he joined the conspiracy of the directors Ducos and Sieyès. The troops which he abandoned in Egypt in 1799 remained there until 1801, when the British finally defeated them and restored Egypt to the sultan.

FRANCE AND EUROPE

The War of the Second Coalition, 1798–1802

Napoleon's invasion of Egypt and his apparent intention of dismembering the Ottoman Empire was one cause of the formation in 1798 of the Second Coalition of European powers against France, for Paul I, tsar of Russia (1796–1801), viewed himself as the protector of Turkish interests and was alarmed by French expansion in the east. Moreover, he resented the French seizure of the island of Malta, since he held the title of grand master of the Knights of Malta. Russia was therefore receptive to Britain's proposals for an alliance against France, which was, in fact, concluded in December, 1798. Austria was also prepared to renew the war against France, having come to realize after the Treaty of Campoformio that the French not only intended to consolidate their domination over territories already acquired but also had further ambitions, particularly in Switzerland and the Italian peninsula.

Early in 1798 the Directory used a disturbance in Rome as a pretext for intervening there, expelling the pope, and establishing a Roman Republic, which was added to the two "sister" republics in Italy already under French control (the Cisalpine Republic and the Ligurian Republic, the name given by the French to the former Republic of Genoa). In the same year the French found a pretext for extending the republican form of government to the Swiss cantons; the centralized Helvetic Republic was proclaimed and brought into the French orbit. In Holland, which the armies of the Convention had invaded and conquered in 1795 and where the Batavian Republic had been established, the provisional government was replaced in 1798 by a regime modeled on the Directory; an alliance imposed upon this new government secured for the French valuable financial and military aid.

Each of these moves added to the suspicion and distrust of the other powers and increased their willingness to enter a new coalition against the French. The most significant change in the composition of the bloc allied against France was the substitution of Russia for Prussia. The latter, having concluded a peace with France in 1795, remained neutral during the war of the Second Coalition.

Geoffrey Bruun, in *Europe and the French Imperium*, has pointed out that the aims of the Second Coalition, summarized in a set of proposals drawn up in 1798 by the English prime minister, William Pitt, foreshadowed the final settlement imposed upon France in 1814–1815.[11] Essentially, the goal of the allies at this time and throughout the Napoleonic era was to restore the balance of power that had been upset by the conquests of France's revolutionary armies. Their aims included the restoration of Holland and Switzerland to independence, the union of the Belgian provinces with Holland under the rule of the *stadholder*, and the restoration of Savoy and Piedmont to the kingdom of Sardinia. Austria was to be compensated with Italian territories for the loss of its Belgian provinces, and Prussia would be permitted annexations in northern Germany. It was tacitly assumed that Russia would acquire territories at the expense of the Ottoman Empire and that Britain would retain all of its colonial conquests.

Such a program should have provided the powers with sufficient incentive to unite in bringing about the defeat of France, but in fact, the Second Coalition and all subsequent coalitions except for the last one, in 1814–1815, suffered from the same weakness: the inability of the allies to coordinate their efforts effectively enough to win the war. Over and over again, alliances fell apart because one or another of the powers was tempted by rewards offered by Napoleon and decided to treat separately with France. Only when France threatened to dominate all Europe, and when the powers had

[11] G. Bruun, *Europe and the French Imperium* (New York, 1938), p. 38.

learned that Napoleon's promises were worthless, did they collaborate to bring about France's defeat.

It can also be argued that France's repeated victories ultimately depended upon the character of its armies, and after 1796, upon the genius of Napoleon as a general. Bonaparte's qualities as a military leader will be discussed in the next chapter. As to the character of the French armies, we have already noted the crusading spirit of the French citizen-soldier after the proclamation of the republic, his sense of fighting for a nation in which he had a personal stake. This attitude apparently inspired in the average soldier greater individual initiative, more confidence in his own resources, than was characteristic of troops fighting in the armies of the absolutist powers. Georges Lefebvre argues that the passion for equality and the hatred of aristocrats common among soldiers during the Jacobin phase of the revolution lasted into the Napoleonic era.[12] One reason for the persistence of this attitude was Napoleon's preservation of the system of promotion through the ranks that had developed in the revolutionary armies. Napoleon did ultimately create a military aristocracy with privileges of its own, but advancement in his armies depended not upon birth, nor even upon education, but upon boldness and bravery in battle. Because officers were drawn from the ranks, a kind of *camaraderie* existed between them and their troops that was found much less often in the armies of France's enemies. These, then, were some of the reasons for the frequent triumph of France's armies over forces far superior numerically.

In the war of the Second Coalition, Tsar Paul I (who had succeeded Catherine the Great in 1796) sent his armies deep into Europe to join with the Austrian and British forces in battles against the French. Russian troops under the command of General Suvorov (1729–1800) fought alongside Austrian armies in a generally successful campaign against the French in the Italian peninsula and later in Switzerland. But a joint Anglo-Russian army under the duke of York failed to drive the French out of Holland because of stiff French resistance and friction between the allied forces. The coalition's principal successes came in the spring and summer of 1799, but a new wave of Jacobin-inspired enthusiasm in the French armies turned the tide even before the *coup d'état* in November. The first ruler to defect from the alliance was the tsar. Disgusted by the strategic errors of his Austrian allies and by their refusal to consult him about the disposition of Italian territories, Paul withdrew from the coalition in October, 1799, and in the following year, irritated by Britain's arrogant use of sea power, he revived the League of Armed Neutrality, a collaborative effort of Sweden, Denmark, Prussia, and Russia to protect neutral shipping against arbitrary search by British naval vessels. Paul even showed some disposition toward concluding an alliance with France, but his assassination in March, 1801, brought about

[12] Georges Lefebvre, *Napoléon*, fourth ed. (Paris, 1953), p. 192.

an end to any such project. The other allies fought on for a while longer, but as we shall see, Austria came to terms with France in 1801 and Britain did so in 1802, thus dissolving the Second Coalition.

REACTION OUTSIDE FRANCE, 1792–1799

In discussing the history of the republic from its proclamation in September, 1792, to the *coup d'état* of Brumaire we have had occasion to see the profound influence which France's war with the First Coalition had upon its internal development. But we have said little about the spirit in which the war was fought, the policies of French governments toward conquered territories, and the continuing reaction of other powers to the revolution and to France's conquests.

With the proclamation of the republic a change occurred in Frenchmen's attitude toward the war. It was still viewed, as it had been at the outset, as a defensive war against the European monarchs bent on crushing the revolution. But a new note is detectable in some of the decrees of the Convention issued in the latter part of 1792. In November, for example, the Convention declared in the name of the French nation that it would ". . . grant fraternity and aid to all peoples who wish to recover their liberty . . ."[13] Another decree, occasioned a month later by resistance in the Austrian Netherlands to French annexation, was even more specific:

> In territories which are or may be occupied by the armies of the Republic, the generals shall proclaim immediately, in the name of the French nation, the sovereignty of the people, the suppression of all established authorities and of existing imposts or taxes, the abolition of the tithe, of feudalism, of seigneurial rights, both feudal and *censuel*, fixed or contingent, of *banalités*, of real and personal servitude, of hunting and fishing privileges, of *corvées*, of nobility, and generally of all privileges.
>
> They shall announce to the people that they bring it peace, aid, fraternity, liberty, and equality, and they shall convoke it thereafter in primary or communal assemblies, in order to create and organize a provisional administration and justice. . . .

The French nation declares that it will treat as an enemy of the people anyone who, refusing liberty and equality, or renouncing them, might wish to preserve, recall, or treat with the prince and the privileged castes; it promises and engages itself not to subscribe to any treaty, and not to lay down its arms until after the establishment of the sovereignty and independence of the people upon whose territory the troops of the Republic have entered, who shall have adopted the principles of equality and established a free and popular government.[14]

[13] *A Documentary Survey of the French Revolution*, p. 381.
[14] *Ibid.*, pp. 382–383.

Clearly the war had become, as the French armies took the offensive, a crusade for the liberation of subject peoples from their royal or feudal oppressors. And here the French found a pretext for the annexation of conquered territories, which might, if left unprotected, be reconquered by their former rulers. It would be unfair to conclude that the idealistic proclamations served merely as a cloak for more cynical territorial ambitions. Some of the republican leaders were sincerely determined to bring the benefits of the revolution to the peoples of Europe, but the fact remains that the liberated peoples were not normally given an opportunity to choose between their liberators and their former oppressors. The customary procedure was for a minority of republican or French sympathizers in an occupied region to petition the Convention for annexation to the republic. Another justification for the incorporation of border regions into the republic was the claim that they lay within France's "natural frontiers"— the Pyrenees, the Alps, the Rhine, the Atlantic, and the Mediterranean. For example, when a delegation from Savoy presented its petition for annexation, the Convention accepted it on the grounds, first, that the people of Savoy shared the sentiments of France, and second, that the territory of Savoy lay within "the limits set by the hand of nature to the French Republic."[15]

The ease with which the border regions were assimilated into the republic varied from place to place. In general, the annexation of Savoy and Nice met with little resistance. The Savoyards were mostly French-speaking anyway and their way of life was quite similar to that of Frenchmen in neighboring Dauphiné. Although the inhabitants of Nice were of Italian stock and spoke an Italian dialect, they had no strong objections to incorporation in the French state. In the provinces of the Rhineland, pro-French orientation and sentiment among the bourgeoisie had been strong even before the revolution, and the granting of full ownership of the land to the peasantry won them over to French control.

The French ran into the greatest resistance in the Belgian provinces conquered from the Austrian empire. Despite their abortive revolt against Austria in 1791, the people of the Austrian Netherlands were not eager to submit to French domination. The leaders of a pro-French minority, exiled by Austrian authorities after the suppression of the revolt, returned with the conquering armies of Dumouriez late in 1792. Supported by the French armies, this group set up Jacobin clubs throughout the conquered provinces and embarked upon an anticlerical campaign which quickly antagonized the devout. When the Convention sent in commissioners to confiscate Church and royal lands and impose new taxes, a rash of civil disturbances and general discontent resulted. The retreat forced upon the French in 1793 meant a temporary respite, but when the armies of the republic returned in

[15] Quoted by Gershoy, *The French Revolution and Napoleon*, p. 241.

1794, the methods of the occupying authorities were far more ruthless. Now the provinces were annexed outright and integrated completely into the French administrative structure. The republic was well on its way toward using methods later employed by the Napoleonic dictatorship in conquered territories.

The initial responses in Britain and Germany to the French Revolution, and the steps leading to the outbreak of war between France and the First Coalition, have already been described. Once they were actively involved in a war with France, the British, Prussian, and Austrian governments found it easier to deal with revolutionary sympathizers in their own countries, who could now be branded traitors. All European rulers denounced the threat of "Jacobinism," viewing it as an international conspiracy subsidized by French money and supported by French agents. To what extent an international conspiracy actually existed is very difficult to determine, but there is no question that its ramifications were exaggerated by contemporary rulers. Where revolutionary sentiment existed outside of France—and it was rare after the September Massacres, the aggressive decrees of the Convention, and the execution of the king—it was encouraged by a minority of native sympathizers rather than by paid French agents. Even governments not actively at war with France proceeded against such individuals with great vigor. In central and eastern Europe they were arrested for the most insignificant political offenses and given heavy penalties. For example, a Hungarian Jacobin who dared to translate into Magyar the "Marseillaise," the French revolutionary song, was condemned to death. To prevent the infiltration of French ideas, the most rigid censorship was instituted in the Austria of Francis II and the Russia of Catherine and Paul.

In Britain, where the legal tradition afforded greater protection for individual liberties, the government had a more difficult time proceeding against supposed Jacobins and radical societies. Even after the war with France had begun, a number of such organizations, supported primarily by artisans and tradesmen, continued to express their sympathy for the revolution and to pursue the cause of parliamentary reform. Pitt, the prime minister, increasingly exasperated by these agitators, finally decided to proceed against them. In a series of state trials in 1794 twelve leaders of the two most prominent London societies—the Corresponding Society and the Society for Promoting Constitutional Information—were charged with treason. Despite overwhelming anti-French sentiment in the country, the juries refused to condemn the accused because of insufficient evidence. The defendants were political reformers eager to change the existing regime, but no real evidence that they intended violence or were actively promoting the overthrow of the monarchy was produced in the trials. As the war contin-ued, Pitt managed to secure legislation from Parliament which gave him greater powers in dealing with the radical opposition. The Two Acts passed in 1795–1796 widened the definition of treason to include writings and speeches as well as actions and banned all large public meetings except those held by special authority. Further regulations in 1799 forbade the existence of secret associations or federations, including trade unions, instituted press censorship, and required the registration of all printing presses. With this legislation the Tory government effectively stifled radical agitation.

By and large, the revolution was not responsible for immediate changes in the political and social institutions of the countries pitted against France. Except for a tightening of censorship restrictions and judicial procedures, the governments of Prussia, Austria, and Russia remained immune to change, their privileged aristocracies even more committed than before to preserving the *status quo*. The principal impact of the revolution in Britain was not on governmental institutions, but rather on the balance of the two political parties in Parliament. The Whigs, who were divided even before the war with France, were further split by Fox's stand of sympathy with the principles of the revolution and his opposition to Pitt's repressive measures. When the duke of Portland defected to Pitt's government in July, 1794, taking a majority of the Whigs with him, there was practically no opposition left in Parliament; the Tory government had the backing of both the landed gentry and of the newer moneyed interests. During the years of the revolution was formed the rigid Toryism, characterized by opposition to reform of any kind, that persisted until well after the defeat of Napoleon.

A FINAL APPRAISAL

Despite the initial attraction of the revolutionary ideals of liberty, equality, and fraternity to sympathizers in countries other than France, their primary impact during the decade 1789–1799 was on Frenchmen, and they have continued to affect Frenchmen ever since. In a nation highly conscious of its own history, the revolutionary tradition has come to mean different things to different groups, but it has persisted, being repeatedly invoked in the series of revolutions that France underwent during the nineteenth century and in the political crises of the twentieth. The key to a Frenchman's political outlook may still be found in his attitude toward the great revolution.

What impressed contemporaries more than anything else was the fact that revolution had struck in France, the state regarded as the oldest and best established on the continent. For this very reason the uprising seemed to constitute a deadly blow to the cause of absolutism and to the feudal institutions which still prevailed in most of Europe. If the venerable French monarchy and the elite of the European nobility could not withstand such assaults upon their privileges, other European rulers and aristocrats might well doubt their capacity to meet similar challenges in their own countries.

The attempts of the revolutionary armies after 1792 to liberate the rest of Europe by force heightened their fears and ultimately stiffened their will to resist any changes in the old order.

In the long run, no country entirely escaped the impact of the French Revolution; indeed, its influence continues to be felt even today. It not only shattered long-standing traditions and deep rooted institutions but also proclaimed new ideals which have powerfully affected succeeding generations both inside and outside of France.

For the "revolutionary virus" (as it was described by conservatives) could not be confined to France indefinitely. Despite the efforts of European rulers to quarantine the "disease," many individuals were infected by it and became its carriers in the Restoration era following the defeat of the revolutionary and Napoleonic armies. The 1789 Declaration of the Rights of Man, and the successive constitutions of revolutionary France, became major sources for ideologies and ideological movements in the nineteenth century. The debt of liberal and nationalist movements to the French Revolution is obvious. Socialists have drawn heavily upon its heritage for theory and strategy. Even conservatives have found it a source of inspiration, since their social and political philosophies often take as their starting point a refutation of the doctrines that inspired the great revolution. It will be the task of chapters that follow to make precise the legacy of the French Revolution to nineteenth-century Europeans, showing more particularly how it provided ideals, slogans, and models for the revolts that punctuated the era from 1815 to 1848.

CHAPTER 2

Napoleon

WHATEVER VIEW one takes of the character of Napoleon Bonaparte, whatever aspect of his achievement is emphasized, whether one admires him as a superb military leader or condemns him as the forerunner of twentieth-century dictators, one cannot deny that he dominated his age. He barely qualified as a native Frenchman, for he was born in Corsica into a family of impoverished nobles in 1769, just a year after the island had been taken over by France from Genoa. As a youth, he secured a state scholarship and studied in military schools in France. Partly because he considered himself an alien in a foreign country, he was forced to rely on his own resources and worked assiduously. He became a conscientious student of history and geography as well as of military strategy and tactics. In 1785, when he was only sixteen years old, he was appointed a second lieutenant in the artillery, but because of his foreign extraction his chances for promotion in the royal army were not particularly good. The advent of the revolution suddenly opened up new prospects for him. He returned to Corsica and devoted his energies for the next three or four years to the movement for Corsican independence, which had been his dream since childhood. This phase of his career ended when he broke with Pasquale di Paoli (1725–1807), the leading Corsican patriot, and his entire family was banished from the island. Abandoning his earlier plans, he now became an ardent French patriot and Jacobin.

His role in recapturing the port of Toulon from the royalists and the English in the winter of 1793 earned him a promotion from captain to brigadier general and attracted the notice of the influential politician Barras, who later proved of assistance to him. The fall of Robespierre brought Bonaparte a temporary reversal of fortune. He was arrested as a Terrorist, deprived of his commission, and briefly imprisoned. Subsequently, however, Barras had him put in charge of the defense of the Convention when it was threatened by the uprising of October, 1795, and his success in this enterprise led to his appointment as commander in chief of the Army of the

Bonaparte, the Consul. *An unfinished but most celebrated portrait of Napoleon in his prime. By David, 1798.*

Interior. At this point he met Joséphine de Beauharnais (1763–1814), the attractive widow of an aristocratic general who had died on the guillotine during the Terror. She was six years his senior, had two children, and was without a fortune, but the young Napoleon fell violently in love with her and married her on March 9, 1796.

Two days before his marriage he was appointed to command the army in Italy, where he first demonstrated his qualities as a military genius; brilliant in offensive warfare, he put emphasis on great speed and mobility and on surprise attacks to disconcert the enemy. He emerged from the Italian campaign a national hero, and the failure of the Egyptian expedition in 1798–1799 did not dim his reputation, partly because the full story of its failure was not known until later.

What manner of man was Napoleon at the time of his accession to power in 1799? From the mountains of conflicting testimony written by his contemporaries, almost invariably biased, it is nearly impossible to arrive at a composite picture. Count André François Miot de Melito (1762–1841), a French councillor of state, who met Napoleon for the first time during his Italian campaign in 1796, recorded his impressions in his memoirs:

> I was quite astonished at his appearance. Nothing could be more unlike the idea my imagination had formed of him . . . I saw a man below the middle height and of an extremely spare figure. His powdered hair, oddly cut and falling squarely below the ears, reached down to his shoulders. He was dressed in

a straight coat, buttoned up to the chin, and edged with very narrow gold embroidery, and he wore a tricolored feather in his hat. At first sight he did not strike me as handsome; but his strongly-marked features, his quick and piercing eyes, his brusque and animated gestures revealed an ardent spirit, while his wide and thoughtful brow was that of a profound thinker. He made me sit near him and we talked of Italy. He spoke in short sentences and, at that time of his life, very incorrectly.

Most of his contemporaries agreed that he had a remarkable intelligence and an unusual capacity for sustained effort and intense concentration. The following comment by Jean Chaptal (1756–1832), his minister of the interior, who knew him perhaps as well as anyone, discusses his performance as First Consul immediately after the *coup d'état* of Brumaire:

We met in the First Consul's rooms almost every evening, and deliberated fom 10 till 4 or 5 A.M. It was in these conferences that I came to know the great man to whom we had just entrusted the reins of government. Though still young, and with little experience of administrative detail, he brought to our discussions an astonishing clarity, exactness, power of argument, and width of view. An untiring worker, and full of resource, he collected and co-ordinated facts and opinions relating to every part of a huge system of administration with unrivalled sagacity.... Though he worked as much as twenty hours out of the twenty-four, he never showed signs of mental or physical fatigue.[1]

[1] Quoted by James M. Thompson, *Napoleon Bonaparte: His Rise and Fall* (Oxford, 1952), p. 150.

Josephine de Beauharnais at the time of her marriage to Bonaparte.

He manifested some of these same qualities as a military commander, his decisions being based on careful planning and detailed knowledge rather than intuition. What seemed to be sudden flashes of insight were actually the fruit of painstaking rational analysis. "Every operation must be done according to a system," he said, "because chance cannot bring about success."[2] This reliance upon reason led many to view Napoleon as a good son of the Enlightenment, but another side of his character made him one of the great heroes of the romantic era. Although he adhered to no established religion, he still felt that his life was guided by what he called his "star," and he referred frequently to the workings of "destiny." And although he might employ careful calculation to achieve specific goals, his ultimate aims seem to have been limitless and undefined. He admired Alexander the Great, Caesar, and Charlemagne not so much for their specific achievements as for their visions of universal empire, which fired his own imagination and inspired his actions. Georges Lefebvre, suggesting the romantic dimension in Napoleon's personality, says, ". . . [the realist] determines his goal, taking into account the possible, and if his imagination and the desire for glory drive him on, he knows where to stop."[3] Napoleon quite clearly was not a realist in this sense, for he recognized no limits to his ambition, and this, in the long run, proved his undoing.

One of the questions most often raised in discussions of Napoleon's domestic policies is whether his regime carried on and—as he said— "crowned" the revolution, or whether it constituted a reversal or denial of the revolution. The answer depends in part, of course, on one's definition of the revolution: on whether one is thinking primarily of the accomplishments of the National Assembly and the Legislative Assembly during the moderate phase between 1789 and 1792, or viewing it as the whole succession of regimes between 1789 and 1799, including the Terrorist government and the Directory. Apologists for the view that Napoleon was a true "son of the revolution" argue that the constructive achievements of the initial period were cut short or interrupted during the rule of the Convention and the Directory, and that with his accession to power as First Consul, Bonaparte undertook to complete the work of the revolution. Opponents of this view grant that many measures completed during the Consulate and Empire stem from reforms initiated under the constitutional monarchy, but they argue that the character of Napoleon's political institutions, the way in which he dealt with the opposition, the strict control of opinion during his regime, and indeed the entire spirit of his administration were in direct contrast with the ideals of 1789. Some contend further that Bonaparte really had far more in common with the enlightened despots of the eighteenth century than with the revolutionaries. According to this view, he displayed

---

[2] Quoted by Georges Lefebvre, *Napoléon*, fourth ed. (Paris, 1953), p. 67.
[3] *Ibid.*, p. 68.

the same passion for rationalization and systematization that characterized Frederick the Great and Joseph II of Austria, and whatever reforms he instituted were enacted on his initiative within the framework of a despotic government which permitted no criticism. He was, it is argued, the ruler who carried the principles of enlightened despotism to their logical extreme. Like so many other historical questions, this problem of interpretation has no simple solution; we shall be examining in the sections which follow evidence in support of these opposing views.

THE CONSULATE, 1799–1804

The government which emerged from the *coup d'état* of Brumaire was merely a provisional regime. It was up to the three victors who had been named "consuls"—Bonaparte, Sieyès, and Ducos—to provide France with a new constitution and a stable government. After a decade of revolution, civil disorders, and foreign wars, most Frenchmen were willing to sacrifice what appeared to them the illusory benefits of liberty for a regime that could ensure internal tranquility and peace. On the day following the *coup d'état*, the consuls swore to end the civil conflict which had continued sporadically in the west, stabilize finances, codify the laws, and terminate the foreign war with an honorable peace. Most of the energies of the First Consul and his government during the next five years were devoted to the fulfillment of these promises.

The Constitution of the Year VIII (1799), drafted by Sieyès with Bonaparte's collaboration, provided a set of institutions that appeared to preserve republican forms but at the same time gave considerably increased powers to the executive. Although the constitution stipulated that the three consuls who held the executive power were to be elected to ten-year terms by the Senate, it specifically designated as the first incumbents of these offices Bonaparte and the two men he had chosen as his colleagues—Jean Jacques Régis de Cambacérès (1753–1824) and Charles François Lebrun (1739–1824). Instead of two chambers, the national legislature now had three—the Senate, the Tribunate, and the Legislative Body. But their activities were circumscribed and the ways in which their members were chosen made them relatively ineffective. The Senate consisted of eighty men named for life. Initially, a majority of them were to be appointed by the outgoing second and third consuls, who became senators themselves. This group, in turn, was to select the remaining senators from lists presented to them by the Legislative Body, the Tribunate, and the First Consul. What in fact happened was that both the original list of senators and the remainder were selected, with Bonaparte's approval, by Sieyès, one of the outgoing consuls. He, too, named the members of the first Legislative Body and Tribunate.

The Senate had no direct legislative powers unless the constitutionality of a measure was at issue, but it had the power to name the members of the other two chambers from a list of "notables." The notables were chosen through universal suffrage—the only feature of the constitution that was ostensibly democratic—but the privilege of voting was now even less meaningful than it had been under the Constitution of 1791 or the Directory. The voters could elect only a group of notables in their own commune, who then elected one tenth of their number to serve as notables of the department. These, in turn, elected one tenth of *their* number to become the notables of France, from whom the Senate chose the members of the Tribunate and the Legislative Body. The Tribunate, consisting of a hundred men, had the power to discuss measures submitted to it by the First Consul or his advisers, but did not have the power to vote on them. The Legislative Body, three hundred men, had the power to accept or reject measures, but could not discuss them. Since membership in all three bodies was appointive rather than elective, the consuls had little to fear in the way of opposition.

Despite this elaborate set of legislative institutions, the actual work of drafting laws fell to the Council of State, a group of experts appointed by the First Consul and directly dependent upon him.

If there were objections to the authoritarian character of this constitution, they were hardly expressed, for the popular vote registered 3,011,007 in favor and only 1,562 opposed. There is little question that the regime was popular with a great majority of Frenchmen. The new First Consul considered the plebiscite an overwhelming vote of confidence, since his name had appeared in the constitution.

NAPOLEON'S ADMINISTRATION

Napoleon revised his initial constitution in 1802, when he had himself proclaimed consul for life, and in 1804, when he became emperor. In each case he sought approval for the increase of his powers through plebiscites which returned him overwhelming majorities. As First Consul, and later as emperor, he carried out an impressive series of administrative, financial, educational, and legal reforms.

Those who view Napoleon as a son of the revolution point out that he completed the administrative system whose main lines had been laid down by the National Assembly. It is true that he retained the basic geographical divisions established in 1789, but in many other respects, his contributions in this sphere marked a reversal of the basic principles of administration which had guided the revolutionaries. For example, he substituted for the elected officials and local self-government of the years 1789 to 1792, the centrally appointed bureaucrats who have been at the heart of France's administrative system ever since—prefects for the departments, subprefects for the districts, and mayors for the communes. Though local councils still functioned to assist the appointed officials, they too were named from Paris rather than elected. The French have apparently come to prefer such a centralized bureaucracy to the kind of federal structure found in the United States and to the decentralized institutions characteristic of Britain, but such a preference is not in harmony with the intentions of the pioneers of the revolution.

The same emphasis on centralization can be seen in Napoleon's approach to financial problems. The Directory had attempted to restore fiscal stability to France by withdrawing the inflated paper currency which had plagued preceding revolutionary governments and by repudiating two thirds of the national debt. Despite these measures no way had been found to augment revenues, and the credit of the government had been seriously impaired. Napoleon realized that an effective method of assessing and collecting taxes was essential. Therefore, instead of leaving with municipal officials the power to draw up the tax rolls and collect taxes levied by the central government, he turned this responsibility over to representatives of the central government—a general director at Paris, deputy directors for each department, and inspectors and assessors in each commune. In this way the entire machinery of taxation was tightened up, receipts were increased, and the government could predict its expected revenues more precisely. Although the French have proved remarkably ingenious in devising means of evading taxes, the basic system established by Napoleon has persisted to this day. Another means by which Napoleon succeeded in raising revenues to meet his enormous expenditures was through the revival of indirect taxes on consumer articles such as liquors, tobacco, and salt. In addition, he could draw upon what was termed the *domaine extraordinaire,* a fund supplied by contributions, subsidies, and confiscations from conquered countries. In 1800 Napoleon decreed the creation of the Bank of France, which was intended to ease the problem of government borrowing, stabilize the currency, and facilitate the payment of annuities. In 1803 it was given the exclusive right to issue bank notes in Paris; not until 1848 could it do this for the entire country. Technically a private institution, it acquired a special status because its shareholders included the First Consul, members of his family, and leading state officials.

In economic matters Napoleon was essentially a mercantilist—that is, he wanted to strengthen France economically and was prepared to do this through regulation of the economy and direct state intervention wherever it appeared necessary. The needs of war and the supplying of his armies were, of course, of primary importance to him, but he was also preoccupied with insuring a regular food supply, particularly to Paris, where shortages or high prices might result in discontent or disorders. The suppliers of food, the peasants, generally flourished under the Consulate and the Empire, especially those who were called upon to produce substitutes (such as sugar beets) for foodstuffs that could no longer be imported from overseas. Napoleon vigorously supported the expansion of French industry, but his measures toward this end were not an unqualified success. Under the leadership of Chaptal, his minister of the interior, a society for the encouragement of national industry was established and efforts were made to enlist the support of French scientists and engineers in developing new manufacturing techniques. The results were particularly striking in the textile industry where the copying or adaptation of English machines led to dramatic progress in the manufacture of cotton. The government claimed, probably with some exaggeration, that output of French cotton mills quadrupled in the four-year period from 1806 to 1810. The development of the mining and metallurgical industries was less impressive. Despite the need for armaments, much of France's iron needs continued to be supplied by small, inefficient hand foundries that produced low-grade work. Many manufacturers prospered under the Napoleonic regime, but they complained of the regulation and petty restrictions upon their operations. Perhaps the group least satisfied with Napoleon's economic policies were merchants, who saw their overseas trade dwindle as France succumbed to British control of the seas. Attempts were made to find new sources of supply and new markets on the Continent, but the volume of foreign trade never achieved the total under Napoleonic rule that it had attained under the Old Regime.

Napoleon is often given credit for continuing and elaborating upon the system of public education inaugurated during the revolution. The principle of free, elementary education for all children had been first proclaimed in the Constitution of 1791 and was reaffirmed by the Convention, but little progress was made during the revolutionary years in the establishment of primary schools. Nor was the Napoleonic government much more successful in expanding the system of primary public education. It has been estimated that only one out of every eight children of school age could be accommodated in primary schools existing in 1813.[4] At the secondary level the Convention provided for the establishment of state-supported "central schools," one for each department and five to be located in Paris. Although some difficulties were encountered in getting these into operation the quality of the teaching in them was high and they were flourishing during the early years of the Consulate. However, in 1802 Napoleon abolished the central schools and substituted for them *lycées* under more direct government supervision. He also permitted the existence of a limited number of private secondary schools. The *lycées* were intended quite frankly as "nurseries of patriotism." The Napoleonic regime prescribed the curriculum and the teaching schedules, appointed the teachers, and set up a system of inspectors to enforce the regulations. Discipline in the schools was on military lines: students wore uniforms, classes began and ended with the

---

[4] Cited by G. Bruun, *Europe and the French Imperium, 1799–1814* (New York, 1938), p. 146.

rolling of drums, and students received military instruction from retired officers. In 1808, Napoleon further centralized education by establishing the *Université*—not a university in the usual sense of the term, but a single system incorporating the whole range of public schools from the elementary level up through institutions of higher learning. Again, the purpose was to ensure greater control over education and promote loyalty to the regime. Private and church schools continued to exist under limited supervision by the state even after 1808, but the *Université* embodied the principle recognized during the revolution that education, controlled and supported by the state, should be available to all citizens.

In Napoleon's own opinion, and in the opinion of subsequent generations, one of the most significant achievements of his administration was the compilation of a series of five law codes, begun when he was First Consul, although not entirely completed until after the establishment of the Empire. Of these the Civil Code—referred to simply as the *Code Napoléon*—was the most important. The revolution had prepared the way for the First Consul by sweeping away most of the statutes and legal privileges of the Old Regime, but the various revolutionary assemblies had made relatively little progress in the drafting of new legal codes. With his passion for order and speed Napoleon in August, 1800, appointed a committee of several of France's most prominent lawyers to draft a Civil Code, and he made sure that it was completed within six months. Keenly interested in the enterprise, the First Consul presided over about half the sessions of the Council of State in which provisions of the draft were discussed in detail. The promulgation of the code was delayed until early in 1804, however, because of opposition to certain articles by the Tribunate and the Legislative Body—one of the few instances in which these chambers delayed proposed legislation.

The finished product has been termed a compromise between some of the most important ideals of the revolution and the needs of the authoritarian Napoleonic regime. One of the fundamental principles of the revolution was retained: the equality of all citizens before the law. The code provided a uniform system of law for the entire country, guaranteed religious liberty and the supremacy of the secular state, and asserted the right of the individual to choose his own profession. In some of its other provisions the code showed the influence of Napoleon's authoritarian outlook. For example, the sections relating to family life reinforced the authority of the father over his children and provided for the subordination of the wife, whose property was legally placed at the disposal of her husband. Revolutionary legislation had required the equal division of property among heirs, but the code permitted greater freedom to the head of the family in disposing of his estate. The right of divorce by mutual consent was recognized but was restricted in the interests of family unity.

Some of the later codes—for example, the Code of Civil Procedure promulgated in 1806—bore a close resemblance to laws under the Old Regime. Both the Code of Criminal Procedure and the Penal Code, begun under the Consulate but not completed until 1810, reflected the increasing despotism of the Napoleonic regime in that they prescribed strict penalties for political offenses as well as for crimes against persons and property. Where revolutionary legislation had changed criminal procedure so that the defendant was presumed innocent until proved guilty, the code reversed this change, restoring the presumption of the defendant's guilt. A Commercial Code, drawn up in 1807, was much less complete than the other codes and merely retained many of the ordinances of the monarchy.

Criticisms have been leveled against the Napoleonic codes, but as a whole they were a remarkable achievement. For brevity and clarity of expression the Civil Code was unmatched; any citizen could look up any point with a minimum of difficulty in a volume so small that it fitted into his pocket. Although the lawmakers assumed that their codes conformed to nature and were therefore universally applicable—just as the *philosophes* and the revolutionaries had supposed that the principles they set forth were "natural laws"—the codes were in fact strongly national in their origin. They drew upon earlier distillations of Roman law that had prevailed in the south of France and upon the Teutonic customary law common to the northern provinces. These were combined and blended with the laws promulgated during the revolution which had so drastically undermined the hierarchical structure of French society and altered the status of the individual. The resulting amalgam was a set of legal codes adapted to the bourgeois-oriented society that came into being with the revolution, a society which stressed the equality of all citizens before the law but at the same preserved the principle of private property. This adaptation explains, in part, why the French codes were borrowed or imitated so widely during the nineteenth century. They were of course, applied directly by the French to many of their conquered territories, including the Austrian Netherlands, Holland, Switzerland, Luxemburg, and a number of the German states. But the influence of the codes spread farther, to the New World where it affected the laws of Canada, Louisiana, and parts of Central and South America, and even as far as Japan.

The Napoleonic Regime as a Police State

Critics of the point of view that Napoleon continued and completed the work of the revolution do not deny his achievements with respect to the administrative system, education, and law, but they emphasize aspects of the Napoleonic regime which seemed directly to reverse the intentions of the original revolutionaries. To begin with, the political system established in 1799—the Consulate—constituted a denial of the doctrine of popular sovereignty which was at the heart of the Declaration of the Rights of Man.

Although French citizens were given the right to vote, their vote was essentially meaningless since members of the Napoleonic assemblies were appointed rather than elected. Moreover, the legislative bodies themselves, restricted in their functions by Napoleon's first constitution, were progressively shorn of their limited powers in the ensuing years. Bonaparte could argue that his mandate from the people came in the form of periodic plebiscites, but these plebiscites were inevitably invoked to ratify decisions already made. By contrast, the initial constitution of the revolution (the Constitution of 1791), though it too fell short of the ideal of popular sovereignty because of its restrictions on the franchise, did provide for an assembly that had genuine legislative powers and truly shared sovereignty with the king. Napoleonic parliamentary institutions were from the beginning little more than window dressing for what was essentially a dictatorship.

The Napoleonic regime was marked, too, by drastic curbs upon freedom of expression. Article II of the Declaration of the Rights of Man had proclaimed: "Free communication of ideas and opinions is one of the most precious rights of man. Consequently, every citizen may speak, write, and print freely, subject to responsibility for the abuse of such liberty in the cases determined by law." No principle was violated more consistently by the Bonapartist government. A few months after Napoleon came to power the number of Paris newspapers was reduced from seventy-three to thirteen. Eventually, the remaining papers in Paris and the provinces were little more than government organs printing official news dispatches and suppressing any information considered detrimental to the regime. The government was also on guard against literary works that might prove politically harmful. Particular attention was paid to the theater, which was placed under the general supervision of agents who subjected all plays, old and new, to rigorous censorship.

In order to enforce such regulations, a large and elaborately organized police force was necessary. Supervision of the police was entrusted to the notorious Joseph Fouché, who had been dismissed from his post as a deputy on mission under the Terror because of his excessive brutality. Fouché created what the Empress Josephine termed "a vile system of espionage" for the surveillance of the personal lives of thousands of individuals suspected of harboring subversive sentiments. The constitutional prohibition of the arbitrary detention of individuals was—in practice—consistently violated. Some political opponents of the regime were kept under close watch in assigned residences; others were detained in insane asylums. After 1810 they were held in "state prisons," where the number of political prisoners rose by 1814 to an estimated 2,500. The resulting atmosphere—reminiscent of Paris under the Terror—was certainly at odds with the principles of individual liberty and freedom of speech proclaimed in 1789.

Because he was first and foremost a soldier, Napoleon reserved a special place in French society for the military. Indeed, his top-ranking officers were showered with favors and came to form an elite which staffed his court and enjoyed special privileges in the Empire. Appointment as a marshal of France was the highest honor Napoleon could confer, and it was received by relatively few. Some were given this title as a reward for personal loyalty or to pacify a particular army clique, but the most outstanding marshals were brilliant generals like Louis Nicolas Davout (1770–1823), a superb tactician who never lost a battle; André Masséna (1758–1817), who distinguished himself in a number of battles, and particularly at Wagram (1809); and the celebrated Michel Ney (1769–1815), termed by Napoleon "the bravest of the brave" for his exploits as a general in numerous campaigns of the revolutionary and Napoleonic eras. Although many marshals had begun their lives as sons of peasants or members of the petty bourgeoisie, they were created dukes or princes, with titles recalling their victories or the provinces they had conquered. Holders of such titles were also rewarded with generous pensions, large bequests, and grants of "fiefs" in Germany or Italy. Some even became kings. Thus Joachim Murat (c.1757–1815), husband of Napoleon's sister Carolina and one of Napoleon's most flamboyant marshals, was named king of Naples in 1808. Napoleon's ideal of the "career open to talent" was strikingly realized in the lives of many of his marshals.

Peace with the Church: The Concordat

After his accession to power, Bonaparte made no immediate public statement about the status of the Roman Catholic Church in France. But he was convinced that the religious issue had to be settled, if possible by a concordat with the pope. The French clergy remained divided into two groups: the constitutional clergy, who had taken an oath to the revolutionary government, and the legitimate—or refractory—clergy, who were either in hiding or in exile, but who retained the sympathy of many French Catholics. Napoleon realized that to win the support of the refractory clergy he would need the aid of the pope. He was further led to seek a settlement with the Church by concern for those Frenchmen who had acquired nationalized Church lands during the revolution and were anxious to have the Church formally renounce its title to these lands. Although Napoleon had no firm religious convictions—he was the first to admit his own opportunism in this respect—he was convinced that France was fundamentally Catholic and that the support of the authority of a revealed religion would be useful in securing the submission of French citizens to law and order.

In 1800, after a successful military campaign in northern Italy had reinforced Napoleon's domination there, he opened negotiations with representatives of Pius VII, pope between 1800 and 1823. The threat of military force and the possibility of a further reduction of the papal territories loomed in the background of the discussions. Nevertheless, the

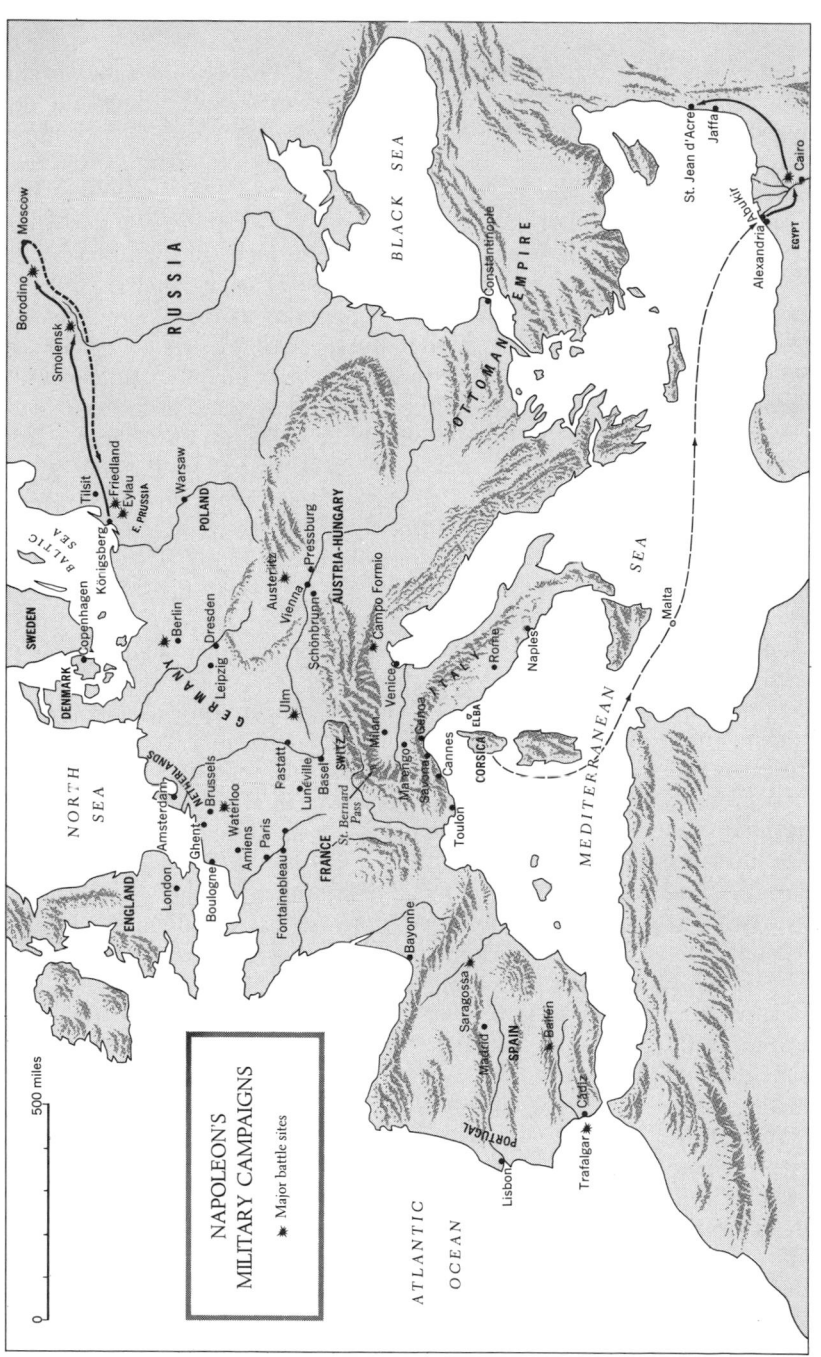

pope's diplomats engaged in delaying tactics and the Concordat underwent some twenty-one drafts before it was acceptable to both Rome and the French state. While the Concordat of 1801 was something of a compromise, the Napoleonic state was the principal gainer. Catholicism was recognized not as the state religion, but as the religion of "the great majority of French citizens" and of the three consuls of the republic. The semiprivileged status given the Catholic faith sufficed to reconcile the papacy and the refractory clergy. Priests were permitted the free exercise of the Catholic worship "in conformity with the police regulations which the government shall deem necessary for the public tranquility." The pope agreed to recognize as valid the titles of all those who had bought Church lands confiscated by the revolutionary government. Since the relinquishment of these lands, together with the abolition of the tithe, left the Church with much reduced revenues, the state agreed, as it had under the Civil Constitution of the Clergy, to pay the salaries of bishops and priests, who were required, before assuming their functions, to take an oath of fidelity to the government. French bishops and archbishops were to be nominated by the government and canonically instituted by the pope; they, in turn, had the right to name members of the lower clergy.

In the Concordat, Napoleon achieved his principal goals. The agreement ended the division within the French church, reconciled the refractory clergy to the republic, and gave the necessary security to owners of former Church lands. The principal gain for the Church, in addition to state salaries for the clergy, was the assurance that Catholic worship could be practiced freely once again in France. Yet the reservation to this right—the agreement concerning police regulation—left an opening by which the government could (and did) control the Church in France. One other concession to the Church was French recognition of the Papal States; however, the pope did not regain the territories of Ferrara, Bologna, and the Romagna, which had been incorporated into the Cisalpine Republic in 1797. The Concordat was not universally popular in France, but it had the enthusiastic support of well over half the nation, and the reconciliation of France and the papacy was celebrated on Easter Sunday in 1802 by a *Te Deum* at Notre Dame.

As a corollary to the settlement with the Catholic Church, Napoleon established a working arrangement with the Protestant Churches in France, which were organized into consistories (one for every 6,000 of the faithful); like the Catholic clergy, Protestant ministers received salaries from the state. Toward Jews, of whom there had been an estimated 40,000 in France in 1789, Napoleon pursued a somewhat more complex policy because he regarded them more as a people than as a religious group and hoped ultimately for their assimilation. By decrees passed between 1806 and 1808 they, too, were grouped into local consistories and these were supervised by a Central Consistory in Paris, headed by the Emperor. During the Revolution, Jews had attained civil status and the right to enter all offices and types of business, but many had continued to serve as livestock traders and money-lenders. Because of complaints against high interest rates charged by Jews in certain parts of France, the Napoleonic government subjected them in all but a few regions to special legislation relating to loans as well as to certain other restrictions. Jews resented these decrees as discriminatory, but the purpose of the Emperor seems to have been, in part, to reduce hostility toward the Jews and thereby to promote their assimilation into the community.

INTERNATIONAL DEVELOPMENTS

The End of the Second Coalition: Peace with Austria and Britain

After his accession to power as First Consul, Napoleon made offers of peace to Austria and Great Britain, the two remaining members of the Second Coalition. When these were spurned he decided upon a major campaign against Austria. With his armies striking again through both Germany and Italy, Napoleon took personal command of a French force of forty thousand in a dramatic march across Great St. Bernard Pass into Italy. There he fell upon the Austrian flank and took the city of Milan. He encountered the main body of the Austrian army in the Battle of Marengo (June, 1800), where only the timely arrival of a relief force under General Louis Desaix (1768–1800) enabled him to turn what appeared to be a catastrophe for France into victory. When Napoleon followed up his defeat of the Austrian armies in Italy by pressing the invasion of Austria through Germany, the Austrian emperor was ready to sue for peace. The treaty concluded at Lunéville in February, 1801, reaffirmed the cessions Austria had made in the Treaty of Campoformio and forced Austria to abandon its remaining possessions in the Italian peninsula (with the exception of Venice and the surrounding region) and to recognize the independence of the Batavian, Helvetic, and Ligurian republics. Gone was the earlier promise of French support for Austria's claims to Bavarian territory, and France now asserted the exclusive right to settle the question of indemnification of the German princes who had lost territories along the left bank of the Rhine.

Once again Britain was the sole member of the coalition to hold out. Although the British had reconquered the island of Malta from Napoleon, had expelled the French from Egypt, and had taken a number of former Dutch and Spanish colonies, their sentiment for peace was strong, for British merchants hoped to regain access to continental markets. Napoleon, too, was anxious to secure an honorable peace, which would leave him free to consolidate his position in France and in Europe. In the ensuing negotiations, the British were at a disadvantage because Pitt had resigned as prime minister in the spring of 1801 and his successor, Henry Addington (1757–1844), was a much inferior statesman whose representatives were no match for the French. * The Treaty of Amiens (March, 1802), was greeted with dismay in Great Britain; it seemed that the British had conceded everything and the French nothing. Among the more important provisions were the following: Great Britain returned to France or to its allies (Spain and the Batavian Republic, or Holland), all the colonial territories won since the beginning of the war with the exception of Trinidad (taken from Spain) and Ceylon (ceded by the Batavian Republic).

The French agreed to evacuate the kingdom of Naples and the Papal States and recognized the return of the island of Malta, captured by Napoleon and later retaken by the British, to the Order of the Knights of Malta. France also recognized the independence of the Ionian Islands. These seven islands lying in the Ionian Sea off the western coast of Greece had been occupied by the French in 1797. But the Russian fleet seized them in 1799 and established them as the Septinsular Republic, under Turkish protection and Russian guarantee. The Russians, in fact, occupied them until 1807. From the British point of view, the treaty's omissions were more significant than its provisions. For no mention was made of France's many conquests on the Continent. France was left in control of Holland, Belgium, the left bank of the Rhine, Switzerland, and most of the Italian peninsula. The independence of the various republics which had been set up under French authority was not guaranteed; they were clearly nothing more than satellites of the French state. Most important, France was left a free hand in reshaping Germany. Nor did British negotiators secure any agreement from the French concerning the restoration of commerce with the Continent, although most continental ports were now in French hands. British merchants who had looked forward to the revival of trade with the Continent were among the treaty's bitterest critics.

In attempting to understand why the British government accepted the terms of the Treaty of Amiens, we must recall both its overwhelming desire for peace after nine years of war and the relative weakness of the new ministry. Furthermore, the treaty did leave intact Britain's strongest weapon, its navy. Britain's mastery of the seas was unaffected; in fact, the war had heightened its superiority in this respect. Whereas the French had lost close to half of their fleet, the British had almost doubled the strength of their navy. Therefore, they were now in a position to renew hostilities against the French whenever it seemed desirable to do so. Meanwhile, they could wait to see whether Napoleon would be satisfied with his conquests or whether he was ambitious for further expansion.

---

* The change of prime ministers provoked the following comment from a contemporary: "Pitt is to Addington as London to Paddington."

The Reorganization of Germany, 1803

Napoleon profited from the brief interlude of peace afforded by the Treaty of Amiens to reshape drastically the map of Germany. His power to do this stemmed from the Treaty of Basel (concluded by France with Prussia in 1795) and from France's treaties with Austria—Campoformio in 1797 and Lunéville in 1801. Through these treaties France had acquired all the German territories lying along the left bank of the Rhine, an important step in the fulfillment of its long-standing goal of expanding to its "natural frontiers." As far as Germany was concerned the central problem created by these treaties was how to compensate or indemnify those princes who had lost territories to France. The treaties themselves had suggested a solution by proposing the secularization of at least some of the old ecclesiastical principalities of Germany—which had been ruled for centuries by archbishops or bishops with temporal as well as spiritual powers—and their annexation to states which had been promised compensation.

Prussia and many of the lesser states favored the proposed secularization, and even Austria, despite long-standing ties with the Roman Catholic Church, cast covetous eyes upon the archbishopric of Salzburg and some of the smaller ecclesiastical territories. An imperial congress summoned in 1797 at Rastatt in accordance with the provisions of the Treaty of Campoformio failed to produce agreement among the German states on the problem of indemnification. To end the deadlock, the imperial Diet agreed to turn the problem over to an imperial deputation (*Reichsdeputation*) consisting of eight members. Before this body could meet, however, Napoleon proceeded to make his own arrangements for Germany. Talleyrand, his foreign minister, having accepted bribes and gifts from German rulers who hoped to acquire this or that piece of territory, drew up the terms of the settlement. After concluding separate treaties with Prussia and some of the states of secondary rank, Napoleon imposed the entire arrangement upon the imperial deputation and eventually upon the Austrian emperor.

The final terms were embodied in a document known as the Imperial Recess of 1803. In accordance with its provisions, 112 states of the Holy Roman Empire went out of existence, their territories being incorporated into neighboring states. Of the ecclesiastical states, all but one, Mainz, were destroyed—and even the archbishop of Mainz lost some of his territory. Of approximately fifty free cities, only six remained: Frankfurt, Augsburg, and Nuremberg, and the three Hanseatic cities—Lübeck, Hamburg, and Bremen. The principal beneficiaries of the settlement in Germany were Prussia and Bavaria, each of which gained about five times as much territory as it had lost on the left bank of the Rhine, and the southwestern German states of Baden and Württemberg. Although Austria gained territory in the south to compensate for the loss of imperial possessions in the west, the overall settlement further undermined the Austrian position with respect to Germany by eliminating the ecclesiastical states which had traditionally supported the Habsburgs and by strengthening Prussia and some of the secondary states. Certainly part of Napoleon's intention in intervening in Germany had been to decrease both Austrian and Prussian influence by attracting to France's orbit a group of secondary states indebted to France for territories they had acquired and willing to accept French leadership in the hope of further favors. In this he was successful, since Bavaria, Baden, and Württemberg tended to look to France for leadership during the following decade.

THE EMPIRE, 1804–1814

In 1802 the French had reason to be grateful to Napoleon, for in less than three years he had brought about the apparent pacification not only of his own country but of Europe as well. The ratification of the Treaty of Amiens, concluding peace with France's last remaining enemy, was followed in a few days by the celebration of the Concordat with the papacy. Many of the former opponents of the regime had become reconciled to it as success followed success during the first years of the Consulate. Others—principally die-hard Jacobins and republicans who accused Bonaparte of having betrayed the revolution—had been exiled or imprisoned. Toward monarchists and *émigré* nobles Napoleon's policy was much more lenient. After the victory of Marengo in 1800, Napoleon removed the names of some fifty thousand from the list of *émigrés* drawn up during the revolution. (This list included some nobles who had not actually left the country but were nevertheless classified as *émigrés*.) In the spring of 1802, after the conclusion of peace, he extended full amnesty to another fifty thousand on condition that they return to the country by September, 1802, and take an oath of loyalty to the constitution. To those whose estates had been seized but not sold he promised full restoration of their property. Only a thousand intransigent nobles were excluded from this amnesty. These measures served to eliminate practically all organized opposition within the country. Bonaparte was now ready to take the first steps toward the establishment of the Empire.

The Proclamation of the Empire, 1804

As early as 1800 Napoleon's brother Lucien had tried to determine the popular reaction to the establishment of hereditary rule for the Bonapartes, and had concluded that such a move would be premature. In 1802 circumstances seemed more auspicious, and the Tribunate was prompted to declare that the nation owed "a signal pledge of gratitude" to the First Consul for his work of pacification. The Senate responded to the suggestion, but instead of offering to retain Napoleon as First Consul for life, merely proposed to extend his term by ten years. Keenly disappointed, Bonaparte seized the initiative and referred the decision to the people in a plebiscite. The question, as finally formulated by the all-powerful Council of State, was simply this: "Is Napoleon Bonaparte to be made Consul for life?" The French people responded with an overwhelming affirmative (3,568,885 in favor, 8,374 opposed), and the Life Consulate was proclaimed in August, 1802. To accompany this change the Senate approved alterations in the constitution which increased the powers of the First Consul and strengthened the Senate (now clearly under Bonaparte's control) at the expense of the Tribunate and the Legislative Body. Although two other consuls remained in office, ostensibly sharing power with the First Consul, the Consulate was now a monarchy in all but name.

However, Napoleon felt that further preparations were essential before he could assume a royal title. He had to be made to appear as the indispensable ruler of the nation, the only bulwark between France and a state of anarchy. This impression, he decided, would be created by the discovery of a conspiracy, a plot to restore the Bourbon dynasty, which would appear to threaten the very existence of the regime. Many *émigrés* still in exile did indeed favor such a restoration. In due course, secret agents of the Napoleonic government, posing in England as monarchist sympathizers and supplied with funds from the treasury to finance the project, approached the leaders of a planned coup who were also receiving a subsidy from the British government, anxious to encourage any plot for the removal of the First Consul. With the conspirators now on French soil, the so-called Cadoudal conspiracy was suddenly exposed; at the proper moment early in 1804, government agents swooped down and arrested Georges Cadoudal (1771–1804), a royalist from Brittany; General Charles Pichegru (1761–1804), one of the former revolutionary generals; and General Jean Victor Moreau (1763–1813), Napoleon's chief rival as a military commander, whom the first two secretly in Paris had attempted to persuade to join the conspiracy. All three were imprisoned, and the details of the plot were bared in the newspapers. Pichegru was subsequently found strangled in his cell. Cadoudal and several other conspirators were tried and executed. General Moreau, who in point of fact refused to participate in the plan, was found guilty but permitted to go into exile in America. Even after the leaders of the plot had been exposed no specific representative of the Bourbon family could be found implicated. The only clues that were picked up seemed to lead to the duke of Enghien (1772–1804), a Bourbon prince of the collateral line of Condé, who had been living in the German state of Baden and had allegedly come to Strasbourg to communicate with English agents. On the flimsiest of evidence Napoleon ordered a contingent of troops to invade Baden, a neutral territory, arrest the duke of Enghien, and bring him to Paris. He had firmly decided on condemning the duke to death, and although he discovered even before Enghien reached the capital that the charges against him were false, he went ahead with the summary military trial and had him

December 2, 1804, a bright but cold winter morning. *At ten o'clock precisely, the royal carriage leaves the Tuileries to proceed through the crowded streets of Paris, passing the Tribunal (Palais Royal) on its way to Notre Dame for one of the most celebrated coronations of all time.*

executed within twenty-four hours of his arrival. The speed and brutality with which this action was taken caused a temporary revulsion against Napoleon in some quarters, but most Frenchmen were relieved that the plot had been discovered and the apparent threat to the regime overcome. All who had a stake in the maintenance of the *status quo*—peasants who had acquired nationalized lands during the revolution, merchants and businessmen who benefited from the prosperity and order achieved under the Consulate, bureaucrats and military men whose fortunes were tied to those of Bonaparte—were willing to approve when the Tribunate proposed that Napoleon be proclaimed emperor and that the imperial dignity should be hereditary in the Bonaparte family. A plebiscite once again approved overwhelmingly what was, in fact, a *fait accompli*.

In the newly revised constitution (sometimes referred to as the Constitution of the Year XII), the first article began, "The government of the republic is entrusted to an emperor," and the document went on to specify the method to be followed in determining the succession within the Bonaparte family. This curious amalgamation of political forms appeared also on the coinage, which subsequently bore on one side the words *République Française* and on the other, *Napoléon Empereur*. Napoleon's reasons for choosing to be "emperor" are not hard to determine. He could hardly call himself king; the Bourbon pretender had not abandoned his claims to the throne, and in any event that title would have been inconsistent with the revolutionary origins of Napoleon's government. Besides, "emperor" carried more grandiose overtones, recalling both the rulers of Rome and Charlemagne, who had been emperor as well as "king of the Franks." Certainly the title suggested that his dominion would extend far beyond the borders which had circumscribed the France of the monarchy.

Napoleon's ambitions also led him to seek a legitimization of his title greater than could be conferred by the French Senate. Accordingly, he succeeded in persuading Pope Pius VII to come to Paris to lend the papal presence to his coronation in December, 1804. Such an act required the pope to abandon certain scruples since a legitimate Catholic prince still claimed the throne of France, but the good will of the most powerful ruler in Europe was not to be dismissed lightly. Besides, Pius was assured by Napoleon's representatives that he would both anoint and crown the emperor. But a few hours before the coronation, the pope was informed that the procedure had been changed. In the climax of the impressive ceremony in Notre Dame, Napoleon took the crown from the pope, turned his back upon him, and facing the audience, placed the crown upon his own head. In this manner he proclaimed to the pope and to all others present his independence of any earthly authority.

The crucial moment of the coronation. *Napoleon abruptly turns his back to the Pope (right) who was to crown him, faces the audience, and, with a theatrical gesture, places the crown on his head. Sketch by David for his celebrated painting now in the Louvre.*

War with Britain and the Third Coalition

Historians have speculated on what would have happened to the Napoleonic Empire if it had enjoyed a decade of peace. Frenchmen were, on the whole, satisfied with the ruler who had ended the insecurity of the revolutionary era and provided them with a stable regime and relative prosperity. But could Napoleon Bonaparte have survived a decade of peace? His reputation had been built initially upon his military victories. And despite his active program of domestic reforms in the years after 1799, his power was based essentially on his command of the army and on the military glory surrounding his name. Moreover, there was a romantic element in his character which made it impossible for him to limit his ambitions. Could one who in a few short years had achieved mastery over the French nation and had successively defeated the other major powers of Europe have settled down to the relatively prosaic tasks of government and administration? Napoleon was impelled by an almost compulsive drive toward further military exploits and the expansion of his newly founded empire.

Responsibility for the renewal of war between France and Britain in May, 1803, lay almost entirely with France. The rest of Europe may well have been ready to settle down to an era of peace after the decade of wars which had ravaged the Continent. The territories which France had annexed by 1803 could largely be regarded as lying within France's "natural frontiers." True, French influence extended to the so-called sister republics in Holland, Switzerland, and Italy, but the peoples of these regions still had a degree of autonomy, and at least some of them benefited from the introduction of French institutions into their territories. The other major European powers had apparently acquiesced in the extension of French influence into these regions; at least, they had signed treaties with France which did not specifically withhold approval of French acquisitions. Addington, the British prime minister, certainly regarded the Treaty of Amiens as more than a temporary truce, but the same cannot be said for Napoleon. For a number of reasons he regarded a resumption of the war with Britain as inevitable, or rather, he took certain steps which made it inevitable. In the first place, he revealed fairly soon that he had no intention of maintaining the *status quo* on the Continent. Even before the peace with Britain had been formally signed, he imposed a new constitution on the Cisalpine Republic (henceforth called the Italian Republic) and had himself appointed its president. A few months later France formally annexed the neighboring state of Piedmont. Dissension between centralists and federalists in the Helvetic Republic gave him a pretext for intervening there, mediating the dispute, and establishing a new state, the Swiss Confederation, which became a close military ally of France. His drastic reorganization of Germany has already been discussed.

Second, and even more alarming to the British, there was evidence of renewed French designs in the eastern Mediterranean. Napoleon sent one of his officers, Colonel Horace Sébastiani (1772–1851), to that region as a military observer, and saw to it that a report of his findings was published (January 30, 1803) in the official government newspaper, the *Moniteur.* Sébastiani's most provocative conclusion was that Egypt, because of its weakened military condition, could easily be recaptured by the French.

A third cause for continued antagonism between France and Great Britain was Napoleon's stubborn refusal to accept British commercial and colonial supremacy. He regarded his own hopes for the economic domination of the Continent as doomed to frustration as long as Britain retained this superiority. How to destroy it was a problem that occupied Napoleon for the remainder of his career.

First he tried to build up a colonial empire in the western hemisphere. His intention was to consolidate French control over the rich sugar-producing island of Haiti and to expand French influence from there into North and South America. The principal obstacle to his designs was the native Negro leader Toussaint L'Ouverture (1743–1803), who had established his control over the island in the 1790's and made it virtually independent of France. In 1802, Napoleon sent an expeditionary force to Haiti to reestablish French supremacy, and announced the restoration of slavery, which had been abolished during the revolution. These measures, and the deposition and deportation of Toussaint, provoked a violent uprising among the natives. An epidemic of yellow fever among the French soldiers completed the decimation of the military force, which finally capitulated to the natives in 1803. Faced with this catastrophe, Napoleon abandoned his plans for a western colonial empire and cut his losses by withdrawing from Haiti and selling the Louisiana Territory to the United States in 1803.

He decided to concentrate instead on undermining Britain's commercial supremacy. Having been brought up in the mercantilist tradition, he was convinced that continental markets lost to British manufacturers would go to the French and provide a further stimulus to French industry and commerce. In effect he was merely continuing policies dating from the Anglo-French commercial and colonial rivalry of the seventeenth and eighteenth centuries. His principal innovation, as we shall see, was his attempt to apply to the entire continent of Europe a policy which had hitherto been restricted to France and, during the 1790's, to those regions immediately dependent upon France. Now France would become the senior partner in a European-wide economic system. But the success of such an enterprise depended upon domination by the French of the entire Continent, and upon their ability to enforce the restrictions imposed on trade with the British. Not until 1806 did Napoleon control enough of Europe to inaugurate his famous Continental System, whose purpose was the destruction of British trade and the achievement of economic mastery of the European continent. His policy in 1802 foreshadowed the Continental System, for he refused to supplement the Treaty of Amiens with any sort of commercial agreement which would have permitted British merchants to trade with France, and he tried to extend this ban to France's allies. Probably no other action by Napoleon did more to consolidate British opinion in support of a renewal of the war with France.

Tensions between Britain and France culminated in the outbreak of war in May, 1803. Napoleon used as a pretext for renewing the conflict Britain's refusal to evacuate the island of Malta. This was a technical violation of the terms of the Treaty of Amiens, but the expansion of his own domination over Italy and his designs elsewhere on the Continent certainly provided the British with adequate grounds for retaining control over this island outpost in the Mediterranean. The war that began in 1803 dragged on indecisively for two years. Napoleon found himself unable to achieve a quick victory, partly because the French fleet was bottled up in its own ports by superior British squadrons, but also because Britain was soon joined by other nations, forming the Third Coalition.

At first, Napoleon seriously entertained the idea of invading England. In the fall of 1803 he concentrated a force of 150,000 men on the coast at Boulogne and ordered the construction of a flotilla of 1,200 flatboats to transport the troops across the Channel. Subsequently, he decided that the invasion forces required support and devised a plan for several French squadrons to escape from the blockaded ports, lure units of the British fleet to the high seas, evade them, and return to the Channel to join the invasion forces. In March, 1805, he was finally able to put this plan into operation. A French squadron under the command of Admiral Pierre Villeneuve (1763–1806) slipped out of Toulon and joined a Spanish squadron (Spain, too, had become involved in the war against Britain), and the combined fleet made for the West Indies. As Napoleon had hoped, the British took the bait. Admiral Horatio Nelson set out in pursuit with a British fleet. But when Villeneuve attempted to evade Nelson and return to Europe to support the projected invasion, the plan began to go awry. For Nelson ascertained the direction of the French fleet and managed to warn the British admiralty, which promptly stationed ships off the northwest coast of Spain to intercept Villeneuve's squadron. Villeneuve took refuge in the port of Cádiz, where he was promptly blockaded again by British units.

Although Villeneuve was blamed for the failure of the project, Napoleon had decided to abandon the invasion even before he got word of his admiral's retreat. Publicly he claimed that French troops stationed at Boulogne were needed on the Rhine to counteract the mobilization of Austrian armies, but probably the decisive factor was the return of Nelson's fleet, for he knew that the Franco-Spanish fleet would be no match for it.

Napoleon's fears were dramatically confirmed later that year. Admiral

The death of Lord Nelson at the Battle of Trafalgar, October 21, 1805. *The British admiral was fatally wounded while commanding the battle from the quarterdeck of his ship, the Victory. Painting by Turner. Tate Gallery.*

Villeneuve, contemptuously ordered by the emperor to make for a Mediterranean port, sailed out of Cádiz. Admiral Nelson intercepted Villeneuve's signals and prepared to meet him at the strait of Gibraltar. On October 21, 1805, off Cape Trafalgar, Nelson's ships overwhelmingly defeated the enemy fleet in six hours of ship-to-ship fighting. At the end of the battle only eleven of the thirty-three French and Spanish ships managed to regain their harbor. The British lost no ships, but they did lose their admiral; Nelson was fatally wounded in the first hour of fighting. The Battle of Trafalgar was unquestionably one of the decisive battles of the Napoleonic wars, for it ended definitively all French hopes of challenging Britain's mastery of the seas.

By one of those ironic twists of history, France's defeat at Trafalgar coincided almost to the day with the surrender of twenty thousand Austrian troops to Napoleon at Ulm, in Bavaria. For Napoleon had lost no time in moving his Grand Army (as he now called the forces hitherto intended for the invasion of England) to the Rhine and invading German territory. His goal was now the defeat of the Third Coalition, which had been formed against France during 1804–1805.

Among the leaders of this coalition was Tsar Alexander I of Russia, whom the British government had approached in 1804 with a view to forming an alliance against France. Alexander, one of the most colorful individuals of this era, had ascended the throne only three years earlier, at twenty-three. His role as ruler of Russia from 1801 to 1825 will be examined in detail in a later chapter; here it is important to note that his actions as a military leader and diplomat, like his polices at home, were frequently marked by unpredictability and inconsistency. Son of the unstable autocrat Paul I, Alexander had been brought up by his grandmother, Catherine the Great, who saw to it that he was given a liberal and humanist education by his Swiss tutor, Frédéric César de La Harpe. The principles inculcated in Alexander by this training were at odds with the respect for the army and the pride in himself as a soldier which he had derived from his father. His instability (some have diagnosed his condition as schizophrenia) was further heightened by the sense of guilt he felt over his father's violent death. Although he played no direct role in Paul's assassination, he is known to have been aware of the plot to depose him and to have done nothing to stop it. Upon his accession, he surrounded himself with liberal advisers and even talked of granting Russia a constitution, but little came of his promises except for some administrative and legal reforms. As he grew older and as Russia became involved in wars against France, Alexander turned more and more conservative. Ultimately he regarded himself as a divinely appointed savior of Europe destined to defeat Napoleon, the Antichrist.

In 1804 he was receptive to Britain's proposals for an alliance for two reasons. First, he felt the French emperor was violating certain accepted standards of conduct in international relations—in his abduction of the duke of Enghien from the independent state of Baden for example. Second, he was convinced that Napoleon posed a threat to Russia's interests in the Ionian Islands, in the Balkans, and in central Europe, where Alexander looked forward to becoming an arbiter. The alliance formally concluded between Britain and Russia in 1805 reiterated some of the aims of the Second Coalition—an independent Holland which would include the Belgian provinces and constitute a barrier against France in the north, and an independent kingdom of Sardinia, controlling Savoy, Piedmont, and the former Republic of Genoa, which would serve the same function in the south. Other goals, less carefully defined, included the elimination of French influence in both Germany and Italy and the strengthening of Prussia on the Rhine. Alexander also expressed his intention of establishing a reconstituted Polish state, and proposed that some sort of international body be set up after the war to enforce the peace settlement. _

Francis II of Austria was understandably hesitant about renewing the war against France, having lost so much territory in the wars of the First and Second coalitions. Nevertheless, steps taken by Napoleon to consolidate French control over northern Italy led Austria in November, 1804, to conclude a defensive treaty with Russia which provided for joint resistance against any further French aggression in Italy or Germany. When Napoleon decided in 1805 to transform the Italian Republic into a kingdom of Italy, with himself as king, Austria prepared to join the coalition with Britain and Russia. As we have seen, Austria's mobilization of its armies gave Napoleon the excuse he needed for transferring his troops from the Channel coast to the Rhine border.

General Mack (Baron Karl Mack von Leiberich, 1752–1828), commander of the Austrian forces in Germany, played from the start into Napoleon's hands by penetrating far ahead of his reinforcements; thus the French were able to outflank and encircle his troops at Ulm. From Ulm, Napoleon moved on without hindrance to the Austrian capital of Vienna. There he heard the news of the defeat at Trafalgar and became aware that his enemies of the Third Coalition—Russia, Austria, and Britain—might be joined by another ally, Prussia. The king of Prussia had preserved his neutrality for a little more than a decade, but the expansion of Napoleon's influence in the German states and the violation of Prussian territory by French forces under General Jean Baptiste Bernadotte (*c.*1763–1844) during Napoleon's campaign against Austria drove the Prussians to threaten support of the coalition. Before these plans could materialize, however, Napoleon met the main armies of the Russians, supported by the Austrians, near the little Moravian village of Austerlitz, and on December 2, 1805, the first anniversary of his coronation as emperor, achieved one of his most brilliant victories. Weakening the right wing of his own forces in order to provoke a Russian attack upon it, he concentrated the full strength of his own attack on the Russian center. His strategy worked perfectly, for having destroyed the center, he was able to turn and annihilate the Russian forces which had advanced on his right. The defeat at Austerlitz cost the allied forces between 25,000 and 30,000 casualties; Napoleon lost fewer than 9,000, including dead and wounded.

The stunning victory at Austerlitz brought about the collapse of the Third Coalition, for the Russians pulled back their troops and informed the Austrians they could count on no more Russian support. Austria saw no alternative but to sue for peace. Prussia hastily dropped its plan for opposing France, and instead, entered into negotiations with Napoleon which resulted in an alliance and the cession to France of minor territories in return for Prussian annexation of Hanover. The terms imposed upon Austria were contained in the humiliating Treaty of Pressburg (Decembr 26, 1805), which deprived Austria of virtually all its remaining possessions in Italy and awarded its imperial territories in western Germany to Bavaria, Württemberg, and Baden as rewards for their support of Napoleon in the war just ended.

Defeat of Prussia and Russia: The Treaties of Tilsit, 1807

The victory at Austerlitz at the end of 1805 and the formation of a Franco-Prussian alliance in February, 1806, brought little more than a brief respite for the Napoleonic armies. Within a few months Napoleon was at war with Prussia, the one power that had managed to remain at peace with France for over a decade.

One explanation for the change in Prussian policy lies in the personality of its monarch, Frederick William III, who had come to the throne in 1797. Though a man of good intentions, he was characterized by weakness of will and vacillation, traits that are particularly unfortunate in an absolute ruler. Frederick William preserved the governmental institutions that had been shaped by his great-uncle, Frederick the Great, among them a cabinet of councillors. But whereas under a strong monarch these officials had executed the will of the ruler, under Frederick William they exerted their own influence upon the king. Unfortunately for the Prussian state, these officials were divided in their counsel, some favoring a policy of conciliation and compromise with Napoleon, others urging an alliance with Austria or Russia and resistance to the French. Prussian policy was consequently erratic during the first years of Frederick William's reign, though the group advocating compromise with Napoleon generally held the upper hand. By the summer of 1806, however, those favoring resistance to France could point to developments that made war with Napoleon appear the only possible course of action.

Prussia's resentment arose in part from the domination which Napoleon now exercised over all parts of Germany that lay outside the boundaries of Prussia and Austria. For it was at this time (July, 1806) that Napoleon established the Confederation of the Rhine, a union of fifteen German states, including Bavaria, Württemberg, Baden, Hesse-Darmstadt, and Berg. The rulers of the confederation states had little choice but to submit to French control since the probable alternative would have been direct absorption into the French Empire. With Napoleon as its protector, the union was later expanded to include practically every state in Germany except Austria and Prussia. One consequence followed less than a month after the establishment of the confederation, when Napoleon finally announced the end of the thousand-year-old Holy Roman Empire. When the rulers of states belonging to the confederation declared that they no longer recognized the empire, Francis II was forced to abandon his traditional title; he retained only the new title that he had assumed two years before: Francis I, emperor of Austria.

Another source of trouble between France and Prussia was to be found in the alliance itself. The treaty had awarded the state of Hanover to Prussia in return for territories on the right bank of the Rhine which Prussia turned over to France and its allies. When, in the course of the next few months, the Prussian king heard that Napoleon had offered to restore Hanover to Great Britain in exchange for the withdrawal of British protective forces from the island of Sicily, he naturally viewed this proposed bargain as a betrayal of the worst sort. The fact that the Anglo-French negotiations broke down did not diminish Frederick William's resentment over Napoleon's duplicity.

In response to these and other provocations the Prussian king concluded a secret agreement with Tsar Alexander which assured Prussia of Russian support in the event of an attack by France. Even before Russia had ratified the treaty, Prussia mobilized its army against the French. The final blow to Franco-Prussian relations was Napoleon's ruthless execution of Johann Philipp Palm, a Nuremberg bookseller who had circulated a pamphlet entitled *Germany in Her Deepest Humiliation*; the tract had called upon Saxony and Prussia to save Germany from destruction at the hands of the French emperor. The disparity between the relative insignificance of the crime and the severity of the punishment offended almost all Germans and helped to arouse Prussian sentiment against France. The war began in October, 1806.

Frederick William's decision to mobilize his troops before he had been assured of adequate Russian support was a mistake. Prussian troops were outnumbered two to one, and they turned out to be no match for the well-trained armies of Napoleon. On October 14, 1806, before the Russians could arrive to support them, the Prussians were defeated simultaneously at Jena and at Auerstedt. After this decisive victory the French pursued the Prussian armies through their own country until they had captured Berlin. The king was forced to take refuge in East Prussia.

Having extended his domination to northern as well as central Germany, Napoleon now stood face to face with Tsar Alexander's Russian armies. His inclination was to engage the Russians immediately and put an end to the war, but the terrain and general conditions were much less favorable than they had been in the Prussian campaign. Winter was approaching, and he feared the losses that would be involved in fighting on the muddy reaches of East Prussia. When he nevertheless took the chance, at Eylau in February, 1807, he lost fifteen thousand men in a battle which settled nothing. The Russians suffered even heavier casualties, and both sides were forced to fall back and wait until spring to renew the conflict.

As was so often the case, Napoleon profited more from the delay than did his enemy. While the Russians and Prussians waited for subsidies from the British and tried vainly to persuade the Austrians to join them, Napoleon called up some eighty thousand new recruits from France and Italy and thus achieved the numerical superiority which helped him to win a decisive victory at the Battle of Friedland in June, 1807.

Despite his heavy losses, Tsar Alexander could have continued the war against the French, but he decided instead to sue for peace. He had been disappointed by the reluctance of Austria and Britain to support him more actively, and feared that continued fighting might provoke an uprising by the Poles. In addition, a pro-French faction of advisers which was gaining strength in his entourage was encouraging him to reach an understanding

Meeting of Tsar Alexander I and Napoleon on the Niemen River, July 25, 1807. *The Treaties of Tilsit resulted from this celebrated encounter of the two emperors on a raft anchored in the middle of the river.*

with Bonaparte. Napoleon was receptive to the tsar's peace overtures partly because of the heavy losses his armies had suffered in the year just past, but also because he hoped that an agreement with Russia would permit him to close Baltic ports to British shipping and goods.

The negotiations between Napoleon and Tsar Alexander constituted one of the most dramatic episodes of the Napoleonic era. On a raft moored in the middle of the Niemen River, the two young emperors met for a series of conferences in which they appeared to contemporaries to be dividing up the European world. And as if to heighten the drama, the hapless Frederick William of Prussia was left on one of the river banks, riding up and down the shore, waiting for the outcome of conversations which would determine the fate of his country. For several days the two rulers matched wits, and in the end, each felt he had triumphed over his opponent.

Two treaties—the treaties of Tilsit (July, 1807)—resulted from the discussions: one concerned France and Prussia; the other settled issues between France and Russia. In the former, Napoleon carried out his intention of humiliating the ex-ally who had dared to oppose him. The king was allowed to retain his throne, but Prussia lost some of its most valuable territories and half its population. Prussian lands to the west of the Elbe were ceded to France; these, with some adjacent areas, formed the new kingdom of Westphalia, which was given to Napoleon's brother Jerome. In the east, Prussia lost the Polish provinces that it had secured in the eighteenth-century partitions of Poland; they were established as the duchy of Warsaw and assigned to the king of Saxony. A separate military convention reduced the Prussian army to a minimum force and provided that French troops would occupy key Prussian fortresses until an indemnity or war contribution had been paid to France.

In the treaty with Russia, the tsar formally accepted the Napoleonic conquests in central and western Europe by recognizing the Confederation of the Rhine and the claims of Napoleon's brothers to the thrones of Holland, Naples, and Westphalia. Napoleon led the Russian emperor to believe that in return for this recognition of the French hegemony in Germany and Italy, he was acknowledging Russia's claim to an eastern European empire. Specifically, the treaty provided that Napoleon would offer his good offices as a mediator in the conflict between Russia and Turkey that had broken out in 1806, a war which he had himself helped to provoke by encouraging the sultan. A secret clause stipulated that if mediation failed, Napoleon would make common cause with Russia in a war against the Ottoman Empire and that France would agree to the cession of the Turkish European provinces of Moldavia and Walachia to Russia. Meanwhile, Russia agreed to withdraw its fleet from the Mediterranean and to yield control over the Ionian Islands to the French. Finally, the tsar offered to mediate between France and Britain. But if the British refused to restore all conquests they had made since 1805 and to respect the freedom of the seas, Russia would declare war on Britain, close the Baltic ports to British products, and call upon the Baltic States, Austria, and Portugal to join in the struggle. Since there was little likelihood of Britain's accepting the suggested conditions, Napoleon thought he could count on Russian support of his efforts to eliminate British trade with the Continent.

The question of who benefited most from the treaty turns less on the actual terms than on the subsequent interpretations made of the agreement by the two rulers. We shall discover that neither Napoleon nor Alexander lived up to the promises made at Tilsit, and each rapidly became disappointed with his new ally. How much faith either ruler put in the alliance is difficult to say. Perhaps neither had too many illusions about its permanence. By 1810, both were coming to the conclusion that a renewal of the war between them was inevitable.

Napoleon's Grand Empire

After the Battle of Austerlitz, in 1805, Napoleon began to speak openly of the Grand Empire which he was constructing in Europe to replace the practically defunct Holy Roman Empire. Indeed, as we know, Francis of Austria, the Holy Roman emperor, had seen the handwriting on the wall as early as 1804, when Napoleon crowned himself emperor of France, and had taken the precaution of naming himself hereditary emperor of Austria as well.

Napoleon's Grand Empire included, first of all, the French Empire proper: metropolitan France and the areas formally annexed to France, such as a sizable strip of Italian territory extending down the western coast to a point halfway between Rome and Naples. In 1810 Holland was eliminated as a satellite state and directly incorporated into the Empire. This nucleus was administered directly from Paris; as new territories were added, they were simply divided into departments ruled by prefects, just like the original eighty-three departments. Beyond the borders of the French state, Napoleon established a series of dependent, or satellite, states; their relationships with France were not uniform, but their rulers were all appointed by Napoleon (indeed, many were members of his own family), and owed allegiance to him. Among these states were some of the "republics" created during the revolutionary era. A third category of states, later added to the Grand Empire, included those which retained their independent status but became "allies" of France, forced to submit to its economic and military directives and to join in the wars against its enemies. For a time both Prussia and Austria fell into this category.

The process of assigning rulers to the dependent states began in 1805, on the Italian peninsula. Once Napoleon had taken the title of emperor he could hardly remain merely "president" of the Italian Republic. He therefore decided to convert this republic into the kingdom of Italy, and after pretending to offer the throne first to his older brother Joseph and later to his stepson Eugène de Beauharnais, announced that because of their refusals he would assume the title himself. He added that his kingship was only provisional: ultimately the new kingdom would go to his chief heir, who would abandon his rights to the French empire as a condition of becoming king of Italy. Eugène de Beauharnais, for the time being, was named viceroy of Italy. At the end of the year, after the Battle of Austerlitz, he added a second state to the Grand Empire, the kingdom of Naples. Angry at the Bourbon ruler of Naples for having violated his promise of neutrality by inviting British and Russian forces into Neapolitan ports, Napoleon declared that "the dynasty of Naples has ceased to reign." In March, 1806, within a month after a French detachment had taken over the kingdom, Napoleon proclaimed his brother Joseph king of Naples and Sicily. In 1808, Joseph moved on to Spain, and Joachim Murat, Napoleon's brother-in-law, received the crown of Naples.

The pattern established in Italy was also followed elsewhere on the Continent. In 1806 Napoleon dissolved the eleven-year-old Batavian Republic and named his younger brother Louis to the throne of the short-lived

"The Plumb-pudding in danger; or State Epicures taking un Petit Souper." *Cartoon, published in London, 1805, showing William Pitt and Napoleon carving up the world.*

kingdom of Holland. To his brother-in-law Murat, in 1806, went the newly created duchy of Berg, in the Rhineland, which was later expanded at the expense of Prussia. To his brother Jerome he assigned the kingdom of Westphalia, created after Tilsit, in 1807. These royal relatives of the emperor were of course bound to him by personal ties, although they were nominally independent of France.

To what extent did the establishment of this sprawling empire spread French institutions to the rest of Europe? Did the dependent states of Germany and Italy, forced to contribute men and money to the support of Napoleon's armies, derive some compensating advantages from French rule? The extent to which French reforms and legislation were introduced varied as greatly from one part of the Empire to another as did the characters of the individual administrators and rulers named to govern the several territories. In regions directly annexed to France institutions were established that were, in theory, the same as those existing in metropolitan France itself, though some adjustments were inevitably made to language and local circumstances. In the newly created departments—and in the dependent states as well—the emperor or his vassal rulers attempted to introduce the Napoleonic codes, the French administrative and financial system, and forms of political representation comparable to those existing at home. It was the general policy, also, to abolish serfdom, eliminate feudal dues, and prohibit the inheritance of large estates. With respect to the church, Napoleon hoped to apply throughout the Empire the policies which had been developed in France: the insistence upon the supremacy of the lay state over the church, the abolition of monastic institutions, the establishment of a system of public instruction, and so on. Resistance to the secular control of education was, as one might expect, particularly strong in parts of Italy. Often the rulers of the dependent states, in closer touch than the emperor with the problems of their particular regions, proved more flexible in the matter of imposing French institutions. When Louis Bonaparte, the ruler of Holland, protested to Napoleon that several provisions of the *Code Napoléon* should be dropped in Holland because they ran counter to Dutch prejudices, his advice was refused with the words, "If you revise the *Code Napoléon* it will no longer be the *Code Napoléon*. . . . The Romans gave their laws to their allies; why should not France have hers adopted in Holland?" [5]

Many peoples of the Grand Empire benefited from the introduction of more efficient administrative institutions, more equitable laws, a more just distribution of the burdens of taxation, and other improvements brought by French rule. The changes were particularly advantageous to those who had been living under the antiquated hierarchical institutions of some of the petty states of Germany or in a state such as the kingdom of Naples. At the same time, the attempt to impose from above institutions that affected established prejudices, personal relationships, and daily routines met with a mixed reception even from those who might have gained most from such changes. It is one thing for a people to achieve reforms as the result of its own efforts; another, to have those reforms bestowed by a conqueror.

In the last analysis, Napoleon came to be viewed more as a conqueror than as a liberator. For membership in the Grand Empire brought disadvantages as well as rewards. As the Napoleonic wars progressed, the vassal states were required to contribute more and more heavily to their support, providing not only financial subsidies but recruits to supplement the imperial armies. (Of the 600,000 men in the forces which invaded Russia in 1812 only a third were native Frenchmen; the rest were of twenty different nationalities.) Regions which did not suffer directly the ravages of warfare were often required to support armies of occupation. Most annoying to the business and trading classes were the galling economic restrictions that formed a part of Napoleon's Continental System, and the hordes of French agents and inspectors required to enforce those restrictions.

In later years, after his defeat and exile, Napoleon tried to create the impression that during his reign he had championed the nationalist aspirations of Germans, Italians, Poles, and other scattered peoples. He could thus contrast himself with the restored rulers of Europe, who after his downfall, held these peoples in subjection or thwarted their hopes for unity. To what extent was this claim justified? Can Napoleon, as some have contended, be viewed as the architect of German and Italian unity, the defender of Polish nationalism?

In two respects he did stimulate the nationalist sentiments of certain European peoples, though perhaps not in the ways he later suggested. His rearrangement of the map of Europe, by decreasing the number of states in Germany and Italy, may have contributed to a greater sense of unity among

---

[5] Quoted by Bruun, *Europe and the French Imperium*, p. 136.

both peoples. Where Germany consisted of some three hundred states, principalities, and lesser political entities at the end of the eighteenth century, the conquests of the revolutionary and Napoleonic armies left only the truncated states of Prussia and Austria, the Confederation of the Rhine (fifteen states at the outset), and a few lesser territories. In addition, Napoleon's decree of 1806 put an end to the anachronistic Holy Roman Empire. He thus cleared the way, unintentionally, for those who subsequently espoused the cause of a united Germany. In the Italian peninsula, the political organization established by the French was destroyed in 1815, but the fact remained that Italians could look back to a time under Napoleon's rule when the numerous states had been combined into only three separate parts: the regions directly incorporated into the French Empire, the kingdom of Italy, and the kingdom of Naples and Sicily. Italy had not known so great a measure of unity since the era of the Roman Empire. Also, by establishing the duchy of Warsaw in 1807 and adding western Galicia to it in 1809, Napoleon revived the hopes of the Polish people for an independent state.

A second, and more important, way in which Bonaparte contributed to the growth of nationalist sentiments among Europeans was by arousing patriotic resentment among the peoples subjected to French domination. How strong such feelings were among the rank and file is difficult to determine. The soldier who served in an army pitted against the French probably fought because he had to rather than out of any sense of loyalty to his nation. The peasant doubtless resented the requisition of his crops or the physical damage to his property caused by warfare, but this reaction did not necessarily result in a new allegiance to his ruler or a new sense of unity with his compatriots. However, among a minority of intellectuals during this era can be detected a new patriotic spirit. The philosopher Johann Gottlieb Fichte, for example, sought to inspire German national sentiment through his *Addresses to the German Nation,* delivered in Berlin in 1807 and 1808, and Ernst Moritz Arndt, a poet and historian, toward the end of the Napoleonic era published a series of poems calling upon Prussia to liberate all Germany from the yoke of the French tyrant. In Italy, the *Carbonari* ("Charcoal Burners"), a conspiratorial organization later devoted to the cause of Italian unity, began as a group devoted to resistance to the French occupation. None of these individuals or groups attracted a mass following before 1815, but the seeds sown during the Napoleonic era bore fruit in the nationalist movements of the nineteenth century.

As for Napoleon's own feelings toward these various national groups, his actions during his years of rule speak louder than any later words. His ruthless subjugation of the peoples of the Grand Empire to French national aims and aspirations, his imposition of French rulers and French institutions upon the dependent states, suggest no profound understanding of national differences or sympathy with nationalist goals. When he destroyed traditional institutions and upset the dynasties of petty rulers in central Europe, he did so not in order to encourage German or Italian national aspirations, but rather to rule the peoples of these territories more effectively and to exploit their resources for his own military or economic advantage. If Bonaparte was motivated in his conquests by any transcendent ideal, it was the ideal not of a federation of equal nations, but rather of a universal empire, like the Roman Empire or that of Charlemagne.

The Continental System, 1806

The Continental System did not emerge suddenly, but was the culmination of a policy of restrictions on trade with Britain adopted by France during the revolution and continued by Napoleon after his accession to power. Only at the end of 1806 did Napoleon feel secure enough in his control over Europe to undertake an all-out effort to destroy British trade with the Continent. In that year, having acquired the kingdom of Naples, he was able to close one of the major remaining points of access for the British, the Neapolitan ports. Even more important was the French defeat of Prussia, which gave Napoleon control of the north German ports, the principal entrepôts for British goods going to the Continent. With the famous Berlin Decree of November, 1806, he formally inaugurated the Continental System, banning all commerce with the British. Hereafter, British subjects on the Continent were subject to arrest; all goods belonging to Great Britain or coming from its factories or its colonies were subject to confiscation. Any vessel, regardless of nationality, coming directly from the ports of Britain or its colonies was forbidden access to continental ports. Since the decree was binding on all of France's dependent states and allies, Napoleon was, in effect, trying to establish a barrier extending from the north German ports to the tip of the Italian peninsula. Because of the condition of the French fleet, Napoleon could not hope to enforce a blockade of British ports; the principal intention of the decree was to prevent all vessels (neutral as well as British) from bringing British or colonial goods into continental ports. The emperor's aim was to secure for continental—preferably French—manufacturers and merchants, markets that had formerly been controlled by the British.

Even before the Berlin Decree, the British had instituted a blockade of their own on goods flowing in and out of continental ports on the North Sea and English Channel. After the decree, Britain retaliated by announcing that all neutral ships plying between coastal ports from which English ships were excluded would be considered liable to capture and condemnation as lawful prizes. The economic struggle between the French and British lasted until about 1812, but the principal goal of the Continental System—the destruction of British trade—was never achieved. Napoleon's plan was basically sound: if he had really succeeded in excluding British commerce from Europe, British credit would have collapsed. But British commerce never was excluded from Europe; British goods continued to flow in by a variety of means. Smuggling operations were carried out on a large scale, particularly through Holland and northwestern Germany. In many instances, customs officials were bribed to allow prohibited goods to enter. By 1810 the British were selling a great many "licenses of trade," which guaranteed neutral ships immunity from capture by British vessels and thus permitted them to carry British goods safely to the Continent. Such ships could be provided with false papers which certified their departure from a non-British port and the non-English origin of their cargo.

In the last analysis, Napoleon simply did not have the navy or the vast corps of loyal civil servants and customs inspectors required to make the system work throughout the entire continent. Frenchmen might respond to his patriotic appeals to defeat the British by adhering to the restrictions imposed by the Continental System, but there was much less reason for the natives of the dependent and allied states to heed such regulations. Merchants who saw their volume of business reduced and consumers who were deprived of products they desired were only too willing to find loopholes by which they could evade the restrictions. Most discouraging to the emperor was the fact that instead of increasing, French trade and business activity declined. For the British blockade achieved its principal purpose, which was not to prevent imports from reaching the Continent, but to weaken the enemy by destroying his commerce and shipping. Numerous French shippers and merchants went out of business as their vessels languished in continental ports blockaded by the British navy.

By 1810, the Continental System was working so badly that Napoleon decided to take advantage of its weaknesses and exploit them to the profit of France. What he did, in effect, was to become a smuggler himself: he authorized the auction of prize cargoes (including goods formally prohibited from entry) if the purchaser paid a duty of 40 percent. Then he instructed his customs agents to admit prohibited goods on condition that they had been falsely labeled by their sellers as prize cargoes. In this way he increased the revenue from duties and permitted the entry of those goods which were particularly in demand. However, this step constituted the abandonment of the purpose of the Continental System and obviously undermined the entire operation. Thus at a time when Napoleon was still enjoying political and military victories, he had already suffered a major economic defeat.

The Peninsular War, 1808–1813

In 1807, with peace temporarily assured in central and eastern Europe, Napoleon became involved in warfare in an entirely different quarter of the Continent. He had long resented the loyalty shown by the ruler of Portugal toward his British ally and was determined to crush the Iberian kingdom and make it conform to the Continental System. To fight Portugal, Napoleon had to secure passage for French troops through Spain. This he did by vaguely promising its senile Bourbon monarch, Charles IV (ruled 1788–1808), that he would divide Portugal between France and Spain. But as we shall see, once French troops had secured a foothold in Spain, Napoleon found a pretext for overthrowing the Spanish monarchy as well. The invasion of Portugal was merely the prelude to the subjugation of the entire Iberian peninsula.

The Peninsular War is important in the context of Napoleon's entire career, for many historians have viewed the beginning of this war as the turning point in the emperor's military fortunes. For the first time he seems seriously to have underestimated the degree of resistance he would arouse and the difficult nature of the warfare he would encounter, the result, in this instance, of the mountainous terrain. Some of the initial French defeats can be ascribed to the ineptitude of the military commanders; when Napoleon took personal command, he was more successful. But the Spanish campaign proved a steady drain on his resources and dragged on indecisively until the final ejection of the French in 1813.

Although the Portuguese royal family fled to Brazil in the face of the invasion, resistance to the French continued, and the Portuguese soon had the support of a British army under the command of Sir Arthur Wellesley (1769–1852), later duke of Wellington, who defeated the French in his initial encounter with them. Meanwhile, a force of 100,000 French troops had crossed the Spanish border, ostensibly to protect the Spanish coasts against the British. In March, 1808, an opportune rebellion against King Charles IV, stemming from the unpopularity of the queen's favorite, Manuel de Godoy (1767–1851), caused Charles to abdicate in favor of his son Ferdinand VII. Profiting from the unsettled situation and from antagonisms within the royal family, Napoleon refused to recognize Ferdinand and succeeded in getting him, as well as his father and Godoy, across the Franco-Spanish border, presumably to settle the dispute among them. The outcome of this maneuver was the forced abdication of the son, which left the throne vacant. Napoleon thereupon arranged for a petition to be drawn up by a number of responsible Spanish officials requesting that the throne be given to Joseph Bonaparte. Only too happy to comply with this request, the emperor agreed, and Joseph abandoned his rights to the kingdom of Naples to become king of Spain.

What Napoleon failed to recognize was that the antipathy shown by the Spaniards toward their ruler did not necessarily imply a corresponding enthusiasm for rule by the French, for the deposition of the Bourbons was greeted by a general uprising which drove the French from Madrid. After a number of reverses during the summer of 1808, Napoleon decided to take personal command of the forces in Spain and succeeded in recapturing the capital. But failing again to understand the character of the Spanish, he undertook a series of reforms—including measures against the Catholic Church, such as ending the Inquisition and decreasing the number of monastic establishments—which merely alienated the people further. Despite a number of victories against the Spanish and the British, who had come to their aid, Napoleon was unable to bring the war to an end. Many of the inhabitants took to the hills to engage in guerilla fighting, and because the country was decentralized and disorganized, opposition was particularly difficult to overcome. Indeed, the city of Cádiz in southwestern Spain, never submitted to French control, and it was here that a national assembly was elected in 1810 to draw up a new constitution for Spain.

The Short War with Austria, 1809

The unexpectedly strong resistance to Napoleon's armies in the Iberian peninsula, and the difficulties he encountered there, served to encourage his enemies elsewhere on the Continent. When, in 1808, Napoleon was forced to withdraw large contingents of the Grand Army from Germany for use in the Spanish campaign, the war party in the Austrian court urged Emperor Francis to seize the opportunity to embarrass his traditional enemy. After Austria's defeat at Austerlitz, Francis' younger brother, Archduke Charles Louis, had undertaken a partial reorganization of the army; this step had been matched by corresponding administrative reforms designed to strengthen the country in a future conflict with Napoleon. Francis himself was reluctant to renew the conflict with the French without allies, and he rightly guessed that no significant support would be forthcoming. Tsar Alexander was still formally allied with France; indeed, the agreements of Tilsit had been reaffirmed at a meeting between the two at Erfurt in September, 1808. Prussia, its territory still occupied by French troops, was engaged in a series of drastic reforms and was in no position to take arms against the French. Despite these misgivings, Francis was persuaded to take the risk. It was pointed out to him that France had half of its forces tied up in Spain, that the war was increasingly unpopular at home, and that the German peoples could not fail to respond to an appeal to liberate their territories from French domination.

Throwing caution to the winds, Austria began the war in April, 1809, by invading Bavaria. Napoleon was aware of the danger of his position. When it became clear that no support would be forthcoming from Russia, he hastily called up fresh recruits and ordered two divisions from Spain rushed to the east. Despite the improvised character of these forces, Napoleon's first moves showed that he had lost none of his skill as a military leader. Within a matter of days he had counterattacked and halted the Austrian advance. He followed up his advantage by marching his armies down the Danube to Vienna at a pace of twenty miles a day. Meanwhile, Archduke Charles Louis was regrouping his troops on the left bank of the Danube. When Napoleon crossed the river and attacked, he met with vicious resistance from the Austrian forces, and after two days of fighting, he was forced to recross the Danube, having lost some twenty thousand men. The Austrians also suffered heavy casualties, but they took satisfaction from the battle because they had beaten back an army commanded personally by Napoleon. After this encounter both armies remained at a standstill for seven weeks while reinforcements were brought up. When Napoleon attacked again, his was the superior force, and he carried the day with a victory at Wagram. The battle was not nearly so decisive as Austerlitz had been, but the archduke saw no purpose in continuing the war and a week later he asked for an armistice.

Austria had challenged the conqueror and had been defeated by him for the fourth time. By the Treaty of Schönbrunn (October, 1809) it lost an additional 32,000 square miles of territory, with some 3.5 million inhabitants. A good part of the ceded area went to Bavaria, and the duchy of Warsaw was strengthened by the annexation of western Galicia. To the south, Napoleon combined formerly Austrian territories with the Ionian Islands to constitute a new state, the Illyrian Provinces. A final provision of the treaty forced Austria to adhere to the Continental System and to break off all ties with Great Britain.

The Empire in 1810

In terms of square miles of territory under French control, the year 1810 marked the apogee of the Napoleonic Empire. The defeat of Austria at Wagram in 1809 extended the domination of the French southward and eastward down the Adriatic coast. Because his brother Louis had shown himself as king of Holland more sympathetic to Dutch than to French interests and had consistently violated the Continental System by allowing British goods to be smuggled in through Holland, Napoleon deprived him of his throne in 1810 and incorporated the Dutch kingdom directly into the French Empire. With other areas along the North Sea coast also added to it, the French Empire proper now consisted of 130 departments (instead of the original 83) and extended in a great arc from the Baltic Sea at the base of the Danish peninsula to a point on the Italian coast south of Rome. The Grand Empire stretched from the southwest coast of Spain to the limits of the duchy of Warsaw, on the border of the Russian empire.

Napoleon appeared to be at the height of his power, practically unchallenged throughout Europe. Except for the continuing war in the Spanish peninsula and the economic struggle with Great Britain, the period from 1810 to 1812 was relatively peaceful for the Empire. By this time he had also taken steps toward the solution of a problem which had been plaguing him for years—the absence of a son to inherit his vast domain. His marriage with Joséphine, contracted in 1796, had failed to produce an heir. More than once since becoming emperor he had considered the possibility of securing a divorce; neither partner to the marriage had remained faithful to the other. Yet Napoleon seems to have been reluctant to separate himself definitively from the woman who had inspired in him his greatest passion.

Nevertheless, marriage with the younger sister of Alexander of Russia was discussed at Tilsit in 1807 and again in 1809; the offer was finally refused by the tsar, ostensibly because the girl was too young. After the defeat of Austria in 1809, the emperor's representatives entered into negotiations with the Austrian court to arrange his marriage to the eighteen-year-old Austrian princess, Marie Louise (1791–1847). Prince Metternich, Austria's foreign minister, immediately took up the proposal, seeing in it a chance for Austria to achieve at least temporary security in its relations with France. For Napoleon the marriage offered not only the hope for a male heir but the prestige of affiliation with the oldest royal house on the Continent. Unable to obtain the consent of Pope Pius VII to the annulment of his marriage with Joséphine, he secured the annulment from a subservient ecclesiastical body in Paris, retired Joséphine to her château at Malmaison, and married Marie Louise in April, 1810. Within a year she had borne him a son, who was given the title of king of Rome. The dynasty now appeared secure.

Beneath the apparent stability of the Empire in the years 1810–1812 lay a number of signs of weakness and deterioration. We have spoken of the resentment aroused in the dependent states by the Continental System and the enforced levies of men and money to support Napoleon's wars. Even in France there were signs of growing discontent. A business recession in 1810–1811 diminished the regime's standing with the bourgeoisie, hitherto Napoleon's strongest supporters. The war in Spain was never popular with the French and aroused considerable opposition to the emperor. The burden of conscription in France reached down to younger and younger men during the Spanish campaign and the Austrian war of 1809, and by 1810 there were disturbing rumors of an impending war with Russia. Finally, devout Catholics, who had regarded Napoleon at the time of the Concordat as the restorer of the faith in France, were shocked by his dealings with the papacy in the years following the proclamation of the Empire. Relations between the pope and the emperor deteriorated steadily after 1805 because of difficulties in the administration of the Concordat and the high-handed action of Napoleon with respect to papal territories in Italy. Gradually, what had been left of the lands of the Church after the establishment of Napoleon's kingdom of Italy was either absorbed into that kingdom or occupied and administered by the French. In May, 1809, when Napoleon proposed formally to incorporate the remaining Papal States into the French Empire, the pope threatened him with excommunication. Napoleon's response was to have Pius VII arrested and taken to Savona, near Genoa, where he was held prisoner. From there he was transferred in 1812 to Fontainebleau. Such an act, culminating the entire series of aggressive moves against the Church, earned Napoleon the bitter enmity of devout Catholics throughout Europe.

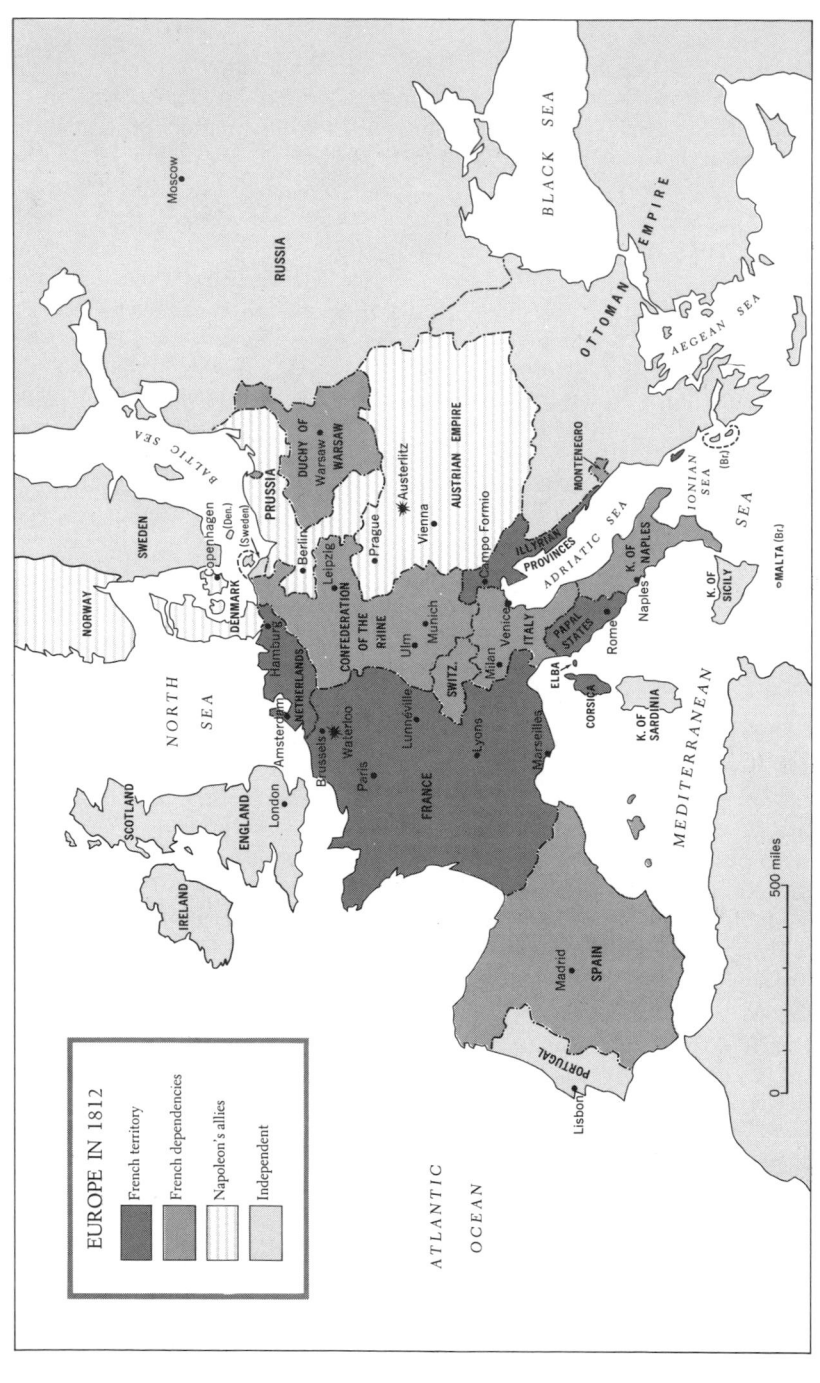

EUROPE IN 1812

French territory
French dependencies
Napoleon's allies
Independent

ATLANTIC OCEAN

IRELAND

SCOTLAND

ENGLAND
London

NORTH SEA

NORWAY

SWEDEN

BALTIC SEA

Copenhagen
DENMARK
(Den.)
(Sweden)

Moscow

RUSSIA

PRUSSIA

Berlin

DUCHY OF WARSAW

Hamburg
NETHERLANDS
Amsterdam
Brussels
Waterloo
Lunéville
Paris
Lyons
FRANCE
Marseilles

CONFEDERATION OF THE RHINE
Leipzig
Prague
Munich
Ulm
SWITZ.
Milan

Austerlitz
Vienna

AUSTRIAN EMPIRE

Campo Formio
Venice

ITALY

ILLYRIAN PROVINCES

MONTENEGRO

ADRIATIC SEA

IONIAN SEA

BLACK SEA

OTTOMAN EMPIRE

AEGEAN SEA

(Br.)

K. OF NAPLES
Naples

K. OF SICILY

MALTA (Br.)

PAPAL STATES
Rome

ELBA

CORSICA

K. OF SARDINIA

MEDITERRANEAN SEA

SPAIN
Madrid

PORTUGAL
Lisbon

500 miles

0

Charles Maurice
de Talleyrand.
Drawing by David.

As early as 1809 a number of individuals saw the handwriting on the wall and began to lay the groundwork for the regime which would succeed Bonaparte's. Among those most active in such plotting was the consummate opportunist Charles Maurice de Talleyrand, who managed to serve and to survive most of the governments that succeeded one another between 1789 and his death in 1838. Born to an aristocratic family in 1754, Talleyrand began his career as a liberal priest and was awarded the bishopric of Autun on the eve of the revolution. As a member of the Estates-General he sided with the Third Estate; in the National Assembly he supported the confiscation of Church lands and the Civil Constitution of the Clergy. In 1791, having been placed under the ban of the Church by the pope, Talleyrand entered the diplomatic service. Upon the execution of Louis XVI, he sought refuge in the United States, returning to France only after the establishment of the Directory in 1795. After serving for two years as minister of foreign affairs for the Directory, he resigned in 1799, in time to help Bonaparte to power in the *coup d'état* of Brumaire. As Napoleon's minister of foreign affairs from 1799 to 1807 he helped assure French supremacy in Europe, and in 1806 was rewarded by the emperor with the title prince of Benevento. In 1807 he resigned his post as foreign minister and in 1809 established contact with the Austrian diplomat Metternich, with a view to providing for future contingencies. He was to play an active role, as we shall discover later, in persuading the victorious allies to accept the restoration of the Bourbon dynasty in 1814, served again as foreign minister—this time for the Bourbon king, Louis XVIII—and represented France at the Congress of Vienna in 1814 and 1815. Before his death he assisted one more French ruler—Louis Philippe—to the throne, in 1830; he ended his career as French ambassador to Britain in the 1830's.

Talleyrand's reputation has suffered at the hands of historians who view him as the prototype of the Machiavellian statesman and faithless diplomat. They charge that his primary concern was enriching himself and ensuring his survival in power in the bewildering succession of French governments from 1789 to 1830. Even his defenders concede his egotism and attribute his survival to the facility with which he adapted his utterances, public and private, to the ideology prevailing at a particular moment. This was perhaps easy for him since, in the last analysis, he adhered to no abstract ideals or principles. But his apologists have also contended that one consistent thread underlay his actions throughout his long career: his concern for France and his loyalty to its interests. His skills as a diplomat and a negotiator were always directed toward improving his country's international position. He deserted Napoleon, it is argued, when he found himself unable to restrain the emperor's insatiable ambition and realized it would ultimately destroy his country. Cutting his ties with the emperor, he laid the groundwork for the restoration of the Bourbon dynasty, and in the peace settlement following the Napoleonic wars he was remarkably successful in restoring his defeated country almost immediately to the ranks of the great powers.

The Invasion of Russia, 1812

Despite the evidence of mounting dissatisfaction with his regime, Napoleon began preparations in the spring of 1812 for the campaign against Russia which ultimately was to prove disastrous for him. Like Adolf Hitler

The Café Frascati in 1807, favored meeting place of the wealthy. *Note the dress and decor, typical of the Empire era.*

The Handwriting on the Wall. *This satirical English cartoon by Gillray recalls the biblical Feast of Belshazzar. Paris, the new Babylon, capital of all vices is doomed to destruction. On the banquet table where Napoleon and a hideous Josephine are dining, several choice morsels are served: the head of George III, the Tower of London, and the Bank of England. A hand points to the fateful words:* Mene, Mene, Tekel, Upharsin.

almost 130 years later, Napoleon saw two powers blocking his plans for complete European domination—Great Britain and Russia. Like Hitler, he tried unsuccessfully to subdue Great Britain, and when his attempt failed, turned eastward, convinced that if Russia were defeated, Britain must also succumb.

We have seen that the relationship between the two emperors, Napoleon and Alexander, was an uneasy one from the start. The ink was hardly dry upon the agreements made at Tilsit in 1807 when Napoleon annexed the newly created duchy of Warsaw to the Confederation of the Rhine and sent thirty thousand troops into the region, a move that appeared very threatening to the Russian empire. His interest in consolidating his control over the Poles was further revealed when, after the defeat of Austria in 1809, he incorporated western Galicia into the duchy of Warsaw, leading Alexander to suspect his designs upon territories taken by Russia from Poland in the eighteenth-century partitions. It also became clear to Alexander that Napoleon was far from willing to concede to Russia the free hand in the dismemberment of Turkey which the tsar thought he had obtained at Tilsit. Alexander realized, as Russia's war with Turkey dragged on, that even if he were victorious, Napoleon would probably block his plans for expansion into Turkey's provinces in southeastern Europe. The nature of Napoleon's own designs in the Balkans is not entirely clear, but there can be no doubt that he was determined to prevent Russia from taking Constantinople. Finally, Napoleon's marriage with Marie Louise in 1810, and his consequent alliance with Austria, were viewed with misgivings by Alexander.

Napoleon's principal grievance against the tsar was Alexander's failure to enforce the Continental System in his own ports. True to the agreement made at Tilsit, Russia declared war on Great Britain, but Alexander never pursued the war actively and his administration of the regulations against British trade left much to be desired. When Napoleon asked Russia in 1810 to confiscate all neutral ships in its ports on the ground that they were carrying British goods, Alexander refused. Instead, he issued a decree later in the year which specifically encouraged the entry of neutral ships into Russian harbors. It was clear to Napoleon that the alliance was nearing its end. Late in 1810, Russia formally withdrew from the Continental System.

Anticipating conflict, both rulers sought allies. Each hoped for the support of Austria and Prussia, but the presence of the Napoleonic armies in Germany and the recent defeats which both Prussia and Austria had suffered at Napoleon's hands left them little choice but to submit to his demands. Accordingly, in 1812 Prussia pledged to contribute twenty thousand men, and Austria thirty thousand, to Napoleon's Grand Army. Unable to win support in Germany, Russia formed an alliance with Sweden. According to its terms, Sweden agreed to join Russia in the war against Napoleon in return for a promise of Russian assistance in annexing Norway, then in Denmark's possession, at the end of the war. Denmark was to be compensated with other territory. Ironically, Sweden's decision to join Russia was made by Crown Prince Bernadotte, once one of Napoleon's generals, who in 1810 had been named heir to the throne by the Swedish Estates. During this period, also, Russia ended the wars against Turkey and Great Britain, and concluded an alliance with Great Britain against France.

In preparation for the invasion, Napoleon assembled his Grand Army in eastern Europe. Its strength at the time of the invasion in June, 1812, was approximately 450,000; by the time reinforcements were brought up, it numbered about 600,000—and was probably the largest military force that had ever been brought together. In its ranks were not only French soldiers but contingents of Italians, Poles, Swiss, Dutch, and Germans (from the Confederation of the Rhine, Austria, and Prussia). Napoleon planned to have the predominantly French contingents of the army advance in the center, supported by an Austrian army to the south and a Prussian army to the north. Crossing the Niemen River in June, he hoped to drive a wedge between the two main Russian armies, surround them, and defeat them separately. His objective for the campaign of 1812 was Smolensk, where he hoped to impose terms on the tsar. If Alexander refused to submit, Napoleon would winter at Smolensk and renew the war in the spring of 1813 with a drive on Moscow.

He proceeded according to this plan. What disrupted his calculations was

The last remnants of the Grand Army en route to Smolensk, November, 1812. *At the beginning of November, cold weather set in and caused additional suffering for the hungry, beleaguered French forces.*

his failure to engage the main body of the Russian armies before he was deep into Russia. The Russian generals, fearing the numerical superiority of the enemy, repeatedly avoided giving battle. Advancing relentlessly across the Russian plains under a blazing July sun, Napoleon lost thousands of men through the ravages of heat, disease, and hunger, and through desertion. When his troops finally reached Smolensk in mid-August, the Russians fought only a rearguard action and then left the city to the invader. According to his original plan Napoleon was to halt here, and he was urged to do so by some of his subordinates. Instead he made the fatal decision to press on to Moscow. General Mikhail Kutuzov (1745–1813) had been given orders to halt the advance on Moscow at Borodino, and there, on September 7, Napoleon met the main Russian force. The two armies fought bitterly, in a battle which left some seventy thousand dead and wounded. In the end, both sides claimed victory, but it was the Russians that retreated, leaving the path to Moscow open. When the French finally reached Moscow on September 14, they found it practically deserted; within a few hours, fires broke out in the city, set presumably by those who had stayed behind for this purpose by order of the retreating military governor. Because most Moscow dwellings were built of wood, the fires spread swiftly, and within a week almost three quarters of the city had burned to the ground. For five weeks Napoleon remained in the empty, devastated city, as the morale of his troops rapidly deteriorated. His offer of a truce having been rejected by Alexander, he waited in vain for the tsar to come to terms.

Finally, unable to supply his troops so far from their bases, frustrated in his hope of achieving a decisive victory, and fearing the onset of the Russian winter, on October 19 he began his celebrated retreat from Moscow. His troops were harassed by attacks by Kutuzov's army and prevented from following a shorter southern route to Smolensk. At the beginning of November, cold weather set in and caused additional suffering for the hungry, beleaguered French forces. By the time they reached Smolensk, only half of the troops who had left Moscow remained. The climax of the catastrophe came in late November when the retreating forces, attempting to recross the Berezina River, were subjected to murderous fire by Russians both behind and ahead of them. From this point on, the retreat became a rout as the army lost all semblance of organization and disintegrated. On December 18, the last remnants of the Grand Army straggled across the Niemen River, from which they had set out in June. Of 600,000 men, only 100,000 remained. The rest had been killed or captured.

Napoleon had left the army early in December, before it reached the Niemen, and had hastened back to Paris. The full extent of the disaster was not known in France immediately, but rumors were trickling back and Napoleon wished to be present personally to quiet misgivings in the capital. His main reason for returning, however, was to organize a new army. Far from being shattered by the defeat he had just suffered, he was more determined than ever to renew the war against his two enemies, Russia and Great Britain. Three weeks after he got back to Paris he demanded from the Senate a draft calling up 350,000 new recruits.

The rout of Napoleon's army at the Berezina River, November 26, 1813.

The War of Liberation, 1813–1814

Fifteen months elapsed between the end of the disastrous Russian campaign and the triumphal entry of the allied armies into Paris on March 31, 1814. What is perhaps surprising is that the French managed to hold off their enemies for so long. That Napoleon succeeded in raising a force of a quarter of a million men by the spring of 1813 was a miracle, but of course the men in this army were not the seasoned troops he had used at Austerlitz and Jena. Moreover, the final campaigns of the emperor were seriously handicapped by shortages of arms, ammunition, and equipment. Indeed, some military historians argue that France's defeat was caused as much by the lack of materiel as by the lack of men. A final reason for the defeat of Napoleon was that his enemies, after almost two decades of intermittent wars against France, succeeded in temporarily setting aside their differences and uniting to achieve victory.

The cornerstone of the coalition which defeated Napoleon was laid in March, 1813, when Prussia and Russia formed an alliance and called upon Austria and Great Britain to join them. The response was not immediate, but the potentialities of the coalition were augmented by an agreement at about the same time between Great Britain and Crown Prince Bernadotte of Sweden. Bernadotte promised, in return for a large subsidy from the British, to furnish thirty thousand Swedish troops to be used against the French. The war between the allies and Napoleon's reconstituted army began in the spring of 1813. Despite two nominal victories in May, Napoleon's losses were heavy, and he willingly agreed in June to an armistice, which lasted most of the summer. This pause turned out to be of greater advantage to his opponents than to himself, for when the fighting began again in August, Metternich had decided to take Austria into the war on the side of the coalition and Great Britain had signed a treaty providing the allies with heavy subsidies. Metternich's decision was reached after Napoleon refused to accept an agreement calling for the abandonment by France of most of its conquests in the interest of a balance-of-power settlement for the Continent. For the first time in his career Napoleon found himself confronted by the united forces of four major powers. Besides his French troops, he had only contingents from the Confederation of the Rhine supporting him. Nevertheless the emperor attacked, and within two weeks, had inflicted a defeat on one of the allied armies at Dresden (August, 1813), in his last major victory on German soil. From that time on, however, the campaign went badly for the emperor, as his subordinate commanders met with a series of reverses. Early in October, Bavaria withdrew from the Confederation of the Rhine and joined the alliance against the French. The climax of the fall campaign came in a series of decisive battles around Leipzig in mid-October, when all the allied armies converged upon the French in what came to be known as the Battle of the

Nations. After several days of preliminary fighting, the allies, in a single nine-hour engagement, drove the French armies back to the gates of Leipzig, winning a shattering victory. Deserted by his remaining German allies, Napoleon was forced to retreat across the Rhine; the Confederation of the Rhine had come to an end.

What made the debacle in Germany even more serious was a series of setbacks in other parts of the Empire. A revolt in the Dutch provinces, followed by an allied invasion there, resulted in the restoration of the prince of Orange as ruler in Holland. An army raised by Eugène de Beauharnais in northern Italy at Napoleon's instigation met with defeat by the Austrians. Finally, the year 1813 saw one reverse after another in Spain, as the duke of Wellington advanced against a French army weakened by the transfer of important contingents to the German front. By the middle of the year, Joseph Bonaparte had fled to France and the French were retreating from region after region. In November, Wellington crossed the frontier into France and laid siege to the city of Bayonne.

Before the allies invaded France from the east, they made an offer of peace to Napoleon which would have left France with its "natural frontiers" of the Alps and the Rhine. Metternich later admitted in his memoirs that the allies had no intention of keeping this promise, that it was made in the belief that Napoleon would refuse, thereby assuming responsibility for continuing the war. Metternich's assumption proved correct. Napoleon did not reject the offer outright, but stalled in such a way that the allies could withdraw it and still blame him for the prolongation of the conflict.

In the beginning of 1814 the allied armies, 200,000 strong, crossed the Rhine. Napoleon, left with only 90,000 soldiers, many of them mere youths, fought a brilliant defensive campaign in these desperate circumstances. Shifting his troops swiftly in order to attack the divided allied forces piecemeal, he managed still to win isolated victories against the Prussian general Gebhard von Blücher (1742–1819) and the Austrian prince Karl Philipp zu Schwarzenberg (1771–1820). But the rawness of his troops, their numerical inferiority, and the lack of equipment finally decided the issue. While he made a desperate attempt to throw himself on the rear of the allied forces in Lorraine, the leading contingents of the invaders pressed on toward Paris. With the final storming of Montmartre by the allies, the French were forced to capitulate. On March 31 Tsar Alexander and King Frederick William made their triumphal entry into the capital. Napoleon had meanwhile hastened back to Paris, hoping to make a last-ditch stand, but he arrived too late and retired to Fontainebleau. Even at this stage he urged his marshals to join him in an assault on the city, but they refused. Prince Talleyrand, who had remained in Paris, now used his position as vice grand elector to summon the Senate, and influenced that body to declare that Napoleon and his family had forfeited the throne of France. Hoping to salvage something, Napoleon thereupon announced his abdication in favor of his son. But the allies would have none of it, and forced him to make his abdication unconditional. Within a month he had departed for the tiny island of Elba, off the Italian coast, where the allies, with a certain degree of irony, granted him sovereign control.

The Bourbon Restoration and the Hundred Days

Although during the final stages of the war, there had been differences among the allied leaders about the selection of a successor to Napoleon, these had been largely resolved by the time of his defeat. Partly because of the skillful machinations of Talleyrand, who was the spokesman of a royalist minority in Paris, the allies settled upon the count of Provence, a younger brother of the beheaded Louis XVI to rule as Louis XVIII. The news that a Bourbon would occupy the throne was not greeted with particular enthusiasm by the French people, but the king's initial pledge that he would not discriminate against individuals because of their past opinions and that he intended to grant a liberal constitution to France helped reconcile those who feared the consequences of a royalist restoration. Moreover, the relatively lenient treatment given France by the allies in the Treaty of Paris (May 30, 1814) was expressly designed to facilitate the resumption of power by the Bourbons.

Despite these advantages, the regime encountered difficulties from the start. The way in which the new constitution, the Charter of 1814, was presented irritated popular sensibilities, for the king expressly stated that the Charter was a "gift" to the French people granted by the king "in the nineteenth year of our reign." By this move, Louis XVIII appeared not only to be denying the principle of popular sovereignty but also to be ignoring the fact that the revolution and the Napoleonic interlude had even existed. The provisions of the Charter itself belied this view, for the document incorporated many features of the Declaration of the Rights of Man and the Constitution of 1791 and maintained the administrative institutions of the Empire. But the uneasiness of the more liberal elements in France was enhanced by the growing influence in court circles of the king's younger brother, Charles Philippe, count of Artois (1757–1836), who was far more conservative than the king and was the unofficial leader of the faction known as the Ultraroyalists, or Ultras. This group openly regarded the Charter as a mere stopgap and called for the establishment of an absolutist regime and the restoration of the Roman Catholic Church to its former privileges. Finally, certain measures taken by the new government alienated specific groups of Frenchmen. Army officers and soldiers suffered from the conversion of the army to a peacetime footing, with a consequent reduction of pay; manufacturers resented the sudden tariff reductions, which subjected them to foreign competition; peasants looked on uneasily as the government returned large tracts of unsold national land to the original owners.

Many of the ills from which Frenchmen suffered in 1814–1815 were attributable to the transition from a wartime to a peacetime economy, but the new government received the blame for them.

Napoleon Bonaparte, who had become increasingly restive under the restraints imposed upon him at Elba, was kept well informed of the mood of his former subjects and had decided by the midwinter of 1815 that the moment had come for his return to power. Taking advantage of the British commissioner's absence from the island, he commandeered several vessels and embarked for France. He landed at Cannes on March 1, 1815, and made his way northward through the mountain passes of Dauphiné, encountering practically no resistance. Indeed, most of his former soldiers rallied to his standard and the cities that lay on his route opened their gates to welcome the former emperor. By the time Napoleon reached Paris on March 20, Louis XVIII and his entourage had fled across the border to Ghent, and the Empire was once again proclaimed. In this way began the period known as the Hundred Days; it lasted until Napoleon's defeat at Waterloo in June.

In an effort to win the support of those groups which had formerly opposed his regime, Napoleon adopted during this period the liberal pose which he was to elaborate further during his final years in exile. Claiming that he had been prevented from offering reforms earlier by the need to defend France against European kings and aristocrats, he provided in his new constitution for an extension of the suffrage, the institution of a responsible ministry, and the elimination of press censorship. The announcement of these changes was greeted with a certain amount of skepticism, and Napoleon was aware that, in the last analysis, what he needed to ensure his position was a military victory.

News of Napoleon's escape from Elba struck the capitals of Europe with the force of a bombshell. March 1 found many of Europe's leaders in Vienna, where they had assembled at a congress in the fall of 1814 to deliberate on the disposition of Napoleon's former empire. Within an hour

February 17, 1814. *Wounded soldiers are brought back to Paris shortly before the city capitulated.*

March 20, 1815. *Napoleon arrives in Paris after his escape from Elba. He is cheered by an enthusiastic crowd.*

after the reception of the news, Metternich had secured agreement from the monarchs of Austria, Russia, and Prussia to renew the war against Napoleon. Great Britain subsequently branded Napoleon an "outlaw" and joined the three eastern powers in a new alliance directed against him.

Napoleon realized that his situation was precarious. Against the combined allied forces, which were estimated at 700,000, he was able to marshal an army of only 200,000, of whom more than a third had to police the interior and defend his frontiers. Nevertheless he determined once more to strike boldly. On June 15 he crossed the Belgian border, seeking to make contact with the armies of Blücher, commanding the Prussians, and the duke of Wellington, commanding a combined force of Belgian, Dutch, German, and British troops. He hoped to split the two armies and defeat them individually. An initial victory against Blücher caused the Prussians to retreat, and Napoleon, having dispatched thirty thousand of his own troops to pursue them, turned to support Marshal Ney* against the forces of the

---

* Michel Ney, duke of Elchingen (1769–1815), was one of Napoleon's most celebrated generals. Created a marshal of the empire in 1804, Ney distinguished himself at the Battle of Friedland in 1807 and at Borodino in 1812. In May, 1814, he was among those who persuaded Napoleon to abdicate, and he became a peer of France upon Louis XVIII's restoration. He initially denounced Napoleon's escape from Elba, but less than two weeks later, Marshal Ney impulsively rejoined his old commander, and participated in his final campaign. After Napoleon's defeat and exile Ney was tried by the Chamber of Peers for treason, and he was executed in December, 1815.

duke of Wellington. But the emperor had miscalculated the direction of Blücher's retreat. The Prussian troops evaded the pursuing French forces, and Blücher succeeded in regrouping them in a position from which he could lend support to Wellington. Thinking that the Prussians were no longer in the area, Napoleon, handicapped by the absence of thirty thousand of his own troops, launched an attack on Wellington at Waterloo. Wellington had the numerical advantage, and because he was fighting from the shelter of a ridge, was able to conceal the strength of the forces massed at his rear. What for a time appeared to be a deadlock between the two armies was turned into an allied victory by the return of Blücher's divisions, which were thrown upon the French right. By the end of the day, there remained only half of the forces Napoleon had taken into battle at noon, and these fled in undisciplined panic. This was a defeat which even Napoleon could not survive. Four days later he abdicated once again, and frustrated in an attempt to escape to America, he surrendered to the captain of a British warship off La Rochelle. To the British fell the responsibility for serving as Napoleon's jailer and he was shipped off to the lonely island of St. Helena in the South Atlantic.

THE ACHIEVEMENT AND THE LEGACY OF NAPOLEON

During the six years that remained to Napoleon, he had little to do beyond reliving and reviewing his epic career. An individual of lesser stature might have engaged in sterile regrets over mistakes made, opportunities lost, and betrayals by trusted individuals, and indeed Napoleon's memoirs are not altogether free of regrets of this sort. But he was more concerned with arranging and ordering his version of the events of his career so as to impose an appearance of unity and coherence upon his achievements. The fruits of this effort are to be seen in his memoirs, sometimes referred to as "the gospel according to St. Helena," which often bear scant resemblance to events which actually took place and are particularly distorted when they deal with the emperor's intentions and motives. But they are nonetheless important, since the account of the emperor's life constructed at St. Helena forms the basis for the Napoleonic legend that emerged after his death and was embellished by successive biographers and admirers.

The essence of the myth which the dethroned emperor attempted to construct was that he had been a liberal and a son of the revolution, aiming to carry on and complete the reforms begun during the revolutionary era and to bring these benefits to the peoples of Europe still living under the antiquated institutions and reactionary rulers of the Old Regime. Writing during an era which witnessed the restoration of many of these very rulers and institutions, he sensed that this image would have a particular appeal.

We have already seen that a number of Napoleon's measures under the Consulate and the early Empire—the *Code Napoléon*, the overhaul of administrative structures, and the stabilization of finances—can be interpreted as bringing to completion reforms initiated during the revolutionary years. In these respects, Napoleon could pose legitimately as the consolidator of the achievements of the revolution. Furthermore, the attempt to introduce many of these changes into the vassal states as well as all of the French Empire seems to justify his claim that he was the standard-bearer of the revolution throughout Europe.

On the other hand, these reforms were made within the context of a political system that denied the individual citizen any real voice in his government and consistently stifled the free expression of opinions, through censorship and surveillance of those suspected of opposition to the regime. Such an atmosphere certainly constituted a betrayal of principles embodied in the Declaration of the Rights of Man, and its existence seems to weaken Napoleon's argument that he was a true son of the revolution.

In assessing Napoleon's long-range impact upon Europe as a whole, it is difficult to separate his policies and their influence from those of the revolutionary governments that preceded him, but there is no question that the Europe of 1815 was very different from that of 1789 and that the Napoleonic regime was responsible for many of the changes. Particularly in those regions that had been directly incorporated into the French empire, many Napoleonic institutions lasted after 1815. Mention has already been made of the persistence of the Napoleonic codes in the Low Countries, in Rhineland Prussia, in the kingdom of Naples, and in various smaller German principalities. Even where the codes were suppressed, they exercised an influence upon laws which replaced them. Although the administrative division of the empire into departments, districts, and communes was abandoned after 1815 by most regions that no longer formed a part of France, Napoleon's highly organized bureaucracy with its appointed officials following the orders of the central government was admired and imitated by rulers seeking greater control and efficiency in their states. Other Napoleonic institutions that survived or were imitated elsewhere include his police system, his tax-collection organization, his Concordat with the Catholic Church, and, of course, the Napoleonic army and system of military education.

As far as social changes were concerned, the abolition of serfdom and of other features of the feudal regime (decreed in some cases by the revolutionary governments, in others by the Napoleonic regime) helped to transform the old order in the Low Countries, the Rhineland, and in a number of German and Italian states. We have seen that the defeat of Prussia by the French armies stimulated the Prussian king to order a series of reforms including the abolition of serfdom in 1807. All these changes, combined with the impact of the Napoleonic codes, with their emphasis upon equality before the law, freedom of land ownership, and the safeguarding of private property, worked ultimately to the advantage of the bourgeoisie and even of the peasantry. In other words, the pattern of social life in western Europe and in parts of central Europe had been significantly altered. Attempts might be made after 1815 to restore the political systems that had existed prior to the Revolution, but the social changes were, for the most part, irreversible.

Napoleon had initially been welcomed, at least in some quarters, as a liberator intent upon freeing the non-noble classes from traditional obligations and restrictions. In the long run, however, enthusiasm turned to resentment as it became clear that the member states of the Grand Empire were merely satellites of France, their chief function being to supply the emperor with men, money, and supplies for his further conquests. Napoleon's new order, if considerably less brutal than Hitler's in the following century, was hardly more appealing to contemporaries. Certainly there were few Europeans outside of France who lamented his downfall in 1814.

But just as time altered the image of Bonaparte in France, so did it transform his reputation in the rest of Europe as well. To be sure, "the gospel according to St. Helena" was never universally accepted: Napoleon did not come to be viewed as the apostle of liberal and nationalist causes. What captured the popular imagination of succeeding generations instead was the vision of Napoleon as a man of the people who made his way to the top, or as the daring general, the brilliant strategist, who commanded hundreds of thousands of men and succeeded in mastering for a time an entire continent. In the relatively prosaic age that followed his downfall, an era of prolonged peace, the exploits of Napoleon the soldier, the limitless quality of his ambition, made of him a romantic hero more glamorous than any creation of fiction.

CHAPTER 3

The Concert of Europe, 1815–1848

THE VIENNA SETTLEMENT of 1815 has been ranked with the Peace of Westphalia (1648), the Peace of Utrecht (1713), and the Peace of Paris (1919) as one of the four most significant international agreements in the history of modern Europe. Merely in terms of square miles of territory affected, such a judgment appears justified; the task of the statesmen at Vienna was nothing less than to dispose of all the lands that had been conquered by the French armies over two decades. The settlement is also notable for its durability. Some adjustments were made shortly after 1830, and more significant changes accompanied the revolutions of 1848 and the movements for German and Italian unification later, but no war among the major European powers occurred until the Crimean War in the 1850's, and a general European conflict comparable to the Napoleonic wars was avoided until 1914. Perhaps even more interesting in retrospect is the fact that the allied statesmen created in 1815 the system of international relations which came, in time, to be known as the Concert of Europe. This system, which provided for periodic conferences among the so-called Great Powers (Great Britain, Russia, Austria, and Prussia) to discuss problems affecting the peace of Europe, lasted, with some alterations, until well past the middle of the century. France, after an initial probationary period, joined the ranks of the Great Powers in 1818. Ultimately the system was replaced by a diplomacy of alliances and alignments, associated with Bismarck, but the precedent of holding general international conferences for the peaceful settlement of differences had been established, and would be revived in the twentieth century.

THE SETTLEMENT OF 1815

We have referred to the settlement of 1815 as the Vienna settlement, and it is quite true that some of the major decisions concerning the disposition of territories were reached in the celebrated Vienna congress which lasted —with interruptions—from September, 1814, until June, 1815. But we shall use the term "settlement of 1815" in a broader sense, to designate the several agreements reached by the European powers during 1814 and 1815, whether or not they were actually made at Vienna.

The Treaty of Chaumont and the First Treaty of Paris

In March, 1814, even before the war with Napoleon had ended, representatives of the four major powers—Great Britain, Russia, Austria, and Prussia—met in Chaumont, France, to conclude the treaty which became the cornerstone of the Quadruple Alliance. In it the allies pledged to remain united not only until France was defeated but for twenty years after the conclusion of hostilities, in order to ensure France's observance of the forthcoming peace. Viscount Castlereagh, the British foreign minister, was primarily responsible for getting his allies to bury their differences and participate in the coalition. Each of the allies agreed to contrbute 150,000 men to the struggle against France; Britain, furthermore, pledged 5,000,000 pounds to the cause of victory.

After the coalition had achieved its initial purpose, the defeat of France, the allies concluded with the government of Louis XVIII what is known as the first Treaty of Paris (May, 1814). The most striking feature of this peace treaty is its relative leniency toward the defeated power, for which several explanations have been given. Hoping to establish a balance of power, the statesmen who drew up this treaty saw that reducing France to second- or third-rate status would serve no useful purpose. More important, perhaps, was the unwillingness of the victors to handicap the restored Bourbon dynasty with an excessively harsh peace. The new king had not, after all, been responsible for the aggressive conquests of France in the wars just ended; his government should not be required to pay the penalty. Accordingly, France was allowed to retain the territories that it had held on November 1, 1792; these included parts of Savoy, of Germany, and of the Austrian Netherlands, as well as a few enclaves such as Avignon. But France was forced to recognize the independence of the remainder of the Austrian Netherlands, Holland, the German states, the Italian states, and Switzerland. All of France's colonies, with the exception of Trinidad, Tobago, St. Lucia, and Mauritius (Ile de France) in the Indian Ocean, were returned to her by Great Britain. Britain also retained the island of Malta. Perhaps most surprising is the fact that France was not required to pay an indemnity to the victorious powers, or even to give back the art traesures that Napoleon had pirated from foreign cities during the wars.

There had been some hope that the Treaty of Paris would settle the fate of territories which France had conquered in central Europe, but disagreements among the allied statesmen prevented immediate decisions about these areas. When the disagreements persisted into the summer of 1814, it was decided to defer further discussion of the territorial settlement until the opening of the Congress of Vienna in the fall. The most important issue creating suspicion among the powers at this time, an issue which continued to be of crucial importance throughout the congress, was the fate of Poland. Russian troops had occupied the former duchy of Warsaw, and Tsar Alexander hoped to establish a Polish kingdom under Russian protection. The tsar's reconstituted Poland would include not only the duchy of Warsaw but also the territories which Prussia and Austria had acquired during the partitions in the last decades of the eighteenth century. Alexander harbored this plan for some time and encouraged Polish leaders— among them Prince Adam Czartoryski (1770–1861), whom he had appointed as his own foreign minister—with promises of a liberal constitution for the revived kingdom. Frederick William III of Prussia knew of the tsar's project and had no objections to it, even though Prussia would have to yield the lands it had taken during the partition, so long as compensation was provided in the form of other territory—preferably that of the kingdom of Saxony, whose ruler, Frederick Augustus I (ruled 1806–1827), had sided with France once too often during the final stages of the Napoleonic wars.

Fearing the reaction that his proposal would provoke, Tsar Alexander avoided making an open statement of his intentions, with respect to Poland even after the war with France was over. His reticence merely served to increase the misgivings of both Viscount Castlereagh and Prince Metternich over the entire issue. Metternich naturally viewed with distrust any proposal which would involve Austria's abandonment of territory acquired during the partitions. Both Castlereagh and Metternich were skeptical about Alexander's reassurances to the Poles that they would retain their freedom, and saw the entire scheme as a plot for extending Russian influence in central Europe. With Poland in the Russian orbit, Alexander's troops would be within easy striking distance of both Berlin and Vienna. The tsar would then replace Napoleon as the principal threat to European peace and stability. The fate of Poland was, then, one of the principal problems facing the statesmen who assembled at Vienna in the fall of 1814.

The Congress of Vienna

ORGANIZATION AND LEADERSHIP

The Congress of Vienna was not really a congress, for the delegates never met in plenary session. Invitations were extended to "all the Powers engaged on either side in the present war," but a secret article of the Treaty of Paris (where the congress was first mentioned) stipulated that the disposition of territories and other important decisions would be left to the four Great Powers of the Quadruple Alliance. The initial hope was that the congress would last only four weeks, after which the decisions of the major powers would be submitted to all the delegates for ratification. But the closed negotiations aroused the resentment of the lesser powers: their representatives had come to the congress under the impression that they would participate actively in its deliberations, or at least be consulted on matters affecting their own interests; now they found, instead, that though some were called to serve on committees dealing with specific problems, in general they were ignored.

One of the unforeseen consequences of this policy was the obligation which fell upon the host of the congress, Emperor Francis of Austria, to entertain the delegates of the smaller states throughout the winter of 1814–1815. Sir Harold Nicolson, in his lively study of the Congress of Vienna, describes the obligations confronting the emperor and his court officials.

In the Hofburg itself he (the Emperor) was obliged, day in and day out, to entertain an Emperor, an Empress, four Kings, one Queen, two Hereditary Princes, three Grand Duchesses and three Princes of the blood. Every night dinner at the Hofburg was laid at forty tables; special liveries and carriages were provided for all the royal guests; the horses in the stable numbered no less than 1,400. Each monarch or head of a family had brought with him a crowd of chamberlains and equerries, and the royal consorts were attended by mistresses of

The Congress of Vienna, 1814–1815. *Seated in the left foreground: Hardenberg; standing next to him: Wellington; standing in the left foreground: Metternich; seated to the left of center foreground: Castlereagh; seated on the right at the table: Talleyrand.*

The Emperor entertains. *A masked ball in the Hofburg, 1815.*

the robe and ladies-in-waiting.... In order to amuse this horde of miscellaneous visitors the Emperor Francis had appointed from his court officials a Festivals Committee who were driven to distraction by the task of inventing new forms of amusement and by the excruciating problems of precedence.[1]

Socially active though Vienna was that winter, accounts of the congress which emphasize only its more glamorous aspects—the balls, banquets, and theatrical performances—are misleading; the principal statesmen and their staffs regularly put in long and hard hours of work hammering out the details of the final settlement.

To a large extent the decisions were the outcome of the interaction of the chief representatives of the five major powers—France and the members of the Quadruple Alliance. The only ruler who took part personally in the negotiations was Alexander I, who was convinced that Russia's major share in the victory against Napoleon entitled him to the dominant role in drawing up the peace. Moved alternately by idealism, religious mysticism, and shrewd calculations of what would best serve Russia's interests, this erratic prince was the despair of those who had to deal with him. His determination to consolidate Russian control over Poland and generally to extend Russia's influence in Europe aroused the suspicion and antagonism of diplomats who were already wary of his professions of liberalism.

[1] Harold Nicolson, *The Congress of Vienna: A Study in Allied Unity, 1812–1822* (New York, 1946), pp. 159-160.

Klemens von Metternich.
Portrait by Lawrence,
painted in London, 1814.

Emperor Francis of Austria, though host to the congress, preferred to leave the burden of diplomatic negotiations to his chief minister, Prince Klemens von Metternich (1773–1859). In 1814 Metternich was already an experienced diplomat. He had served the Austrian foreign office since 1801, first as minister to Saxony, then as minister to Prussia, and from 1806 to 1809 as ambassador to the court of Napoleon in Paris. In 1809 he was appointed foreign minister, a position he held without interruption until 1848. A handsome man who wore the uniform of a knight of Malta and had finely powdered hair, he was known to all his contemporaries for his conceit and pompousness. He wrote in his memoirs in 1819, "There is a wide sweep about my mind. I am always above and beyond the preoccupation of most public men; I cover a ground much vaster than they can see. I cannot keep myself from saying about twenty times a day: 'how right I am, and how wrong they are.'" He has been called a supreme opportunist, but he himself denied the charge, claiming that his actions sprang from certain "principles" to which he consistently adhered. Among these the most important was the idea of "equilibrium," which he applied to his conduct of both domestic and foreign policy. According to Metternich, all society rested ideally in a kind of equilibrium, or "repose," which was periodically upset. In his own time, the balance had shifted too far in one direction with the violence attendant upon the French Revolution and the Napoleonic conquests. Now it would be the task of Europe's rulers to restore equilibrium, for which a period of peace was essential. To some degree he felt that Europe's stability would be ensured by the return to their thrones of "legitimate" rulers who had an interest in the preservation of established institutions; however, his adherence to this principle has been exaggerated, for many parts of the Vienna settlement to which he agreed violated the principle of "legitimacy." Metternich was assisted in 1814–1815 by Friedrich von Gentz (1764–1832), who acted as secretary general for the congress and whose brilliantly written memoirs and letters are a rich source for information about the period.

Great Britain was represented in the negotiations at first by its foreign minister, Viscount Castlereagh (Robert Stewart, second marquis of Londonderry, 1769–1822), and after February, 1815, by the duke of Wellington, who came as first British plenipotentiary. Castlereagh was a fundamentally lonely individual who concealed his shyness behind a screen of formal good manners. To many he appeared aloof and condescending. We have already seen him as one of the chief architects of the final coalition against Napoleon; because of Britain's unique position among the powers, he also played an important role in the territorial settlement of Vienna. The British government was as determined as the other powers to prevent a resurgence of French aggression, and had made a heavy financial contribution to the winning of the war, but Britain, unlike the others, had no territorial ambitions on the Continent. As long as his country's maritime and commercial interests were secure, Castlereagh could play the role of a disinterested mediator among the conflicting continental states. His position was enhanced, moreover, by the fact that Britain had restored to France almost all of its colonial possessions and could therefore call for comparable generosity on the part of the other allies.

Prussia played only a small part in the deliberations at Vienna, partly because the deafness of its chief representative, Prince Karl August von Hardenberg, made it difficult for him to follow the discussions closely, and partly because the Prussian king, Frederick William III, was personally subservient to the tsar. The king was not only ready to support Alexander's claims in Poland but showed himself prepared to follow Russian dictates on other matters of policy as well.

Since the peace treaty with France had been concluded before the congress assembled, France was invited to send a representative. This turned out to be Prince Talleyrand, who had survived the downfall of Napoleon and now served Louis XVIII, whom he had assisted to the throne. Though the four allies had certainly not intended to admit the defeated power to their deliberations, Talleyrand's skill as a diplomat never showed to greater advantage than at the Congress of Vienna. By exploiting the resentment of the lesser powers over their exclusion from the discussions, and posing as their champion, the indefatigable Talleyrand gradually managed to worm his way into the councils of the big four, and to participate in the making of some of their decisions. Indeed, by the middle of the winter he was able to take advantage of a split that developed among the victorious powers in the Polish-Saxon crisis to conclude a secret agreement with Britain and Austria directed against Russia and Prussia.

THE POLISH-SAXON SETTLEMENT

The inability of the allied representatives to come to an agreement over the status of Poland and Saxony in the early summer of 1814 meant that the whole issue was still very much alive when they assembled in Vienna in the fall. Castlereagh did his best to persuade Tsar Alexander to scale down his demands for Polish territory and to arrange some sort of compromise, but he failed. Metternich's attempt at direct negotiations with Alexander resulted in a scene so violent that the tsar threatened him with a duel and refused to speak to him directly for three months thereafter. Even Hardenberg entered into discussions with Alexander which were designed to bring about a compromise, but Prussia's insistence on the acquisition of the whole of the kingdom of Saxony did not predispose the tsar to moderate his own demands. By December the atmosphere between Britain and Austria, on one side, and Russia and Prussia, on the other, was so tense that there was open talk of the possibility of war. At this point Prince Talleyrand stepped in with a stratagem which appeared at first to heighten the crisis but ultimately resulted in its solution. He proposed to Metternich and Castlereagh a secret alliance to be directed against Russia and Prussia. The agreement, signed on January 3, 1815, provided that France, Austria, and Great Britain would support one another in the event that any of them should be attacked by Russia or Prussia, and went on to specify the number of troops each would contribute to the joint defense. Although the detailed terms of the alliance remained secret, rumors of its formation were allowed to leak out, and they reached the rulers of Russia and Prussia almost immediately. The expectation that further attempts to push through their designs would result in a general European war was sufficient to convince the tsar and his Prussian supporters to back down, and the crisis was effectively ended.

Would the three signatories really have resorted to war if the tsar had persisted in his designs? It is known that Castlereagh was acting against the orders of his government in signing the agreement, and France would certainly have had difficulty in mustering the forces promised for the defense of Poland and Saxony; but the bluff worked, and the way was paved for a peaceable settlement of the dispute. Perhaps the most amazing feature of the entire episode was the fact that France, which had been defeated a mere six months before, had formed an alliance with two of its conquerors directed against the other two. Immediately after the conclusion of the agreement, Talleyrand wrote to his monarch, Louis XVIII, "The Coalition is dissolved. France is no longer isolated in Europe." [2] From this time on, Talleyrand sat with the inner group at the congress.

Late in January, Metternich made the proposal that was the basis for the final agreement on Poland and Saxony. Poland emerged as an ostensibly independent kingdom, but it was a greatly reduced version of the state Alexander had hoped for, since Prussia was allowed to retain Posen, and Austria to keep Galicia, territories they had taken during the partitions. Krakow, with the area immediately around it, was established as a free city under the joint protection of Austria, Prussia, and Russia. The rest of the former duchy of Warsaw constituted the new Polish state, with Alexander as its ruler. In time, the tsar conferred upon the Polish kingdom a liberal constitution, which guaranteed full independence and a separate political structure to the Polish people, but the preamble made clear that the constitution was being granted not as a right, but as a favor. Furthermore, the kingdom was to be a hereditary possession of the Romanov dynasty, and its foreign policy was to remain under the control of Russia.

Prussia may not have come away with all that it had hoped for, but it fared reasonably well, receiving two fifths of the territory of Saxony, with a population of 850,000; the remainder of Saxony was restored to its former ruler, who retained the title of king. Prussia also received additional territories in Germany—Swedish Pomerania, and portions of Westphalia and the Rhineland—in part, as compensation for lands ceded to Hanover and Bavaria.

THE FINAL SETTLEMENT

Once the Polish-Saxon issue had been disposed of, the diplomats at Vienna were able to reach agreement on other aspects of the territorial settlement without further crises. Their decisions were embodied in a document known as the Final Act, which was completed and signed in June, 1815. Traditional interpretations of the Vienna settlement have emphasized the adherence of its architects to certain fundamental principles: legitimacy, the balance of power, and compensation. According to this view, the negotiators at Vienna set as one of their tasks the restoration of "legitimate" rulers to their thrones. In fact, however, this principle was frequently disregarded, particularly with respect to the former German states, for no statesman seriously contemplated the restoration of all the petty rulers to their thrones. The intention of establishing a balance of power was unquestionably more important than considerations of legitimacy in the settlement of 1815. From it stemmed both the unwillingness of the Great Powers to weaken France unduly and the insistence by Britain that Prussia be strengthened so as to serve as a counterweight to Russia in

[2] Quoted by Nicolson, *The Congress of Vienna*, pp. 177–178.

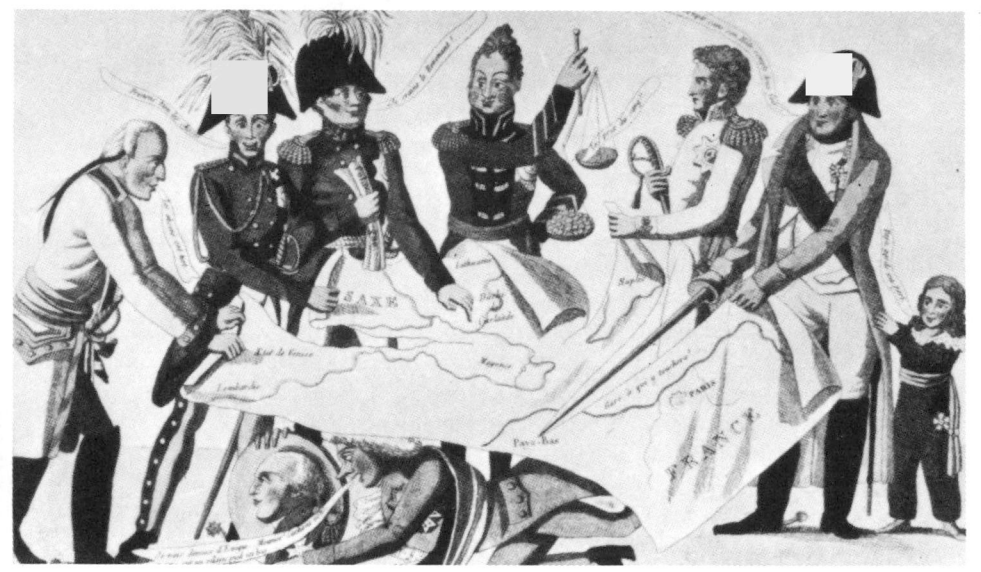

"Dividing the Cake." *Anonymous drawing (Vienna, 1815).*

the east and France in the west. The principle of compensation merely supplied one means for preserving the balance of power. When a victorious nation gave up a piece of territory, it received compensation in the form of other territory. Thus in the Polish-Saxon crisis Prussia received Saxon lands in return for relinquishing some of its Polish possessions. Austria acquired territories on the Italian peninsula in return for yielding the Austrian Netherlands to an enlarged kingdom of Holland.

But in the last analysis the Vienna statesmen were probably less concerned with following principles than with pragmatically ensuring that France would not trouble the peace of Europe in the future. To this end they established around France two defensive barriers made up of the neighboring states. At the northernmost end of the first of these barriers, which was formed by states touching France's borders, was the new kingdom of the Netherlands, consisting of the former Dutch republic and the Austrian Netherlands, under the rule of the ex-*stadholder* of Holland (the heir of the house of Orange), who was given the title King William I. This reunification of the two regions of the Low Countries, formally separated since the Peace of Westphalia in 1648, was one of the less durable achievements of the congress. Linguistic and religious differences contributed to the dissatisfaction of the people of the southern provinces, and in 1831 they revolted and proclaimed their independence as the new kingdom of Belgium.

Along the eastern boundary of France were ranged a number of German states (including Prussia, in that it was given control of the territories along the left bank of the Rhine); Switzerland, which was reestablished as an independent confederation of cantons; and the kingdom of Sardinia, which included not only the island of Sardinia but also the territory of Piedmont on the mainland. The kingdom of Sardinia (also referred to as the kingdom of Piedmont) was enlarged and strengthened by the addition of Genoa, Nice, and a part of Savoy. On France's southwestern border Spain was again under Bourbon rule; Ferdinand VII had been restored to the throne by Wellington in the final stages of the Peninsular War.

Reinforcing the states along France's borders was the second defensive barrier, lying farther to the east: Prussia proper, Austria, and the remaining German states. The British intended Prussia to emerge from the settlement as a formidable power in central Europe, standing as a bulwark against both French and Russian aggression. Ultimately Metternich agreed to support this policy even though it was strongly attacked by other Austrian statesmen as a threat to Austrian domination of the German states.

Austria received major territorial restorations in the south. These included on the Italian peninsula the provinces of Lombardy and Venetia, and on the Dalmatian coast the Illyrian Provinces—all of which were directly incorporated into the Austrian empire. Austria also recovered Salzburg and the Tyrol, both lost to Bavaria during the Napoleonic wars. A *Deutscher Bund* ("Germanic Confederation") was established as a kind of successor to the defunct Holy Roman Empire. It was composed of thirty-eight states, including four free cities, and Austria and Prussia (except for their non-German territories), bound together in a loosely organized union under the presidency of Austria.

On the Italian peninsula, beyond the second defensive barrier, a number of rulers were restored to their thrones. The Papal States were returned to the pope. In central and northern Italy, three small duchies—Tuscany, Parma, and Modena—were put under princes related to the Austrian royal family, and Austrian influence was to remain strong throughout the peninsula in the years after 1815. The kingdom of Naples and Sicily (the kingdom of the Two Sicilies) was ultimately restored to the Bourbon ruler, Ferdinand I, after remaining under Joachim Murat, Napoleon's brother-in-law, until he made the mistake of rallying to the emperor's standard during the Hundred Days.

In other provisions of the Vienna settlement, Sweden was allowed to retain Norway, acquired from Denmark in the preceding year, but was forced to accept Russia's conquest of Finland. Great Britain voluntarily abandoned all colonial conquests with the exception of those taken from France in the first Treaty of Paris, Helgoland and the former Dutch colonies of Ceylon, the Cape Colony, and Demerara, in Guiana.

The Second Treaty of Paris and the Holy Alliance

Napoleon's escape from Elba and the episode of the Hundred Days delayed the discussions at the Congress of Vienna but did not affect the

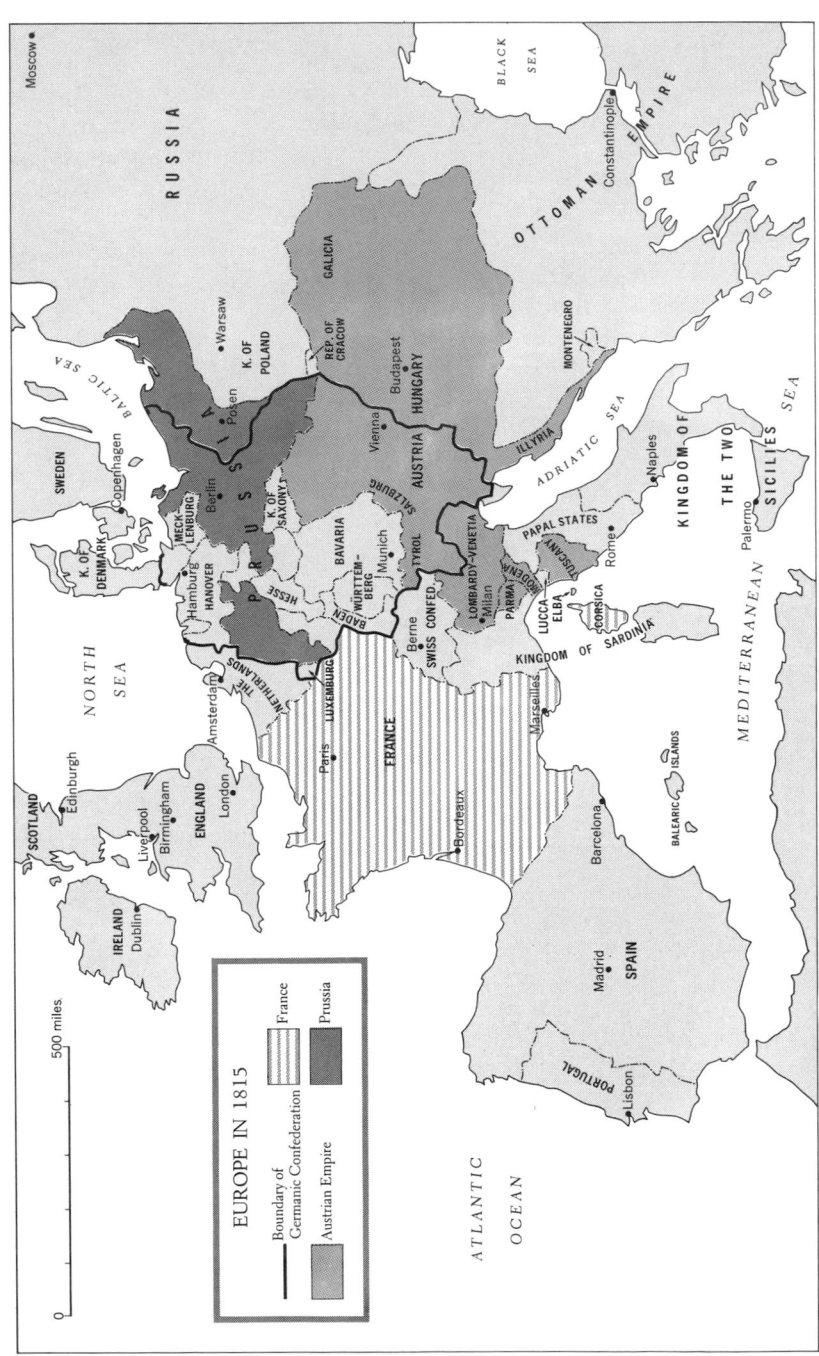

EUROPE IN 1815

overall territorial settlement. Indeed, the Final Act of the congress was signed before the Battle of Waterloo. The principal consequence of Napoleon's return for the settlement of 1815 was the change it brought about in the terms imposed upon France. The failure of the French to oppose Napoleon—indeed, the enthusiastic reception which many Frenchmen gave him—seemed to call for harsher punishment than the first Treaty of Paris had imposed.

Quick action by the British brought about a second restoration of Louis XVIII, who returned, according to the current phrase, "in the baggage of the allies." Because they had played the principal role in the final battles against Napoleon, the British and the Prussians took the lead in drafting the second Treaty of Paris, which was signed only in November, 1815, after five months of wrangling among the allies. Hardenberg had to contend with the vigorous demands of the Prussian general staff for a treaty which would strip France of Alsace-Lorraine, the Saar Valley, and the rest of Savoy and impose a crushing indemnity. These demands for a vengeful peace were also resisted by Castlereagh, who hastened to Paris in July and remained there until November, patiently working for a moderate settlement. In his view the considerations that had made lenient treatment of France desirable a year earlier were still present. The resulting treaty, somewhat of a compromise, was nevertheless notable for its moderation. The first treaty had cut France back to the boundaries of 1792; this one specified the boundaries of 1790, which meant the loss of several fortresses, a few small strips of territory on the Belgian and Swiss frontiers, and an additional slice of Savoy, ceded to the kingdom of Sardinia. The first treaty had imposed no indemnity, this one required France to pay 700,000,000 francs to the victors and to support an army of occupation of 150,000 troops for five years. (This force was reduced to 30,000 in 1817 and removed entirely in 1818.) Finally, France was required to return the art treasures it had kept under the first treaty.

France's renewed defiance of Europe during the Hundred Days made a reaffirmation of the Quadruple Alliance appear essential. A declaration signed on the same day as the second Treaty of Paris was designed as a guarantee of that treaty. In it each of the four powers pledged to supply sixty thousand men in the event of a violation of the Treaty of Paris, particularly another attempt at a restoration of the Bonapartist dynasty. Of special interest is the article of this document calling for periodic conferences of the contracting powers for discussion of their "common interests" and for "the examination of measures which . . . will be judged most salutary for the repose and prosperity of peoples, and for the maintenance of peace in Europe." In this statement were contained the germs of the conference system which persisted well into the nineteenth century.

The Quadruple Alliance was reaffirmed for the limited purpose of preventing violations of the Treaty of Paris, not to guarantee the broader settlement made at the Congress of Vienna or the more general goals of the contracting monarchs. But it was to become confused in the popular mind with another alliance, which had been proposed by Tsar Alexander and signed by the monarchs of Prussia and Austria in September, 1815. The other rulers of Europe were invited to adhere to the three monarchs' agreement. Precisely where Alexander got the idea for this Holy Alliance has never been determined, though it is clear that considerable influence was exerted upon him by Baroness Barbara von Krüdener (1764–1824), a Pietist mystic, who had acquired temporary ascendancy over him. The concept of a general agreement among the European states for the renunciation of war and the establishment of international order seems to have been in his mind for at least ten years, and the religious sanction which underlay the proposal reflected his mood at this time.

The general reaction of European diplomats to Alexander's proposal seems to have been one of amused cynicism, summed up by Castlereagh's oft-quoted comment, "A piece of sublime mysticism and nonsense." Metternich appears to have shared this view, yet Emperor Francis joined Frederick William of Prussia in signing the document, since they felt this act could do no harm and would please the tsar. Indeed the only rulers who failed to adhere formally to the Holy Alliance were the future George IV of Great Britain, acting as prince regent, who excused himself on the ground that his signature would be unconstitutional without the accompanying signature of a minister; the sultan of the Ottoman Empire, who refused on the ground that he was not a Christian; and Pope Pius VII, who commented acidly that "from time immemorial the papacy had been in possession of Christian truth and needed no new interpretation of it."[3]

In the Holy Alliance, the three contracting monarchs declared "their fixed resolution to take no other guide for their conduct . . . than those precepts of that holy religion, namely the precepts of Justice, Charity and Peace . . . as being the only means of consolidating human institutions and remedying their imperfections." It went on to state that the three monarchs, acting as Christian brothers, would on all occasions and in all places lend each other aid and assistance to protect religion, peace, and justice.

Whatever the motives behind the Holy Alliance, there is no question that within a few years it was serving Metternich and the tsar as an instrument for the repression of liberal and revolutionary movements throughout Europe. Perhaps most unfortunate was the confusion in the public mind between the Holy Alliance and the Quadruple Alliance: the conference system delineated by the Quadruple Alliance consequently came

---

[3] Quoted by F. B. Artz, *Reaction and Revolution, 1814–1832* (New York, 1934), p. 118.

to be viewed merely as a device for enforcing reactionary policies. The defense of reaction had certainly not been the intention of Viscount Castlereagh. Indeed, the history of Britain's relationship with its allies during the next few years consisted largely of Castlereagh's repeated attempts to prevent the transformation of the Quadruple Alliance into an instrument for repression.

The Settlement of 1815 Appraised

During the nineteenth century the settlement of 1815 was widely criticized by liberals and nationalists. For one thing, it was associated in the popular mind with Metternich, who came to symbolize for his critics all that was antiliberal and antinationalist. It was also attacked because of the apparently callous way in which territories had been shifted from one state to another with no consideration for the wishes of the inhabitants. This sort of cynical maneuver, it was felt, was typified by the annexation of the Italian provinces of Lombardy and Venetia by the Austrian empire, a move which appeared to have no other justification than the principle of compensation: Austria had given up its provinces in the Netherlands in order to permit the formation of a strengthened kingdom of Holland, and therefore received territory elsewhere; whether the Italian-speaking peoples of Lombardy and Venetia favored submission to the Habsburg emperor of Austria had seemed irrelevant to the peacemakers. The continued domination of large blocs of Poles by Prussia and Austria (to say nothing of the sham character of Polish "independence" under Russian tutelage) was another example of the Vienna statesmen's indifference to nationalist aspirations.

What can be said in response to these charges against the statesmen of 1815? The most obvious reply is that the accusations were anachronistic. Such transfers of territories and peoples had been practiced for centuries and were entirely consistent with the traditions of European diplomacy. Nor did the peoples affected react as their descendants a generation or two later would have done. True, the French revolutionaries had emphasized the doctrine of popular sovereignty and the feeling of Frenchmen toward their nation changed during the revolutionary years, but it would be a mistake to assume that the attitudes of all other European peoples underwent a corresponding transformation during the same era. To be sure, as we have noted, Napoleon did arouse resentment among the peoples he conquered, and German, Italian, and Polish patriots attempted to arouse nationalist sentiments among their fellow countrymen. In Prussia and in Poland they were partially successful, but only slowly did a strong sense of national identity emerge among the masses. It is therefore unreasonable to criticize Metternich, Castlereagh, and their colleagues for failing to appreciate the potential strength of feelings which were frequently no more than embryonic in 1815.

The settlement achieved in 1815 has inevitably been compared with the one reached by the Paris Peace Conference in 1919. Both followed general European wars; both involved major territorial adjustments; both had to deal with the difficult problem of how to treat a defeated power whose aggression was believed to have been responsible for the war. The peacemakers of 1919, aware of the parallel, set out consciously to avoid the "mistakes" made by their predecessors a century earlier, and the disintegration of the Paris settlement in the 1930's after little more than a decade led to a reappraisal of the work of the Congress of Vienna and to a more favorable judgment of its achievements. Perhaps the Vienna statesmen had a less difficult task than their successors after the First World War precisely because they did not have to reckon with the strong nationalist feelings generated during the nineteenth century.

Many circumstances help to determine whether a treaty lasts, yet it is hard to escape the conclusion that the relatively judicious treatment accorded France by the peacemakers in 1815 had something to do with the permanence of the settlement. The unwillingness of the victors to handicap the restored Bourbon ruler with a punitive peace, coupled with their conviction that France must inevitably take its place once again among the major powers, led them to draw up a treaty which the French were able to live with for close to half a century. When one compares this result with the fate of the Treaty of Versailles, imposed on Germany in 1919, the peacemakers of 1815 do not appear as benighted as their critics have charged.

Finally, in assessing the positive accomplishments of the statesmen of 1815, we must return to the plan of the Quadruple Alliance for periodic conferences of the Great Powers to deal with questions affecting the peace of Europe. Beneath this proposal lay an assumption concerning international relations which differed from the view that had prevailed before 1789. This changed point of view was reflected by Metternich in 1824 when he said, "For some time Europe has had for me the character of my own country." By this statement, and perhaps more by his actions, he seemed to suggest that the Great Powers had a responsibility for maintaining the welfare of Europe as a whole—not just for pursuing their own interests— and that an important part of their obligation was the avoidance of war. This idea was at the heart of what was called the Concert of Europe.

THE FATE OF THE CONFERENCE SYSTEM

In the years immediately following 1815, the Great Powers met regularly in a series of conferences dealing with problems of mutual concern. The last of these was held in 1822. By that date—and indeed, even earlier—Great Britain's differences with Austria, Russia, and Prussia over the nature and purpose of the alliance had reached a stage where collaboration on a permanent basis was no longer possible. Yet the collapse of the plan for regular meetings did not end the Concert of Europe. For the continental powers—joined occasionally by Britain—continued to assemble whenever specific crises developed, and the idea persisted that any threat to peace in Europe was automatically of concern to all. The period following 1815 was certainly not free of tensions, but the fact that no war was fought among the major powers may be attributed at least in part to this new system of European diplomacy.

The Congress of Aix-la-Chapelle

For the first three years after the conclusion of peace the primary task of representatives of the Quadruple Alliance was to supervise the enforcement of the Treaty of Paris and the occupation of France. By 1818 France.had arranged for the final payment of its indemnity and the allies decided that the time had come to evacuate the occupation troops and adjust relations between France and the other powers. This was the principal task of the Congress of Aix-la-Chapelle, which brought together in 1818 the rulers of Russia, Austria, and Prussia, along with delegations of diplomats from the four Great Powers and France. To all appearances the congress went smoothly and achieved its stated purpose. The withdrawal of troops from France was agreed upon, and as a token of complete reacceptance by the treaty nations, France was included in a newly formed Quintuple Alliance with the four other powers. Lest the French should disturb the peace again, the Quadruple Alliance was retained. But this was merely a safeguard; the diplomats generally agreed that France had fulfilled its obligations and was ready to assume its privileges and obligations as a Great Power. A number of other questions were dealt with by the powers, and the general impression was that the hopes which had been placed in the conference system were now being realized. Thus Metternich could comment, "Never have I known a prettier little congress."

Yet the testimony of others who participated in the Congress of Aix-la-Chapelle belied this general impression. For the discussions at the congress brought out sharp differences between the British and Russian views of the alliance and its purposes. Tsar Alexander had taken the opportunity to propose an *Alliance Solidaire*, by which the powers of Europe would guarantee not only each other's borders and possessions but also the security in each country of whatever form of government then existed. Castlereagh's sharp rejection of this proposal was accompanied by an explanation of the position which the British had held since 1815, and which they were to reiterate more than once in the years that followed. The British representative made it clear that the Quadruple Alliance had never been more than a specific commitment to prevent French military aggression. To interpret the alliance as a broad instrument for the preservation of established regimes and the suppression of revolutions wherever they occurred was to go far beyond the treaties to which Britain adhered. In the face of this determined stand, Tsar Alexander withdrew his proposal.

The Revolutions in Southern Europe, 1820–1823

Two years later, in 1820, the unity of the Great Powers was tested more concretely when a series of revolutions broke out in Spain and on the Italian peninsula. For the first time the differences among the Great Powers were brought into the open. The first of the revolts was directed against Ferdinand VII of Spain, the Bourbon ruler who had been restored in 1814. He had been returned on condition that he would observe the liberal Constitution of 1812, which had been drawn up by an elected national assembly, the Cortes, in Cádiz, the one region of Spain that Napoleon had never subdued. Yet as soon as he had been restored he dissolved the Cortes, abandoned the constitution, and proceeded systematically to persecute the liberals who had been responsible for it. The general inefficiency of the government, evidence of corruption in high places, and an economic crisis provoked further antipathy to the regime. The rebellion began in the army, among regiments about to be sent to the Spanish colonies in Latin America to suppress revolts which had erupted there, but it quickly gained the support of upper-middle-class merchants whose business had dwindled in the postwar era and of a handful of liberal intellectuals sympathetic with the ideals of the French Revolution. Although the revolution was in no sense a popular movement, the rebels were strong enough to force their will upon the king, who agreed in March, 1820, to respect the constitution and to summon the Cortes once again. For two years, until the French rescued him, the king remained the captive of the revolutionaries.

The response of the Great Powers to news of the revolt in Spain was far from uniform. The strongest reaction, not surprisingly, came from Tsar Alexander, who before the revolution succeeded, sent notes to the other allies suggesting some sort of joint intervention in defense of Ferdinand VII. Among the most amenable to this proposal was France, which had a particular interest in Spain because of its proximity, and saw intervention as an opportunity to counteract British influence in the Iberian peninsula. Prussia, although less directly concerned, was also willing to follow Russia's lead. Given Metternich's general horror of revolutions, it is a little surprising that he hesitated to support the tsar's proposal, but his conviction that the Iberian peninsula was Britain's particular sphere of influence led him to await the British reaction. The British position was unequivocal. Although Castlereagh had no sympathy for the revolution, the British were determined for several reasons to prevent joint allied intervention in Spain. In the first place, intervention was contrary to Britain's view of the Quadruple Alliance. Second, the presence of the allies in Spain might threaten British commercial interests there. Finally, Britain saw that intervention by the allies might lead to an attempt to wrest from the South American colonies the independence they had recently won from Spain, and in the process hinder the increasing British trade with the western hemisphere. Acting upon motives of principle and pocket, the British government on May 5, 1820, circulated a memorandum to the other powers opposing allied intervention in Spain and reiterating the view that the alliance had originally been directed against France and that it had never been intended as "an union for the government of the world or for the superintendence of the internal affairs of other States."[4] In the face of such categorical opposition, the Russian proposal was temporarily dropped.

When a series of revolts, apparently inspired by the Spanish example, erupted later in 1820 in other parts of Europe, Alexander's appeals met with more enthusiastic support. Indeed, Metternich, resorting to his most extravagant metaphors, referred to the revolutions as "conflagrations," "torrents," and "earthquakes." Spain's neighbor, Portugal, was affected in August. Here a peculiar situation existed; John VI, the king, was still in Brazil, where he had fled during the Napoleonic wars, and the government was in the hands of a regent who had the support of Marshal William Carr Beresford (1768–1854), the British general commanding troops stationed in the country. Taking advantage of the temporary absence of Beresford, a group of Portuguese army officers raised the standard of rebellion and established a provisional government which announced its support of the king, provided he returned to his country. Meanwhile, a newly summoned assembly began to draft a constitution on the Spanish model.

More alarming to the powers, particularly to Metternich, was a concurrent revolt in Naples that threatened Austrian control of the entire Italian peninsula. Metternich spoke of this as the "greatest crisis" of his career. The rebellion was directed against Ferdinand I, the restored king of Naples and Sicily, who was an uncle of the king of Spain, and resembled him in many respects. Like the Spanish king he had broken the promises made to his people upon his return in 1815 by abolishing reforms introduced during the French occupation and restoring the nobility and clergy to their privileged positions in the state. Further, since Metternich had helped place him upon the throne, he was regarded as subject to Austrian influence. Opposition to Ferdinand came in large measure from the same groups that supported the rebellion in Spain: army officers and members of the business class. They had the additional support of nationalist secret societies like the *Carbonari*, which had emerged during the Napoleonic occupation and now directed their attack against Austrian influence as well as the reactionary government of Ferdinand. The demands of those who revolted in Naples were vague and primarily negative. The rebels did press for a constitution based on the Spanish Constitution of 1812, but there is some evidence that they were ignorant of its actual provisions.

[4] Quoted by Charles K. Webster, *The Foreign Policy of Castlereagh, 1815–1822* (London, 1925), p. 238.

The Neapolitan revolt aroused great excitement throughout the peninsula, but only in the northern Italian kingdom of Sardinia did an actual insurrection break out. Here the hopes of the revolutionaries were focused on Charles Alber (1798–1849), nephew of King Victor Emmanuel I and heir to the throne, but the irresolute behavior of the young prince when the rebels sought to make him their leader in March, 1821, helped doom the revolt to failure.

Metternich was horrified by the revolt in Naples; yet he delayed taking measures to suppress it. It would have been relatively simple for an Austrian army to invade the kingdom and crush the rebels, but Metternich preferred to win the support of the Concert of Europe before adopting such a course of action. Despite Britain's refusal to condone intervention in Spain, Metternich now appealed to Castlereagh for backing in Italy. The British foreign minister's reaction is interesting. While he fully sympathized with Metternich's concern over a revolt which might easily spread to the rest of the peninsula, and affirmed that Britain would have no objection to armed Austrian intervention in Naples on behalf of Ferdinand, he opposed here—as he had in Spain—the principle of joint allied intervention. Rebuffed by the British, Metternich turned somewhat reluctantly to a quarter where he knew he could get support. He arranged for a congress of the rulers of Austria, Russia, and Prussia to be held at the Austrian village of Troppau in the autumn of 1820. Both Britain and France refused to participate officially but sent observers to the meeting. Apparently Metternich would have preferred to limit the discussion to the question of intervention in Naples, but Alexander insisted that the congress draw up a more general statement. The result was the Troppau Protocol, which in effect asserted the general right of the European powers to intervene in states that had undergone revolutions and to bring them back, by force if necessary, to the "bosom of the Alliance." This document referred throughout the "European Alliance," never specifying whether the congress was acting in the name of the Holy Alliance or the Quadruple Alliance.

In accordance with the protocol, the eastern powers agreed to authorize intervention in Naples, but they postponed determination of the form it should take until January, 1821, when the congress reconvened at Laibach, with Ferdinand of Naples invited to consult with them. There it was decided that an Austrian army, acting in the name of the allies, should be sent to Naples. Quickly dispatched, the army suppressed the revolt and restored Ferdinand to his throne. Then it moved northward to join the royalists in Sardinia, and the two forces defeated the rebels there.

Metternich had apparently achieved his goal of securing international support for the suppression of the Italian revolutions, but the victory was sealed at the cost of British friendship. For Castlereagh, incensed that the action in Italy was undertaken in the name of the allies, issued an official statement in January, 1821, dissenting from the action of the other powers and proclaiming publicly the British position. Repudiating the Troppau Protocol, the declaration stated that the British government "cannot admit that this right [of interference in the internal affairs of another state] can receive a general and indiscriminate application to all revolutionary movements, without reference to their immediate bearing upon some particular State or States, or be made prospectively the basis of an Alliance." The statement was hailed by liberals throughout Europe with great enthusiasm. They looked upon Britain as the champion of the liberal cause against the leaders of the Holy Alliance, whose apparent intention was to police the European continent and suppress liberal movements wherever they existed.

Those who viewed Britain as the defender of liberal aspirations throughout Europe were mistaken, for the Tory government headed by Lord Liverpool (Robert Banks Jenkinson, 1770–1828) had no such intentions. Its actions reflected instead the growing rift between Britain and the three eastern powers. Castlereagh had worked more closely with his continental colleagues than any British foreign minister before him; he had been, indeed, the prime mover behind the Quadruple Alliance and the conference system which grew out of it. But when he saw that system being perverted, being exploited for purposes for which it had never been intended, he felt that there was no alternative to withdrawing Britain's support. Castlereagh had already embarked upon the policy that was later to be characterized as "splendid isolation." When he committed suicide as a result of overwork and fatigue, George Canning, his successor at the foreign office, continued with enthusiasm the policy which Castlereagh had adopted with regret.

Canning's acceptance of the post of foreign minister preceded by only a few weeks the Congress of Verona in 1822, the last in the series of regular postwar conferences among the allies, and the meeting at which the split between Britain and the other powers was formally confirmed. The congress was summoned to discuss further measures to be taken in Spain and to deal with still another revolution, the Greek war for independence from the Ottoman Empire, which had begun in the preceding year. By the time the congress met, a temporary settlement of the Greco-Turkish affair had been reached, but sentiment for intervention in Spain was strong, since Ferdinand's position was steadily worsening. In the forefront of those urging action in Spain was France. France's attitude during the 1820–1821 crisis had been ambiguous. Like Britain, it had sent only an observer to the Congress of Troppau, but, although not formally adhering to the Troppau Protocol, France had made no protest against it. In the interim between Troppau and Verona, the Ultraroyalist faction had gained the upper hand in Paris. It advocated a French invasion of Spain to restore the king and to extend French influence in the Iberian peninsula. At Verona, France got the support of all three eastern powers and was authorized by them to act on behalf of the Concert. Before the agreement was completed, however, Canning instructed the duke of Wellington, the British delegate to the congress, to inform his colleagues that the British would not be a party to any intervention in Spanish internal affairs, "come what may."

Britain could protest, but could not prevent the action decided upon by the others. When the Spanish revolutionary government refused to modify its constitution at the request of the continental powers, a French army crossed the Pyrenees (April, 1823) and drove the revolutionary government from Madrid. By autumn the last resistance of the rebels had been crushed at Cádiz and the king was restored to his throne. Ignoring the advice of the French to maintain a moderate constitutional regime, Ferdinand VII proceeded to eliminate the last vestiges of constitutionalism and to carry out mass reprisals against the liberals. Those who escaped torture and execution were imprisoned or driven into exile. Spain had been restored, in the words of the Troppau Protocol, to the "bosom of the Alliance."

Having failed to thwart intervention in Spain, Canning still hoped he could prevent the restoration of the Latin-American republics to Spain. This aim was shared by President James Monroe of the United States, which in 1822 had recognized these new republics. Somewhat suspicious of British designs on Cuba, Monroe refused a British proposal for joint action and proceeded alone. In December, 1823, in a statement which came to be known as the Monroe Doctrine, he proclaimed that the Americas were henceforth closed to European colonization and intervention. Great Britain subsequently recognized the independence of the Latin-American republics from Spain and Portugal. Because British sea power helped guarantee this independence, Canning could boast in 1826, "I called the New World into existence to redress the balance of the Old."

The Greek Revolt, 1821–1832

The revolt of the Greeks against Turkish domination and the reaction of the European powers to this revolt were aspects of a larger problem that was to plague European diplomats throughout the nineteenth century. This was the "Eastern Question," which had its origin in the continuing decline of the Ottoman Empire and the weakening of its authority over its outlying territories. Each European government had to decide whether to stem the disintegration by bolstering up the sultans, or to hasten it and exploit the decay to its own particular advantage. No power pursued a perfectly consistent course with respect to the Sublime Porte (as the court of the sultan was called). The Russians clearly hoped to profit from their proximity to the Turkish empire and from the religious tie between Russians and Greek Orthodox Christians living within the empire to acquire special privileges from Turkey. The British, suspicious of Russian ambitions in the Near East, more than once defended the sultan against his enemies; their support of the Greek revolt was an exception to this general policy.

The Greeks had been living under Turkish rule since the middle of the fifteenth century, and to most Europeans, Greece was merely a province of the Ottoman Empire. Actually, Greece had enjoyed a privileged position within the empire from the seventeenth century onward, for the sultans used educated Greeks from Constantinople (the so-called Phanariot Greeks) in their administrations and permitted Greek merchants (along with Armenians and Jews) a near monopoly of trade in the eastern Mediterranean. Moreover, within Greece the Turks permitted the teaching of the Greek language and the exercise of the Greek Orthodox faith. The Greeks, then, had never entirely lost sight of their past and their identity. In addition, a marked revival of Greek national sentiment and of interest in the past occurred at the end of the eighteenth and the beginning of the nineteenth centuries, and with this came a growing desire for independence from Turkish rule. The immediate impetus for revolt came in 1821 from a secret society known as the *Hetaíria Philiké* ("Society of Friends"); the society had been organized in 1814 and consisted primarily of Greeks living outside of Greece who hoped for a revival of the Greek empire of the early Middle Ages. The leader of the society was Prince Alexander Ypsilanti (1792–1828), son of a Greek provincial administrator and himself a former general in the Russian army. Having been given the impression by the tsar's Greek-born foreign minister, Count Johannes Antonius Capodistrias (1776–1831), that he would get Russian support for a Greek uprising, Ypsilanti led a band of volunteers into the Turkish province of Moldavia, where he summoned the native Rumanians as well as his fellow Greeks to revolt against their Turkish masters. Ypsilanti's attempt failed because the Rumanians refused to respond to his call and because the tsar disavowed him. Two weeks later a more spontaneous revolt erupted in the Morea and spread to some of the Aegean Islands and to central and northern Greece. The avowed goal of the revolutionaries was complete independence from the Ottoman Empire and the creation of a new Greek state.

Representatives of the major powers were still assembled at Laibach when they received news of the Greek revolt early in 1821. Their response was practically unanimous. They had no particular sympathy for the Greeks, and they considered the revolt one more threat to established authority that had to be suppressed. Chiefly at Metternich's urging, the tsar denounced the rebels and dismissed Capodistrias. Not even Britain, on whom some liberals had counted for support, showed any inclination to aid the Greeks. Indeed, the principal goal of Castlereagh and the British government was to see order restored in the Ottoman Empire and to forestall the possibility of Russian intervention.

But a new force became involved in the Greek revolt, a force that did not come into play in the revolutions in Spain and Italy and that gradually compelled the governments of Britain, Russia, and France to repudiate their initial stand and throw their support to the rebels. This was a ground swell

Massacre at Chios.
Painting by Delacroix.
The Louvre, Paris.

of popular backing for the rebels—the movement known as Philhellenism, which included admirers of Greece all over Europe and America. To generations brought up on the classics, the Greek revolt had a romantic appeal unlike that of any other. Moreover, the fact that the Greeks were Christians struggling to free themselves from Moslem domination gave the entire movement the flavor of a crusade. Unable to express opposition to their own regimes, liberals throughout Europe rallied to the cause of Greek independence and organized committees to provide the rebels with money, supplies, and even volunteers. And the success of the Philhellenic cause was in no small part due to the fervent support of some of the leading romantic writers of the era—Byron and Shelley foremost among them. Byron had gone to Greece in 1810 and subsequently expressed his hope "that Greece might still be free." To this cause he devoted his last years, and he died in Greece in 1824.

Sympathetic to Greek independence though they were, the Philhellenes were thoroughly horrified by the brutality of the Greeks in the Morea revolt. But they were quickly stirred to renew their sympathy by the vicious retaliatory measures taken by the Turks, who on Easter Day, 1821, hanged the Greek patriarch in his sacred vestments at Constantinople, and in 1822

massacred most of the hundred thousand Greeks living on the island of Chios, an event commemorated by Delacroix in a famous painting.

Despite popular sympathy for the Greek cause, several years of public pressure and protracted negotiations were required before any European government actively intervened. During this time Sultan Mahmud II (ruled 1808–1839), unable to defeat the Greeks with his own forces, called upon his vassal, the powerful Mehemet Ali (1769–1849), pasha of Egypt, to lend military and naval assistance. Mehemet Ali's son Ibrahim Pasha (1789–1848) was put in command of a force that invaded and subdued the Morea in 1825. Although the odds against the rebels were heavy and internal quarrels at times brought them to civil war, the Greeks continued to hold out, hoping for intervention by the European powers. Only in 1827 did this become possible. In that year, France joined Russia and Britain in signing the Treaty of London, which stated that if Turkey refused to accept an armistice, the three powers might support the Greeks with their naval forces. When Turkey did indeed reject an armistice, a joint force of British, Russian, and French ships bottled up Ibrahim's fleet in the bay of Navarino, on the west coast of the Morea, in October, 1827. Unable to force either Greeks or Moslems to stop fighting, the allied naval commanders finally moved into the bay itself, met Ibrahim's fleet in a close artillery engagement, and almost completely destroyed it. Philhellenes cheered the news of the victory at Navarino. But the conservative governments of Great Britain, France, and Russia were somewhat embarrassed by it, and the duke of Wellington, who had succeeded Canning as prime minister of Great Britain and was much less sympathetic to the Greek cause, apologized to the sultan for the action of the allied naval commanders.

A few months later, in April, 1828, Tsar Nicholas I, who had come to the throne in 1825, used a hostile statement by the sultan as a pretext for declaring war on Turkey. The tsar was interested not so much in achieving Greek independence as in capitalizing on the weaknesses of the Ottoman Empire, which appeared near collapse. Yet during the conflict, which lasted for more than a year, the Russians seemed to undergo a change of heart. Turkish resistance proved to be stronger than anticipated and the tsar came to realize that even if he succeeded in defeating the sultan, the other powers would not stand idly by while he despoiled the Ottoman Empire. Accordingly, the Russians stopped short of Constantinople and in September, 1829, in the Treaty of Adrianople, concluded with the Ottoman Empire a peace which imposed certain restrictions on the Turkish government in the administration of its European provinces of Moldavia and Walachia (present-day Rumania), making them virtually Russian protectorates, but involved no significant territorial concessions.

The Treaty of Adrianople also stipulated that the Ottoman Empire must abide by decisions which Russia, France, and Britain would reach concerning Greece. The three powers met in London in 1830 to settle the Greek

situation. They declared Greece an independent kingdom under their protection, but two years of negotiations were necessary before the boundaries of the new state were definitively settled and a ruler named. The crown of the new kingdom was refused by two German princes before it was finally accepted by Otto, the son of King Ludwig of Bavaria, in February, 1832, eleven years after the outbreak of the revolt.

The revolt of the Greeks and their ultimate achievement of independence made a great impression on contemporary Europeans. For this was the first successful breach of the *status quo* after 1815 and seemed to mark a significant victory for the idea of nationality as well as for the cause of liberalism. That these were not necessarily the motivating concerns of the British, French, and Russian governments is indicated by their decision to name a German-born ruler for the new Greek state, but factionalism among the Greeks would have made it difficult for the guaranteeing powers to find a native ruler whom all could support. In any event, European liberals, temporarily disillusioned by the defeat of the revolutions of 1820–1821, derived new hope from the success of the Greeks and the support given their cause by Britain, France, and Russia. The way had been prepared for a new wave of uprisings in 1830.

THE BELGIAN REVOLT, 1830–1831

Before the Greek question had been settled, the European powers were confronted by another crisis, which appeared to threaten the *status quo* much more directly. Indeed, it was the first real challenge to the territorial settlement reached at Vienna and was therefore a matter of vital concern to all the Great Powers. This was the revolt of the Belgian provinces against the Netherlands, to which they had been annexed in 1815 as a barrier to French aggression. The Belgians had never been enthusiastic about the union. Differences in traditions, language, religion, and economic interests naturally separated the two peoples. The Dutch, proud of their two centuries of independence, were contemptuous of the Belgians, who had been subjected to Spanish, and then Austrian, rule. The policies of King William of Orange further aggravated tensions between them. The predominantly Catholic population of the Belgian provinces resented the Protestant king's policy of equality for all religious denominations. The establishment of Dutch as the official language of the realm except in the French-speaking Walloon districts of Belgium annoyed the Flemings, whose dialect was very different from Dutch. And although the economic activities of the two parts of the kingdom actually complemented each other rather well—the industry and agriculture of the southern provinces finding outlets through the commercial centers of the northern—Belgian manufacturers felt that the Dutch tariff system did not sufficiently protect their industries.

Battle of Navarino, 1827. *British, Russian, and French vessels practically destroyed the Turkish fleet in this engagement.*

Opposition to the Dutch was concentrated mainly in two political groups, the Clericals and the Liberals, themselves often at odds. The Liberals were resentful of the constitutional structure of the state because it gave an equal number of representatives in the elected States-General to the Dutch and the Belgians, even though the Belgian population was nearly 3.5 million and the Dutch a mere 2 million. They were critical of the high-handed way in which the king dealt with the States-General and often dispensed with the advice of his ministers; they protested government persecution of the opposition press. The Clericals resented the creation of state secondary schools and the extension of state control over independent (that is, ecclesiastical) schools through a system of government inspection. In 1828, Liberals and Clericals managed to bury their differences and formed a "union of parties," which drew up a common program demanding freedom of the press, freedom of teaching, and ministerial responsibility in government. Neither group contemplated the overthrow of the dynasty; rather, they hoped to achieve their demands within the framework of the existing regime.

The success of the July Revolution (1830) in neighboring France, which overthrew the reigning monarch, Charles X, and substituted a broader constitutional regime under King Louis Philippe, quickened the spread of discontent in Belgium. Moreover, a temporary economic decline brought particular hardships to the working classes in Belgium's larger cities. But the

Belgian revolt was actually touched off by the performance of an opera. After a stirring rendition in Brussels of *La Muette de Portici*, an opera by Eugène Scribe and Daniel Auber about a revolt in Naples, students left the theater shouting "Down with the Dutch!" and "Down with the Ministry!" The student riot turned into revolt, and the revolt spread. The king sent troops to Brussels, but after three days of bitter fighting, they were forced to withdraw, leaving the city in the hands of the rebels. By October a provisional government had been established and a national congress summoned to draw up a constitution for the new state. Belgium was to be a constitutional monarchy, but members of Holland's house of Orange were explicitly excluded from the throne.

The independence of Belgium clearly violated the settlement of 1815, and it was on this basis that King William of Holland appealed to the Great Powers for their help in reestablishing his authority in the Belgian provinces. As might be expected, Tsar Nicholas of Russia was eager for intervention, and he appeared to have the support of Metternich and Frederick William III of Prussia. Before they could act, however, Talleyrand, newly arrived in London as French ambassador, warned the duke of Wellington that France would not tolerate intervention by the eastern powers in a territory lying on its borders. Wellington agreed to oppose intervention and notified the eastern powers of the British and French position. He further proposed a conference of the five Great Powers in London to discuss the future of the Belgian provinces, an invitation which the eastern powers accepted reluctantly. Metternich apparently hoped that Wellington might be persuaded to support joint military action, but by the time the conference met in November, 1830, Wellington's ministry had fallen and had been succeeded by the Whig cabinet of Earl Grey.

Although Lord Palmerston, the Whig foreign minister, was hardly enthusiastic about the revolt in Belgium, he concluded in November that it could no longer be reversed. Moreover he was not eager to see troops of the eastern powers move into an area where Britain traditionally had interests. The French, having just emerged from their own revolution, were sympathetic to the cause of Belgian independence and hoped it would result in an increase of French influence in the region. At the same time, a revolt of the Poles against their Russian overlords in November distracted Tsar Nicholas from Belgian affairs; he was now far more interested in suppressing the revolution in his own territory than in intervention in the Netherlands. Both Austria and Prussia were concerned about the possible spread of the Polish revolt to subject Poles living within their own borders, and by early 1831 Metternich was also preoccupied with revolts in Italy. In the end, Russia, Prussia, and Austria played only a small role in the settlement of Belgium's status. By stipulating that Belgium would remain a neutral state under the permanent guarantee of the Great Powers, Britain and France succeeded in persuading them to accept a protocol which virtually recognized Belgium's independence.

The collaboration between Britain and France was threatened early in 1831 when the newly elected Belgian national congress offered the throne to the duke of Nemours (1814–1896), second son of the French king, Louis Philippe. The French government was not innocent of maneuvering on behalf of the duke's candidacy, seeing in it a means of making Belgium subservient to France's interests. But Palmerston's strong reaction to the offer, including a threat of war, led Louis Philippe to refuse the throne for his son. It was then offered to Leopold of Saxe-Coburg, a German prince but a British subject, the widower of Princess Charlotte of England and uncle to the future Queen Victoria. Accepted by all parties at the London conference, Leopold was proclaimed king in July, 1831. Only King William of Holland was unreconciled to this solution. In August, 1831, he sent a sizable army into Belgium in an effort to reconquer the lost provinces. The Concert thereupon authorized joint Anglo-French intervention to eject the Dutch. William continued his resistance for another year and a half and did not finally acknowledge Belgium's independence until 1839.

The handling of the Belgian revolt suggested that the Great Powers could act together in reaching a solution to a thorny diplomatic crisis despite the sharply opposing points of view of the several governments. Credit for the outcome must go to Lord Palmerston for his skillful conduct of the negotiations. But the Russian and Austrian governments may have been more willing to accept his solution for Belgium because of the restraint shown by both the British and French governments toward the revolts in Poland and the Italian states. Despite impassioned pleas from liberals in

Lord Palmerston. *British Foreign Secretary, subsequently Prime Minister. Photographed in his later years.*

both the House of Commons and the French Chamber of Deputies for intervention on behalf of the Poles and the Italians, neither government had seriously considered going to the support of the rebels against Russia and Austria. Each of the major powers appeared determined in 1830–1831 to avoid any action which might precipitate a general European war.

THE "EASTERN QUESTION," 1832–1841

To contemporaries, one of the most notable features of the international crisis created by the Belgian revolt was the way in which it seemed to underline the growing division between the three absolutist powers of eastern Europe and the two constitutional states of western Europe. This alignment, signs of which had existed ever since the conclusion of Alexander's Holy Alliance in 1815, had not been maintained consistently throughout the 1820's. Indeed, France under the Bourbon monarchs had more than once sided with the eastern powers, as it did, for example, on the question of intervention in the Iberian peninsula. The revolution of 1830 in France appeared to heighten the chances of Anglo-French collaboration, for it brought to power a regime whose institutions were similar, at least superficially, to those of Britain, and the new monarch, Louis Philippe, paid lip service to the individual liberties and guarantees traditionally respected in Britain. Yet a close look at the relationship between France and Britain in the 1830's and the 1840's reveals that it was far from cordial; indeed, outright hostility prevailed during the diplomatic crisis which occurred in 1840. The friction between the two powers arose in part from conflicting economic interests; French manufacturers feared British competition and therefore sought to maintain tariff schedules that would exclude or limit British imports. In addition, as Louis Philippe became more firmly established on his throne, his outlook grew increasingly conservative, and he turned more frequently to Metternich, seeking an understanding between France and Austria which he hoped would heighten the legitimacy of his regime.

The revival of the so-called Eastern Question after the Greek settlement of 1830 most clearly illustrates the tenuous character of Anglo-French relations and the degree of flexibility still present in the European Concert. This time the trouble arose out of the conflict between the sultan of Turkey and his powerful vassal, Mehemet Ali, pasha of Egypt, whose aid he had secured during the Greek revolt. As a reward for his support, Mehemet Ali now demanded the cession of Syria, and when the sultan refused, he proceeded in 1832 to send an army, led by his son Ibrahim, into this territory. The sultan appealed to Britain for support against his rebellious vassal, but Palmerston, still occupied with the Belgian situation, turned him down. After a number of victories by Mehemet Ali's forces seemed to threaten the sultan's regime, Russia decided to intervene on behalf of the

Mehemet Ali, pasha of Egypt. *Lithograph from a drawing by the Count of Forbin at Alexandria, March, 1818.*

sultan, and early in 1833 sent a squadron to Constantinople. The French and the British, alarmed by the threat of Russian domination over Turkey, marshaled their fleets in the eastern Mediterranean and joined Russia in imposing a settlement on the sultan and his vassal. Turkey was saved from collapse, but the sultan was forced to cede Syria to Mehemet Ali. The crisis had apparently been surmounted. Soon afterward, in July, 1833, Russia and Turkey concluded the Treaty of Unkiar-Skelessi for mutual assistance in the event of attack. In a secret clause, Turkey was excused from fulfilling its obligation in return for closing the Dardanelles to all non-Russian vessels of war. When France and Britain discovered the existence of this clause a short time later, they protested the treaty because it gave a favored position to Russian warships in the Straits and seemed to leave Turkey at the mercy of Russia. But for the time being, they did nothing.

A second crisis developed when, in 1839–1840, the growing power of Mehemet Ali once again appeared to endanger not only the sultan but also other powers with interests in the eastern Mediterranean. Lord Palmerston, now convinced of the seriousness of the threat from Mehemet Ali and suspicious of Russia's designs on Turkey, decided that Britain should support the sultan more effectively. But France, whose interest in Egypt dated back to the Directory, was sympathetic to Mehemet Ali and encouraged him in his ambitions for an empire in the Near East. The issue came to a head in 1839 when the sultan renewed hostilities by invading Syria. His forces proved no match for those of his enemy; his army was defeated by Ibrahim, and his leading admiral shortly afterward deserted with the fleet to Mehemet Ali. At this crucial point the sultan died, leaving the Ottoman Empire in the hands of a young boy, Abdul-Medjid I, who was prepared to yield to his more powerful vassals, Mehemet Ali and Ibrahim.

The crisis brought renewed attempts to revive the Concert. Even before the outbreak of hostilities Palmerston had tried to secure a general guarantee of Turkish integrity from the Great Powers. But he encountered French hostility to the sultan and he could get no support from Russia, which was still adhering to the unilateral promise of aid to Turkey made in the Treaty of Unkiar-Skelessi. In September, 1839, after the defeat of the sultan's forces, Tsar Nicholas had his representative in London approach Lord Palmerston with a proposal for settlement of the crisis. Palmerston was initially wary of the Russian plan since he suspected that the tsar would attempt to drive a wedge between Britain and France by insisting that France's protégé, Mehemet Ali, back down despite his victories and return his conquests to the Ottoman Empire. But he welcomed the tsar's simultaneous offer to abandon the Treaty of Unkiar-Skelessi and substitute a general guarantee of Turkey's integrity.

Accordingly, Palmerston invited the other Great Powers to London to join in a general settlement. Austria and Prussia quickly agreed. But France, now under the premiership of Adolphe Thiers (1797–1877), demurred. Public opinion in France was running strongly in favor of the Egyptian pasha, and Thiers was convinced that Britain would not act independently of France in the Near East. He was soon proven wrong, for Palmerston was convinced that "for the interests of England, the preservation of the balance of power and the maintenance of peace in Europe" a settlement of the sort proposed had to be reached. Overcoming opposition within his own cabinet by threatening to resign, he forced acceptance of his position and the four-power Treaty of London was signed in July, 1840. Mehemet Ali was offered Egypt as a hereditary possession, and control over southern Syria for the remainder of his life, but he was to relinquish everything else he had conquered from the sultan and return the Turkish fleet. Counting on French support, the Egyptian pasha refused to accept the terms of the treaty and announced that he would stand firm. The result was renewed conflict in the Near East. The British bombarded the Syrian coast and landed troops. But France, despite repeated threats of war with Britain, which kept international tension at a fever pitch for three months, never did join the conflict. Realizing that war with Britain would not be in France's interest, Louis Philippe dismissed Thiers from office in October, 1840, and entered into negotiations with the other powers. No longer supported in his intransigent position by France, Mehemet Ali was persuaded to conclude an agreement with the sultan which embodied the provisions of the Treaty of London, except that it did not give him control even over southern Syria. In July, 1841, the five Great Powers signed the Straits Convention, which stipulated that the Straits, both the Bosporus and the Dardanelles, were to be closed to *all* foreign warships when Turkey was at peace. France's participation in this agreement signified its return to the Concert of European powers and the end of the diplomatic crisis.

What was perhaps most interesting about the crisis of 1839–1840 was the diplomatic alignment of powers which were at ideological extremes. The principal antagonists in the crisis were Britain and France, whose political systems were more alike than those of any other two powers. Britain's principal collaborator was Russia, whose absolutist government was anathema to liberals throughout Europe. At the height of the crisis Metternich seems to have suspected Britain and Russia of planning war against France and even considered seceding from the London agreement, drawing Prussia with him and concluding a separate agreement with France. Moreover, it was Metternich who was instrumental in bringing France back into the Concert of Europe by mediating between it and the other powers. Ideological considerations seem, then, to have played a relatively minor role in the relationship among the Great Powers in this crisis, as in others before 1850.

Perhaps the most interesting question concerning international relations during this period is why no war occurred among the major powers for almost forty years after the Vienna settlement, despite numerous diplomatic crises and threats of conflict. Gordon Craig, who has recently suggested a number of explanations for this absence of war, emphasizes particularly the remarkable consensus that existed among the powers despite their ideological differences.[5] All of them accepted the principle of the balance of power and the implied assumption that no state should expand its powers or influence without the consent of the others. Each government was therefore willing to exercise a certain degree of restraint in its dealings with others, as for example, Russia did in 1833 in exacting only one relatively minor concession from Turkey in return for support. The general respect for treaties also contributed to European stability. Finally, there was the willingness of the powers to participate in joint efforts to maintain peace. For example, though Britain's diplomats refused to make commitments to a stated policy in advance, they realized that their nation had an obligation and an interest in European affairs and therefore intervened at times when the balance of power was threatened or peace endangered. As long as the major powers were willing to adhere to such a code of behavior, peace among them could be preserved.

To these explanations may be added one more. Evidently no government saw a particular advantage to be gained by war. All except France were concerned with maintaining the settlement of 1815, and even France had been treated well enough by the victorious powers, so that it had no overwhelming desire for revenge or for rectification of its boundaries. If aggressive sentiments existed in France, they were found most often among members of the opposition, who did not exert a significant influence on

[5] Gordon Craig, "The System of Alliances and the Balance of Power" in *New Cambridge Modern History*, Vol. X (Cambridge, Eng., 1960), pp. 266–267.

government policy. Perhaps the greatest potential threats to peace in this era came from the liberals in France and Britain, eager to champion the cause of oppressed nationalities whether in Poland or in Italy, but their governments were generally unwilling to endanger the stability of Europe by undertaking crusades for the liberation of subject peoples.

CHAPTER 4

The Industrial Revolution and Its Impact on European Society

IN THE INTRODUCTION to this volume it was argued that the Industrial Revolution undoubtedly transformed more profoundly the lives of Europeans during the era 1789–1850 than did the French Revolution. In countries affected by industrialization, fundamental changes took place in the way human beings earned their livelihood, in the conditions of their material existence, and in the pattern of their daily lives.

Like many capsule phrases, the term "Industrial Revolution" has been the subject of considerable controversy and a wide variety of interpretations. For a long time the Industrial Revolution was viewed as a relatively sudden flurry of technological innovations or inventions, particularly in the manufacturing of textiles, that occurred in England during the second half of the eighteenth century. T. S. Ashton, one of the leading scholars of the phenomenon, suggests the traditional or popular conception of the Industrial Revolution when he quotes the English schoolboy who began an essay on the subject, "About 1760 a wave of gadgets swept over England." [1] Modern scholars regard the Industrial Revolution as a much more complex series of developments which occurred first in eighteenth- and nineteenth-century England but which were repeated, with variations, in the northwestern tier of states of the European Continent in the first half of the nineteenth century, in some states of Germany and northern Italy after 1850, and reached eastern and parts of southern Europe only at the end of the nineteenth century or the beginning of the twentieth century. Indeed, some of the developments associated with the Industrial Revolution are continuing today in Asia, Africa, and Latin America under the label "economic development" or "economic modernization."

Despite important differences among the societies in which industrializa-

---

[1] *The Industrial Revolution, 1760–1830* (New York, 1964), p. 42.

tion has occurred, in methods by which changes have been achieved, in the rate of development, and in the social impact of industrialization, it is possible to find some common denominators in the process—particularly in those European countries first affected. Essentially the Industrial Revolution in England and on the Continent involved the substitution of machines driven by water power or steam for simple tools operated by hand or foot. This, in turn, resulted in significant changes in the organization of production. For example, the shift in textile manufacturing from spinning and weaving by individual laborers in their homes to production of cloth by machinery required workers to be concentrated in factories whose location was determined by proximity to the sources of power. Such a change yielded tremendous increases in productivity, but it was fraught with important material and psychological consequences for the laborers. For it required mass migrations of population, led to the emergence of new cities and the expansion of old ones, and wrought major changes in the worker's mode of life.

Besides textile manufacturing, two other industries were particularly important in the Industrial Revolution in Britain and normally played a key role in industrialization on the Continent: coal mining and the manufacture of metals. Innovations in these industries stimulated and were stimulated by changes taking place in the production of textiles. The development of an effective steam engine by the 1770's and its introduction in textile mills required improved exploitation of Britain's coal resources as a source of fuel. Iron was the raw material essential for the construction of machinery and engines used in the mills and mines.

POPULATION GROWTH

Even before the Industrial Revolution wrought a transformation of European society, a dramatic increase in population began to disrupt Europe's traditional way of life. Beginning in the eighteenth century, particularly after 1750, the population of most European countries began to grow rapidly. During that century the Hapsburg Empire expanded from twenty to twenty-seven million, Spain grew from five to ten million, and Prussia from three to six million. France's population increased somewhat less rapidly, from twenty to twenty-nine million, and Britain's from nine to sixteen million. This growth continued through the nineteenth century but at significantly different rates. Britain and the states that joined to form the German Empire in 1871 continued to grow very rapidly, each trebling its population during the nineteenth century, while the growth of France's population slowed down markedly. Some of the states of southern and eastern Europe had to wait until after 1870 for their major growth. For Europe as a whole, the population doubled between 1800 and 1900. The cumulative effect of this population explosion after 1750 was tremendous, particularly when one considers that the rate of population growth in Europe as a whole had been only 3 per cent during the century from 1650 to 1750. Even without industrialization European society would have been subjected to unprecedented stresses.

In the absence of detailed population statistics for the eighteenth century, demographers differ in their explanations of this sudden population increase. Some have noted in its initial stages an increase in the birth rate, at least in some countries, but most have laid greater stress upon a significant drop in the death rate after 1750. More children survived infancy, and more adults lived to an older age. For this a number of reasons have been offered. Improved hygiene and advances in medicine spared Europeans from some of the worst endemic diseases and plagues. An increase of the food supply limited the famines that had periodically plagued Europe and provided somewhat better diets. In this connection, the introduction of potato cultivation was one of the most important agricultural innovations

View of a densely populated London slum, 1848.

in western and central Europe since it enabled people to survive even though they might be living in great poverty. The opening up of land not previously under cultivation also contributed in some regions to higher food production and provided an inducement to peasants to increase the size of their families. Finally, improvements in the maintenance of public order and security meant that life was not as hazardous as it had been in an era of greater brigandage and violence; nor were there as many civil and religious wars as there had been in the seventeenth century.

Europe's dramatic population increase had dynamic consequences for European society and institutions. Increased numbers of people inevitably place pressures upon available resources and stimulate competition for those resources. For example, although new land was opened up for cultivation the growth of the rural population ultimately outstripped the supply of land available and forced many peasants or children of peasants to seek their livelihood elsewhere. Population growth, in its early stages, resulted in a higher percentage of youth in society; this may have added vitality but it also contributed to greater social turbulence. In the long run, changing patterns of population growth affected traditional family structure as parents were called upon to support larger families or see the unity of the family disrupted by departure of those seeking their living beyond their traditional home or village. A longer life span meant greater numbers of old people to be cared for.

To what extent did the growth of population contribute to the Industrial Revolution? To what extent was population growth stimulated by industrialization? No easy answers to such questions are possible. A rapidly expanding population undoubtedly created a need for more efficiently produced and cheaper goods such as clothing, yet some countries with a growing population experienced an Industrial Revolution and others did not. A country like Great Britain, which increased its productivity, both agricultural and industrial, in the century from 1750 to 1850, could obviously support a larger population, but was industrialization responsible for population growth? Population increase and industrialization are clearly intertwined, but it would be difficult to establish the precise causal relationship between the two. The most that can be said is that each country affected by an Industrial Revolution appears to have undergone a significant expansion of population in the few decades preceding industrialization and that this growth of population exerted its own pressures upon the society before industrialization took place.[2]

BEGINNINGS OF THE INDUSTRIAL REVOLUTION IN GREAT BRITAIN

Why did the Industrial Revolution begin in Great Britain? What peculiar features of the British society and economy explain the head start

2 Peter G. Stearns, *European Society in Upheaval* (New York, 1967), p. 66.

Sheffield, an English manufacturing town, known for its cutlery.

of this nation? No single answer can be given, for a number of factors, taken together, help explain Britain's primacy.

The Industrial Revolution was closely related to the changes in methods of farming and stock breeding in eighteenth-century England which had constituted an agricultural revolution. These came about when the large landowners, politically secure after their victory over the crown during the revolutions of the seventeenth century, sought to exploit their dominant position and to increase their money incomes. Their efforts to cultivate the land more efficiently and to introduce improved methods of stock breeding were hampered by the system of open fields, common lands, and semicollective methods of farming inherited from an earlier era. For success, their experiments needed large enclosed fields, so the landowners tried to speed up the process of "enclosing," or fencing in, their land by having the so-called acts of enclosure passed. As a result of these acts, which were unopposed in Parliament, vast areas were brought under more efficient cultivation and the landlords did achieve greater productivity—at the expense of thousands of small farmers who were forcibly ejected from their homes and from lands their families had cultivated for centuries. The enclosures brought about a marked increase in food production; British farms could now support a larger population with the work of fewer

Manchester, from the entrance to the London and North-Western Railway.

individuals. Some of those displaced from their farms ultimately sought employment in the new manufacturing centers and thus provided some of the surplus labor without which no industrial revolution can gain momentum.

On the Continent, no comparable source of labor was available until the nineteenth century; in France for example, the persistence of a system of small landholding probably handicapped the development of industry.

Two other requirements for an industrial revolution are adequate sources of the raw materials needed in the manufacturing process and markets to absorb the finished goods. Here, too, Great Britain had several advantages: a long-established fleet of merchant vessels and a vast and growing colonial empire. Although Britain definitely triumphed over France, its closest rival for an overseas empire, only with the defeat of Napoleon, its supremacy in North America had been established by the series of wars fought with France in the mid-eighteenth century. Britain had a thriving class of merchants ready to transport finished goods and raw materials and a reserve of potential customers for the products of its industries.

One more precondition for industrialization is the availability of capital for investment in the development of machinery and the construction of factories. Britain had a banking system and credit facilities that were better developed and more flexible than those on the Continent, and prosperous merchants and landowners who were willing to put up funds to finance new industrial enterprises.

That some of the key inventions which revolutionized the textile industry were British achievements was owing not so much to the native genius of the people as to the demand for greater quantities of goods produced more efficiently and cheaply. British hand labor could not compete successfully with Asian labor in the production of cotton cloth. But if cotton could be spun and woven by machines, British manufacturers could clearly capture the market. This was the stimulus that led to improved spinning devices and more efficient looms.

It was to be expected, therefore, that in the early years of the Industrial Revolution the innovations would be most obvious and the results most striking in the manufacture of textiles, particularly cotton cloth. Of special interest is the way in which improvements in one part of the manufacturing process stimulated advances in another part. The first notable invention, a hand loom which halved the time required for weaving, came in 1733. This loom stimulated the demand for yarn, and thus for a spinning process which could produce yarn in great quantities; the need was filled by James Hargreaves (d. 1778), who developed the spinning jenny, a simple hand device by which six or seven threads could be spun simultaneously. About 1770 Richard Arkwright (1732–1792), a Lancashire barber, further accelerated the spinning process by inventing the water frame, which used waterpower to spin many threads at a time. The introduction of the cumbersome water frame and the later substitution of steam for waterpower required that the spinning process be moved into a mill or factory. Arkwright's first water-driven factory, established in 1771, gave employment to almost six hundred workers. The revolutionary developments in spinning soon caused the production of yarn to outstrip the weaving capacity of the hand looms and thus stimulated the development of a power loom. Within a half century both spinning and weaving had been mechanized. But it took some time for these inventions to be put into general use and for textile production as a whole to be brought within factory walls. Even as late as the 1830's some cloth was still being produced in cottages.

The new technology also found early expression in Britain in two other key industries: coal mining and metallurgy. Coal was a source of fuel for the new engines, and iron was the raw material essential for building the machines themselves. Clearly, advances in textile manufacturing depended upon improvements in both coal production and iron manufacturing. The rich coal deposits of the British Isles had been largely untapped as long as wood was available as fuel. In the early eighteenth century the near

Hargreaves' Spinning Jenny. *Engraving. One of the key innovations in the revolutionizing of textile manufacturing.*

exhaustion of the forests meant that wood was too precious to be used for fuel and charcoal too scarce to be used in smelting iron; a new source of fuel and a new process for smelting iron were required, and coal filled both of these needs. By 1700 the first coal-mining shafts had been sunk, but their depth was limited by the presence of underground water. Until a successful method for removing this water could be found, coal production was restricted. A steam-driven pump invented in 1705 by Thomas Newcomen (1663–1729), and improved upon in the two succeeding decades, made possible the working of seams in and below the watery layers and thus increased the output of the mines. Because of its limitations, Newcomen's invention was used solely for pumping water from the mines. In the 1770's the Scotsman James Watt (1736–1819), with the financial backing of Matthew Boulton (1728–1809), perfected a much more versatile steam engine that was to serve as a new source of power for a great variety of industries.

Britain had adequate resources of iron ore, but until a method of smelting iron without reliance on charcoal (and hence wood) could be found, these supplies could not be exploited. The pioneer in developing a new smelting process for iron was Abraham Darby (1678–1717) of Coalbrookdale. In 1709 he succeeded in smelting quality pig iron with coke instead of charcoal. The consequences of his discovery did not immediately transform the industry, however, because Darby's iron was suitable only for castings and was not thought to be pure enough to serve as material for forges. Only in 1783–1784 did Henry Cort (1740–1800) develop puddling, or rolling, a process in which he used coke to burn away the impurities in pig iron,

Weaving machines in a German textile mill, 1848.

The Rocket. *Print of Robert Stephenson's famous steam locomotive, 1829.*

making it suitable for use in forges. Cort's discovery freed the forgemasters from reliance upon charcoal-produced iron and thus led to a remarkable expansion of the iron industry.

By 1800 then, all of the elements essential for a technological revolution were present. Fuel, in the form of coal, was plentiful; iron of a high quality was available for machines and other uses; and the steam engine provided abundant and dependable power. Perhaps the greatest single remaining need was for speedier and more efficient methods of transportation to bring together the various elements involved in production. Between 1760 and 1830 the building of an extensive system of canals greatly facilitated the movement of goods from one part of England to another and drastically reduced the cost of transporting such heavy commodities as coal, iron, timber, stone, and clay. But it was the advent of the railroad in the 1830's and 1840's that made possible the rapid distribution of raw materials and finished products so characteristic of modern industrial societies. Coal had been transported by horse-drawn vehicles on rails for several decades, but not until the 1820's when a practicable steam locomotive was constructed, could the possibilities of the railway be realized. The successful run in 1829 of George Stephenson's *Rocket* at a speed ranging up to sixteen miles an hour on the newly constructed Liverpool and Manchester Railway marked the real beginning of the railroad age in Great Britain. Within two short decades after 1830 some 6,500 miles of rails were laid, and the impact of the railroad began to be felt in almost every phase of British life.

The Social Impact of the Industrial Revolution

The revolution in technology and in the organization of production inevitably had a tremendous impact upon the societies in which it occurred. Some reference has already been made to changes in class structure caused by the Industrial Revolution: the rapid expansion of the bourgeoisie and the emergence of a new urban proletariat. But it is important to look more closely at the effect of these changes upon the lives of individuals, parti-

Entrance to the railway at Edge Hill, Liverpool, 1831.

cularly those whose destiny it was to spend their lives digging coal or operating the machines in the factories. Perhaps never before in human history had so radical a transformation occurred in men's occupations or in their physical environment. In one country after another an increasing proportion of the working people spent their lives not cultivating the fields and living in small, isolated villages, but toiling in factories or mines and living in large, crowded cities.

It is easy to exaggerate the speed of this transformation even in Great Britain, where it appeared to occur most rapidly. Englishmen did not simply move from farm to city overnight. Although the enclosure of common lands accelerated in the last decades of the eighteenth century, many small farmers stayed on as landless agricultural laborers or tried to eke out a living by spinning or weaving in their cottages. Only gradually did they start drifting to the mills, which were at first located near the streams that supplied the waterpower. Initially, cotton manufacturers in the north had so much difficulty attracting laborers that they resorted to the employment as "apprentices" of groups of pauper children from London and the south. But with the general application of steam power to the cotton industry after 1800, factories tended to be located in towns and cities near the sources of coal, and there a labor supply was more readily available. The phenomenal growth of certain key industrial cities occurred in the first half of the nineteenth century. Between 1801 and 1850, for example, the population of Manchester rose from 77,000 to 303,000; that of Liverpool, from 82,000 to 397,000; and that of Birmingham, from 71,000 to 242,000. Some cities expanded as much as 40 per cent in a single decade. As one might expect, the most rapid growth occurred in factory cities, but port cities expanded with an increase in overseas trade and older administrative centers grew as governments assumed more responsibilities and centralized their functions. Paris and London owed their growth in the nineteenth century not so much to new industrial enterprises as to rising trade, growth of banking facilities for administration of vast amounts of capital, and to the multiplication of administrative personnel needed for governing their respective countries. Also artisans and shopkeepers who had formerly lived in provincial towns gravitated to larger cities where opportunities appeared to be greater. Some older towns and cities, untouched by new industrial enterprises or bypassed by railroads, saw their population dwindle. In short, countries affected by industrialization and population growth underwent vast internal migrations.

Much has been written about material conditions in the new factory cities but less attention has been paid to the quality of life and the psycho-

View of Bute Docks at Cardiff, 1849.

logical responses of urban immigrants.[3] For those who came directly from the countryside, life in the cities marked a real break with the past and required considerable adjustment. The monotonous routine of factory labor, the crowding, and the newness of the environment must have imposed serious strains upon the former country dweller. Charles Dickens (1812–1870) caught the atmosphere of these depressing industrial cities in his celebrated novel *Hard Times* (1854). Here is his description of "Coketown," a fictitional representation (some would say a caricature) of one of the industrial towns of Lancashire:

It was a town of red brick, or of brick that would have been red if the smoke and ashes had allowed it; but as matters stood it was a town of unnatural red and black like the painted face of a savage. It was a town of machinery and tall chimneys, out of which interminable serpents of smoke trailed themselves for ever and ever and never got uncoiled. It had a black canal in it, and a river that ran purple with ill-smelling dye, and vast piles of buildings full of windows where there was a rattling and a trembling all day long, and where the piston of the steam-engine worked monotonously up and down like the head of an elephant in a state of melancholy madness. It contained several large streets all very like one another, inhabited by people equally like one another, who all went in and out at the same hours, with the same sound upon the same pavements, to do the same work, and to whom every day was the same as yesterday and to-morrow, and every year the counterpart of the last and the next.[4]

It is not difficult to imagine the disorientation and loneliness of an individual thrust suddenly into an environment such as this. Moreover the experience of the English laborer was to be duplicated on the Continent during the course of the nineteenth century as vast numbers of country dwellers gravitated to the new industrial cities.

The impact of the city on individuals and families shows up in statistical information. For the cities, rates of suicide, insanity, and crimes against property were notably higher than in rural districts. The divorce rate was three or four times higher in the cities, and there were twice as many illegitimate births. The relative youthfulness of urban immigrants (most 'were between twenty and forty) made for a certain dynamism in the city environment but it also may explain the higher incidence of agitation and riots. Among the first generation of those who moved to the cities many seem to have remained attached to their rural roots and returned to their

[3] One of the best contemporary documents on this subject is Friedrich Engels' *The Condition of the Working Class in England* (originally published in German in 1845; first published in England in 1887). For a stimulating new analysis of Engels' work and its background, see Steven Marcus, *Engels, Manchester, and the Working Class* (London, 1974).

[4] Charles Dickens, *Hard Times* (New York, 1966), p. 17.

Children sent to work in the cotton factories, 1840. *Engraving.*

villages at harvest time or whenever the opportunity presented itself. With the passage of time, however, the city dweller came to view himself as a species apart from his rural cousin differing in outlook, habits, and aspirations. In one country after another affected by the Industrial Revolution the ratio between city dwellers and country dwellers shifted. By 1850 the British population was over half urban; Germany passed this point only in 1900 and France, not until 1930.

Living conditions in industrial cities were frequently deplorable. Some British cities which had made progress earlier in paving their streets and covering their sewers were unable to handle the massive influx of new inhabitants and a deterioration of conditions occurred. In newer urban centers streets were often no better than rutted paths. Municipal governments were unable to meet the need for an adequate water supply and for sewage disposal. Many sewers remained open and rivers were polluted by waste materials. The following is an excerpt from a famous *Report on the Sanitary Condition of the Labouring Population* drawn up in 1842 by Edwin Chadwick, a reformer who was responsible for some of the early public-health legislation passed in Great Britain. This passage describes conditions in Leeds, a factory city located in Yorkshire,

. . . numbers of streets have been formed and houses erected without surface drainage—without sewers—or if under drainage can be called sewers, then with such as, becoming choked in a few months, are even worse than if they were altogether without. The surface of these streets is considerably elevated by accumulated ashes and filth, untouched by any scavenger; they form nuclei of disease exhaled from a thousand sources. Here and there stagnant water, and channels so offensive that they have been declared to be unbearable, lie under the doorways of the uncomplaining poor; and privies so laden with ashes and excrementitious matter as to be unuseable prevail, till the streets themselves become offensive from deposits of this description; in short, there is generally pervading in these localities a want of the common conveniences of life.[5]

Where housing already existed buildings were divided and redivided to the point where the poorest families had only one room or shared a room with another family. Newer housing was no less cramped and was often gerry-built and flimsy. Not surprisingly, disease and epidemics flourished in the new industrial cities and the mortality rate was high.

THE CONDITION OF THE WORKING CLASSES

Among students of the Industrial Revolution one of the most disputed questions has concerned the material and psychological condition of the factory hands employed in the burgeoning industrial cities. Some writers, particularly those of socialist or Marxist persuasion, have contended that workers in the new industries were little better than slaves at the mercy of their capitalist employers, suffering physical and psychological privations of the worst sort. Adherents of this view dwell upon the long working hours, the low wages, and the poor living conditions of the workers. They stress the evils of child and woman labor and the alienation of the worker from his employer. There is no question that workers in the early stages of the Industrial Revolution were badly off compared with their modern day counterparts. But critics of this interpretation argue that the worker's condition should be viewed not in terms of later standards but in a contemporary context. Was the condition of early factory workers really worse than that of agricultural laborers in the same period or the period just preceding? How did the industrial worker view his own situation? That evils existed, particularly in the early phases of the Industrial Revolution in England and on the Continent, no historian denies. But more recent interpretations point out that significant benefits resulted from industrialization even for the workers and have challenged or qualified many of the charges brought against the Industrial Revolution by the traditional school.

First and foremost, the Industrial Revolution brought about a tremendous increase in productivity and, with it, a substantial rise in per capita income. Moreover, as David Landes has pointed out, this rapid growth was self-sustaining:

[5] Quoted in J. F. C. Harrison, Society and Politics in England, 1780–1960: A Selection of Readings and Comments (New York, 1965), p. 155.

Where previously, an amelioration of the conditions of existence, hence of survival, and an increase in economic opportunity had always been followed by a rise in population that eventually consumed the gains achieved, now for the first time in history, both the economy and knowledge were growing fast enough to generate a continuing flow of investment and technological innovation, a flow that lifted beyond visible limits the ceiling of Malthus's positive checks. The Industrial Revolution thereby opened a new age of promise.[6]

Although disputes still continue about wages, the best evidence suggests that factory workers earned higher real wages than were offered in the countryside. Some of their costs, such as rent, were higher but their money wages were higher still. This meant that the factory worker had a higher standard of living than his rural counterpart. His diet was better and more varied; he was apt to be better clothed.

Critics of the school that emphasizes the horrors of industrialization also point out that such writers arrived at their conclusions from evidence with a built-in bias—that is, the reports of parliamentary commissions set up in the early nineteenth century by reformers whose purpose was to expose the worst abuses of the system. They also argue that there was much greater variation in the condition of the workers than had been supposed. Within the same industry it is possible to find laborers working in oppressed conditions whereas others were reasonably well off. Finally, the hardships of the working class in Britain cannot be blamed exclusively on industrialization. Such factors as the postwar depression following the Napoleonic wars and short-term fluctuations of the economy were also responsible for their temporary suffering.

All the above conditions have led to a modification of the traditional view and provide a necessary corrective to the gloomy impression of industrialization gained from novels like Dickens' *Hard Times*. But even if one assumes that the city worker's standard of living was higher than that of his rural cousin, certain deplorable aspects of his situation must still be taken into account. One is the relative insecurity of the industrial worker, who was more susceptible to the fluctuations of the free market economy. Even a relatively well-paid laborer was apt to find himself suddenly laid off owing to an industrial slump. Because all of his income had gone in normal times to pay for the necessities of life he had nothing to fall back on during periods of unemployment or illness. Although charitable organizations or workers' mutual-aid societies might provide temporary assistance, such institutions could not support large numbers of unemployed for prolonged periods. In such circumstances workers might become desperate and resort to violence. It is significant, for example,

[6] David S. Landes, *The Unbound Prometheus: Technological Change and Industrial Development in Western Europe from 1750 to the Present* (Cambridge, 1970), p. 41.

that the Revolution of 1848 in France was preceded by a serious industrial as well as agricultural depression that left many workers unemployed and hungry.

Certain intangibles must also be considered in a comparison of the lot of the industrial worker with that of the agricultural laborer. The farmer or farm hand may have worked just as many hours as the factory hand, his living conditions were undoubtedly crude and primitive, and he was probably subject to just as great a variety of diseases. But he worked out of doors, his daily tasks were probably more varied, and his opportunities for recreation were undoubtedly greater. It was in part to the discipline of the mill and the sheer monotony of his routine that the early factory hand objected. Also, the crowding together of human beings into ugly, hastily built cities, to which reference has already been made, tended to sharpen their discontent. Finally, the extensive employment of women and children in the textile mills and in the mines is a scandalous feature of industrialization which weighed on the consciences of some industrialists as well as of humanitarians and reformers. The revelation that child apprentices, some as young as seven, were forced to work up to twelve and fifteen hours a day, six days a week, in the cotton mills of the north, came as a shock to many Englishmen and inspired legislation to restrict child labor as early as 1802. Yet because of inadequate enforcement of the laws, the exploitation of children continued at least until 1833, when the first effective Factory Act forbade the employment in textile mills of children under nine years of age and restricted the labor of those between nine and thirteen to forty-eight hours a week. Though one cannot contest the long-range benefits accruing from the Industrial Revolution, it must be recognized that the price paid in human suffering during its early stages was great.

EXPANSION OF THE MIDDLE CLASS

The growth in power and prestige of the middle class or bourgeoisie is perhaps the most important single development in the social history of nineteenth-century Europe. Indeed it would not be inappropriate to describe that century as the "century of the middle class." The great French Revolution contributed to the liberation of this class in France in ways which have been described earlier—by eliminating traditional privileges of the aristocracy and the clergy, by establishing institutions of government that gave greater representation to the middle class, by removing many of the legal barriers to bourgeois advancement, and by proclaiming fundamental rights that allegedly belonged to every human being regardless of birth. The spread of French ideals and institutions to other peoples during the Revolution and afterward provided the impetus or, at least, a rationale for similar advancement of non-privileged classes elsewhere in Europe.

Refuge for the Destitute: The Male Ward, *about 1840*.

But the Industrial Revolution, by stimulating the growth in wealth and in numbers of the middle class, undoubtedly had an even greater impact on its conquest of power and prestige. Even before industrialization, the expansion of trade and commerce had led to a significant growth in the economic power of this class throughout Europe, but the bourgeoisie during the century of industrialization from 1750 to 1850 "created," in the words of Karl Marx, "more massive and more colossal productive forces" than had been produced by "all generations put together." The wealth generated by these new productive forces thrust the bourgeoisie into a commanding position and enabled its leaders to assert their power in a decisive way. Of course, this result was achieved at different times in different parts of Europe depending upon the progress of industrialization and the degree of resistance of traditionally established classes and institutions. In Britain, France, and the Low Countries, where its economic strength was the greatest, the middle class succeeded by the 1830's or 1840's in gaining control of the machinery of government. In central Europe, where industrialization lagged behind, the bourgeoisie emerged later as a political force; lacking unity and a coherent set of goals the middle class made a bid for power in the revolutions of 1848 but encountered stubborn resistance from the monarchs and older privileged groups. In the long run, however, wherever industrialization occurred, the middle-class drive for power was irresistible and all the European rulers had to come to terms with the bourgeoisie, whether by granting them political representation, by enacting legislation favorable to their economic interests, or both.

In the foregoing paragraphs the terms "middle class" and "bourgeoisie" have been used without qualification, as though they denoted a homogeneous, unified social group. The reality was, of course, far more complex and makes generalizations difficult and risky. Vast differences in wealth and style of life characterized the various categories of the middle class. Long before the nineteenth century, affluent merchants and bankers constituted an elite within the bourgeoisie whose style of life rivaled or surpassed that of many aristocrats. This group tended to look down upon the new industrialists and entrepreneurs who emerged with the Industrial Revolution though mutual economic interests ultimately narrowed the gap between them. Professionals such as lawyers, doctors, government officials, and writers made up another important element of the middle class that played an active role in the French Revolution and whose political influence increased out of proportion to its numbers during the nineteenth century. To the lower middle class belonged the shopkeepers whose income was far below that of the merchant princes but who had a clear sense of their status as property owners and prided themselves on their avoidance of manual labor.[7] The fortunes of this group varied greatly during the nineteenth century; some of them expanded their enterprises and prospered in the growing cities, while others tended to stagnate or to lose out in competition with larger businesses.

One group—the artisans or craftsmen—does not seem to fit neatly into any of the broader social classes or categories, yet it remained an important element in nineteenth-century society. Some social historians rank artisans in the lower middle class, some classify them as workers; still others view them as a separate social group with their own peculiar attributes and attitudes. Artisans were those who possessed a definite and traditional economic skill such as tailors, printers, butchers, and bakers. Into this same category fell construction workers of various sorts (carpenters, masons, painters) as well as cabinetmakers. Most of these had traditionally been concentrated in towns or cities and were normally organized into guilds, though guild organization had declined in some countries during the seventeenth and eighteenth centuries. Artisans tended to pride themselves on their skill which resulted from a long apprenticeship and enforcement by the guild of high standards of workmanship. Working independently or with a few other craftsmen, the artisan normally carried his productive operation through by himself. It is obvious that his attitude

---

[7] For a good recent discussion of the lower middle class and an attempt to provide a working definition of the term, see Arno J. Mayer, "The Lower Middle Class as Historical Problem," *Journal of Modern History*, 47 (September, 1975), 409–436.

toward his work and the pride he took in his product might differ radically from that of the factory worker or coal miner whose operations were more routine and who frequently contributed only one step toward the completion of the final product.

Many activities of the artisans survived the Industrial Revolution and were relatively unaffected by it. As late as 1850, for example, there were still as many artisans as factory workers in Great Britain.[8] Particularly in France, where an aversion to mass-produced manufactures long persisted, artisans remained an important social group throughout the century. In some instances, however, the process of industrialization threw artisans and craftsmen into direct competition with the newer industries and resulted in their eventual displacement. The fate of the handloom weaver and of others engaged in home manufacture of textiles is perhaps the most obvious example. Within a matter of a few decades the revolution in textile manufacturing described earlier led to the ruin of those who adhered to traditional methods. Unable to compete with cheaper, more efficient mechanized production, some tried to hang on by working even longer hours at home while others gave up and went to work in the factories. In Germany, one of the most serious uprisings during the first half of the nineteenth century was a revolt of handloom weavers (*Weber*) in Silesia in 1844. Exploited by their entrepreneurs, ruined by the competition with mechanized cotton manufacturing plants, several thousand of them burned and looted the houses of their employers. The episode was dramatized at the end of the century by the German playwright Gerhard Hauptmann in a play entitled *The Weavers*. Some artisans, like the so-called Luddites in England at the end of the Napoleonic Wars, directly threatened by mechanization, burned factories and destroyed machinery in an effort to maintain their traditional livelihood. And a closer examination of some of the riots and revolutions that occurred during the first half of the nine-teenth century in France and in central Europe has shown that in many cases revolutionaries who have been labeled "workers" were in fact artisans or even small shopkeepers.

ECONOMIC LIBERALISM

One other factor of importance to the success of the Industrial Revolution was the growing influence of the doctrines of economic liberalism, or *laissez-faire*, in Britain during the first half of the nineteenth century. Industrialization has, of course, taken place in societies where such doctrines do not prevail, in the planned economies of the Soviet Union and Communist China, for example. But proponents of capitalism, the system of free enterprise, argue that the initial success of the Industrial Revolution

[8] Peter N. Stearns, *European Society in Upheaval* (New York, 1967), p. 138.

in Great Britain resulted in large part from the progressive liberation of English manufacturers from government restrictions and their relative freedom from government control. Whether or not one sees a direct causal relationship between *laissez-faire* and industrialization, there is no question that they developed concurrently in Britain. To be sure, capitalism did not emerge only at the end of the eighteenth century. Capitalist forms of organization had existed at least since the end of the Middle Ages, but the incentive for individual enterprise had been thwarted to some degree by the prevailing economic philosophy of mercantilism, according to which the state had extensive powers to control the trade and regulate the economic life of the nation. In the eighteenth century greater opportunities for commercial initiative existed in Britain than in France partly because the new mercantile interests shared control of Parliament, yet the dominant view was still mercantilist.

Toward the end of the eighteenth century, however, mercantilist policies and restrictions on trade came increasingly under attack. Their principal critic was Adam Smith (1723–1790), whose *Wealth of Nations*, published in 1776, proposed instead a "system of natural liberty" which, for the most part, denied to government the right to regulate economic life. Government's primary function, according to Smith, was to maintain competitive conditions, for only within such a framework would the unrestricted self-interest of the individual be forced to operate for the general good. Although the *Wealth of Nations* became the single most influential and widely read economic treatise of its time, the most effective opposition to Britain's restrictive trade policies probably came from manufacturers objecting not so much on theoretical grounds, as because these policies provoked retaliatory measures from other nations and thus hindered the expansion of British trade. Shortly before the French Revolution, William Pitt the Younger made a start toward removing the restrictions on British commerce, but the dislocation of trade caused by the wars with France postponed further action until after 1815.

By the end of the Napoleonic wars, British industry had gained a commanding lead; the British could produce cotton goods, for example, in greater quantities and more cheaply than any continental rivals. A lowering of British tariffs, it was hoped, would lead to a corresponding reduction by foreign powers of tariffs on British manufactured goods. During the severe economic depression that immediately followed the Napoleonic Wars, British manufacturers, burdened with surpluses of goods they could not sell abroad, intensified their pleas for tariff reductions. But the Tory Parliament, heeding only the landowners, who sought not less but more protection, passed the Corn Law of 1815, which virtually excluded foreign grain from England until the price of native grain reached a specified level. We shall discover in a later discussion of developments in Britain from 1815 to 1850 that some progress was made toward the elimination of restrictions on trade in the 1820's but that the corn laws were not finally repealed until as late as 1846.

THE EMERGENCE OF SOCIALISM

Among the more vigorous critics of the bourgeois industrial societies emerging in western Europe in the first half of the nineteenth century were a number of writers who referred to themselves as socialists. Without any significant influence on the working classes, they did call attention to the inequities and injustices of unrestricted competition and proposed alternative methods of economic and social organization. Despite the great variations in their schemes, they are usually grouped together as Utopian Socialists. The term is used in part because they, or their disciples, tried to establish model communities of a Utopian character—many of them in the United States; it also distinguishes these socialists from the followers of Karl Marx, a little later in the century. In Marx's view, the socialism of the Utopians was excessively abstract, not sufficiently grounded in the facts of history.

What was common to all the Utopian Socialists—men like Henri de Saint-Simon, Charles Fourier, and Robert Owen—was the belief that under the existing economic system there was far too much emphasis on the production of goods and far too little on their distribution. The result was that those who were most in need of the products of industry were frequently unable to secure them. This is the way an Owenite publication put the problem in 1821:

England possesses the means and the power of creating more Manufactured Goods than the world can consume; and her soil is capable of furnishing several times the number of her present population with food.

Notwithstanding this power, and this inalienable source of superabundant subsistence, millions of her own people are but imperfectly supplied with some, and are entirely destitute of most, of the necessaries and comforts of life, and of the numberless articles of convenience or of elegance which inventive skill has contrived for the accommodation or embellishment of society.[9]

Socialist writers could also point to the frequent crises, attended by large-scale unemployment and suffering, that seemed to be inherent in a system of unrestricted competition. Where was the basic flaw in the system? The Utopians offered no single answer, but they generally shared the view that excessive individualism and self-seeking were characteristic of capitalism, and proposed in its place systems of social organization based on cooperation and mutual respect.

Henri de Saint-Simon (1760–1825), one of the pioneer socialists in France, maintained that industrial society should be organized on a "scien-

[9] Prospectus to *The Economist* (1821).

tific" basis, in accordance with certain social "laws" which could be discovered through the study of history. Rejecting ideals of political and social equality, he proposed a hierarchy of classes; the dominant class was to be an intellectual and moral elite concerned with the general improvement of humanity. Below it he placed the propertied class—the captains of industry, charged also with governmental and administrative functions. Finally, at the bottom, was the "most numerous" class, the unpropertied laborers, whose welfare was to be the responsibility of those above them. The most important feature of Saint-Simon's cooperative commonwealth was its goal: the improved material condition and moral and intellectual regeneration of the lowest class.

Charles Fourier (1772–1837), another French socialist, was admired by later socialists for his systematic exposure of some of the glaring abuses and wasteful practices of the capitalism of his day. But he is perhaps better remembered for his blueprint of a cooperative community which he believed would so transform men's environment as to bring about a fundamental change in human behavior. His theory was based on the view that men's actions were governed by a set of "passions," or instincts, which under existing conditions were misused or misdirected because of the faulty environment. Accordingly, he proposed the establishment of a number of small communities or self-contained societies, called *phalanges* ("phalanxes"), in which work would be performed and social life organized so as to make the most effective use of the "passions." To make work attractive (*i.e.* satisfying to the passions) jobs would be rotated, giving everyone an opportunity to perform "agreeable" as well as "necessary" tasks in the community.* Despite the communal nature of these enterprises, Fourier did not intend to abolish private property. Indeed, he anticipated that considerable differences in wealth might remain. Fourier, whose own means were modest, announced after the publication of his proposals that he would be at home daily at noon, ready to discuss them with anyone interested in financing a phalanx. He hoped to establish a limited number of phalanxes which would prove so successful that they would be imitated throughout the world. Reportedly, he returned home punctually at noon every day for ten years, but no patron ever appeared.

Utopian Socialism was not confined to France. One leading socialist who had an opportunity to put his theories into practice was the Welshman Robert Owen (1771–1858), a self-made manufacturer who bought a cotton mill at New Lanark, in Scotland, and turned the town into a model community organized on cooperative principles. Like Fourier, Owen believed in man's natural goodness and was convinced that he was corrupted

* One of Fourier's ingenious proposals concerned garbage disposal in the phalanxes: since little boys and girls love dirt, this and other disagreeable jobs in the community would be assigned to the children.—Alexander Gray, *The Socialist Tradition* (London, 1946), p. 188.

Louis Blanc. *The socialist author of* The Organization of Labor *who was named to the Provisional Government in February, 1848.*

only by an improper environment. If man could live in a society based upon cooperation and mutual respect rather than self-interest and competition his true nature would reveal itself. At New Lanark, beginning about 1800, Owen converted a miserable factory town into a clean, orderly community with educational facilities for children and a remarkably high standard of living. The extent to which this achievement resulted from the application of cooperative principles and not from Owen's own benevolent rule is a matter of dispute, but the project has been viewed as one of the first successful socialist experiments. Like Fourier, Owen tried to interest others, particularly his fellow manufacturers, in establishing cooperative communities, but he met with little response. Believing that his ideas might have greater success in the less tradition-bound atmosphere of the United States, he took over an existing community in Indiana in the 1820's and rechristened it New Harmony, but this experiment was marked by internal dissension and collapsed after three years. Owen was subsequently active in the trade-union movement in Great Britain and in founding consumers' cooperatives for workers, but experienced failure and disillusionment in his later years.

Louis Blanc (1811–1882), a Frenchman, has been described as a figure of transition between the Utopian Socialism of the first half of the century and the "proletarian socialism" of the second half. His ideas—as expressed, for example, in his essay "The Organization of Labor" (1839)—were simpler and had a more direct appeal to the working class in France than those of either Saint-Simon or Fourier. Writing in an era plagued by depressions, he charged that under the system of *laissez-faire* the worker was often denied one of his basic rights, the right to work and earn a decent living. To the state belonged the responsibility of guaranteeing this right. Aware that the bourgeois-dominated July Monarchy would never fulfill this obligation, Blanc viewed political reform and the broadening of the franchise as essential prerequisites to social reform. Once the state was sympathetic to the cause of the laboring classes, it would subsidize the formation of "social workshops," cooperative enterprises for production which would in time dominate the most important branches of industry. The workers themselves would assume control of the workshops, repaying the government loans over a period of years. Blanc further hoped that the association of workers for economic ends would lead them into voluntary associations for the satisfaction of other needs as well. In other words, the social workshops would form the nucleus of a fully cooperative society. The simplicity of Blanc's ideas—particularly his emphasis on the right to work and the responsibility of the state to provide work—constituted their appeal. *The Organization of Labor* went through numerous editions in the 1840's and seems to have reached a fairly wide audience. In the Revolution of 1848, Blanc's propaganda was reflected in the demand of Paris laborers for recognition of the "right to work" and in the revolutionary government's establishment of "National Workshops." These turned out, however, to be little more than caricatures of Blanc's original proposal.

With the possible exception of Louis Blanc, these early socialists had relatively little influence upon their contemporaries. Aside from small bands of disciples and a few attempts, almost all abortive, to establish model socialist communities, they were ignored. For this neglect there is a variety of explanations. Yet one assumption, common to all of the Utopian Socialists, may help to explain their failure; this was their belief, derived from certain of the *philosophes* of the eighteenth century, that man was naturally good, so that once his social environment and institutions were changed, all evil and suffering would automatically be eliminated. Adherence to this view clearly resulted in their underestimating the complexity of human institutions and the obstacles to social change.

Later socialists led by Marx and Engels specifically attacked the Utopian conviction that a socialist society could be brought into existence at will, at any time or place, and that if one only propagandized widely enough, or set up enough model communities, socialism would be accepted and substituted for the existing social framework. The Marxists believed instead that to try to establish socialism before conditions were ripe was an exercise doomed to failure. Yet even Marxists were willing to give credit to the Utopian Socialists for a number of insights, and to draw on their critique of the capitalist system. All of the Utopians challenged the principle of economic competition, arguing that it resulted at best in a kind of anarchy of waste and inefficiency, at worst in serious social injustice and acute suffering for the working classes. Saint-Simon, anticipating the Marxist analysis, recognized the importance of social classes and class divisions in history and pointed out the diverging class interests in industrial society.

Finally, all of the Utopians in one way or another felt that the state bore some responsibility for the material welfare of its citizens and concluded that the reform of society was a proper task for government. All of these notions have, of course, become a part of subsequent socialist thought, and one need hardly point out that their influence has also spread beyond the circle of socialists, that they have been accepted in some degree by all democratic industrial societies.

CHAPTER 5

Restoration and Romanticism

HISTORIANS COMMONLY employ the term "Restoration" to characterize the era in European history following the downfall of the Napoleonic Empire. Like most other historical labels, it is applied loosely, being used even in reference to states which did not undergo the restoration of a ruler or a dynasty. The period's end is placed at 1830 in some nations and at 1848 in others. The era was characterized by relative peace in international relations, but within practically every state a struggle was in progress, sometimes hidden, sometimes in the open, between those in power in 1814 –1815 and those who challenged or sought to undermine them. The entrenched groups, in an effort to protect their position, tended to defend the *status quo* or to proceed slowly in making changes. Their opponents, impatient for reforms or greater liberties, took to the barricades when they found their wishes frustrated or denied. The members of each group drew upon earlier writers to justify their position and themselves developed political philosophies or ideologies designed to further their cause.

CONSERVATISM

If the era after 1815 is described as the Restoration, it is important to know what was restored. Certainly, not everything that had existed before 1789. Had the principle of legitimacy been carried to its logical extreme by the statesmen at Vienna, the Holy Roman Empire would have been reestablished, along with the more than three hundred petty states into which Germany was divided before the revolutionary era. Actually, the principle of legitimacy was so haphazardly applied that Napoleon's brother-in-law, Joachim Murat, could have remained permanently on the throne of Naples in the place of the "legitimate" Bourbon ruler if he had not sacrificed his position by rashly supporting Napoleon during the Hundred Days. Nevertheless, hereditary monarchy was regarded by the statesmen at Vienna as one of the fundamental institutions to be restored, for they felt it was the only form of government capable of ensuring continuity and stability in human affairs. Metternich, who is usually viewed as the prototype of all that was conservative in the Restoration, did not subscribe to the divine-right theory of monarchy, but he was convinced that the hereditary succession of kings served as a guarantee for all other social institutions. Tsar Alexander I's Holy Alliance was a union of *monarchs* who pledged to lend each other assistance for the protection of religion, peace, and justice.

In almost every country in Europe, the Restoration also brought a revival in the status of the nobility. In France and the parts of Europe conquered by the French the members of the nobility had, during the revolution, suffered fates ranging from the loss of economic and legal privileges to exile or execution. But even in areas not ruled by the French the events of the 1790's had seriously frightened the aristocracy, who saw traditional prerogatives threatened by the advance of revolutionary ideas. With the advent of the Restoration, the nobles sought to recover the privileges and property that had been lost and allied themselves with monarchs against changes that might further endanger their position in society. There was a particular irony in this drawing together of king and nobility in defense of the established order in a country like France, where the feudal aristocracy had traditionally opposed the centralizing tendencies of the monarchy. But both monarch and aristocracy were now confronted with a strong bourgeoisie intent upon preserving the gains of the revolution and consolidating its political power. In central Europe the threat was less immediate since the bourgeoisie was still weak, but Metternich nonetheless allied himself with the imperial aristocracy against the middle class, which he found seriously infected with the "revolutionary virus." In Britain, where the aristocracy was already an amalgam of landed and commercial interests, a parallel to the conservative reaction on the Continent nonetheless can be found after 1815 in the determined resistance of the Tory leadership to attempts to widen parliamentary representation in the House of Commons to include the new class of manufacturers.

Along with the monarchy and the aristocracy, the churches regained their influence during the Restoration. Support and sympathy for the Catholic Church among the governing classes was unquestionably stronger in 1815 than in 1789, for the revolutionary years witnessed a revival of faith and religious observance among many of the educated who had succumbed during the Old Regime to the rationalism and anticlericalism of the Enlightenment. In particular, members of the nobility who had observed during the revolution the simultaneous assault upon the churches, the aristocracy, and the monarchy often concluded that their own fortunes were closely tied up with those of organized religion. Nor were they unmoved by '' · suffering and martyrdom of members of the clergy at the hands of rev-
·ionary governments and the dignity with which Pope Pius VII with-

Edmund Burke.

stood the harsh treatment inflicted upon him by Napoleon. Whatever the sources of the Catholic revival, the Church was viewed in 1815 as one of the bulwarks of the social order and enjoyed a position of favor with European rulers.

The monarch who occupied a throne in Europe in 1815 typically felt no need to justify his regime to his own people. A source of his strength lay precisely in his unquestioning acceptance of his role as a ruler to whom the subjects owed automatic obedience. Nevertheless he could hardly ignore the fact that legitimate rulers had been toppled from their thrones in many places during the preceding quarter century and that the very institution of monarchy had succumbed in more than one country to a republican regime.

And though the ruler himself may not have seen reason for elaborating theoretical justifications of his authority, many intellectuals did. As we know, the French Revolution had barely begun when one of the most gifted and influential of all conservative political philosophers, Edmund Burke, wrote his *Reflections on the Revolution in France*, which questioned the entire basis of the revolution and became a handbook of conservatism for the generations that followed. During the last decade of the eighteenth century two Frenchmen, Joseph de Maistre (1753–1821) and the viscount of Bonald (1754–1840), both *émigrés*, spent their years in exile writing elaborate treatises in defense of absolute monarchy and the authority of the Catholic Church. Less systematically, Metternich and his aide Friedrich von Gentz, both before and after 1815, joined in the attack upon revolutionary principles and the appeal to traditional institutions. And German philosophers like Fichte and Hegel certainly reflected some of the assumptions of early-nineteenth-century conservatives in their emphasis upon the importance of the state. The philosophy of conservatism that developed between 1790 and 1820 was in many respects far more original than the liberal thought of the era.

Although individual variations existed, there were several common themes and arguments running through the work of practically all the conservative intellectuals. For the most part they took the French Revolution as their springboard, presenting lengthy attacks upon revolutionary principles and criticisms of the philosophy of the Enlightenment, which they held chiefly responsible for the catastrophe of 1789. Then they went on to develop a philosophy that was largely a reaction against the ideas of the *philosophes* and the revolutionaries.

In particular, the conservatives objected to what they considered the excessive reliance of the *philosophes* on reason, especially the kind of abstract reason that was used to justify "natural rights" and the introduction of new political and social institutions. Burke, with his great admiration for Britain's unwritten constitution, took an unmistakable stand against revolutionary programs:

> The science of constructing a commonwealth, or renovating it, or reforming it, is, like every other experimental science, not to be taught *a priori* . . . . The science of government being therefore so practical in itself and intended for such practical purposes — a matter which requires experience, and even more experience than any person can gain in his whole life, however sagacious and observing he may be — it is with infinite caution that any man ought to venture upon pulling down an edifice, which has answered in any tolerable degree for ages the common purposes of society, or on building it up again, without having models and patterns of approved utility before his eyes.[1]

Burke's appeal to "experience" as a guide in politics was echoed by other conservatives, particularly in Britain. It was part of a broader appeal to "tradition" and "history" that could be found at the very heart of conservative political thought. In this view, both society and government, because they are products of a long historical development, must be treated with respect. If changes or reforms are to be made in either, they must come gradually and only with proper consideration for historical antecedents and national traditions. This doctrine, carried to its logical extreme, was used to justify complete adherence to the *status quo* on the ground that tampering with any part of the delicately balanced institutional structure might endanger the whole.

A second weakness that conservatives attributed to the political philoso-

---

[1] Edmund Burke, *Reflections on the Revolution in France*, ed. by Thomas H. D. Mahoney (New York, 1955), pp. 69–70.

phy of the Enlightenment was its emphasis upon the individual and his rights. Under attack came the entire tradition of John Locke and his disciples, both in Britain and on the Continent—the view that society and government are necessary evils or artificial constructions for the preservation of the natural rights of the individual. For conservatives, it was meaningless to talk of "individual liberty," apart from society, since freedom could be achieved only through the community. The individual was not distinct from society, an end in himself, but part of a collectivity which was somehow more than the sum of its various members. Conservative political thinkers handled this theme in many different ways, but almost all shared the view that society was an organism which had evolved over the centuries and that the individuals who composed it were indissolubly bound with those who had preceded them as well as those who were to follow.

Conservatives deplored, in varying degrees, the lack of respect for estabished religion and ecclesiastical authority that had found expression during the revolution in the persecution of the clergy and attacks upon Christian dogma. Some, notably Joseph de Maistre, held the skepticism and anticlericalism of men like Voltaire directly responsible for the revolution. Many conservatives valued religion chiefly as a kind of cement which contributed to the preservation of social order; the Catholic Church was regarded as one of the traditional institutions of society whose fortunes were linked with those of the monarchy and the aristocracy. But for de Maistre, Catholic Christianity was the very foundation of the social order. He believed that all sovereignty is derived from God and is vested in the monarch. Because of the divine origin of his authority, the king is absolute in his realm; his power can be limited in no way by his subjects. Religion provides the people with a motive for obedience and submission to the king and at the same time reconciles them to the natural inequalities which exist in society. Having provided a justification for absolute monarchy, de Maistre went on to argue that church and state must collaborate in promoting man's moral welfare and in preserving order. Should a conflict between the two arise, the authority of the church is higher than that of the monarch. Indeed, de Maistre ended by regarding the pope as the supreme political and religious authority in what amounted to a universal theocracy.

These convictions—that the continuity of political and social institutions had to be respected, that the community took precedence over the individual, and that organized religion was essential to the social order—provided the justification for the conservatives' faith in hereditary monarchy, supported by the authority of the church, as the form of government best fitted to preserve social stability and order.

At least two of the conservatives' arguments came to exert considerable influence beyond their own camp. Their renewed emphasis upon the historical conditioning of all social institutions proved to be a much-needed corrective to the antihistorical outlook associated with the Enlightenment and contributed to the nineteenth-century habit of viewing almost all problems historically. Conservatives were not alone in seeking to explain the present in terms of the past. By mid-century Karl Marx had developed a theory of social evolution whose basic premise was historical. And even "classical" liberals adjusted their thinking to include a historical dimension and a heightened awareness of the past.

In the same way, the conservative stress upon the community (which had been foreshadowed by Rousseau a generation before) gradually weakened the atomistic view of society that had prevailed in the preceding century. Socialists accepted as a basic premise the need for individual self-sacrifice to the community, and some of them moved to the position that a strong state was the only agency capable of achieving social reform. Liberals—at least British liberals—persisted in the view that government was a necessary evil and sought to maximize individual liberty and freedom from social restraints. But even John Stuart Mill (1806–1873), the classical defender of individual liberty, was forced to admit the inadequacy of a totally atomistic view of society and recognized that individuals in society bore a responsibility for the welfare of their fellow citizens and that it might fall to government to see that these obligations were fulfilled.

Opposition to the Restoration

It is easier to enumerate the groups that defended the *status quo* and benefited from the Restoration than it is to classify the opponents of the political and social order that prevailed after 1815. In the conservative camp were monarchs, nobles, and churchmen. But did the opposition, like the Third Estate in France before the revolution, include "everyone else"? Perhaps, if one counts among the opposition all who had a grievance against the existing order. However, there is a difference between mere dissatisfaction with the *status quo* and active opposition, involving attempts to change or even destroy it. The dominant and most vigorous opponents of established institutions were drawn from the middle class; they often referred to themselves as liberals. The middle class in the first half of the nineteenth century was far from being homogeneous in any country, but was not yet the all-embracing social group that it is today. The older financial and commercial leaders were joined at this time—at least in Great Britain, France, and the Low Countries—by a generation of "new men," enterprising manufacturers who sought more aggressively to win political influence. These two groups, along with wealthy lawyers and doctors, constituted the upper middle class, by far the most active segment politically.

Beneath lay various strata of the lower middle class—shopkeepers, artisans, prosperous small farmers—whose outlook differed from that of

The rich and the poor in Vienna in the 1830's. *An upper-class drawing room (above), living and sleeping quarters of a factory worker (below).*

business and professional men, but who certainly did not share the point of view of the lowest classes. Even where elected assemblies existed, as in western Europe, the members of this group played no formal role in politics because normally they could not meet the property qualifications for voting. Yet it was from the lower middle class that various secret societies, such as the *Carbonari* in Italy and the Society for the Rights of Man in France, often recruited their membership and their leaders. And in the revolutions which occurred during and after the 1820's, representatives of this class were found joining in attacks upon the government and the established order.

The peasantry still constituted the overwhelming mass of the population in Europe during the first half of the nineteenth century. Though there was considerable variation in their status, from one country to another and within individual nations, it is safe to say that the members of this class played practically no active part in the political life of the European nations. The revolution had brought about changes in the economic and legal status of the peasantry in France and in areas under French control, and the Industrial Revolution slowly affected some details of existence in western Europe, but the mass of European peasants lived as they had for centuries—in a state of relative isolation, with few secular interests outside of their own particular locality. Only where their land tenure appeared to be threatened did the peasants show any concern about events at the national level.

As the Industrial Revolution proceeded in Britain and, more slowly, in France and the Netherlands, the nucleus of an industrial proletariat began to emerge. But except for the relatively unsophisticated Chartist agitation in Britain during the 1830's and 1840's, one can hardly speak of organized political activity by the working classes in the first half of the nineteenth century. To be sure, the workers had many specific grievances—long hours, inadequate wages, labor by women and children, seasonal unemployment, unsanitary and dangerous conditions in factories and homes—but, deprived of the vote and frustrated in their attempts to organize, they had no means for expressing their discontent except violence and revolution.

Two special groups also belonged to the opposition during the Restoration. One consisted of military men, primarily army officers. They were particularly active in the revolts of the 1820's in countries where there existed no constitutional or legal channels for the expression of opposition. In Spain, Portugal, the Italian states, and Russia, army officers played significant, and in some cases leading, roles in uprisings against their respective regimes. Their motives varied widely, but certainly the dissatisfaction with their reactionary governments stemmed in part from their contact with the more advanced societies of western and central Europe during the Napoleonic wars and their exposure to the ideals of the French Revolution.

The other special group consisted of students, at both the university and the secondary levels. They often took their places on the barricades, particularly during the revolutions of 1830–1831 and 1848, and helped to staff many of the revolutionary societies active throughout the Restoration. As we shall see, the *Burschenschaften*, or student societies, which sought to stir up nationalist enthusiasm, were in the forefront of the opposition to Metternich in the Germanic Confederation just after 1815. In Paris during the Revolution of 1830, students from the upper schools fought alongside workers to overthrow the Bourbon regime. Elsewhere during the 1830's, students flocked into liberal nationalist organizations like Young Italy, Young Ireland, and Young Poland. The repressive policies of the Holy Alliance and the stubborn resistance to change of the reactionary rulers proved particularly hateful to the generation that entered schools and universities after 1815.

EARLY NINETEENTH-CENTURY LIBERALISM

Opponents of the established order during the Restoration were usually termed "liberals," and to an extent they did share a common set of goals or ideals, which constituted the political philosophy of "liberalism." As used then, the term was perhaps not as vague or as emotion-ridden as it is today in the United States, but it was still subject to a wide variety of interpretations. A Spanish officer revolting against the inefficient absolutism of Ferdinand VII hardly shared the goals of a Whig seeking reform of the methods of choosing representatives for the House of Commons; a member of the *Burschenschaften* with hopes for a closer union among Germans differed considerably in outlook from a Russian nobleman intent upon the abolition of serfdom. But all were branded "liberals" by their opponents, and more important, they drew on a common heritage and shared certain goals.

The most obvious of these goals was simply a desire for changes in the existing order. Whether they opposed continued Tory domination in Britain or the autocratic rule of the tsar in Russia, they were dissatisfied with established institutions and disputed the conservative belief that whatever existed had the sanction of time and should therefore be preserved. The suspicions of Metternich and Tsar Alexander notwithstanding, there is little evidence to suggest that the liberals possessed an international organization or even that secret ties existed between the liberal groups of individual nations, but their discontent did give them a common point of view.

Despite the variety of their specific goals, almost all liberals drew in some form upon the heritage of the Enlightenment and the French Revolution. As men of some substance they viewed the more extreme phase of the revolution with disapproval, but most of them subscribed to the general body of ideals commonly described as the "principles of 1789." "Liberty," which was central to their credo, was certainly understood to include individual freedom—freedom from arbitrary arrest and imprisonment, freedom of speech, freedom of assembly, and freedom of the press. These were a part of almost every liberal program between 1815 and 1848. At the same time, even in the application of this concept, wide differences in interpretation and emphasis existed. More than one historian has pointed out that English liberals put a greater emphasis upon the individual and the desirability of individual liberty than did liberals on the Continent. Of tremendous influence upon British liberalism was the argument of Jeremy Bentham (1748–1832) that the "greatest good for the greatest number" would result if each individual were allowed to pursue his own self-interest with a minimum of outside interference. This fundamental principle, reinforced in the economic sphere by the doctrine of *laissez-faire*, gave a character to British liberalism which distinguished it from that on the Continent.

On the Continent, wherever there were peoples who had not yet achieved political unity or who were living under a foreign ruler, "liberty" and "freedom" were apt to denote liberty from foreign control and freedom for the nation. "Freedom" for the Greeks meant freedom from Turkish control; "liberty" for the Italians meant the overthrow of Austrian domination. And many of those in the German states who thought of themselves as liberals sought above all "freedom" for the German "nation"—some form of closer union among the German people, without which personal or individual freedom appeared meaningless. For these peoples, liberalism and nationalism were closely allied; indeed, nationalist aspirations often tended to overshadow, and occasionally overwhelmed, other liberal values.

Popular sovereignty, another of the great principles proclaimed in 1789, was an ideal which liberals generally acknowledged but were seldom ready to carry to its logical conclusion. They were quite willing to invoke it to contest the arguments of de Maistre or Bonald in favor of absolutism, but in practice they were determined to restrict sovereignty to the propertied classes, who alone possessed the right to vote in the countries with elected assemblies. Men like Benjamin Constant de Rebecque (1767–1830), a Frenchman who was one of the foremost spokesmen of the liberals, strongly opposed the principle of universal suffrage, arguing that the tyranny of the mob could be just as dangerous as the tyranny of a king. "Property alone, by giving sufficient leisure, renders a man capable of exercising his political rights." Justifying the property qualification, he argued that the vote was accessible to all men: the poor man had only to acquire the requisite amount of property in order to vote. The liberals, in short, were not democrats.

If the liberals spoke frequently of "liberty" in the first half of the nineteenth century, they spoke less often of "equality." Certainly they saw nothing essentially wrong with the gross inequalities in the distribution of property and wealth which were to be found throughout Europe. The new class of manufacturers in Britain included many who had built up fortunes through their own ambition and enterprise; they were convinced that any individual with similar initiative could better himself by meas of "self-help." What liberals did insist upon, in theory at least, was equality before the law. This principle was already generally recognized in England and was now guaranteed in France by the *Code Napoléon*, but in many parts of Europe where it was still denied, the abolition of the special legal privileges of the nobility and clergy became a central part of the liberal program.

These, then, were some of the more important ideals shared by European liberals after 1815: liberty, for the individual and for the nation; representative government, though in practice this usually meant representation for the propertied classes only; and equality before the law. With respect to specific goals, however, there were wide differences among liberals in the various parts of Europe. In the states of central, eastern, and southern Europe, where constitutions and representative institutions were virtually nonexistent, the goal of liberals was a written constitution which would limit the authority of the ruler and provide for an elected parliament or assembly which would share in the formulation of laws. The word "constitution" took on an almost mystical significance for liberals in some of the German and Italian states, who assumed that by its mere existence such a document would solve all their problems. But in the countries of western Europe where a constitution and an elected assembly already existed in 1815, liberals naturally had different goals. Their primary task was to see that representative institutions functioned in such a way that the government was genuinely responsible to the people—or rather to the propertied segment of the population represented, for example, in the French Chamber of Deputies. Accordingly, they tried to limit the authority of the king and to make his ministers responsible to the elected chamber for their actions. Some even recommended broadening the base of the electorate to include men of lesser wealth.

A further explanation for the divergences among liberal goals lay in the differences in the social structure and class relationships in the various countries. Where the landed aristocracy or the clergy were still entrenched and retained unique privileges, liberals focused their attack upon these privileges. In France most of these prerogatives had been lost during the revolution but from 1815 to 1830 liberals had to remain constantly on guard against attempts by both the nobility and the clergy to recover them. In Britain, where the Industrial Revolution was already causing significant changes in the social structure, representatives of the newer manufacturing interests sought to free themselves of restrictions inherited from a preindustrial era and to compel the older landed and merchant classes to share their control of the House of Commons.

The specific goals of the liberals also depended in large measure on whether they lived in a unified, independent nation, such as Great Britain, France, or Spain, or belonged, like the Germans, Italians, and Poles, to a people that was divided or living under foreign domination. Where nationhood had yet to be achieved, liberalism was normally characterized by strong nationalist aspirations, and the transcendent goal became national unification or national independence.

EARLY NINETEENTH-CENTURY NATIONALISM

Frequently nationalist sentiments were not confined to liberals; they affected social groups and classes other than those usually identified with the liberal cause. Should nationalism be regarded as merely one strand of the liberal ideology, or did it have an identity of its own? It is difficult to say, especially since the terms "liberalism" and "nationalism" were not employed with precision during this period.

Two or three circumstances in the first half of the nineteenth century tended to draw together those working for liberal ideals and those striving primarily for nationalist goals. In the first place, they shared a common heritage; both drew, in part, upon the French Revolution for inspiration. For nineteenth-century nationalists, the French revolutionaries had provided a stunning example of what a people could achieve when they were unified under a government that they themselves had created. The tremendous release of national energy and the stirring patriotism that had characterized the revolutionary armies impressed those Europeans who were still divided or living under foreign rule after 1815. They were convinced that if only they could achieve a similar national consciousness and enthusiasm, they too could overcome the obstacles that stood in the way of independence and unity. The faith in popular sovereignty is perhaps the most important link between liberalism and nationalism. People living under a dynasty or ruling caste whose ends seemed to differ from their own could not feel quite the same stake in their country as people living under a regime which proclaimed, as did the *Declaration of the Rights of Man and the Citizen,* that "the source of all sovereignty resides essentially in the nation." Only when the government was closely identified with all the people could a nation be considered "free."

Furthermore, in the first half of the nineteenth century, liberals and nationalists could be closely allied because nationalism had not yet taken on the exclusive, parochial character that it assumed later. Paradoxical as it may seem, some of the leading nationalists were still influenced by the cosmopolitan heritage of the Enlightenment. Thus for Giuseppe Mazzini, one of the most famous of all nationalist propagandists before 1850, there was no incompatibility between loyalty to one's nation and loyalty to humanity: "In laboring according to true principles for our country we are laboring for Humanity; our country is the fulcrum of the lever which we have to wield for the common good." The achievement by each people of its own "national existence" was merely the prelude to the association of all in a higher community of nations. At the same time, Mazzini shared some of

Giuseppe Mazzini.

the views of liberals concerning the institutions which the nation should possess. The only true country for him was "a fellowship of free and equal men bound together in a brotherly concord of labor towards a single end." Indeed, he went beyond most contemporary liberals, advocating a republican form of government and a radical egalitarianism.

Finally, liberals and nationalists were drawn together after 1815 by the mere fact that both were in opposition to the *status quo*. Because the settlement of 1815 had failed to take into account the aspirations of both liberals and nationalists, both sought to undermine it and inveighed against the powers of the Holy Alliance apparently determined to maintain its integrity. Metternich, in persecuting both liberals and nationalists throughout central Europe, was at least partially responsible for the alliance that was forged between them.

Up to this point early nineteenth-century nationalism has been defined only in terms of its similarities and affinities with liberalism. But nationalism had nonliberal roots and characteristics as well. These are perhaps best revealed in the development of German nationalist thought at the end of the eighteenth and the beginning of the nineteenth centuries. There appeared fairly early in the development of German nationalism a strain of exclusiveness and intolerance and an emphasis upon the transcendence of the state over the individual that ultimately brought about its separation from liberalism. While this separation did not occur exclusively in Germany and illiberal elements could be found also in nationalist movements elsewhere in Europe, the phenomenon is best illustrated in the attitudes toward the nation of a number of highly influential German writers.

The first of these was Johann Gottfried von Herder (1744–1803), a Protestant pastor and theologian who wrote extensively on philosophy, history, and literature. When Herder was born, Germans did of course speak a common language, but because they were divided into hundreds of petty states they generally lacked any conception of Germany as a national entity. On the contrary, German intellectuals tended to share in the cosmopolitan outlook of the Enlightenment and the general admiration for the French *philosophes*. Herder was one of the first to object to what he considered the excessive dependence of the educated classes in Germany on French thought and French manners, and urged his compatriots to develop their native culture. He believed that each people—that is, the body of persons sharing a common language—possessed a unique *Geist* ("spirit," or "genius"), which had to be developed in its own particular way. The national culture, to be authentic, had to arise from the life of the *Volk*, or common people, and draw its inspiration from them. Two features of Herder's nationalism should be emphasized. One was its exclusively cultural character. Herder was not concerned with political questions and never argued that the political unification of Germany had to accompany its cultural renaissance. Second, Herder's theory of national development was applicable to peoples other than Germans; it certainly was not intended to imply that German culture was superior to any other.

Many literary figures of the German romantic school, such as the Grimm brothers, took seriously Herder's injunction to explore Germany's cultural past, and through their writings brought about an awareness of German folklore, law, and religion. But among some of Herder's disciples in the generation after 1800, the character of German nationalism began to change. The philosopher Johann Gottlieb Fichte (1762–1814), twenty years younger than Herder, did much to stimulate the more aggressive brand of German nationalism that was to emerge in the second half of the nineteenth century. His changed outlook resulted in part from his reaction to the French invasions of Germany and particularly to Prussia's humili-

Hegel with his students.

ation by the Napoleonic armies in 1806, which occasioned his famous series of lectures, *Addresses to the German Nation*, delivered in the winter of 1807–1808. In these lectures he called for a system of national education in Germany which would ultimately result in the moral regeneration of the German people. Education was to make Germans aware of themselves as a unique people, reveal to them their national character, and teach them to love the fatherland. In describing the kind of spirit that should prevail in a time of national crisis, Fichte wrote, "[It is] not the spirit of the peaceful citizen's love for the constitution and the laws, but the devouring flame of higher patriotism, which embraces the nation as the vestures of the eternal, for which the noble-minded man joyfully sacrifices himself, and the ignoble man, who only exists for the sake of the other, must likewise sacrifice himself."[2] In his earlier works Fichte was concerned with the problem of individual freedom, but he arrived at a point in his thinking where he regarded a strong, authoritarian state as the prerequisite for true freedom. He offered no simple definition of "freedom," but became convinced that the individual could attain it only by identifying himself with the greater personality of the nation. Moreover Fichte, unlike Herder, attributed to the Germans an originality and a genius not possessed by other peoples. He carried none of these ideas to extremes, but his *Addresses to the German Nation* became a source of inspiration and ammunition for subsequent German nationalists.

Of the numerous other writers who contributed to the broadening stream of German nationalism in this era, none was more important than the celebrated idealist philosopher and professor Georg Wilhelm Friedrich Hegel (1770–1831). Several of Hegel's conclusions, which were based on his philosophy of history, were incorporated into the German nationalist ideology. The first was his strong emphasis on the state. Reacting against eighteenth-century individualism, Hegel regarded the state as far more than an artificial convenience for the satisfaction of individual needs. Rather, it was a manifestation of the "world spirit" operating in history, and its task was to bring a nation to self-consciousness. Since the state was the embodiment of what he termed the "divine idea," the essence of morality, the individual could lead a truly ethical life only by identifying himself with the state. By submitting to the state and rendering it unconditional obedience, the individual could realize true freedom. A second point concerned the special role that the Germanic nations were destined to play in the final stage of the unfolding of the historical process whose purpose was the realization of "freedom." According to his view of history, in the first, or oriental, stage of historical development the *monarch* alone had been free; in the Greek and Roman stages the *few* had achieved freedom;

---

[2] Quoted in *Introduction to Contemporary Civilization in the West*, third ed. (New York, 1961), Vol. II, p. 155.

but only in the last, or Germanic, stage of history, were *all men* destined to be free. This belief in the peculiar historical destiny of the Germanic peoples (whether or not this destiny was interpreted as the realization of "freedom" in Hegel's sense) became an integral part of German nationalism. Finally, Hegel was responsible in some measure for the growing prestige of the Prussian monarchy in Germany as a whole. For although he implied that the Germanic state of the future would be constitutional in form, he threw his full support behind the powerful Prussian state as the agent destined by History to bring the Germanic people to full consciousness.

Like Fichte, Hegel did not attempt to deduce a concrete political program from his philosophical system. But there is no question that he provided a theoretical justification not only for the conservative nationalism of the later nineteenth century but for the state worship characteristic of twentieth-century fascism as well. Paradoxically, Hegel also affected modern socialist theory, through his influence upon Karl Marx (1818–1883). Hegel's confidence that he had discovered meaning and direction in human history and his emphasis upon the dialectical process by which the "world-spirit" realized itself are reflected in Marx's own theory of dialectical materialism.

If German writers were the leaders in the development of nationalist theory, the phenomenon itself was to be found throughout Europe in the first half of the nineteenth century. Herder's injunction to Germans to concentrate upon their own cultural heritage was taken up by writers of other nationalities, who displayed a new interest in their own history, language, literature, and art. For example, among the Slavic peoples of southeastern Europe, many of whom had been living for centuries under the domination of the Austrian or the Ottoman empire, a cultural renaissance beginning at the end of the eighteenth century was in full swing after 1815. Slavic philologists, historians, and literary men devoted themselves to unearthing their respective national traditions by compiling collections of folk legends, poems, and chronicles, and to systematizing knowledge of their languages by writing grammars and dictionaries. Where a language had gone out of use, attempts were made to revive it in the schools and in books and newspapers. Such nationalist movements were at first almost entirely cultural and their leaders were largely intellectuals—scholars, clerics, and liberal noblemen. But as the century proceeded they assumed an increasingly political character. While a revolt of the Serbs against Turkish rule in 1804 did not stem directly from such a cultural revival, the Greek revolt of 1821 was certainly inspired in part by a literary and linguistic renaissance that had begun in the last years of the eighteenth century. In the Austrian empire, the nationalist movements of the Slavic peoples remained primarily cultural, but the revival of the Magyar language and the growing Magyar literary production in Hungary stimulated the demand for greater autonomy of the Hungarian Diet. And Italians whose territories had been annexed to the empire in 1814–1815 grew increasingly restive under the impact of nationalist propaganda in the 1830's and 1840's.

ROMANTICISM

Where in the Restoration era does one place "romanticism"? Was it associated with the political and social developments of the period, or was it a purely literary and artistic movement? Is it possible to establish a workable definition of romanticism that can be applied to Germany as well as Britain, to Russia as well as France? Can one assign chronological limits to so amorphous a phenomenon? It is tempting to accept a recent description of romanticism as a "mood" that pervaded many aspects of nineteenth-century European culture but escapes any rigid definition. To each characteristic attributed to the "romantic school," individual exceptions may be found. Nevertheless, the mood existed and was widely influential.

The romantics reacted against the Enlightenment or against views which they attributed to writers of the Enlightenment. Whereas the *philosophes* had in general stressed the role of reason and the intellect in discovering truth, the romantics ascribed much more importance to feeling and emotion. The reality of human experience for them lay in the soul rather than the mind, in the heart rather than the head. Goethe's Faust, though

Caspar David Friedrich, the ruins of a monastery and its graveyard ("Abtei im Eichwald"), 1809. *In the Schloss Charlottenburg, Berlin.*

created by a writer who defies classification as either classicist or romantic, was nevertheless the prototype for the romantic age: the scholar, disillusioned and discouraged by his long quest for intellectual understanding, who finally turns to sentiment, dreams, and action for the redemption of his soul.

How the romantic mood affected the visual arts can best be discovered through a brief discussion of some individual painters of the period: a German, Caspar David Friedrich (1774–1840); an Englishman, Joseph Mallord William Turner (1775–1851); and a Frenchman, Eugène Delacroix (1798–1863). None of these can be described as the prototype of the romantic artist, but together, their works reveal some of the most prominent features of painting during the romantic era. All of them reacted against existing artistic conventions and rules, in their choice of subjects, the composition of their paintings, or their actual painting techniques. Like almost all painters of the romantic era they believed that the artist must express himself—his instincts and his passions—through his work. A painting was to be not a formalized representation of some preexisting order, but rather the individual artist's vision of the cosmos, the vehicle for his imagination. A successful painting would play upon the feelings and emotions of the viewer and stimulate his own imagination.

Friedrich, who is most noted for his landscapes and seascapes, reflects the romantics' profound interest in nature. His drawings reveal his close familiarity with natural detail, but his paintings of mountains towering in the morning mists or gnarled trees silhouetted against the moonlight end by transforming nature and giving it an almost supernatural or spiritual quality. In his landscapes there is invariably an aura of the mysterious or sinister, a sense of foreboding. Friedrich attempts to convey his vision of the relationship of the individual to the cosmos by placing in the foreground of his landscapes one or two isolated figures with their backs to the viewer, contemplating the grandeur of the natural scene. Through his composition he appears to be indicating the smallness and insignificance of human beings before the vast forces of nature, but he also seems to convey a sense of the individual's longing for the infinite, his desire to lose himself in the cosmos.

Turner, too, is noted for his landscapes and his dramatic paintings of the sea, but a concern with the individual's relationship to nature is less obvious in his work. His subjects are varied: historical and mythological scenes, shipwrecks, dramatic episodes such as the burning of the Houses of Parliament in 1834, and above all, sunrises and sunsets over the water. While Friedrich was not particularly innovative in his painting techniques, Turner developed a new freedom in his brushstrokes and became particularly skilled in the rendering of light. Using watercolors, he succeeded in capturing nuances of light and color in nature, which he later reproduced in oils. As he grew older, he tended more and more to blur the contours of the

Liberty Leading the People. *Painting by Eugène Delacroix. The Louvre, Paris.*

objects he painted, so that a ship, for example, seemed to melt into the surrounding sea and sky. In these techniques he anticipated devices later to be used by the Impressionists, who like him were less concerned with objective detail than with the total impact of a scene upon the viewer.

Delacroix, perhaps the most celebrated of French romantic painters, wrote in his *Journal*, "If by my Romanticism people mean the free display of my personal impressions, my remoteness from the servile copies repeated *ad nauseam* in academies of art and my extreme distaste for academic formulae, then I am indeed a Romantic."[3] In his choice of subjects, his arrangement of figures, and his daring use of color Delacroix liberated himself from established conventions and gave full expression to his aesthetic imagination. He was particularly sensitive to the relationship between poetry, music, and the visual arts, and contended that the color harmonies of a painting could stimulate sensations comparable to those aroused by the combination of sounds produced by an orchestra. He drew many of his themes from Byron, Sir Walter Scott, and Shakespeare. In his choice of subjects, Delacroix, like many other romantic painters, was guided by the

[3] Quoted by Marcel Brion, *Romantic Art* (London, 1960), pp. 134–135.

desire to tell a story or celebrate an event. An ardent political liberal, he commemorated the Revolution of 1830 in France with his "Liberty Leading the People," a dramatic painting dominated by the bare-breasted figure of a woman standing on the barricades, holding aloft the tricolor in one hand and a gun in the other, as she spurs the revolutionaries on. Beneath her lie the disheveled corpses of those who have fallen; the entire scene is illuminated by the flames of buildings burning in the background. The same theatricality and sense of movement is revealed in many of the oriental scenes he was fond of painting, such as the famous "Massacre at Chios," depicting the slaughter by the Turks of the Greek inhabitants of the island of Chios during the Greek revolution. Delacroix's fascination with the Orient, which was shared by many of his contemporaries, is an example of the romantic taste for the exotic and the bizarre.

In music, romanticism tended to be less revolutionary than in the visual arts. Historians of music generally identify the period of classicism with the eighteenth century and that of romanticism with the nineteenth, but they stress the continuity between the two periods and point out that the classical forms, developed or refined by Haydn, Mozart, and Beethoven—the sonata, the string quartet, and the symphony—persisted into the romantic era. And though some romantic composers took liberties with it, the classical system of harmony too remained dominant in the nineteenth century. But the early romantic composers—men such as Franz Schubert (1797–1828), Robert Schumann (1810–1856), Felix Mendelssohn (1809–1847), and Hector Berlioz (1803–1869)—infused the traditional forms with new meaning and reinterpreted the function of music. They tried to work directly on the mind and the senses of the listener so as to evoke an infinite range of impressions, emotions, and thoughts. Some, such as Berlioz, sought to do this by using a much more varied and complex orchestration and by developing "program music," in which they attempted to convey, by means of imaginative suggestion, descriptive or poetic subject matter. Mendelssohn, for example, imparted a sunny and vibrant mood to his *Italian Symphony*, while the mood of his *Scotch Symphony* was gray and somber, with a suggestion of the skirling of bagpipes and the sound of heroic ballads. A more explicit attempt to achieve the fusion of poetry and music was made by the German romantics, particularly Schubert and Schumann, in the *Lied* ("song"), an art form in which words and melody are blended in perfect harmony. There is hardly a mood or a nuance of feeling that does not find expression in Schubert's *Lieder*, but the dominant impression is one of sadness, nostalgia, or yearning.

In literature, the revolt against the Enlightenment began as early as the mid-eighteenth century, although romanticism as a literary movement did not come to fruition in most countries until the first half of the nineteenth century. For example, in the growth after 1740 of English Methodism one finds a reaction against the prevalent Deism of the eighteenth century and a return to enthusiasm and emotion in religion. The writings of Jean Jacques Rousseau (1712–1778), himself a *philosophe*, also foreshadowed various aspects of romanticism: extreme sensitivity to nuances of feeling, concern with the individual personality, preoccupation with nature and the "natural." In Germany, the literary movement known as *Sturm und Drang* ("storm and stress") out of which German romanticism developed, dates from the 1770's. By the early 1800's, romanticism as a literary movement was in full sway in Germany and had its representatives in Britain and France as well.

In matters of style, the romantics revolted against strict adherence to discipline and form that had characterized the classical tradition in literature. The measured Alexandrine verses of the seventeenth-century dramas of Racine and Corneille were now considered stilted and "artificial." The romantics regarded their own literary creations as freer and more "natural." The attitude of most romantic writers toward the individual also differed from the point of view prevalent in the Enlightenment. Although the *philosophes* had expressed an interest in the individual and his rights, their main concern had been to discover what qualities men had in common, what characteristics united them. In other words, they sought to generalize about human nature. Most romantic writers, on the other hand, were

Peter von Cornelius, illustration to Goethe's *Faust. Faust and Gretchen meet in Marthe's garden. Pen drawing, 1811.*

convinced of the uniqueness of the individual personality and suspicious of the kind of generalizations made by their predecessors. To them, diversity was not only natural but right and desirable. Carried to an extreme, this attitude led to a sense of isolation or alienation on the part of the individual, to self-dramatization and self-pity. Many a romantic figure, like the hero of Goethe's novel *The Sorrows of Young Werther* (1774), suffered from this sense of isolation and self-pity, though not all resorted, like Werther, to suicide as the only way out. The emphasis on individuality also found expression, in some of the romantics, in revolt against society and its conventions.

For others romanticism meant a return to the past and a sentimental nostalgia for earlier eras of history, particularly for the Middle Ages. Where writers of the Enlightenment like Voltaire had felt nothing but contempt for the Middle Ages as an era of superstition and obscurantism, François René de Chateaubriand (1768–1848) in France, Novalis (Friedrich von Hardenberg, 1772–1801), in Germany, and Sir Walter Scott (1771–1832) in Britain all romanticized the medieval period and compared it favorably with their own. Not all of them found the same virtues in the medieval past, nor did they all object to the same things in their own age. But the vogue of the Middle Ages was in part a reaction against the ugly, materialistic, and heartless industrial civilization that seemed to be emerging. In the Middle Ages the romantics thought they found a society in which the individual had security and a sense of belonging, an organic community in which the poor were contented with their station and deferred to their betters and the noble lords recognized their responsibility to protect those dependent upon them.

Perhaps, above all, they saw the Middle Ages as a time when faith prevailed, not the cold reason and skepticism of the Enlightenment. Romantic writers of a conservative turn were especially likely to look back nostalgically to an era in which faith had provided a sense of cohesion and unity that was missing from their own society. Certainly a return to religion, and particularly to Catholicism, was an important feature of romanticism. For many, it was less the beliefs than the colorful ceremonial, or ritualistic, aspects of Christianity that exercised a particular appeal. In this period also can be found the roots of the Gothic revival in architecture, which a few decades later saw the construction of the British Houses of Parliament and other monuments in Gothic style and the restoration of long-neglected Gothic cathedrals.

The romantic mood affected writers of practically all political and ideological persuasions and cannot be identified exclusively with any one group. Clearly, political conservatives shared many of the assumptions and points of view that have been attributed to the romantics: the reaction against the Enlightenment and its undue emphasis on reason, the return to the past, and the reversion to orthodox forms of Christianity. Particularly in Germany the major writers of the romantic school were conservative in their outlook; indeed, the German conservative tradition owes a great deal to romanticism. The admiration of romantic writers like Novalis for the organic society of the Middle Ages led them away from another romantic trait, the stress on the individual, and prepared the ground for the doctrine of the total submission of the individual to the state. Romanticism in Germany was both conservative and nationalist in tone. Yet exceptions may be found even to this generalization. The romantic writer Heinrich Heine (1797–1856), often called modern Germany's greatest lyric poet, was devoted to the cause of individual liberty and violently opposed the extreme positions taken by German nationalist writers in the first half of the nineteenth century. In Great Britain, some of the most noted romantic poets began their careers as radicals and ended as conservatives. William Wordsworth (1770–1850), an outspoken admirer of the French Revolution in its early stages, gradually turned against it, and in the end became a die-hard conservative opposed even to parliamentary reform. Samuel Taylor Coleridge (1772–1834) experienced a similar change of views. But in the second generation of English romantic poets, George Gordon, Lord Byron (1788–1824) championed the cause of oppressed nationalities everywhere and led the movement for Greek independence, and Percy Bysshe Shelley (1792–1822) shocked his contemporaries with views that caused him to be branded an atheist and an anarchist.

The element of nationalism in the romantic point of view was another expression of the reaction against the Enlightenment. Whereas the *philosophes* tended to be cosmopolitan in their outlook and to emphasize the similarities among men and nations, romantic writers turned with curiosity to their own national origins and traditions. As creative writers they were naturally interested in their native languages and often sought inspiration from folk tales and legends. Consequently, they became increasingly aware of differences among cultures, and tended to stress their national distinctiveness.

A similar pride in the nation appeared in the writing of romantic historians, though there may be disagreement as to which historians deserve this label. Few would question the term "romantic" when applied to the French historian Jules Michelet (1798–1874), best known for his multi-volumed *History of France*, a work which revealed his passionate devotion to his nation and its past. Like other romantic historians, Michelet viewed history as literature, or even art, and his histories abound in imaginative, detailed, descriptive passages full of color. A man of the people himself, he intended his history of the nation to reveal the life and soul of the French people rather than to be a chronicle of its kings and queens or a history of its institutions. In England, Thomas Babington Macaulay (1800–1859), a Whig statesman as well as historian, revealed a comparable pride in his own nation whose moral and material progress he attributed to the English love of liberty. Characterized by its vigorous language, its sense of drama and movement, and its author's profound knowledge of his nation's past, Macaulay's *History of England* became a classic, read by generations of Englishmen. In Germany, where romanticism was so closely tied to the revival of a German national consciousness, historians wrote of Germany's medieval past, recounting the exploits of the Franconian and Hohenstaufen emperors as well as of the Teutonic knights who had settled Prussia. But the most noted German historian of the nineteenth century, Leopold von Ranke (1795–1886), though sharing the romantics' interest in Germany's past, went beyond them by developing a new approach to historical study. Rejecting the traditional reliance on earlier historical narratives, Ranke stressed the importance of going to the sources—contemporary documents and other records—and using them critically. In his *History of the Popes* and his *German History in the Era of the Reformation* he exploited hitherto unused materials, such as the diplomatic reports of the Venetian ambassadors, in such a way as to "get inside" the eras he was studying and deal with them in their own terms. Although his work was certainly not devoid of interpretation, his ideal was objectivity in dealing with past events and he insisted that conclusions must arise strictly from the historical evidence. From Ranke stemmed the concept of professional or "scientific" history which has had a profound influence on historians ever since.

Finally, the romantic mood influenced the cause of social reform particularly during the 1830's and 1840's. Reformers appealed to the humanitarian feelings of their contemporaries by dramatizing the plight of Negro slaves and the sufferings of their own poor. The sense of conspiracy and adventure associated with the activities of republican secret societies in France after 1830 was consonant with the current romantic atmosphere and contrasted strongly with the prosaic qualities of the established order. The dreams of socialists for the creation of Utopian communities, perfect societies here on earth, though comparable in some ways to the visions of the *philosophes*, had an irrational appeal that distinguished them from the Utopias of their eighteenth-century predecessors.

Romanticism was a many-faceted, pervasive phenomenon that left almost no doctrine or ideology untouched. Some have attributed to the influence of the romantic mood the soft-mindedness and fuzziness of so much of the thinking and writing of the first half of the nineteenth century. In this view the romantic era marked an interlude between the more disciplined, rationalist *Weltanschauung* of the eighteenth century, which reflected the order and regularity of the Newtonian universe, and the positivist, science-oriented outlook that was to triumph in the second half of the nineteenth century. But whether one was a romantic conservative yearning for the rebirth of a society that had disappeared, a romantic liberal serving the cause of freedom for oppressed peoples, or a socialist reformer dreaming of the establishment of a society free of poverty and social ills, what remained of the romantic mood was shattered by the mid-century revolutions of 1848. For the abortive uprisings of that year seemed to prove that ideals were not enough, that in the last analysis physical force, material resources, and power were what counted in human relations.

CHAPTER 6

The Transformation of the European States during the Restoration Era

ATTEMPTS TO PRESERVE the *status quo* during the Restoration era lasted longer in some parts of Europe than in others. In Great Britain, France, and the Low Countries, major changes in the political climate or alterations of the 1815 settlement took place in 1830 and 1831. In the rest of Europe, despite temporary and isolated disturbances in the 1820's and about 1830, the political arrangements of Vienna persisted at least until the revolutions of 1848. Economic and social changes did occur in central and eastern Europe during this era, but they proceeded more slowly than in western Europe and their political consequences were not openly manifested until at least the middle of the century.

REACTION AND REFORM IN GREAT BRITAIN

Tory Rule, 1815–1830

The end of the Napoleonic wars found George III, who had assumed the crown in 1760, still on the throne in Great Britain. But since he was subject to recurrent fits of insanity, his son had become prince regent in 1811, and after his father's death, ruled in his own right as George IV, from 1820 to 1830. During this reign the prestige of the British monarchy sank. A clever but disreputable individual, George earned the enmity of a good part of the nation when he attempted to divorce his wife Caroline, from whom he had been separated for many years, and prevented her from being crowned as queen in 1820.

The irresponsibility of the ruler served to increase the importance of the Tory ministers, who had held office almost without interruption during the three decades prior to 1815. Although both Whig and Tory parties were still dominated in 1815 by members of the aristocracy, the Tories were more inclined to sympathize with the conservative view of British society and institutions that Burke had praised in his *Reflections on the French Revolution*. Moreover, their leadership of Britain during the prolonged wars against France had made them profoundly suspicious of radicalism and movements for reform. The Whigs received support from the newer moneyed interests and from Protestant dissenters. They were therefore more amenable to the gradual reform of laws and governmental institutions and the removal of mercantilist restrictions on commerce and industry.

In the years immediately after 1815 the Tory view prevailed; indeed, the government of Lord Liverpool, which lasted from 1812 until 1827, was one of the most reactionary in modern British history. Its actions and policies between 1815 and 1820 must be seen against the background of the severe depression that attended the transition from a wartime to a peacetime economy. The sudden drop in government expenditures and the loss of wartime markets for British manufactures and grain brought a period of falling prices, unstable currency, and widespread unemployment. The government's remedy for this situation, hardly calculated to meet with general approval, was a protective tariff, the Corn Law of 1815, which prohibited the importation of foreign grain until the price of English grain rose above a specified level (eighty shillings per quarter). This measure, unabashedly favoring the landowners, naturally antagonized urban laborers who were forced to pay a higher price for their bread in circumstances that were already difficult. No one in either party came forward to champion the cause of the working classes, so the task fell to radical agitators and writers and to clubs organized for reform. Some men, among them William Cobbett (1763–1835), the most famous of the radical pamphleteers, attacked all kinds of abuses, but most radicals concentrated on trying to reform the methods of selecting representatives to the House of Commons. For they were convinced that as long as control of the lower chamber remained in the hands of the aristocracy, which also controlled the House of Lords, there was no hope for legislation that would benefit the country as a whole.

Acute economic distress after 1815 led to a series of public meetings at which radical orators called for the repeal of the Corn Law of 1815 (along with earlier corn laws still on the statute books) and for parliamentary reform. Although almost no violence was associated with these demonstrations, the Tory ministry, taking alarm and seeing the danger of revolution everywhere, acted against the reform societies in 1817 by temporarily forbidding all public meetings, suppressing all societies not licensed by government, and suspending the Habeas Corpus Act. These measures brought a brief lull in popular agitation, but a new economic slump the following year resulted in a series of mass meetings in some of the larger cities of the north and Midlands. The most famous of these was held,

Peterloo Massacre, 1819. *A contemporary caption to this print referred to the "wanton and furious attack by that brutal armed force The Manchester & Cheshire Yeomanry Cavalry."*

despite a government ban, in St. Peter's Fields in Manchester in August, 1819. Local authorities sent a squadron of cavalry into the crowd of sixty thousand to arrest the fiery radical orator, Henry Hunt (1773–1835). In the resulting panic, eleven people were killed and several hundred injured. The incident was immediately branded the Battle of Peterloo, or the Peterloo Massacre. To the popular outcry that greeted this episode the government responded only with further measures of repression. In November, Parliament passed the famous Six Acts, a series of drastic restrictions intended to eliminate large public meetings, suppress or seriously weaken the radical press, and speed up conviction of offenders against the public order. As if to justify these measures, the government three months later uncovered a radical plot organized by one Arthur Thistlewood (1770–1820) for the assassination of the entire cabinet, the seizure of the Bank of England, and the establishment of a provisional government. Betrayed by an agent provocateur, the conspirators were arrested in a house on Cato Street in London; as might be expected, the Tory ministry gave widespread publicity to the Cato Street Conspiracy, pointing out how narrowly the country had escaped disaster.

Perhaps because of the repressive measures, perhaps because the economy picked up, after 1820 the radical movement in Britain subsided for almost a decade. During this period the Tory ministry was broadened considerably when Lord Liverpool, upon the death in 1822 of the foreign minister, Castlereagh, added to his cabinet three men who were a good deal more amenable to change than their colleagues: George Canning (1770–1827) as foreign minister and leader of the House of Commons; William Huskisson (1770–1830) as head of the Board of Trade; and Sir Robert Peel (1788–1850) as secretary for home affairs, the beginning of his long career. None of these men went so far as to favor major parliamentary reform at this time, but they were ready to carry out a series of pragmatic, piecemeal changes in laws and institutions that helped bring the British government into closer touch with economic and social realities.

Peel was responsible for a long-needed revision of the criminal code, which still carried the death penalty for some two hundred offenses, among them pocket picking, sheep stealing, and forgery. Because juries refused to convict offenders for such petty crimes when the punishment was death, disregard for the law had become widespread. Peel reduced the number of capital crimes and made the penalties more nearly commensurate with the offenses. This achievement, combined with his introduction in 1829 of a regular metropolitan police force in London (called "Bobbies" after him), led to a considerable reduction in the crime rate in Britain.

Huskisson was primarily responsible for the elimination of restrictions on British trade inherited from the mercantilist era. He was able to reduce the tariff on many items needed by British manufacturers as well as on some consumer goods, such as wine, coffee, and sugar. Many restrictions (including those on the importation of corn) still remained, but his policy was continued by subsequent ministries and in the 1840's culminated in complete free trade.

Although others prepared the way, Peel and Huskisson also deserve some credit for the repeal in 1824 of the Combination Acts, which had prohibited the formation of labor organizations. The impact of this repeal was reduced somewhat when, after a year of strikes and violence, Parliament in 1825 passed a law that restricted labor unions to bargaining over wages and hours and effectively prevented them from striking. But the right of labor to organize had been recognized.

Despite the gains achieved through these laws, the Tory ministry remained unpopular. Lord Liverpool's death in 1827 opened the way for the

brief ministries of Canning (who died after a few months in office) and the ineffectual Lord Goderich (Frederick John Robinson, 1782–1859). The appointment in 1828 of the duke of Wellington, the celebrated national hero, as prime minister prolonged the Tories' incumbency, but Wellington's alliance with the most reactionary elements in the party alienated young Tory liberals and contributed to the growth of the Whig opposition. During Wellington's ministry one more major reform was achieved, despite his personal distaste. This was the passage in 1829 of the bill for Catholic emancipation, which permitted Catholics to sit in Parliament and to hold all public offices except those of lord chancellor of England and lord lieutenant of Ireland. This reform, proposed many times before, had been repeatedly thwarted by the opposition of the king or the House of Lords. Now the pressure from an active movement in Ireland, led by the Irish barrister Daniel O'Connell (1775–1847), forced the issue. Wellington and Peel, convinced that civil war would result if they tried to hold out, pushed the bill through the House of Lords, and Wellington's threat to resign brought the king's assent. Passage of the bill did not solve the problem of England's relationship with Ireland, particularly since the ministry immediately raised the property qualification for voting there, but it was an important step in the long process of eliminating religious discrimination.

The Catholic Emancipation Act was the last significant contribution of the Tories before they left office after almost a half century of rule. Two events in 1830 helped to topple the Wellington ministry and prepare the way for passage of the Reform Bill of 1832. One was the news of the July Revolution in France, which overthrew the restored Bourbon regime and brought to power a government supported by the middle class. The other was the death of King George IV and the accession of his brother William IV, an event which according to constitutional tradition required the holding of a general election. The election resulted in sizable gains for those favoring reform. But more significant than either of these events was the cumulative effect of the Industrial Revolution upon British society; it had created social groups, forces, and problems which the old Tory leaders were incapable of handling. To the Whigs fell the task of breaching the old order and of taking into partnership with the older aristocracy the new "captains of industry."

As we have just seen, the growing sentiment for free trade among manufacturers and workers met with some response when Huskisson secured a reduction of duties on certain imports and set a precedent for further reductions. In 1828 a change in the corn laws allowed the importation of grain according to a sliding scale of duties. Yet as long as landowners remained dominant in both houses of Parliament, the new manufacturers (the "Manchester men" as they were called) could not hope

to achieve free trade. For this reason, reform of the methods for choosing representatives to the House of Commons became the overriding concern of the manufacturers.

Parliamentary Reform, Free Trade, and Chartism, 1830–1848

The Reform Bill of 1832, passed under Whig leadership, constituted the first recognition in British political life of the tremendous changes wrought in British society by the Industrial Revolution. In the years before 1832, the migration of workers from one region to another as industrialization progressed, the emergence of new cities, and the dramatic growth of some old cities accentuated the injustices of a system that had remained practically unaltered since the seventeenth century. The most glaring weakness was the underrepresentation, and sometimes the lack of representation, of new centers of population in the northern and western parts of England. Old boroughs lying in the eastern and southern counties had declined markedly in population but still sent two members each to the House of Commons. Among the most celebrated of the "rotten boroughs" was Old Sarum, which was still represented although no town existed there at all. Thriving new cities like Manchester, Birmingham, Leeds, and Sheffield, on the other hand, sent no representatives to Parliament. There were also "pocket boroughs," in which no real election took place because the seats were "in the pocket" of powerful landlords who used their influence to name their own candidates. As long as the Tories remained in office the cause of reform was stalled. But in 1830 the death of King George IV and the accession of William IV made a general election necessary, and the campaign was fought at least in part on the issue of reform. The Tories lost some fifty seats in the House of Commons, most of them to Whigs or to other advocates of reform; Commons was now in the control of the Whigs. The duke of Wellington, who had remained adamant in his opposition to reform, finally left office in November, 1830, and was succeeded by Earl Grey (1764–1845), a Whig committed to the cause. But for Grey to get the Reform Bill through Parliament took another year and a half—a stormy period characterized by mounting popular violence, strenuous measures on the part of the Whig leadership, and last-ditch resistance by Tory peers in the House of Lords. Only the threat of the king, under pressure from Grey, to create enough new peers to secure passage of the bill in the House of Lords finally persuaded the intransigents to abandon their opposition.

The Reform Bill of 1832 did not immediately revolutionize British political life. Indeed, one contemporary admitted that the House of Commons named in the first general election after the act turned out "to be very much like every other parliament."[1] Certainly those who voted for the

[1] Charles Greville, quoted by A. Briggs, *The Age of Improvement* (London, 1959), p. 261.

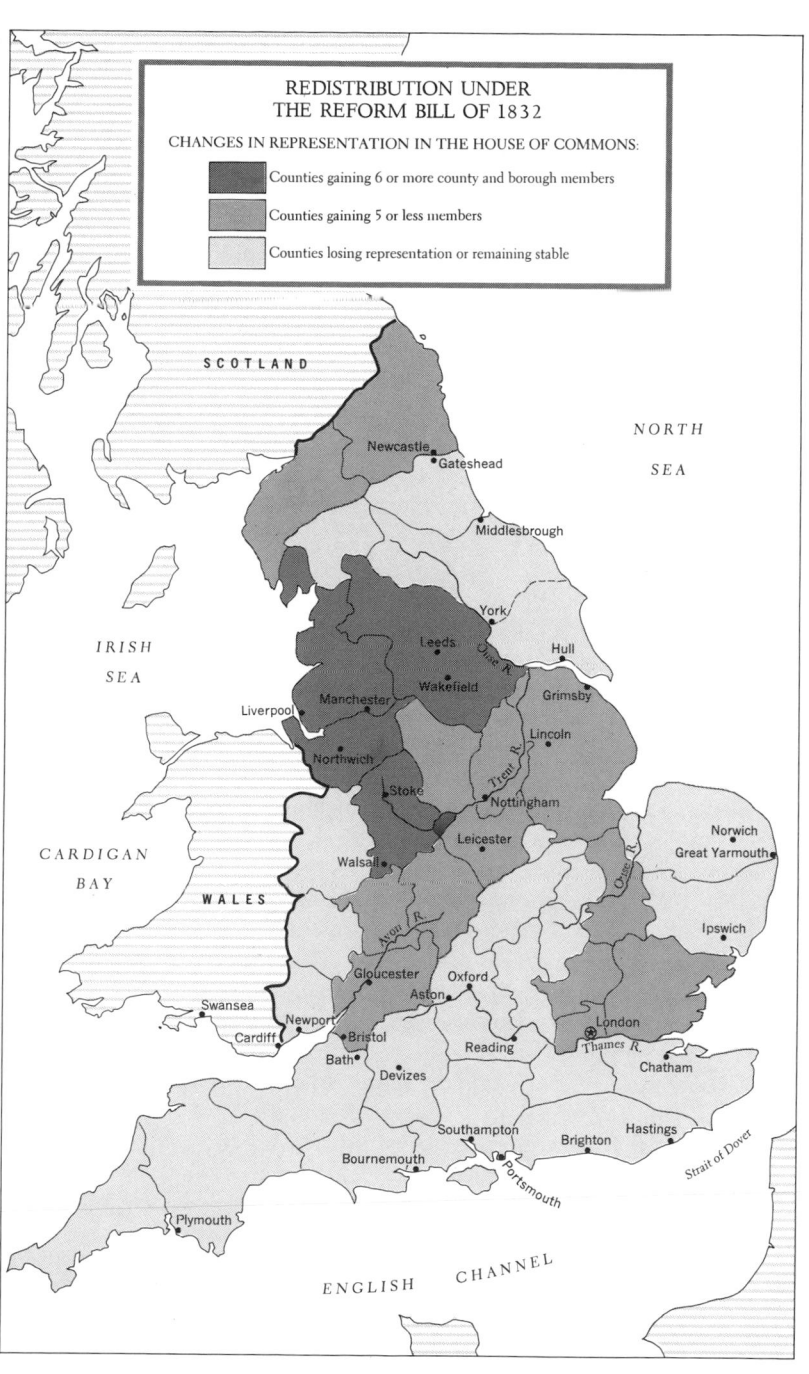

REDISTRIBUTION UNDER
THE REFORM BILL OF 1832

CHANGES IN REPRESENTATION IN THE HOUSE OF COMMONS:

Counties gaining 6 or more county and borough members

Counties gaining 5 or less members

Counties losing representation or remaining stable

SCOTLAND

NORTH SEA

Newcastle
Gateshead

Middlesbrough

York

Leeds
Wakefield
Manchester
Liverpool
Northwich
Stoke
Leicester
Walsall
Gloucester
Oxford
Aston
Swansea
Newport
Cardiff
Bristol
Bath
Devizes
Reading

Hull
Grimsby
Lincoln
Nottingham
Ouse R.
Trent R.
Avon R.

Norwich
Great Yarmouth
Ipswich

London
Thames R.
Chatham

IRISH SEA

CARDIGAN BAY

WALES

Southampton
Bournemouth
Portsmouth
Brighton
Hastings
Strait of Dover

Plymouth

ENGLISH CHANNEL

bill had no intention of creating a thoroughly democratic political system in Great Britain. While the electorate increased by about 50 per cent after 1832, only one in five Englishmen had the privilege of voting and the franchise still depended upon possession of a minimum of property. Yet the Reform Bill of 1832 was one of the most significant measures in the evolution of modern Britain. By redistributing seats in the House of Commons to increase representation of the new towns and cities, it admitted to partnership with the older landed and commercial aristocracy the new class of industrialists and manufacturers. The latter certainly did not take over the government of Britain in 1832, but in succeeding decades the balance of power gradually shifted to them. In two other respects the Reform Bill of 1832 was of great importance. It opened the way for a series of reforms in other spheres of British life—municipal administration, relief of the poor, and church-state relations—and more important, it established a precedent for further extensions of the franchise. If representatives of the manufacturers were to be taken into partnership in the governing of the nation, why should not the more prosperous and reliable workers be represented? This question was raised within a decade by the organizers of the Chartist movement.

The reform of Parliament made possible the eventual triumph of economic liberalism in Great Britain by giving greater legislative voice to the proponents of *laissez-faire*. Yet the new economic doctrines did not take hold at once. The principal demand of the economic liberals—the repeal of the corn laws—was not met for a decade and a half despite vigorous action and massive propaganda campaigns by proponents of repeal. The main opposition to repeal came, of course, from the landlords, who feared that an influx of cheap foreign grain would ruin British agriculture. The proponents of repeal joined together in 1838 to form the Anti-Corn-Law League, a well-financed and highly effective pressure group. Prominent among its supporters were such manufacturers as John Bright (1811–1889) and Richard Cobden (1804-1865), who argued not only that repeal was in the national interest but that free trade would promote international understanding and the cause of peace. Yet the campaign might have failed had it not had the support of the laboring classes, who were convinced that repeal would lower the price of bread. A turning point came with the conversion of Sir Robert Peel, the leading Tory minister of the period, to this cause, once he became convinced that continued maintenance of the corn laws was not essential to British prosperity. Further impetus was given by the failure of the Irish potato crop in 1845; a threat of famine hung over Britain, which could be dispelled only by supplementing British wheat with foreign grain. In 1846 the corn laws were finally repealed. That year marks the beginning of a free-trade era for Britain that lasted until the First World War. The abolition or reduction to a minimum of duties on practically all other imported goods followed the repeal of duties on grain.

If free trade was one of the principal goals of the liberals, elimination of government regulation of the domestic economy was the other. Adam Smith emphasized this aspect of *laissez-faire* less than has been generally supposed, but it became an important principle for the group of writers in England known as the classical economists, who elaborated Smith's doctrines. These thinkers "discovered" a comprehensive system of economic "laws" which operate in a competitive economy, comparable to the laws governing the physical universe. They believed that government interference with the natural operation of these economic laws was harmful to the economy. This point of view was adopted, for example, by the economist David Ricardo (1772–1823). Although his ideas concerning wages were interpreted more rigidly by his followers than he intended, he did advocate a strict *laissez-faire* position with respect to the rise and fall of the price of labor. Workmen might be doomed to an eternal cycle in which higher wages resulted in larger families and an increased supply of labor, followed by a corresponding increase in competition for jobs and an inevitable drop in wages, but it was not the function of government to try to interfere with free competition in order to maintain wages at a high level; the fluctuation of wages would be determined by the law of supply and demand operating in the labor market.

To what extent did a *laissez-faire* attitude prevail in Britain in the first half of the nineteenth century? This view, without question, became increasingly influential during this period. Yet a closer look at the role played by government in the British economy of the mid-nineteenth century reveals that during the years of expansion of the free-enterprise system there developed also a tradition of state intervention and regulation of industry on behalf of the working class which was clearly at odds with the *laissez-faire* position. There was never a lack of critics to attack the excesses of a system which seemed to leave the wage earner at the mercy of economic "laws." Ironically, a year after the Reform Bill, when manufacturing interests had increased their representation in the House of Commons, Parliament passed the first effective Factory Act, curbing the hours of employment of children in the textile mills and prescribing other regulations for their treatment. The following decade saw the passage of further legislation, restricting the employment of women and children in the mines and enforcing the introduction of safety devices and of better methods of sanitation in the factories. The Ten Hours Act of 1847 applied officially only to women and young persons, but had the practical effect of limiting the working day of adult males as well. Such statutes, involving interference by government with the functioning of free competition, were generally opposed by manufacturers. But the fact that they were passed and enforced suggests that the philosophy of *laissez-faire* never held undisputed sway in Great Britain.

It would be tempting for the sake of simplicity to view the opposition to economic liberalism in purely class terms. Thus, it could be argued that while bourgeois manufacturers clearly favored the application of *laissez-faire* doctrines and opposed restrictions upon their activity, members of the landowning aristocracy, seeing their political and economic domination threatened, sought to retain government restrictions or impose new ones upon the rapidly growing industries. According to this view, the members of the working class were in an ambiguous position. They sided with their employers on the issue of free trade, in the hope that lowered tariffs would reduce the cost of living; on the other hand, they viewed the manufacturers as exploiters bent on securing maximum profits at labor's expense, and consequently sought an alliance with the landowners as a means of imposing regulations on industry.

There is just enough truth in this interpretation to make it appealing. Landowners did stubbornly resist the repeal of the corn laws until finally forced to capitulate by growing pressures from the manufacturers and workers. The Tory leaders, who defended the property holders' interests, did support legislation regulating working conditions in retaliation against the manufacturers for their opposition to the corn laws. Finally, the working-class movement was indeed divided over its goals.

But the divisions on class lines were not so clear-cut as this interpretation suggests. The movement for restricting the working day of women and young persons to ten hours, for example, had the support of a variety of individuals. The two principal leaders of the movement in Parliament, Michael Sadler (1780–1835) and Lord Ashley (Anthony Ashley Cooper, later earl of Shaftesbury, 1801–1885) were Tories. Sadler had been a businessman before becoming a social reformer, and Ashley, though a landowning aristocrat, appears to have been motivated not so much by a desire for revenge against the manufacturers as by religious and humanitarian impulses linked with a traditional sense of *noblesse oblige*. The campaign for the Ten Hours Act had the active support of many who called themselves radicals, but it also was backed by some maverick manufacturers, such as John Wood of Yorkshire, and John Fielden of Lancashire. Reform was not, therefore, exclusively the goal of one social class or group.

The most important single manifestation of working-class sentiment in these years, the Chartist movement, seems to have sprung not from discontent with *laissez-faire* economic policies or from specific grievances against the new manufacturers, but rather from a generalized distress in the 1830's and 1840's for which the workers saw one principal remedy—political representation. Finding inadequate the Reform Bill of 1832, for which they had agitated along with the middle classes, they sought further parliamentary reform. Chartism drew its support from at least three different groups among the working classes. One of these consisted of the rather moderate, quite respectable artisans of the London Workingmen's Association founded in 1836 by a cabinetmaker, William Lovett (1800–1877). They

A Chartist procession in London, April 10, 1848.

were joined by members of the more radical Birmingham Political Union, a propagandist group dating back to 1816, which, was revived in the 1830's by a radical Birmingham banker, Thomas Attwood (1783–1856). The third group, led by Feargus O'Connor (1794–1855), a fiery Irish landowner and demagogue, appealed to the most distressed elements of the population of Leeds and the northern counties. All three groups threw their support behind the People's Charter, the document which gave its name to the Chartist movement. The Charter, a list of political demands to be presented to Parliament, called for universal manhood suffrage, equal electoral districts (that is, districts with equal numbers of inhabitants), vote by secret ballot, annual elections to Parliament, the abolition of the property qualification for members of Parliament, and the payment of stipends to those elected to the House of Commons. The last demand was important since workers or those representing them could hardly afford to run for Parliament as long as its members were unpaid.

During 1838–1839 a massive campaign to enlist support for the Charter was organized, complete with large public meetings, inflammatory speeches, and torchlight processions. This culminated in the spring of 1839 in the assembling in London of a National Convention (the name was chosen for its associations with the French Revolution) and the presentation to Parliament of a huge petition on behalf of the Charter signed by several hundred thousand individuals. Despite this wave of agitation which was attended by great publicity, Parliament refused even to consider the petition. The Chartists found themselves in a dilemma. Some of the more radical branches of the movement staged riots and local strikes, but the majority were not prepared to resort to violence to gain their ends. After 1839 the movement split into rival factions and temporarily collapsed. The National Chartist Association continued to uphold the principles of the Charter and presented the demands again in 1842 and in 1848, the year of revolutions on the Continent, but Chartism was never as strong in the 1840's as it had been at the outset and fell into the hands of less responsible leaders, such as Feargus O'Connor, ready to use the movement for the advancement of personal ends.

The Chartist movement failed in its own time, but the goals of the Chartists, were realized between 1858 and 1918. Only the requirement of annual elections to Parliament has not become a part of the English electoral system. Perhaps most interesting about the Chartist agitation is the fact that although it arose from severe economic distress, the average English workingman was convinced that he could improve his condition not by direct action against his employer or a generalized attack on *laissez-faire* policies, but rather by peaceful, legal means and direct representation in Parliament. His counterpart on the Continent resorted to more violent tactics.

THE RESTORATION AND THE JULY MONARCHY IN FRANCE

The Bourbon Restoration and the Revolution of 1830

It is hardly surprising that some of the bitterest political struggles between 1815 and 1830 took place in France, the birthplace of the revolution and the most important country in which the restoration of a monarch occurred. The opposing forces were the Ultraroyalists, who sought to wipe out all the revolution had achieved, and the liberals and their allies, who were intent upon preserving the reforms secured between 1789 and 1814. Between them stood Louis XVIII (ruled 1814–1824), basically sympathetic with the Ultras, but shrewd enough to realize that any attempt to wipe out the gains of the revolution would end in disaster for his dynasty. The new constitution—the Charter of 1814, Louis' "gift" to the people—recognized the major achievements of the revolutionary years. It specifically guaranteed the principle of equality before the law and the retention of the Civil Code. It confirmed the titles to their property of those who had purchased national land during the revolution, and preserved the Napoleonic Concordat, along with the principle of religious toleration.

The Charter did not determine where the real power should lie, and this question was debated by political theorists, whose views ranged from the defense of absolute monarchy to the assertion of popular sovereignty, and fought out at a less theoretical level by politicians. Specifically at issue were the powers of the bicameral Assembly: the Chamber of Peers, whose members were appointed to hereditary tenure, and the Chamber of Deputies, whose members were elected in accordance with a highly restricted franchise based on property ownership. What was to be the relationship of the Assembly to the king? Executive power was vested in the king and his ministers, but legislative power did not clearly rest with the chambers. The king (or his ministers) had the sole power to initiate legislation; the chambers could only petition the king to do so. According to the Charter, the chambers could reject a bill proposed by the king but could not amend it without royal consent. Nor was the position of the ministers clearly defined. According to the Charter the ministers were officers of the king, appointed by him and charged with the execution of his policy. Nowhere did the Charter say that the ministers must represent the majority in the legislature. Yet, in fact, between 1815 and 1830 the leading minister did represent the majority group in the Chamber of Deputies except on two occasions, one in 1815–1816 and the other in 1829–1830. The principle of ministerial responsibility was thus gradually established, although it was never explicitly conceded by the king.

Some fundamental procedures of parliamentary government developed in France during the Restoration, and a generation of statesmen gained valuable political experience. But the basic issue was left unresolved, for the restored Bourbon rulers failed to establish a working compromise between the traditional claims of monarchy and the revolutionary principle of popular sovereignty. The regime foundered over this issue in 1830.

Politically, the fifteen-year era falls into three periods. During the first, which lasted for only a year (1815–1816), the Assembly was dominated by the Ultraroyalists, who won a majority in the Chamber of Deputies and embarrassed the king and the moderate-royalist ministry by announcing their intention of sweeping away a number of institutions inherited from the revolutionary and Napoleonic eras and restoring confiscated estates to their prerevolutionary owners. Actually they achieved very few of their goals, though they did set up special courts to try Bonapartists and revolutionaries whom they charged with treason. Even before the Ultraroyalist Chamber of Deputies was elected, an unofficial White Terror erupted, a counterpart of the Terror of 1793–1794, carried out by royalists during the summer of 1815 in the south of France. Bands of royalist volunteers, remnants of an army organized at the time of Napoleon's escape from Elba by a nephew of the king—Louis Antoine de Bourbon, duke of Angoulême (1775–1844)—now arrested, imprisoned, or massacred hundreds of individuals suspected of Jacobin or Bonapartist sympathies. The White Terror spread from Marseilles to other parts of Provence and Languedoc. At Nîmes and in the department of the Gard the victims included many Protestants suspected by the Catholic royalists of disloyalty to the Bourbon monarchy.

It appears that the White Terror was neither instigated nor directed by the restored monarchy, but government officials looked the other way as the royalist bands carried out their vigilante purges. When Louis XVIII realized that the extremism of the Ultraroyalists was alienating the nation from the monarchy, he dissolved the Chamber of Deputies, in September, 1816, and called for new elections.

In the new chamber the majority consisted of moderate royalists, and between 1816 and 1820 they supported the ministries headed by the duke of Richelieu (1766–1822) and his successor, Duke Élie Decazes (1780–1860). This second period of the Restoration was one of relative calm despite frequent verbal attacks on the ministry by both Ultraroyalists and liberals. New electoral laws extended the franchise somewhat, though there were still only about 100,000 voters out of a total population of 30,000,000.

This tranquility was shattered in 1820—the year of revolutions in Spain, Portugal, and Italy—by the assassination of the duke of Berry, the son of Louis' younger brother and presumably the last of the Bourbon line. (The hope of the assassin that he was putting an end to the Bourbon dynasty was frustrated when the duke's widow was discovered to be pregnant, and in due course produced a male heir.) Although the murder was the act of an isolated fanatic, the Ultras charged the king's minister, Decazes, with responsibility for the crime because of his alleged laxity in dealing with the opposition. So strong was the pressure put on the king that he was forced to abandon Decazes and appoint a new ministry. At this point began the final period of the Restoration in France, an era of growing reaction that lasted until 1830. During this period Louis took a less active role in government, and the initiative gradually passed to his younger brother, the count of Artois, who became Charles X upon Louis' death in 1824.

The assassination of the duke of Berry was used as an excuse for imposing restrictions on the press and for revising the electoral law to give increased influence to the landed aristocracy at the expense of the bourgeoisie. Between 1822 and 1828, under the ministry of the count of Villèle (1773–1854), the Ultras were finally able to secure legislation favorable to their own interests. For example, the Law of Indemnity (1825) compensated nobles who had emigrated during the revolution for the loss of their landed estates. This measure was doubly offensive to the members of the bourgeois opposition because they were the principal holders of the government bonds whose interest rate was reduced to provide funds for the indemnity. Although the Law of Indemnity finally ended the controversy over the revolutionary land settlement, it was not viewed in this favorable light in 1825.

One of the principal features of Charles X's reign was the close tie established between throne and altar. The Law of Sacrilege (1825) imposed the death penalty for offenses of an allegedly sacrilegious character and for the theft of sacred objects from churches. The law was particularly odious to liberals because it appeared to put the state at the service of the Church in a manner reminiscent of the Old Regime. Villèle also did his best to undermine the *Université*, the state educational system founded by Napoleon, by placing a bishop at its head and dismissing many of its liberal teachers. At the same time he encouraged the growth of Catholic seminaries outside the state system. Their function was ostensibly to train priests, but in fact they competed with the state secondary schools for students. Finally, although the Jesuit order was still formally banned in France, the government openly countenanced the presence of Jesuits as teachers in Catholic schools. Indeed, liberals were convinced that Jesuits had infiltrated everywhere and were secretly directing government policy.

Developments like these resulted in steadily mounting opposition to the Villèle ministry. Liberal newspapers, such as the *Constitutionnel* and the *Journal des Débats*, contributed to the struggle. In 1827 was formed a liberal political society called *Aide-toi, et le ciel t'aidera* ("Heaven help those who help themselves") whose goals were to prevent falsification of electoral lists by government officials and to spread liberal propaganda. Formerly enthusiastic backers of the regime now began to join the opposition. So too did a number of wealthy bankers and manufacturers who resented legislation that favored the nobility and the clergy.

In 1827 Charles X made the error of dissolving the Chamber of Deputies and calling for new elections. When a majority of moderate royalists was returned, the king reluctantly yielded to the principle of ministerial responsibility by dismissing Villèle and summoning the moderate viscount of Martignac (1778–1832) to take his place. Martignac relaxed the restrictions on the press and dismissed some of the more notoriously reactionary Ultraroyalists from the civil service. However, the heckling of this ministry by both the Ultra and the liberal extremes made its existence difficult and ultimately provided the king with a pretext for dismissing Martignac in 1829. He then named the prince of Polignac (1780–1847), clearly flouting the will of the Assembly. For Polignac, who in 1816 had refused to swear to uphold the Charter, was one of the most notorious of the Ultras and could not possibly command a majority in the Chamber of Deputies.

From this time on, the alternatives for France seemed to be royal despotism and revolution. A protest against the Polignac ministry by a majority of the deputies in the spring of 1830 merely provoked the king to dissolve the chamber and call for new elections. But the result was an even larger majority for the opposition.

Confronted with the prospect of a recalcitrant Assembly, Charles decided to seize the initiative, and before the new body could meet, issued the royal decrees known as the July Ordinances. The decrees dissolved the newly elected Assembly, established a new electoral system, arbitrarily deprived the wealthy bourgeoisie of the right to vote, and imposed a rigid censorship on the press. Though the king could argue that the Charter gave him the

Scene from the July Revolution of 1830, Paris.

right to issue such decrees, the opposition correctly interpreted the July Ordinances as an attempt to abandon the Charter. The promulgation of the decrees gave rise to an insurrection—the July Revolution of 1830.

The revolution occurred with a minimum of violence, partly because the government, not anticipating trouble, had made few preparations to resist. What fighting there was occurred in Paris and was all over in three days. It began in Paris on July 26, when spontaneous demonstrations greeted publication of the royal ordinances. The following day unemployed workers, joined by students and some republican agitators, threw up barricades in the streets of Paris to prevent the passage of government troops. On July 28 the insurrectionists captured the Hôtel de Ville and raised the tricolor flag. The king, who was hunting on his estate at Saint-Cloud, offered to withdraw the ordinances and dismiss the ministry, but it was already too late. A group of liberal leaders, who had been meeting daily since July 26, fearing a republican seizure of power, announced the formation of a provisional government. Favoring a constitutional monarchy, this group proposed giving the crown to the duke of Orléans, cousin of Charles X. The duke was a natural rallying point for monarchists dissatisfied with Charles X. He had remained in France during the first stages of the great revolution, fought with the revolutionary armies before going into exile early in 1793, and professed liberal views. At first, he hesitated because the legitimate king had not abandoned his title to the throne, but he agreed to serve as "lieutenant-general" of the realm until the succession was settled. Then the agreement of the marquis de Lafayette, the aged hero of the American and French revolutions and an unofficial leader of republican forces in Paris, was secured. In a dramatic scene on July 31, the duke of Orléans entered the capital and paraded through streets lined with silent and sullen workers until he reached the Hôtel de Ville. There he met Lafayette for an interview, and then they appeared together before the crowds with a tricolor flag draped over their shoulders. Lafayette had satisfied himself that the duke would sit on a "throne surrounded by republican institutions." To no avail did Charles X announce that he was abdicating in favor of his young grandson. Next, a majority of the old Chamber of Deputies met and formally offered the throne to the duke of Orléans, so Charles had no alternative but to go into exile in England. Within a few days the new king accepted a revised version of the Charter which eliminated the preamble stating that the document was the "gift" of the king to his people. Instead, his title—"king of the French People"—clearly implied that he owed his throne to the popular will. The July Revolution had put an end to the Restoration in France.

Louis Philippe and the July Monarchy, 1830–1848

Although those who had engineered the July insurrection were under the impression that they had carried out a genuine revolution, the constitu-

Deputies calling the duke of Orléans to the throne. *Painting by Heim. Scene from the Revolution of 1830 in France. Musée de Versailles, Versailles.*

tional changes that resulted in France from the change of dynasty were relatively slight. As "king of the French People" Louis Philippe presumably recognized the principle of popular sovereignty, but in point of fact he never fully accepted this doctrine. The Charter of 1814 was retained with only slight modifications, and the right to vote was still restricted to substantial property owners. The suffrage was extended from about 100,000 to 170,000 in a nation of 30,000,000. Nonetheless, the July Revolution represented the final triumph of the *haute* ("upper") *bourgeoisie* over the nobility. It was, after all, representatives of the bourgeoisie who had helped bring the new king to power and who thereafter held a privileged position in his regime. The constitutional embodiment of their victory lay in the provision that appointments to the Chamber of Peers, the upper house, would henceforth be held for life only, instead of being hereditary. A few liberal members of the noble class continued to play a role in politics but most of them viewed the new regime with contempt and retired to their homes in the exclusive Faubourg Saint-Germain of Paris or to their country estates.

Louis Philippe's regime is often termed "the bourgeois monarchy." It drew its principal support and its allegedly drab, materialistic character from the middle class, and the monarch himself appeared to embody many of the virtues exalted by this class—thrift, sobriety, a propensity to hard work. A devastating, if somewhat exaggerated, portrait of the vices of bourgeois society under the July Monarchy may be found in the novels of Honoré

The Rise of the Bourgeoisie. *This 1810 drawing shows the Parisian restaurant* Boeuf à la mode. *Note the woman cashier on the right.*

de Balzac (1799–1850). In works like *Eugénie Grandet, Le Père Goriot,* and *Cousine Bette* (all part of his vast *Comédie Humaine*), Balzac exposed a society obsessed with the acquisition of money and the power it could bring. At all social levels, but especially among the bourgeoisie, the class from which he himself came, Balzac found ambition, greed, and corruption poisoning the relationships among human beings. The policies of the government favored the interests of the wealthier manufacturers and tradesmen, and after an initial wave of enthusiasm for the new regime, disillusionment began to set in among the *petite* ("lesser") *bourgeoisie,* who were still excluded from political participation, and among the Parisian working class, whose contribution to the Revolution of 1830 had apparently counted for nothing. The history of the July Monarchy is, in large part, the history of the mounting dissatisfaction of these social groups with the government and the consolidation of opposition to it which culminated in the Revolution of 1848.

Even among the upper bourgeoisie who were represented in the Chamber of Deputies there were different opinions about the direction the regime should take. Led by François Guizot (1787–1874), a group designated as the right-center which came to be known as the Party of Resistance, supported the view that France had now arrived at the perfect and final form of government, a balanced system in which the monarch, the peers, and the elected representatives of the propertied classes each played their allotted role. Anyone excluded from political participation had only to "get rich" (in a phrase often attributed to Guizot) in order to secure the privilege of voting. Now that France had achieved this state of perfection, further changes in its institutions were unnecessary. The other group, the left-center, or the Party of Movement, was represented by Adolphe Thiers, a statesman whose political career spanned the better part of the nineteenth century; its members argued that the Revolution of 1830 was merely a stage in the political evolution of France and that the electoral base should be gradually broadened. At first these two factions were evenly matched, but by 1840 the right-center (with which the king was in sympathy) had won the day. Guizot was the premier during the last eight years of the king's reign and effectively suppressed opposition to the regime in the Chamber of Deputies.

Outside of the chamber the opposition was vigorous, particularly in the early years of the regime. It came from a number of sources. There were the Legitimists, who remained loyal to the dynasty which had been overthrown and hoped for a restoration of its heir. Then there were the Bonapartists, and in these years the Napoleonic legend won increasing popularity among Frenchmen. A new, young generation tended to contrast their own prosaic, money-grubbing society and the cautious foreign policy of Louis Philippe with the dramatic exploits of the Napoleonic regime when life had been exciting and opportunities for heroism and glory had existed for the young.

The fascination that Napoléon had for the post-Napoleonic generation can be seen in the novels of Stendhal (pseudonym for Henri Beyle, 1783–1842). Of his major works, only *Lucien Leuwen* was set in the era of the July Monarchy, but the heroes of *The Red and the Black* and *The Charterhouse of Parma* embody the energy, the intelligence, and the will that Stendhal found in Bonaparte.

The death without heirs of the duke of Reichstadt, Napoleon's son, in 1832, temporarily weakened the Bonapartist cause, and at first nobody took very seriously the claims of the emperor's nephew, Louis Napoleon, as his successor. Two ill-planned and rather ridiculous attempts by the young pretender to seize power, one in 1836 and another in 1840, were quickly thwarted by the government. Arrested and tried after the second of these, he was condemned to life imprisonment, but he escaped to England in 1846 and remained there until 1848.

The only group that appeared potentially dangerous to the July Monarchy consisted of those who favored the establishment of a republic. In 1830 they were still few, mainly students and young radicals drawn from the lesser bourgeoisie. Having initially accepted the new regime, they quickly became disillusioned with it and began to renew their republican propaganda, multiply their secret societies, and attract new recruits from the discontented. Except for the aim of eliminating the monarchy, their program was not particularly extreme; they advocated extension of the suffrage, salaries for members of the Chamber of Deputies, and free public education.

Since censorship was one of the issues about which the Revolution of 1830 was fought, the July Monarchy began by allowing considerable freedom of expression in the press. The result was an outburst of political commentary and criticism. In this age political and social satire was a powerful weapon, and the caricaturist Honoré Daumier (1808–1879) was only one of the more successful social satirists. Daumier's caricatures of Louis Philippe shaped like a pear were so popular that opposition newspapers could be sure of being understood when they spoke simply of *La Poire.* Before long the tolerance of the government (and of the king) began to wear thin and steps were taken to curb the excesses of the opposition press. As we shall see, in defense of its restrictions the government pointed to public demonstrations and riots allegedly inspired by press attacks on the regime and to a series of attempts upon the life of the king which more than once came dangerously close to success.*

In a country where the Industrial Revolution was still in its infant stages, no sizable urban proletariat existed in 1830. But the rapid expansion of

---

* The fact that the king was the target of attempted assassinations on ten different occasions during the first decade of his reign led him to remark, ". . . there seems to be a closed season on all kinds of game except me."—Quoted by Gordon Wright, *France in Modern Times* (Chicago, 1960), p. 152.

Philipon's celebrated caricature of Louis Philippe in which the king's head is gradually changed into a pear. *Other satirical papers took over the representation and even street urchins began to chalk "la Poire" on the walls of Paris.*

French industry in the 1830's and 1840's, and its concentration in a few regions, led to the development of an urban working class. Conditions in industrial areas were as bad, and in some cases worse, than in the corresponding parts of England. The labor of women and children was used extensively in the textile mills of the north, where a fifteen-hour working day was not uncommon. Epidemics were frequent, particularly among children, because of poor hygienic conditions in homes and factories. Periodic economic crises led to temporary unemployment and consequent suffering for laborers living at a bare subsistence level. In contrast with Great Britain, France made practically no effort to regulate conditions in the factories and mines. With the bourgeoisie firmly in control, the government's *laissez-faire* policy went largely unchallenged. The few reforms that reached the statute books such as a child-labor law passed in 1841, were unenforced. In these circumstances, the working class in France behaved with remarkable restraint.

The only significant working-class disturbances under the July Monarchy

Silk weavers of Lyons, 1850. *The first significant working class uprisings of the nineteenth century in France occurred here in 1831 and 1834.*

took place in 1831 and 1834 at Lyons, the center of the silk industry and the second largest city in France, but their repercussions were felt elsewhere. Because the silk industry was well established, the workers were relatively class-conscious and receptive to programs of political and social reform. The first insurrection seems to have been a largely spontaneous affair resulting from discontent over low wages, but there is evidence of collaboration between the workers and republican secret societies in a more generalized protest during the uprising in 1834. Both outbreaks were suppressed by government troops. In the second one the workers held Lyons for five days and the government had to bombard sections of the city before the rebellion could be quelled. The Lyons insurrections, the most important social uprisings in France since the French Revolution, marked the beginning of an alliance between republicans and the working class against the July Monarchy. One month after the insurrection of 1834, an attempted republican uprising in Paris led to brutal reprisals by government forces. This was the occasion memorialized by Daumier in his famous drawing "The Massacre in the Rue Transnonain," showing a victim of a government raid, clad in his nightshirt and cap, stretched out at the foot of his bed and covered with bayonet wounds.

These insurrections were followed by the mass arrest and trial of republican and radical leaders, and the republican opposition was driven completely underground. The government used the uprisings and the attempts on the life of the king as pretexts for the September Laws of 1835. These brought the press under strict censorship and simplified and speeded up judicial proceedings against those accused of provoking insurrection against the state. The September Laws marked a turning point in the history of the July Monarchy: they did not end criticism but they drastically curbed the opportunities for its expression. With the safety valve of a free press no longer available, pressure built up steadily in the final years of the regime, until it finally exploded in the Revolution of 1848.

Perhaps the most serious charge that can be brought against the leaders of the July Monarchy is that they made no real effort to understand the underlying causes of the insurrections and demonstrations against the regime. Refusing to recognize the legitimacy of republican demands for broader political representation and of working-class demands for an amelioration of social conditions, they simply chose to ignore popular unrest. As premier from 1840 to 1848, François Guizot bears much of the responsibility for the failure of the July Monarchy. Though a brilliant historian and one of the instigators of the Revolution of 1830, he seems to have been incapable of understanding the forces active in his own time. In an era when important economic changes were taking place in French society, he adopted a policy of almost total immobility and resistance to change. In the realm of foreign affairs, his do-nothing policy could be justified on the ground that peace was in France's self-interest, but the absence of adventure and the drabness of France's role in the international scene contributed to the unpopularity of the government. In economic matters he retained the *laissez-faire* policy pursued by the July Monarchy from the outset, though the government did take the initiative in establishing a plan for a national

Massacre in the rue Transnonain, 1834. *Honoré Daumier.*

network of railroads in 1842, offering subsidies to private firms which undertook their construction. No serious attempts were made to regulate or improve working conditions even though abuses were widespread. Where Guizot particularly excelled was in the manipulation of elections and the corruption of elected representatives, activities which were essential if he was to maintain a majority in the Chamber of Deputies. By carefully selecting the time at which elections were to be held, choosing the towns where the voters were to meet, and promising patronage where it would do the most good, he could secure the return of a favorable majority. And to ensure the continuing support of those elected, lucrative government posts, which they could hold while serving as deputies, were offered to them. Political devices like these are employed to some extent in all parliamentary regimes, but Guizot so abused them that the representative system became a farce. One of the most serious consequences of Guizot's method was that the king and the government were prevented from discovering the true sentiments of the French people. Repeated proposals from a minority of deputies for a reform of the electoral system or the elimination of officeholding by deputies were overridden or disregarded by Guizot's majority. With a growing sense of frustration, liberal reformers in the Assembly finally decided they must turn to extra-parliamentary means for achieving their ends. From this resolve were to originate the electoral banquets held in the winter of 1847–1848 throughout the country, in the propaganda campaign for electoral reform which helped precipitate the Revolution of 1848.

METTERNICH'S REPRESSION IN CENTRAL EUROPE

The various peoples inhabiting the central part of the European continent, from the Baltic Sea in the north to the island of Sicily in the south, fell under the domination during the Restoration era of the Habsburg dynasty, or rather of its chief agent, Prince Klemens von Metternich. The Austrian chancellor had his emissaries or his spies everywhere, sending back reports to Vienna, constantly on the alert for evidence of liberalism or subversion that might threaten the *status quo*. In point of fact, in the years immediately after 1815, active opposition was confined to a small minority of students, army officers, liberal nobles, and merchants. The peasants who constituted the great mass of the population were little concerned with political questions. Such grievances as they had were directed primarily against their landlords, not the government. Since industrialization did not get under way until the 1830's and 1840's, and then only in the Rhineland and northern Italy, there existed no numerically significant middle class to assume the leadership of a liberal opposition.

The opposition that did exist in central Europe was as often nationalist as liberal, though no clear-cut distinction between the two was made by

Metternich or, indeed, by those who agitated against the *status quo*. In Austria, nationalist sentiment normally took the form of demands by representatives of non-German groups for greater use of their language in schools and administrative offices. In Italy and the German states, nationalism meant the desire for freedom from Austrian domination and a greater measure of unity for the respective peoples. To all these aspirations, Metternich's answer was the same. They were ruthlessly suppressed as threats to the delicate equilibrium of existing institutions. He was convinced that—particularly within the Austrian empire proper—any attempt to tamper with the elaborate structure might bring the entire edifice tumbling down. If the chancellor's goal was the maintenance of order and a reasonable degree of calm, his policy worked remarkably well during the better part of the period between 1815 and 1848. But by refusing to face up to the real and complex problems existing in the Habsburg realms, and by stifling the growing nationalist desires of Germans and Italians, he merely postponed the explosion, which finally erupted in 1848.

The Germanic Confederation, 1815–1832

The Germanic Confederation, created by the Congress of Vienna, consisted of thirty-eight states; Austria and Prussia were the largest of these, though their non-German territory was not included. The institutional embodiment of this loose federation was a federal diet, or assembly, consisting of delegates appointed by the rulers of each of the member states, which met in the free city of Frankfurt am Main. The function of the diet was ill defined, especially since the Confederation had no executive to implement its decisions, but it soon became clear that the Confederation had been set up as an instrument for the exercise of Metternich's influence throughout the German states. While Metternich seems to have viewed it initially as a kind of defensive alliance against encroachment on German territory by France or Russia, in fact it came to be used primarily for the repression of liberal movements throughout Germany.

Not all of the thirty-eight states had governments quite as reactionary as Austria's. Although Metternich had discouraged them from doing so, rulers in a number of states granted constitutions to their subjects to fulfill promises made during the final years of the Napoleonic era; among them were the medium-sized states of southern Germany—Bavaria, Württemberg, and Baden. These constitutions, like the French Charter, did not acknowledge the principle of popular sovereignty; indeed, in the virtual absence of a middle class, suffrage was confined primarily to the landed aristocracy and the administrative bureaucracy. Where elected assemblies existed, their primary function was merely to ratify legislation proposed by the sovereign.

At first, liberals throughout Germany looked hopefully to Prussia for imspiration. King Frederick William III not only had promised a constitution to his people, on the eve of Waterloo, but had agreed between 1807 and 1814 to a series of reforms that made Prussia appear to be one of the more progressive states in Germany. Leadership in initiating these reforms came from Baron Heinrich vom und zum Stein (1757–1831), who was chief minister in 1807–1808. Although he was dismissed from office in 1808 because of pressure from Napoleon upon the king, Stein's program of reforms was carried on by his successors. Among these, the most important was Baron (later Prince) Karl August von Hardenberg (1750–1822), who served as chief minister beginning in 1810. Stein, and Hardenberg after him, were convinced that Prussia's recovery from the defeat inflicted by Napoleon could occur only as the result of a series of political and institutional reforms comparable, in some respects, to those undertaken by the French during the revolution. After the humiliating defeat of Prussia at Jena in 1806, Hardenberg is alleged to have told the king, "Your Majesty! We must do from above what the French have done from below."[2] By giving its citizens greater opportunity for participation in the affairs of state, Prussia could develop a new patriotic spirit.

Among the reforms were the abolition of serfdom, though landlords retained manorial jurisdiction over the peasants. Some of the more rigid class distinctions were abolished by decrees making it possible for non-nobles to buy land formerly restricted to noble ownership and permitting members of the noble class to go into trade. Stein's Municipal Ordinance of 1808 introduced a system of municipal self-government which permitted towns to control their own affairs through town councils and salaried magistrates. Opportunities in primary and secondary education were broadened by Wilhelm von Humboldt (1767–1835), Prussian minister of education in 1809–1810. Humboldt was also responsible for founding the University of Berlin in 1809. Inspired by a new humanistic educational philosophy, the university became the rallying point of intellectuals seeking Prussia's regeneration and liberation from foreign control. Finally, an important series of reforms in the army was undertaken by Gerhard von Scharnhorst (1755–1813) and Neithardt von Gneisenau (1760–1831), who eliminated some of the barbarous punishments hitherto inflicted upon enlisted men, encouraged promotion by merit in the officer corps, and introduced universal military conscription to create a truly national army. A new emphasis upon infantry and artillery tended to weaken the traditional, feudal character of the Prussian army.

Both Stein and Hardenberg had looked forward to the creation of a legislative assembly as the culmination of this program of reforms, and the king's promise of a constitution establishing some sort of representative government appeared to confirm their hopes. But no constitution was

[2] Quoted by K. S. Pinson, *Modern Germany*, (New York, 1954), p. 33.

The festival of the Burschenschaften at the Wartburg Castle, October 18, 1817. *Engraving by Ferdinand Flor. Some of the students can be seen burning books of anti-nationalist writers in the background.*

forthcoming. After 1815 Hardenberg and others with similar views gradually lost their influence over the king to a more reactionary group. In 1817, when it was announced that the king would form a council of state composed of the royal princes, ministers, heads of departments, and army commanders, the liberals temporarily abandoned their hope for a representative assembly and a constitution. The Prussian government became more efficient than that of any other German state, but it remained absolutist.

Those who had hoped for a closer measure of unity among Germans after the Napoleonic wars were far from satisfied with the Austrian-sponsored Germanic Confederation and resented the particularism of the rulers of the individual states. To spread the ideal of unity and "freedom" for Germans, students organized *Burschenschaften*, or student societies, in a number of German universities. These drew their inspiration from men like Joseph von Görres (1776–1848), an ardent nationalist who edited *Der Rheinische Merkur*; Ernst Moritz Arndt (1769–1860), a poet and Prussian patriot; and Friedrich Ludwig Jahn (1778–1852), who had become famous during the Napoleonic Wars when he organized an association of *Turngemeinden* or gymnastic societies, whose aim was to bring about the physical and moral regeneration of German youth. "Turnvater Jahn" was perhaps the noisiest and most aggressive of the German nationalists of his time and foreshadowed some of the traits of twentieth-century Nazism. Preaching hatred of foreign influence and even of foreign dress, he urged young Germans to return to their Teutonic heritage. His followers wore gray shirts, and he encouraged such unruly behavior as the disruption of lectures by professors who were insufficiently nationalist in their outlook. Jahn was also responsible, along with others, for injecting anti-Semitism into the doctrines of the *Burschenschaften*, though some members of the societies resisted this tendency.

During their brief history the *Burschenschaften* staged a number of popular demonstrations. An assembly in 1817 brought young people from all over Germany to the Wartburg Castle, near Eisenach, where Luther had taken refuge from his persecutors. Timed to coincide with the three-hundredth anniversary of Luther's posting of his ninety-five theses and the fourth anniversary of the German victory at the Battle of Leipzig, the assembly opened with speeches exhorting the students to dedicate their lives to the "holy cause of union and freedom." The group then marched in a torchlight parade to a nearby hilltop to witness the burning of books by conservative and antinationalist writers. Eighteen months later, Karl Sand, a mentally unbalanced theological student who was a *Burschenschaft* member, assassinated the dramatist August von Kotzebue, known for his reactionary views. Sand was condemned to death and Metternich decided the time had come to proceed against the *Burschenschaften*. Acting with representatives of the nine most important German states, Metternich drew up the celebrated Carlsbad Decrees (1819) and submitted them to the diet of the Germanic Confederation for ratification. These decrees dissolved the *Burschenschaften*, set up rigid censorship and press control throughout the Confederation, and created an elaborate system for rooting out subversive individuals in schools and universities.

The enforcement of the Carlsbad Decrees was a serious blow to the liberal and nationalist movements, which had never been very strong, and political opposition to the Metternichian system was practically nonexistent for several years after 1819. With the collaboration of Frederick William III of Prussia, Metternich actively intervened in those states of the Confederation where legislative bodies still existed in order to restrict their influence and to stifle potential opposition. Only in the latter part of the 1820's did nationalist student societies reappear, meeting clandestinely to avoid the secret police.

In 1830 news of the July Revolution in France touched off a flurry of excitement in Germany and inspired minor revolutions in Brunswick, Saxony, and Hesse-Cassel, where the rulers were forced to abdicate in favor of sons or brothers who then granted constitutions to the people. Metternich was convinced that these revolts were part of an international radical conspiracy. In 1832, at an all-German festival at Hambach, twenty-five thousand people drank to Lafayette and denounced the principles of the Holy Alliance; and once again Metternich seized the occasion of a demonstration as the pretext for issuing series of decrees which strengthened the princes in dealing with their parliaments, brought the universities under renewed surveillance, and prohibited all public meetings. Within a year or two, all open opposition had ceased.

Germany in the Vormärz Era: Economic Development Prior to 1848

Because the revolutions that were to disrupt the German states in 1848 occurred in March, the decades in Germany preceding these mid-century upheavals are often referred to as the Vormärz ("pre-March") era. Politically, the 1830's and 1840's were a period of relative stagnation. The German princes, with Metternich's encouragement, clung stubbornly to established institutions and rigorously suppressed dissent. Economically, however, the years between 1815 and 1848 were of great importance for Germany's subsequent progress. Although the development of German industry at this time can hardly be compared with that of Great Britain, France, and Belgium, the groundwork was laid for the major advance that occurred in the second half of the century. Even in these early years, industrial progress was great enough to disturb the existing equilibrium of social forces in certain regions of Germany, thereby creating significant sources of unrest. In addition, the steps taken to break down the economic barriers between the various states of Germany were to have important political as well as economic consequences.

German economic development in the first half of the nineteenth century varied greatly from one region to another. What industrialization there was tended to be concentrated in certain regions, such as the Rhineland and Saxony, while other areas were almost entirely unaffected. Even in Prussia there were vast differences between the Rhine provinces of the west, which enjoyed an industrial development comparable to that of France, and the provinces of the east, where an almost feudal agrarian society persisted well into the nineteenth century. Obstacles to industrialization were many. Although events of the French revolutionary and Napoleonic eras had shattered traditional economic patterns and modes of organization, the period after 1815 brought a revival of the authority of the guilds in many regions, and the handicraft system persisted in most industries. Governments were still dominated by the landed interests, and manufacturers found it difficult to secure the removal of restrictions on business enterprises and trade. Many conservative Germans associated economic liberalism with political liberalism and therefore viewed it with suspicion.

Despite these difficulties significant advances in German industrial development occurred after 1830, particularly in the coal-mining and metallurgical industries. Deep mine shafts were sunk in the Ruhr Valley and coal production increased substantially. By the early 1840's the Krupp works at Essen was producing high-grade steel. Developments in the textile industry were slower since Germany produced mainly linen and woolen cloth, both less adapted to manufacture by machinery than cotton and silk. But there were advances here as well. Industrial growth was supported by new transportation systems; by 1850 the German states could boast of three thousand miles of railroad track, although the first line had been laid only in 1835.

To the German manufacturer or merchant seeking customers beyond his local market, the most serious obstacle was the vast network of tariff barriers that separated the German states and hampered trade even within some of the larger states, such as Prussia. In the early nineteenth century goods shipped from Hamburg, on the North Sea, to Austria had to cross ten different states with ten different customs systems, all exacting transit duties. No wonder the German manufacturer, unlike his French counterpart, was reluctant to produce for national consumption. For this reason the most important single economic development in this era was the establishment of a *Zollverein* ("customs union"), which by 1844 included most of the states of Germany. Prussia took the lead in 1818 by abolishing all tariff barriers among the provinces within its own borders and establishing a uniform tariff rate on imports. Within the next few years Prussia concluded

View of a factory where machinery was manufactured near Munich, 1849.

tariff treaties with a number of neighboring states and provoked the negotiation of similar treaties among some of its rivals. In 1834, seventeen states with a population of 26,000,000, came together in the *Zollverein*, a union which established free trade among them and provided for annual meetings of their delegates. By 1844 all German states except Austria, Hanover, Oldenburg, and the Hanse cities (Hamburg, Bremen, and Lübeck) adhered to the union; the result was a remarkable expansion of the volume of trade among them. Gradually the political implications of this economic collaboration became clear: Prussia's leadership of the *Zollverein* was undermining the hitherto dominant position of the Habsburg monarchy. The *Zollverein* turned out to be of decisive importance in preparing Germany for unification under Prussian leadership.

In estimating the effects of these economic changes upon German society one must remember that as late as 1848 at least two out of three Germans still made their living from the land. Yet even in rural areas the years from 1815 to 1848 were characterized by change and unrest, for in many regions the peasants were trying to adjust to legislation, introduced during the revolutionary and Napoleonic eras, which radically altered their status. Serfdom had been abolished in the parts of Germany under French control and even in some areas, such as Prussia, not annexed by the French. But freedom from personal servitude did not necessarily mean improvement of the peasants' material status, for many were still saddled with manorial dues or other obligations, and only in certain regions and under certain circumstances did they receive clear title to the land they farmed. Indeed, in Prussia the legislation abolishing serfdom strengthened the great landholding *Junker* aristocrat. Freed from his feudal obligation to protect the serf and to provide him with lodging and other necessities of life, the *Junker* took possession of his land and exploited it for his own profit, employing his former serfs, now landless, as agricultural laborers. The condition of the "free" peasant of East Prussia was far worse after his so-called emancipation than before. When the peasant did secure title to a piece of land, it was often so small that he could not farm it productively. Whether the peasant was a freeholder, a tenant farmer, or a landless laborer, he had grievances. And he could hardly hope to secure redress of them from a government dominated by the large landowners.

Among the workers living in the towns and cities, those employed in factories were still in a minority as late as 1848. The majority were artisans working under the traditional handicraft system and it was among this group that there was the greatest unrest. Suffering from the competition of new industries in Germany and abroad, the old craft guilds went into a decline and the artisans found themselves either unemployed or earning starvation-level wages. Their discontent found occasional expression in riots and blind onslaughts upon the machinery which they held responsible for their situation. For example, Silesian linen weavers rioted in 1844, attacking factories and destroying the homes of the owners. By comparison, factory workers in Germany enjoyed steady employment and relatively high wages.

As elsewhere, the impact of industrialism brought a rapid expansion of the middle class during the *Vormärz* era. Neither as large nor as concentrated as the bourgeoisie of England and France, this class assumed in Germany an economic influence far out of proportion to its size. German manufacturers and merchants, denied the right to participate actively in the governing of their respective states, managed to win concessions as their rulers began to be aware of their potential strength. The *Zollverein*, for example, was established largely in response to their pressure. The cause of national unification had no stronger supporters than German businessmen anxious to promote greater efficiency of government and smoother economic operations. A comment in the *Düsseldorfer Zeitung* in 1843 gives an indication of their outlook, "Thus we have instead of one Germany, thirty-eight German states, an equal number of governments, almost the same number of courts, as many representative bodies, thirty-eight distinct legal codes and administrations, embassies and consulates. What an enormous saving it would be, if all of that were taken care of by one central government. . . ." [3]

Comparisons have been made between Germany at the beginning of 1848 and France in 1789, and there are indeed certain superficial resemblances. In both, the nobility was still dominant; if anything, the German nobility was probably more strongly entrenched than its French counterpart under the Old Regime. In both, a rising bourgeoisie had gained significant economic influence but was still excluded from political privileges. In both, there was widespread dissatisfaction among the lower classes, which made them potential supporters of the middle class in the event of revolution. But the parallel begins to break down when one looks at the nature of the grievances of the peasantry and the urban workers. And an even greater difference appears in the organization of the two countries: the decentralization, if not fragmentation, of Germany on the eve of 1848 contrasts markedly with the relatively high degree of centralization in France, where a development in Paris might carry the entire country with it. In the *Vormärz* era Germans were still seeking the unity which the French monarchy had achieved long before 1789.

The Austrian Empire, 1815–1848

Within the Austrian empire proper, Metternich's main problem, though he may not have recognized it, was the emergence of a growing national consciousness among the various peoples under Habsburg rule. This was to remain the central problem for the empire throughout the nineteenth

[3] Quoted by T. S. Hamerow, *Restoration, Revolution, Reaction* (Princeton, N.J., 1958), p. 17.

century and was resolved only with the breaking up of the empire at the end of the First World War. For Austria in 1815 was not a national state like France or Britain, but a collection of peoples and territories united only by their common allegiance to the Habsburg ruler. The broad territorial outlines of the Habsburg empire had been set since the sixteenth century, but only at the beginning of the nineteenth century was it given a name. Until Francis adopted the title emperor of Austria in 1804, anticipating Napoleon's dissolution of the Holy Roman Empire, the territories of Austria were simply referred to as the "lands of the House of Habsburg" or the "lands of the Holy Roman Emperor." Most of the peoples in the empire thought of themselves not as Austrians, but as subjects of the Habsburg emperor.

It is difficult to find agreement on the precise national identities of the peoples that composed the Habsburg empire. However, three major national groups can be specified. The first of these consisted of the Germans; forming no more than a quarter of the population, they were concentrated primarily in the western part of the empire in the old Habsburg lands around Vienna. Large groups of Germans also lived on the fringes of Bohemia, the territory to the north which had once been a separate kingdom, and in all the major cities of the empire. To the extent that there was a middle class in Austria, it was made up of Germans. The growth of German nationalism in the first half of the nineteenth century caused division among the Germans in Austria. The strong nationalists were prepared to sacrifice the Austrian empire, if necessary, in order to join a unified German nation. The moderates hoped to see other states of Germany merge with Austria under the continued rule of the Habsburgs.

The national group second in importance—in influence if not in numbers—consisted of the Magyars, who lived in the crown lands of St. Stephen, in the eastern half of the empire, which included Hungary, Transylvania, and Croatia. The Magyars were proud of their origins, which could be traced to the Middle Ages: their first crowned ruler, Stephen ascended the throne in the year 1001. Traditionally the most independent people in the empire, they maintained their own Diet and their own local administration. Every emperor was still required, by tradition, to go to Budapest to be invested separately with the crown of St. Stephen. Even before 1815, the cultural revival had begun among the Magyars which was to grow into a movement for greater autonomy within the Austrian empire. At the same time, the Magyars constituted a minority in their own lands and were faced with nationalist movements among the Slavic peoples and the other groups subject to them.

The third major group consisted of the Slavs. Including almost half the population of the Austrian empire, the Slavs formed its largest single national group. But they were divided into a number of subgroups and before the nineteenth century had little national consciousness. Of the

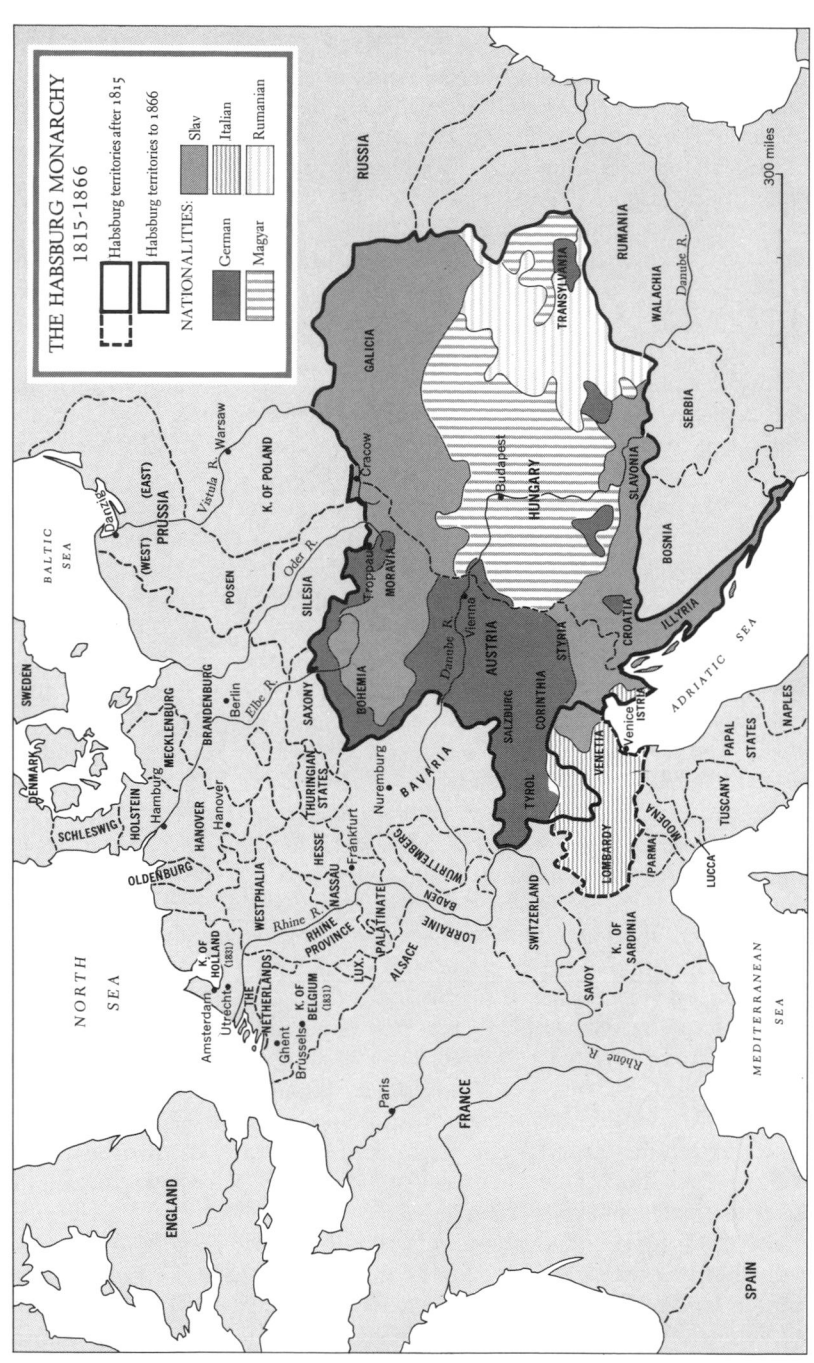

greatest potential political importance among the Slavs were the Poles, who had been attached to the empire only at the end of the eighteenth century and therefore retained a strong sense of national identity, and the Czechs, who had earlier ruled the independent kingdom of Bohemia. Because the great majority of the Slavs were peasants working the estates of German or Magyar masters, their nationalist aspirations were often mingled with social grievances.

To these three major groups should be added the Italians of the provinces of Lombardy and Venetia, which had been annexed to the Habsburg lands by the settlement of 1815, and the Rumanians, a sizable minority concentrated in the eastern part of the Hungarian kingdom.

What policies did Metternich adopt in governing this congeries of peoples under Habsburgs control? In general, he tried to avoid the problems posed by the emerging nationalism, and in the early part of the century, such an attitude served reasonably well. By the 1830's, however, it had become increasingly difficult for the government to ignore the demands of nationalist groups for greater autonomy. Still Metternich did not propose a broad solution; rather he resorted to a number of temporary expedients for neutralizing nationalist sentiment and tried to play off one national group against another. Certainly he did little to forestall the explosion of 1848, which resulted from a combination of nationalism and social discontent. In his defense it may be said that Metternich had the misfortune of serving under two emperors—Francis I and his successor Ferdinand I—who had neither the will nor the capacity to support any program of constructive reform. Ferdinand, in fact, was an imbecile and an epileptic who was allowed to inherit the throne in 1835 because of his father's wish that the direct line of succession not be interrupted. During his reign, which lasted until December, 1848, he was authorized to sign documents presented to him and reacted, on occasion, to events that occurred; but Austria was, in fact, ruled by a body of councillors (of whom Metternich was the most important) acting in the emperors name. But Metternich did not take full advantage of the opportunities this situation offered for exercising his personal control. Indeed, there was much truth in his own admission, "I have governed Europe on occasion; Austria, never."

ITALY: THE BEGINNINGS OF THE RISORGIMENTO, 1815–1848

Events in Italy between 1815 and 1848 were similar in many ways to those in the German states. For the mass of Italians, the change from French to Austrian domination made very little difference. But for the small, educated middle class in the cities of northern Italy and for other groups which had benefited from the introduction of French institutions, the restoration of petty despotic governments taking their directions from

Austria proved a disappointment. Those who had hoped during the Napoleonic era for a closer union among Italian-speaking peoples were reluctant to accept Metternich's view of Italy as a mere "geographical expression." The peninsula was once again divided into a number of lesser states: the kingdom of Naples and Sicily (the Two Sicilies) under the restored Bourbon Ferdinand I; the Papal States, to which Pope Pius VII returned after several years of exile; the smaller principalities of Parma, Modena, and Tuscany, all ruled by relatives of the Austrian emperor who took their directions from Metternich; the provinces of Lombardy and Venetia, directly incorporated into the Austrian empire and administered from Vienna; and the kingdom of Sardinia, ruled until 1821 by Victor Emmanuel I, of the house of Savoy. None of these states possessed constitutions or representative assemblies in 1815 and the restored rulers retained only those French institutions which tended to strengthen their despotic regimes. Then, as now, the northern half of the peninsula was better off economically than the southern. Only in Sardinia, Lombardy, and Venetia was there significant industrialization before 1850, and only in these areas were attempts made to increase agricultural production through experimentation with new techniques.

The failure of the revolutions of 1820–1821 in Naples and Sardinia (discussed in Chapter 3) and the reprisals taken against the rebels tended to weaken and discourage nationalist and liberal opposition. As in Germany, the decade of 1820–1830 saw little overt resistance to established authority, although secret societies like the *Carbonari* continued to operate underground. Again as in Germany, the July Revolution in France was the signal for a series of minor revolts; these occurred in Modena, Parma, and the Papal States, beginning in December, 1830. But unlike their German counterparts, the Italian revolutionaries of 1830–1831 counted on the active support of the new government of Louis Philippe in France, hoping it would oppose any Austrian attempt at intervention. However, Louis Philippe was not willing to risk his international position, and the French Assembly was not prepared to risk a war with Austria. Metternich therefore had a free hand; he sent troops to Modena, Parma, and the Papal States, put down the revolts, and restored their legitimate rulers.

The activities of the revolutionary societies discussed so far constituted the faint beginnings of what came to be known as the *Risorgimento* ("Resurgence"), the movement for Italian national unification. But the failure of the revolutionary movements in 1830–1831, following the suppression of revolts in Naples and Sardinia ten years earlier, tended to discredit the methods of secret societies like the *Carbonari*. The *Risorgimento* entered a new phase in the 1830's, with new leaders and different techniques.

Among the leaders of the *Risorgimento* before 1848, Giuseppe Mazzini

(1805–1872) is unquestionably the most renowned, though recently historians have suggested that classic accounts of the movement for national unification exaggerate his role. With his idealistic, semireligious faith in Italian nationalism, he was undoubtedly the chief inspiration for radical students and intellectuals who hoped to see Italy emerge as a unified republic. Mazzini was born in Genoa, in the kingdom of Sardinia. During his youth he was active in secret societies. In 1821, when he saw refugees streaming northward from Naples after the suppression of the revolt there, he put on a black suit to signify his mourning for the condition of Italy, and he affected this costume for the rest of his life. He participated in the revolts of 1830–1831, and was imprisoned for six months, being released on the condition that he remain outside of Genoa. Instead, he chose exile from all of Italy, and spent most of the remaining forty years of his life in Switzerland, France, and Great Britain. There he wrote inspirational tracts and pamphlets that were circulated in his homeland, and founded Young Italy, the organization particularly associated with his name. The goal of this movement, in which membership was restricted to men under forty living either in Italy or in exile, was the expulsion of foreign tyrants from the Italian peninsula and the establishment of a united republic. However, Mazzini's skills at organization and administration fell short of his ability as a propagandist, and his few attempts to foment uprisings in his native land failed.

Schooled in the writings of the French revolutionaries, Mazzini believed strongly in the principle of popular sovereignty. At the same time, he felt that during the French Revolution the *rights* of man had been emphasized too much and his *duties* too little. Drawing on the heritage of Rousseau and to some extent on the German idealist tradition, he was convinced that a person could be happy only while devoting himself to a collective enterprise. In the work which he appropriately called *The Duties of Man* (published in two parts, 1844 and 1858), Mazzini argued that the highest collective enterprise to which the individual could dedicate his life was the nation. In a lyrical passage typical of his prose, he wrote, "O my Brothers! love your Country. Our Country is our home, the home which God has given us, placing therein a numerous family which we love and are loved by, and with which we have a more intimate and quicker communion of feeling and thought than with others; a family which by its concentration upon a given spot, and by the homogeneous nature of its elements, is destined for a special kind of activity." Yet important as love for the nation was to Mazzini, he regarded national loyalty as part of a higher duty toward "Humanity," to whom men owed primary allegiance. "You are *men* before you are either *citizens* or *fathers*." The nation was for him the vehicle through which men fulfilled their obligations toward humanity as a whole. His concern for other nationalities led him to found in 1834 a movement known as Young Europe, which was to establish national committees for patriotic agitation in Germany, Poland, and Switzerland. Mazzini was convinced that by encouraging nationalist movements among the peoples still divided or living under foreign domination, he was working toward the day when all nations, having realized their national aspirations, would work for humanity at large. For this reason Mazzini is often viewed as the prophet of the ideals that President Woodrow Wilson (1856–1924) tried to embody in the peace settlement of 1919: national self-determination and the association of all peoples in a League of Nations.

Many Italians who desired the unification of the peninsula viewed Mazzini as a dangerous radical whose ideal of a democratic republic implied social revolution and a threat to property. Some of these rallied to the Neo-Guelph movement, which took its name from the papal faction in the medieval struggle between popes and emperors. The principal impetus to the Neo-Guelph cause came from the publication in 1843 of *The Civil and Moral Primacy of the Italians,* by Vincenzo Gioberti (1801–1852), which called for the establishment of a federation of Italian states under the leadership of the papacy, with executive authority vested in a college of princes. To those who were skeptical about the willingness of the pope to lead a crusade for Italian unity, the election of a new pope in 1846 seemed to offer hope, for the man who took the name Pius IX had a reputation as a liberal. His initial measures in the Papal States—granting an amnesty to political offenders and relaxing restrictions on freedom of speech and of the press—suggested that he might indeed become the rallying point for a liberal Italian federation.

A third faction working for the cause of unification consisted of the so-called Moderates, most active in the kingdom of Sardinia, with supporters in Lombardy and Venetia. Principally liberal nobles and members of the bourgeoisie, the Moderates looked to Sardinia for leadership in unification and foresaw the establishment of a constitutional monarchy. They believed that economic unification had to precede political unity. Accordingly, they strove for the elimination of tariff barriers and the stimulation of commerce among the Italian states. While urging industrial development, they nevertheless realized that they must concentrate on improving and modernizing agricultural methods since farming was still Italy's principal industry. Young aristocrats like Count Camillo Benso di Cavour (1810–1861), later prime minister of Sardinia, set up model farms and established agricultural societies to disseminate knowledge of new techniques. Some historians argue that the efforts of northern Italian liberals and Moderates for economic reform contributed more than all the progaganda of Mazzini toward the unification of the peninsula.[4] An elite of educated, influential

---

[4] For example, Kent R. Greenfield, *Economics and Liberalism in the Risorgimento* (Baltimore, 1934).

individuals in a number of Italian states became accustomed to exchanging ideas and collaborating in the attainment of certain limited goals. Their efforts were partially rewarded when Charles Albert, the king of Sardinia, lowered tariffs, reformed the finances of his country, and officially encouraged agricultural improvements, but his liberalism did not extend to political matters until the eve of the revolutions of 1848.

Thus, at least three different movements had been organized in the peninsula before 1848, each working in its own way for greater unity among the Italian peoples. Yet it should be emphasized that the strength of the Neo-Guelphs and the Moderates was concentrated almost exclusively in the northern regions of Italy and that even Mazzini's Young Italy won the support of only a small minority of the population. As yet most Italians were untouched by the *Risorgimento*.

RUSSIA

Alexander I and the Decembrist Revolt of 1825

Despite her reputation as an "enlightened" monarch, Catherine the Great (ruler of Russia from 1762 to 1796) never relaxed her control over her subjects. At the beginning of the nineteenth century, Russia was the most autocratic of the European states. Catherine's son Paul I (ruled 1796–1801) recognized no limitations on his authority and possessed a strong sense of his position as a divine-right monarch. To a foreign envoy he is supposed to have remarked, "Know that no one in Russia is important except the person who is speaking with me; and that, only while he is speaking." In practice, however, the authority of the tsar had certain limits. One of them resulted simply from the size of the vast empire under his rule; it extended from the Baltic Sea to the Caucasus, from the borders of Poland to the Pacific. With the modes of transportation and communication then

View of Moscow from a terrace in the Kremlin. *Engraving by Gabriel Lory, 1799.*

in existence, it was impossible for the central government to extend its control into every corner of the realm.

Recognizing the danger to absolutism posed by western ideas and influences, Paul did his best to isolate Russia, restricting foreign travel by his subjects and forbidding the importation of European, and particularly French, books. He rightly estimated that the greatest threat to his autocratic control came not from the masses—peasants and serfs—but rather from the educated aristocracy, which had been exposed to French culture during the reign of Catherine. And indeed, it was this group that brought his brief tyrannical reign to an end. In 1801 he was assassinated by a cabal of aristocrats seeking to bring to the throne his twenty-four-year-old son Alexander, whose outlook was known to be much more liberal than his father's.

As we have seen, Tsar Alexander I was an unstable figure, characterized by changing moods and inconsistent actions. Viewed by some as a hypocrite and a traitor to the ideals of his youth, he seems rather to have been genuinely torn between the liberal, humanitarian impulses acquired during his unorthodox schooling and the more traditional authoritarian policies of his father. His struggle against the armies of Napoleon undoubtedly contributed to his abandonment of liberal projects after 1812. But in 1801 his accession was welcomed by those who hoped for a liberalization of the regime, and they took heart from his immediate relaxation of many of the restrictions Paul had imposed. At the outset, Alexander surrounded himself with an "unofficial committee" of advisers, men of known liberal views like Frédéric César de La Harpe (his former tutor) and Prince Adam Czartoryski, the Polish patriot who served for a time as foreign minister. The task of this committee was no less than to bring about the regeneration of Russia, and Alexander made it clear to his intimates that the granting of a constitution and the abolition of the institution of serfdom were important parts of his overall program. Despite these laudable intentions, the reforms he did in fact achieve were very limited, partly because he and his advisers failed to appreciate the complexities and practical difficulties involved. The reforms actually carried through were made in two periods in the first half of Alexander's reign, each brought to an end by the renewal of the war against Napoleon.

The most significant reforms of the first period (1801–1805) included changes in the governmental structure, among them the establishment of western-style ministries each headed by a minister responsible to the tsar; the founding of six new universities; and an increase in the number of secondary schools. As for Russia's principal social problem, serfdom, no substantial steps toward abolition were undertaken, probably because the tsar and his advisers were reluctant to mount a full-scale attack on the privileges of the landed aristocracy. However, a government decree of 1803 encouraged the voluntary liberation of serfs by their masters under government supervision. Although fewer than fifty thousand male serfs (about 1 per cent of the total serf population) were freed during Alexander's reign, this was the first step toward the emancipation in 1861.

The second period of reforms (1807–1812) was dominated by Count Mikhail Speranski (1772–1839), who served as a kind of unofficial prime minister to the tsar during these years. The results were again disappointing to those who expected any significant change in the character of the regime. Instructed to draft a constitution, Speranski prepared a moderate scheme which would have introduced self-government in stages, beginning with electoral assemblies at the local level and culminating with a state assembly at the top. However, his plan did not envisage giving real legislative initiative to the state assembly; the law-making powers were to rest rather with a council of state composed of high dignitaries and presided over by the tsar. The establishment of the council of state was, in fact, the only part of the proposal that was realized. Whatever additional reforms Speranski undertook resulted from his thorough familiarity with Russia's bureaucracy, and tended toward improving the efficiency of its operation.

Even if Napoleon had not invaded Russia in 1812, it is doubtful whether Speranski would have remained in office much longer. For in an effort to meet the serious financial crisis from which the Russian government was suffering, he proposed financial reforms and new taxes that aroused the bitter antagonism of the landed nobility. Branded a "Russian Jacobin" by his opponents, he was suddenly dismissed by Alexander in 1812 and sent into exile. He was later recalled to government service and became a member of the council of state in 1821.

Speranski's dismissal did not result in a sudden reversal of imperial policy. The transition from liberalism to reaction was rather gradual and uneven, reflecting the tsar's erratic and even inconsistent behavior. In general, Alexander appeared more liberal abroad and in the outlying parts of his empire than he was at home. To the Polish state reconstituted under Russian hegemony by the Congress of Vienna he gave a liberal constitution modeled in part on Speranski's proposal which had been rejected for Russia. The constitution of 1818 guaranteed individual liberties, including free speech and a free press, and provided for a diet to be elected on a broad franchise. Poland was permitted to maintain its own army and administrative personnel and to use Polish as the official language.

In St. Petersburg, however, the nobility of an older generation—some of whom had been associated with Tsar Paul's government—recovered influence, particularly after 1815, and the regime became increasingly repressive. The changed policy was felt especially in the educational system, which served as a kind of barometer of reaction in nineteenth-century Russia. Universities and schools were put under the control of religious bigots who established an elaborate system of surveillance, expelled professors on the slightest pretext, and prohibited study at foreign universities. Censorship regulations were complex, arbitrary, and absurd. The government not only forbade writing on political and constitutional questions but also sought to pass judgment on the alleged morality or immorality of artistic productions. The measure that aroused the most widespread resentment, however, was the establishment in 1816 of military colonies. Their original purpose was to reduce the cost of keeping an army by setting up self-supporting units of soldiers and their families to cultivate the land. But in many areas peasants were put into uniform and subjected, along with their families, to strict military discipline under the command of troops from the regular army. Bitterly resented by the peasants, the military colonies provoked movements of protest and became one of the principal grievances of opponents of the regime.

The mounting reaction of the last decade of Alexander's reign could hardly fail to arouse opposition among member of the educated classes who had placed such high hopes in the young monarch. Numerous influences helped to create this liberal opposition. To the influx of western ideas during Catherine's reign was added the stimulation of French revolutionary doctrines. During the wars against Napoleon, Russian officers and soldiers, exposed to other European cultures, could not help contrasting the relative freedom of the average western European with the absence of liberty at home. Disappointed by Alexander's failure to provide Russia with a constitution or representative institutions, they were frustrated by their inability to express their criticisms openly. Almost inevitably the opposition was forced to act after 1815 through the secret societies that eventually engineered what has come to be known as the Decembrist Revolt.

From the outset two general tendencies were present in the movement for reform. The more moderate aims eventually found expression in the Northern Union, a group composed primarily of young aristocrats and literary men who sought to establish a constitutional monarchy on the British model. More radical measures were favored by the Southern Union, consisting mainly of impoverished army officers and led by Colonel Paul Pestel, who advocated the assassination of the tsar and the establishment of a highly centralized republican regime patterned after the Jacobin dictatorship of 1793. In some respects Pestel anticipated the Soviet regime. He favored drastic powers for the revolutionary government, to prevent counterrevolution. His program of agrarian reform included the abolition of serfdom and the state confiscation of all land. Thereafter, the land would be divided into a public and a private sector and every citizen would be guaranteed his allotment within the public sector.

The two societies were not tightly organized or disciplined, and little was done to coordinate their activities. The sudden death of Tsar Alexander I late in 1825 found them ill prepared for the revolt which followed, triggered

St. Petersburg. *Parade in front of the royal palace. From a print made in 1815.*

by the confusion that arose over the succession. Constantine, the brother nearest in age to Alexander, was serving as governor-general of Poland and had secretly renounced his claim to the throne in 1823 in favor of the youngest brother, Nicholas. When Alexander died, each proclaimed the other tsar, and a period of uncertainty ensued. Since Nicholas was known to be much more conservative than his older brother, the insurgent leaders of the Northern Union decided to press for the accession of Constantine and in December persuaded two thousand troops of the St. Petersburg garrison to refuse their allegiance to Nicholas. The soldiers marched to the Senate Square shouting "Constantine and Constitution," with many of them apparently under the impression that Constitution was Constantine's wife. Once on the square they were given no further orders, and remained there in the cold all day. It was Nicholas who finally took action, bringing in loyal troops who fired upon the mutinous soldiers and killed many of them. Another uprising, by the Southern Union, also failed.

Not only was the Decembrist Revolt of 1825 badly prepared and badly led; it also lacked real popular support. Its only immediate consequence was to intensify the new tsar's antiliberal sentiments. Hundreds of those involved were arrested, and five of the leaders, including Pestel, were summarily tried and executed. Nevertheless it was a significant episode in Russian history, for it marked the first open challenge to Russian autocracy and this challenge came from some of the best-educated men in Russia— young army officers, including some of the elite Grenadier Guard, and representatives of the liberal nobility. Most important of all, it provided a revolutionary legend and a host of martyrs, for later groups that sought the overthrow of the tsarist regime.

Russia under Nicholas I, 1825–1855

Tsar Nicholas I, who assumed the throne during the Decembrist Revolt and ruled Russia until 1855, is traditionally viewed as the most reactionary of Russia's nineteenth-century autocrats. Strongly impressed by the events at the outset of his reign, he was determined to prevent their recurrence. Personally meticulous and conscientious in the performance of his duties, he carried out a prolonged investigation of the origins of the revolt, interrogating prisoners himself in some instances in order to get an idea of the true nature of the opposition. But this activity, which might have led to reform or the elimination of abuses, resulted instead in an intensification of the repressive policies pursued in the later years of Alexander's reign. Indeed, Nicholas developed an almost pathological fear of revolution at home and abroad, leading contemporary liberals to call him the Gendarme of Europe.

Under Nicholas an attempt was made to freeze the social structure of Russia by discouraging or actively preventing members of any but the upper classes from securing an education. The educational system itself was put under even closer surveillance and suffered a further decline of standards. S.S. Uvarov, Nicholas' minister of education for the better part of his reign, formulated the principles to be inculcated by the schools: autocracy (a belief in the unlimited powers of the tsar), orthodoxy (adherence to the official church and the morality for which it stood), and nationalism (devotion to the traditions of "Russian national life").

Tsar Nicholas I.

Nicholas' particular innovation was the concentration of power in His Majesty's Own Chancery, a bureau that had originally been organized to deal with matters requiring the sovereign's personal participation. He expanded the functions of this body and divided it into several sections. One of these, the notorious Third Section, or political police, was given almost unlimited powers of surveillance over every aspect of Russian life, with the duty of arresting and exiling any "suspicious or dangerous persons," of reporting on the state of public opinion, and of keeping a close watch on all foreigners living or traveling in Russia. The tsar particularly distrusted the intelligentsia—largely writers, teachers, and liberal nobles—since many of them had been involved in the secret societies. The system of preliminary censorship (which required approval by the government censor of all written material before publication) was particularly intense after the revolutions of 1830–1831 and the revolutions of 1848, and effectively stifled the discussion of all political or potentially dangerous social questions.

It is tempting to compare the police state of Nicholas I with the totalitarian regimes of the twentieth century, but such a parallel is false and misleading. In the first place, tsarist control was limited by its own inefficiency. When Nicholas broadened his chancery and established the Third Section, he left numerous existing bureaus and administrative units intact; consequently there was extensive overlapping of functions and confusion of jurisdiction. Second, though the elaborate censorship made clear what subjects were forbidden, it did not attempt to prescribe the subjects writers *should* discuss. The atmosphere of Russia under Nicholas was unquestionably stifling, yet this era paradoxically saw the beginning of Russia's golden age of literature, and counted among its luminaries the poets Alexander Pushkin (1799–1837) and Mikhail Lermontov (1814–1841), the novelist and dramatist Nikolai Gogol (1809–1852), and finally the novelists Ivan Turgenev (1818–1883) and Fëdor Dostoevski (1821–1881), some of whose earlier works were published during Nicholas' reign. True, both Turgenev and Dostoevski were arrested in the reaction following the revolutions of 1848, but until then they had been left relatively undisturbed. As long as writers avoided discussion of proscribed subjects and direct criticism of the autocratic regime, they were allowed to publish their works.

Despite these compensating features, which made Nicholas' reign less oppressive than it has sometimes been thought, the refusal of the tsar to deal with such basic problems as the discontent of the serfs, the low productivity of the farms, and the backwardness of technology and communications meant that Russia lagged seriously behind the western European nations in economic and social development. Its weaknesses in this respect were illustrated dramatically at the end of Nicholas' reign when Russia suffered defeat by France and Great Britain in the Crimean War (1854–1856).

Blindfolded Polish rebels are interrogated by Russian officers, 1830.

Though Nicholas did succeed in preventing further revolts in Russia, he was faced in 1830 by an uprising in Poland, which drastically altered the status of that country. As we have seen, the kingdom of Poland sanctioned by the Congress of Vienna had received from Tsar Alexander I one of the most liberal constitutions in Europe. In practice, however, the autonomy of the Poles was restricted and the will of the diet thwarted by Alexander's brother, Constantine (1779–1831), who commanded the Polish army and interfered frequently in the administration of the country. Compared with the Russians or with those Poles living in territory directly annexed by Russia, the inhabitants of "Congress Poland" were well off; but the violation of their constitution by the tsar, combined with a revival of Polish national sentiment after 1815, made them restive even during Alexander's reign. With the accession of Nicholas in 1825, tension between the Poles and their Russian masters increased. In November, 1830, when a rumor circulated that the tsar was about to march a joint Russian-Polish army into France and Belgium to suppress the revolutions there, a group of army cadets supported by university students revolted in Warsaw.

Only a handful of rebels was involved at first, but the departure of the Grand Duke Constantine opened the way for the establishment of a provisional government dominated by Polish landed aristocrats. Had the Poles been unified, their revolution might well have succeeded, for they controlled a well-disciplined military force. But after the initial victory the revolutionaries divided into the Whites, feudal aristocrats who tried to negotiate with the tsar for moderate reforms, and the Reds, a more radical element drawn from the gentry, who opposed any sort of compromise. The peasants who constituted the mass of the population saw no reason to support the revolt since they had been exploited by both landowning groups. The Polish rebels had counted strongly upon intervention on their behalf by France or Britain, since liberals in these states were clamoring loudly for support of the Polish cause, but neither government was willing to commit itself to such action.

The Poles did win some initial victories, but in September, 1831, the Russians captured Warsaw and ended the revolt. Ruthless reprisals were taken by Nicholas. The constitution granted by Alexander was withdrawn, thousands of Poles were executed or banished to western Europe, and Poland was governed thenceforth by what amounted to a military dictatorship.

Despite two successive waves of revolution, in the early 1820's and in 1830–1831, the Restoration was still intact after 1830 and the old order persisted in most of Europe up to 1848. Only in France, Belgium, and Greece had successful revolutions occurred, and in the latter two, the revolutionaries had succeeded because they were supported by certain of the Great Powers. Great Britain, of course, underwent important changes in her institutions, particularly after 1830. Elsewhere in Europe—in Spain and Portugal, in some of the German states, on the Italian peninsula, in Russia and Poland—revolutions had collapsed or been suppressed. Despite the rallying power of liberal ideals and goals, the revolutionaries had proved no match for the regimes they challenged. Against the secret societies composed of disaffected soldiers, liberal nobles, artisans, students, teachers, writers, and adventurers the rulers could usually muster loyal troops, and they could count on the backing of nobility and clergy in the suppression of the revolts. Often a lack of unity among the revolutionaries, along with poor organization and leadership, turned initial victory into defeat.

But the strength of the dissatisfied groups continued to mount after 1830 under the impact of the two most powerful forces of the age: the Industrial Revolution, which was significantly changing Europe's economic and social structure by bringing new classes into existence and weakening old ones; and the legacy of the French Revolution, which continued to inspire opponents of the old regimes with the ideals of liberty, equality, and fraternity.

CHAPTER 7

The Revolutions of 1848

ON JANUARY 12, 1848, the people of Palermo revolted against their ruler, Ferdinand II, since 1830 king of Naples and Sicily. At the moment, the uprising attracted little attention; yet it was the first of almost fifty revolutions that occurred within the first four months of 1848, disturbances that rocked France, Austria, Prussia, and almost all of the lesser German and Italian states. By April, 1848, no European ruler appeared to be safe on his throne, and Tsar Nicholas I, horrified at the spread of revolution, could write to the English queen, Victoria: "What remains standing in Europe? Great Britain and Russia."[1] Despite differences in language and nationality, in political and economic development, the countries of Europe showed remarkable uniformity in their response to the revolutionary impulse.

Tensions had been mounting throughout the 1830's and 1840's. In France there had been growing resentment of Guizot's manipulation of the electoral machinery, his corruption of the deputies, and his almost total disregard of the distress of the working class. In the German states the bourgeoisie had long been dissatisfied by the continued political division, and the handicraft workers and peasants had been suffering economic deprivation. Within the Habsburg empire and Italy nationalist aspirations had been continually thwarted. With all this combustible material, only a spark was needed to set off the conflagration. A particularly acute economic crisis helped to precipitate the revolutions. The crisis had its origins in low grain production in Britain and Europe in 1845 and 1846 and in the failure of the potato crop in Ireland in 1845. Harvests in the British Isles improved somewhat in 1847, but in France and Germany they were again bad. Food prices, particularly the price of bread, the staple of the lower classes' diet,

---

[1] Quoted by L. B. Namier, *1848: The Revolution of the Intellectuals* (London, 1946), p. 3.

rose markedly during 1847. The crisis in agriculture had repercussions in the world of finance, with bankruptcies and bank closings. In France, where industrial expansion had not been accompanied by a corresponding development of new markets, overproduction in a number of industries led to falling prices for manufactured goods, business failures, and widespread unemployment.

Many have asserted, however, that the revolutions of 1848 were born of hope as much as of despair. Behind them was a whole range of ideals and aspirations for a better world. So pervasive was the idealism of the revolts that it has been argued that they had a common denominator in a uniform ideological outlook developed during the first half of the nineteenth century. Thus, Sir Lewis Namier refers to the events of 1848 as "the Revolution of the Intellectuals." Yet there was no single revolutionary organization or movement encompassing all of Europe, and although revolutionaries everywhere mouthed similar phrases and slogans, the words meant quite different things to different peoples. A broad spectrum of goals motivated the revolutionaries of 1848.

In general, all of the revolutions took much the same course. Though France's February Revolution followed the revolt in Palermo by more than a month, it was this outbreak in Paris that sparked revolts elsewhere in Europe, and the subsequent fate of the revolution in France seemed to foreshadow developments in central Europe. The overthrow of Louis Philippe in February triggered successful revolts during March, first in the Austrian empire, then in many of the lesser German states, and finally in Prussia. During the same period revolts spread northward in the Italian peninsula from Naples and Sicily into Sardinia, Tuscany, the Papal States, and finally the regions directly under Austrian control. In this initial stage the frightened rulers capitulated with practically no resistance to the revolutionary demands, promising their subjects constitutions and representative assemblies and hastily granting the freedoms which had been denied their peoples. Unlike Louis Philippe, the central European rulers managed to retain their thrones while their more unpopular ministers were dismissed or, like Metternich, forced to flee. For the moment the revolutionaries appeared triumphant.

The turning point in the course of the revolts came during the summer of 1848. In France, an insurrection of disillusioned workers against the new government in June was decisively defeated. The victory of "forces of order" in France encouraged counterrevolutionary forces elsewhere in Europe. In most instances the armies of the central European states had remained loyal to their respective rulers during the revolts, and now they were ordered to attack the revolutionaries, whose ranks were weakened by the divisions that inevitably appeared after their initial successes. In this counterrevolutionary assault the rulers were supported by the landowning aristocracy and in some states also by elements of the bourgeoisie who, though they had participated on the side of the revolutionaries at the outset, were now alarmed at the possibility of thoroughgoing social revolution.

By December, 1848, the revolutionaries had been defeated or were fighting rearguard actions almost everywhere in Europe. The overthrown dynasty was not restored in France, but in December the first presidential election under the new republican constitution resulted in an overwhelming victory for Louis Napoleon Bonaparte, who emerged as a savior and symbol of order for many Frenchmen frightened by the bloodshed and social upheaval that had occurred earlier in the year. Another eight months passed before the Habsburg monarchy, with the aid of Russian troops, suppressed the revolt in Hungary. In the early months of 1849 the Sardinians renewed their struggle against Austria for the liberation of Italian territory, and elsewhere in the peninsula the Roman Republic was proclaimed. But these were short-lived episodes which merely prolonged the revolutionary agony but could not reverse the general trend. By the end of 1849 the counterrevolution was everywhere triumphant. To the bitterly disillusioned revolutionaries it seemed that nothing had been gained. In fact, the situation in many countries appeared worse than it had been before the revolts. Where constitutions had been granted they were either suspended or rendered ineffectual. Revolutionary leaders were imprisoned or exiled and the freedoms for which they had fought were systematically denied.

Such were the general outlines of this period of upheaval. But a closer look at the separate revolutions is needed, for 1848 proved to be a watershed in the history of nineteenth-century Europe; in the writings and speeches of the 1850's a new atmosphere can be detected, setting this decade off from those which preceded it.

THE FEBRUARY REVOLUTION IN FRANCE

On January 29, 1848, a little more than three weeks before revolution erupted in France, Alexis de Tocqueville (1805–1859), a noted writer and member of the parliamentary opposition, addressed his colleagues in the Chamber of Deputies:

...I am told that there is no danger because there are no riots; I am told that, because there is no visible disorder on the surface of society, there is no revolution at hand. Gentlemen, permit me to say that I believe you are mistaken. True, there is no actual disorder; but it has entered deeply into men's minds. See what is preparing itself amongst the working classes, who, I grant, are at present quiet. No doubt they are not disturbed by political passions, properly so-called, to the same extent that they have been; but can you not see that their passions, instead of political, have become social? Do you not see that they are gradually forming opinions and ideas which are destined not only to upset this or that law, ministry, or even form of government, but society itself, until it totters upon the foundations on which it rests today? . . . This, gentlemen, is my profound conviction: I believe that we are at this moment sleeping on a volcano. I am profoundly convinced of it. . . .[2]

De Tocqueville's speech was greeted with ironical cheers from the majority; no one took seriously his prophecy of catastrophe.

Yet signs of the forthcoming troubles were certainly not lacking. The combination of food shortages, a rising cost of living, and widespread unemployment had led to an increasing number of working-class demonstrations during the winter of 1847–1848. Sometimes sheer hunger was to blame. Yet because the workers were not effectively organized, their demonstrations attracted relatively little attention. The most obvious expressions of opposition to the July Monarchy were banquets to popularize the cause of electoral reform. Political leaders, frustrated in their attempt to effect changes through normal legislative channels and forbidden by law from organizing political rallies, used the device of the dinner meeting to focus opposition to the regime. Participating in these dinners were not only members of the so-called parliamentary opposition, such as Adolphe Thiers, but also men of known republican views. Some seventy banquets were held all over France during the winter, and this campaign was to culminate in a large banquet scheduled for February 22, 1848, in Paris. On the very day of the banquet, Guizot's government banned both the dinner and the procession that was to precede it. This was the episode that precipitated the revolution.

The revolt lasted only four days. At first the crowds that gathered on the Paris boulevards were dispersed without difficulty. Gradually the movement gathered momentum, as regiments of the bourgeois National Guard joined the opposition. Inhabitants of working-class districts began to tear up the paving stones in the streets in order to erect barricades.

Louis Philippe, now seventy-five, refused to take the first demonstrations seriously. But by February 23 the situation had become so acute that he dismissed the unpopular Guizot and replaced him with an old personal friend, Count Louis Molé (1781–1855). Guizot's dismissal might have placated the middle-class opposition; it did not satisfy the Parisian working class, which became ever more radical in its demands. By February 24 the situation in the capital was so serious that the king decided to abdicate in favor of his ten-year-old grandson, the count of Paris. But his decision came too late, for the popular forces now controlled most of the city and were approaching the Tuileries, the royal residence. The king escaped through the garden to a waiting carriage, which started him toward exile in England.

A crucial point in the revolution had been reached. The symbol of authority was gone, and the new form of the French government had to be determined. The Chamber of Deputies was still in session, and the king's daughter-in-law, the duchess of Orléans, decided to attempt to have herself

[2] Alexis de Tocqueville, *The Recollections of Alexis de Tocqueville*, trans. by Alexander Teixeira de Mattos (London, 1948), pp. 12–13.

The February Days in Paris. *Revolutionaries, ill equipped with arms.*

proclaimed regent for the count of Paris. When the duchess appeared on the rostrum with the young count and her brother-in-law, the duke of Nemours, the poet-turned-politician Alphonse de Lamartine (1790–1869) was speaking. Some members of a mob had forced their way into the assembly hall and stood menacingly at the rear, behind the deputies. The fate of the royal family rested with Lamartine, who at this point abandoned the dynasty and declared his support of a republic. The crowd responded by swarming over the hall; deputies retreated hastily, and the duchess fled with her son. In this chaos a provisional government was chosen. As Lamartine read aloud names that had been proposed for the new government, the mob shouted its acceptance or rejection of each, in a kind of impromptu election. When the list was complete, the crowd adjourned to the Hôtel de Ville, where revolutionary ritual demanded that the republic be proclaimed.

Those who had been named to the provisional government at the Chamber of Deputies were moderate republicans, men generally sympathetic to the program advocated by the republican newspaper *Le National*, which had called for electoral reform in the last years of the July Monarchy. When they arrived at the Hôtel de Ville, however, they found a delegation from a more radical republican newspaper, *La Réforme*, which was far more concerned than *Le National* with social issues. Since the radical republican group had named its own provisional government, the two lists had to be combined. To the original moderate republicans, therefore, were added three men supported by the radical faction: the socialist Louis Blanc, a mechanic named Albert, and the astronomer François Arago.

In the moment of victory the moderate and the radical republicans had closed ranks and agreed on the provisional government for the Second French Republic. But in the months that followed the cleavage between the two factions broadened. The moderates were concerned primarily with political questions, such as the nature of representation, qualifications for suffrage, and the working of the electoral system. The radicals, while they did not neglect political issues, talked largely of social reform. They had no well-formulated program—indeed, their proposals were vague and amorphous —but their basic concern was improvement of the condition of the working classes. The history of the first four months of the republic is the history of a growing divergence between the moderate republicans, who had the confidence of a majority of the French, and the radical republicans, who had the support of the Paris working class.

One question which confronted the provisional government immediately, and about which moderates and radicals disagreed, was what to do with the vast numbers of unemployed who were concentrated in Paris and who had contributed to the success of the revolution. One of the few coherent demands of the members of the Paris mob in the February Revolution had been for recognition of the "right to work"; they expected the new government to provide employment for all who wanted it. Pressed by the Paris mob for an immediate solution, the provisional government announced the establishment of "National Workshops," on the pattern outlined by the socialist Louis Blanc in his *Organization of Labor*. It would have seemed natural to confide the direction of this project to Blanc himself, especially since he was already a member of the new government. But the task of establishing the National Workshops was given to Alexandre Marie, the minister of public works, while Louis Blanc was sidetracked in a newly created "Workers' Commission." Instead of being autonomous cooperative enterprises operated by the workers, as envisioned by Blanc, the National Workshops became in fact vast relief projects in which the unemployed were put to work on hastily contrived road-construction jobs. To complicate matters, the number of unemployed far exceeded the number of jobs the government was able to provide and the surplus laborers were put on what amounted to a dole. Although the moderate republicans in the government may have been sincere in their desire to provide jobs, their decision to entrust the program to Marie, an avowed antisocialist, proved that they had no intention of making the National Workshops the nucleus of a social transformation. Instead, one of their motives was to immobilize the Paris mob and thus avert the threat of further social revolution. Ironically, this is precisely what they failed to do. The enrollment in the National Workshops jumped from an initial 10,000 in March, to 70,000 in April, 100,00 in May, and an estimated 120,000 in June. Unable to provide employment for such vast numbers, the government discovered it had created a huge army of idle proletarians in Paris ready to support radical leaders and demagogues in further demands upon the republic.

The split between moderates and radicals was further widened in a national election held on April 23, to name the National Assembly, which was to draw up a constitution for the republic. In the general state of euphoria immediately following the February Revolution, the provisional government had proclaimed universal manhood suffrage. By a stroke of a pen the electorate was increased from the 200,000 qualified to vote by the end of the July Monarchy to 9,000,000. How would this vastly expanded electorate vote? The results of the election showed the essentially moderate and even conservative character of the country as a whole as opposed to the radical complexion of the capital. Out of nine hundred seats, approximately five hundred went to moderate republicans and only one hundred to radicals. Most surprisingly, the remaining three hundred seats were won by avowed monarchists, supporters of either the Legitimist Bourbon dynasty or the recently overthrown Orléanist succession. The elections had proved conclusively that the provinces of France were far more conservative than the capital; the French peasantry, alarmed by radical statements that implied a threat to property, had united with the bourgeoisie against the radical republicans and the Paris proletariat. The new five-man executive committee chosen by the National Assembly to replace the provisional government included no representative of the working class. Indeed, Lamartine, the committee's head, was an outspoken opponent of Blanc.

In the face of direct defeat in the elections, the workers of Paris staged a demonstration on May 15 that looked at first like a repetition of the February Revolution. Again the workers overpowered guards and invaded the hall where the assembly was meeting. After listening to harangues by Armand Barbès and Auguste Blanqui, leaders of two revolutionary clubs, they moved to the Hôtel de Ville, where a provisional government was proclaimed. But the established government was better prepared than its predecessor had been in February and used the National Guard and a newly formed mobile guard to clear the assembly hall and reoccupy the Hôtel de Ville. Barbès, Blanqui, and a number of other leaders were imprisoned, and their radical clubs were dissolved. The abortive uprising increased the government's fear of the left and precipitated a decision to dissolve the National Workshops. Anticipating a violent reaction, the government delayed announcing the liquidation of the workshops until reinforcements had been mobilized. On June 22, just four months after the outbreak of the February Revolution, the termination of the National Workshops was proclaimed. The reaction of the Paris workers was immediate and spontaneous. Disillusioned by the government's failure to fulfill its promise of work for all, many workers disobeyed the order to disband and took up arms instead. So began the bloody June Days.

In February workers and members of the lesser bourgeoisie had fought side by side. Now the class lines between them were rigidly drawn. For three days Europe witnessed some of the bloodiest street fighting of the nineteenth century, as the Paris proletariat battled the government forces. A state of martial law was declared in the capital and General Louis Cavaignac (1802–1857), former governor of Algeria, became virtual dictator of Paris. Benefiting from the experiences of 1830 and of February, 1848, Cavaignac allowed the fighting to spread before moving in with guns trained on the barricades. At the end of three days, the toll of dead and injured was estimated at ten thousand. And this was not all. Cavaignac used his emergency powers to carry out vigorous reprisals against those suspected of leading the insurrection. Most of the eleven thousand prisoners taken were deported to the French colony of Algeria. Cavaignac could boast that order had been restored.

The June Days constituted a clear-cut victory for the moderate republicans over the radicals. But it was an expensive victory, for it left great bitterness among the working classes and opened up wounds that took many years to heal. The propertied classes were convinced that they had barely escaped the overthrow of the entire social order; thus the June Days strengthened what came to be known vaguely as the Red Fear. In the months that followed, conservatives capitalized upon this fear by introducing legislation to curb the freedom of the press, limit the right of political association, and outlaw secret societies. The reaction to the June Days was also reflected in the constitution of the Second Republic, which was finally completed in November. In providing that the president should be elected by universal manhood suffrage and that the executive and legislative powers should be separated, the framers of the constitution intended to create a strong executive who could deal effectively with any future proletarian uprisings.

A final effect of the June Days was to strengthen the appeal of one of the candidates for the presidency in the first election, held under the new constitution on December 10, 1848. Charles Louis Napoleon Bonaparte (1808–1873), who had returned from exile in England, entered the lists against candidates whose names were associated with the early months of the Second Republic. These included, in addition to Lamartine and General Cavaignac, Alexandre Auguste Ledru-Rollin (1807–1874), who had been minister of the interior in the provisional government, and François Raspail (1794–1878), who had been active as a republican as early as the Revolution of 1830. Posing as the defender of order, Napoleon's nephew won a landslide victory: 5,500,000 votes compared with the 1,500,000 of his nearest opponent, Cavaignac.

Louis Napoleon had not been taken very seriously by his opponents. In his two personal appearances before the National Assembly his awkward bearing, his German accent, and his halting speech had made him a subject of ridicule. Apparently some monarchists voted for him, as a harmless stopgap who could serve as president until France was ripe for a royalist restoration. Although he had written vaguely socialist tracts during his years of imprisonment and exile, it is doubtful that these views won him many working-class votes. His great appeal unquestionably lay in the magic of his name. In the more than three decades that had elapsed since the defeat of the first Napoleon, Frenchmen had had an opportunity to forget the unpleasant aspects of the Napoleonic regime. The Napoleonic legend had grown particularly during the drab years of the July Monarchy, when Louis Philippe's foreign policy had appeared timorous and inglorious. In contrast, the name Napoleon symbolized an era when France's power had been second to none. But the three years following his election revealed that Louis Napoleon had been greatly underestimated by those who hoped to use him. Like his uncle before him, Louis Napoleon saw himself as the instrument of destiny, and he was determined to make himself the master of France.

THE REVOLUTIONS OF 1848 IN THE GERMAN STATES

When news of France's successful February Revolution crossed the Rhine, a wave of popular discontent spread through the states of Germany, beginning in the south and west, then extending into the central areas, and reaching Prussia and the north by the middle of March. Most of the German rulers, frightened by the fate of the French king, capitulated even before the opposition had a chance to organize, and replaced their conservative ministers with men of known liberal views. Many promised constitutions and other reforms, and offered to give their subjects a share in government. These concessions did not eliminate the threat of violence, however, for the causes of the revolutions in Germany were social as well as political. The smoldering bitterness of handicraft workers against the industrialization which had deprived them of a livelihood burst forth in attacks upon machinery and factories. In rural areas the peasants' pent-up resentment of manorial dues and obligations, the hunting and forest privileges of the nobility, and inadequate land allotments, found expression in orgies of looting and burning. The first task faced by the new liberal ministers in many states was the suppression of popular disturbances and the restoration of order.

Prussia

Prussia was most seriously affected at the outset, in part because of the irresolute behavior of King Frederick William IV (ruled 1840–1861). The king's accession to the throne had given rise to hopes for constitutional changes and for Prussia's leadership in a movement for national unification, but these hopes proved groundless. Although the king talked of national unity for the Germans, he appears to have had merely a romantic feeling for a common German past, and even retained his loyalty to the Habsburgs as the traditional imperial dynasty. His conception of political representation was not based on any current liberal theory, but rather on an idealized medieval view of the state as a structure in which the various estates of the realm were to be grouped under a king whose position derived from divine right. In 1847 Prussian liberals were temporarily encouraged when the king summoned the *Landtag*, or United Diet, which brought together representatives of provincial diets named by the long-established estates. But in his first speech to the diet he showed that he had no intention of relinquishing any real control over legislation or the budget, and the diet was prorogued shortly afterward, to the disillusionment of the liberals.

When popular demonstrations broke out in Berlin in the middle of March, 1848, the king refused to believe that they were directed against himself and ordered his troops not to fire on his "beloved Berliners." Nevertheless he decided that concessions were in order; on March 18 he announced his readiness to participate in the drawing up of an all-German constitution, indicating also that the United Diet would be reconvened. Serious trouble for the government might have been averted had it not been for an episode which occurred later the same day. An apparently good-na-

Revolution of 1848 in Berlin. *One individual is writing "National Eigenthum" (National Property) on the palace of the prince of Prussia in order to protect it from the mob.*

tured crowd that had gathered outside the royal palace was being dispersed by the cavalry when two shots rang out from an unknown quarter. Within minutes, the crowd had been transformed into an angry mob, which engaged the troops in eight hours of bitter street fighting. So disturbed was the king over the violence and loss of life that he yielded to popular demands and ordered the departure of the troops from the city. Without armed protection, he was left in Berlin a captive of the aroused citizenry and was subjected to a series of humiliating experiences which he was never to forget. On one occasion he was summoned to the palace balcony with the queen to view the mutilated corpses of those who had died in the street fighting. As each body was thrust toward the monarch, the name of the victim and the manner of his death were intoned.

During this crisis the king issued a proclamation declaring his willingness to assume leadership among the German princes and added that Prussia would "merge itself" into a new German empire. For the moment he was not called upon to fulfill this promise. But he did agree to the election by universal manhood suffrage of an assembly, which met in May to draw up a constitution for Prussia. This constituent assembly, which included a generous representation of liberals and democrats, became increasingly radical in its deliberations during the summer and fall. Meanwhile the king, encouraged by the mounting counterrevolutionary trend elsewhere in Europe, regained his nerve and consolidated the conservative groups around him. In November he was strong enough to order troops back into the capital and to banish the constituent assembly to a nearby town, where it was finally dissolved on December 5. Curiously enough, the efforts of this body were not entirely without results. For Frederick William in December, 1848, promulgated a constitution of his own which was quite similar in many respects to the one drafted by the assembly. It included safeguards for the liberties of Prussian subjects and provided for a bicameral legislature whose lower house would be chosen by universal manhood suffrage though through a system of indirect election. However, in the following year modifications of the electoral system made the provision for universal suffrage almost meaningless. The voters were divided into three categories, or classes, according to the amount of taxes they paid, and the votes of the wealthy counted far more heavily than those of the poor. Indeed, two thirds of the delegates to the lower house were chosen by about 15 per cent of the population. In this way the authority of the king and the privileged orders was preserved in the lower as well as in the upper house, whose members inherited their seats or were appointed to them by the king. Prussia retained this constitution until 1918.

The Frankfurt Parliament

The revolution in Prussia had its counterpart in virtually every one of the thirty-eight German states, including Austria. During 1848 liberals from all

German National Assembly, Frankfurt am Main, 1848. *Contemporary wood engraving. The procession moves into the Paulskirche (St. Paul's Church) for the opening of the Frankfurt Parliament on May 18, 1848.*

over Germany made a concerted attempt to establish a unified nation under liberal auspices. The vehicle for unification was to be the Frankfurt Parliament (sometimes called the Frankfurt Assembly), and the failure of this body to unify Germany in 1848 marked a significant defeat for German liberalism and a major turning point in the development of modern Germany.

The origins of the Frankfurt Parliament help, in part, to explain its weakness. It emerged not from any official action by the governments of the German states but from a spontaneous gathering of about fifty German liberals inspired by the March revolts, who met in Heidelberg. They issued invitations to a preliminary parliament (*Vorparlament*); this group, in turn, arranged for elections to be held in each of the German states for delegates to an all-German national parliament. Voting was to be by universal manhood suffrage, and each delegate was to represent fifty thousand Germans. The elections were duly held, though the electoral laws and methods varied considerably from state to state. When the delegates came together for the first time on May 18, 1848, in the free city of Frankfurt am Main, the event attracted great excitement. The galleries of the old St. Paul's Church, where the assembly met, were crowded with journalists from all over Europe; the altar was draped with a huge portrait representing "Germania." The spectators and delegates believed that they were witnessing the birth of a new nation.

The professions and social origins of the 830 delegates are of particular interest. The overwhelming majority were university-educated members of the upper bourgeoisie. Among those elected were more than a hundred professors and teachers and numerous lawyers, doctors, ministers, bankers, merchants, and manufacturers. Some of Germany's leading scholars, writers, and publicists were present. Particularly noteworthy was the paucity of statesmen and of men with experience in practical politics, a shortcoming which handicapped the assembly throughout its brief history: far too much time was spent in arguments over theoretical or doctrinaire issues, while practical problems tended to be neglected.

The assembly was also hampered from the start by the conflicting aims of its members. With no established political parties to marshal a consensus on particular issues, it was extremely difficult for the assembly to take any concerted action. The delegates did all agree that their goal was a unified German nation. But they disagreed on the form of government—whether it should be a federation or a unitary state, a monarchy, an empire, or a republic—and on who, if a monarchical or imperial regime was selected, would be the German ruler. They disagreed, furthermore, on what the boundaries of the new state should be; indeed, this proved to be a particularly divisive issue.

Perhaps the most serious weakness of the Frankfurt Parliament was its anomalous position in regard to existing German governments and their princes. For the assembly did not conceive of its purpose as merely the drafting of a constitution for a united Germany but claimed to be a government speaking and acting for the German people as a whole. Yet its relationship to the rulers and governments of the German states was undefined, and these did not accept its leadership. The diet of the old Germanic Confederation, for example, continued to meet for several weeks after the formation of the Frankfurt Parliament. At the root of this general question of sovereignty was the fact that the Frankfurt Parliament had no armed forces at its disposal. The armies of the individual states were left intact. When it became necessary for the assembly to use force—as, for example, when it declared war on Denmark in response to the appeal of German-speaking inhabitants of the territories of Schleswig and Holstein for protection against the Danes—Frankfurt had to call upon Prussia to supply the necessary troops. The lack of a consolidated armed force under its control also hampered the new German government's dealings with foreign powers. Nevertheless the assembly did attempt to pursue an independent foreign policy, to the annoyance of the Prussian and Austrian governments, which maintained their own foreign offices and diplomatic relations.

There were other fundamental weaknesses. In their excitement and enthusiasm over the prospect of founding a new nation, the delegates to the Frankfurt Parliament failed to take into account the power relationships in Germany. With Austria and Prussia the strongest states, no enduring nation could be founded without the approval and support of at least one of these. Misled by the temporary weakness of the Prussian and Austrian governments after the March revolts, the delegates assumed that the two rulers would follow Frankfurt's lead and permit their states to be absorbed into a new German nation. They were wrong. In the end, neither government was willing to merge with the new nation and neither ruler was willing to accept its leadership.

The delegates considered the drafting of a constitution for the new Germany their principal task, and because so many of them were scholars, professors, and lawyers, they threw themselves into this project with great enthusiasm. Members of the committee writing the constitution spent six months constructing a statement of the "Fundamental Rights of the German People." Drawing on the French Declaration of the Rights of Man, the American Declaration of Independence, and other similar documents, they incorporated into their statement the major principles of mid-nineteenth-century liberal philosophy. The result became a part of the constitution completed in March, 1849, which guaranteed the basic liberties of speech, assembly, and the press; it was particularly advanced in its provisions for public education and religious toleration. But by the time the deliberations were over and the draft was completed, circumstances in Germany had changed so significantly that there was little chance for its acceptance.

One issue divided the members of the assembly and prevented them from concluding their task sooner—the question of the boundaries of the new state. One group of delegates favored what came to be known as the *Kleindeutsch* ("Little-German") solution: the inclusion in the new Germany only of Prussia and the lesser German states. Another group of delegates favored the *Grossdeutsch* ("Big-German") solution: the incorporation into the new state, in addition to the territories just named, of the German provinces of Austria (including Bohemia, with its large Slavic population). A compromise was reached in October, 1848: all German territory would be joined in the new nation, but any state with non-German possessions (*i.e.* Austria) would be accepted as part of the new Germany only by abandoning its non-German possessions or by holding them exclusively through a personal union in the crown. This condition meant that Austria could not join the German nation unless the emperor abandoned his Hungarian territories as an integral part of his empire. Such a possibility was remote, and Francis Joseph I (ruled 1848–1916) indicated his attitude toward this solution early in March, 1849, by promulgating a new constitution that reaffirmed the unity and integrity of the Habsburg empire and thus precluded any possibility of the inclusion of Austrian territory in the new Germany. The *Kleindeutsch* faction appeared to have won out, and the Frankfurt Parliament voted not long afterward to offer the crown of the "emperor of the Germans" to the king of Prussia. At first Frederick William IV refused to give a direct reply to the offer, on the grounds that he needed the consent of the princes of the lesser German states. But when twenty-eight princes indicated their willingness to accept the constitution, the king rejected the offer outright and ordered the Prussian delegates to quit the Frankfurt Parliament. He refused to accept what he had earlier termed a "crown picked up from the gutter," like that worn by Louis Philippe.

Austria, too, withdrew its delegates, and a number of lesser states followed. There remained only a "rump" parliament of radicals; these subsequently moved to Stuttgart, in Württemberg, whence they issued appeals to the German people and tried to foment new uprisings. Revolts did occur in a few of the lesser states of Germany in May, 1849, but these were quickly suppressed—in some instances with the support of Prussian troops. The remaining members of the Frankfurt Parliament finally dispersed ignominiously in June, 1849.

Thus ended the attempt of the liberals to establish a united Germany. Had the nation been unified under liberal auspices in 1848 rather than under Prussian leadership, by Bismarck, in the 1860's, the subsequent history of Germany might have been different. It is often argued that instead of becoming an aggressively nationalistic and militaristic state, Germany would then have joined the company of peace-loving nations. But how peace-loving were German liberals? An examination of the deliberations and actions of the Frankfurt Parliament with respect to other nationalities and national groups shows that these liberals were far from tolerant and peace-loving; on the contrary, their speeches reveal exactly the strain of aggressiveness and contempt for other nationalities that recurred in the declarations of succeeding German statesmen.

A case in point involves the attitude of the assembly members toward the Polish minority in the eastern provinces of Prussia. Before 1848 German liberals, like other European liberals, were sympathetic to Polish aspirations for an independent state. As late as April, 1848, in the *Vorparlament*, they talked of a restored Poland with the boundaries of 1772. But, when put to the test, these German liberals reversed their stand. The Poles living in the Prussian province of Posen (where they outnumbered Germans 8 to 5) became restive after the king made some vague promises. They began to demand the autonomy or independence of Posen as a preliminary to the restoration of an independent Poland. A Polish National Committee was set up, but Polish peasants became impatient and rose up against Prussian officials administering the region. When the Prussian government responded by sending in troops, the Poles appealed to the Frankfurt Parliament for support. In the ensuing full-scale debate, in July, 1848, one speaker after another denounced the Polish pretensions and supported Prussian suppression of the revolt. The overwhelming majority of the assembly renounced their earlier sympathy for Polish nationalism because it now appeared to conflict with German national aims. If the eastern provinces of Prussia (such as Posen) were abandoned to the Poles, they would be lost forever to the new German nation. Some of those most emphatic in their speeches were precisely the liberals who had a few months earlier spoken in favor of Polish independence. To justify their position some argued that the Poles had shown themselves unable to maintain their existence as an independent nation and therefore deserved to be subjected to the rule of another people. One delegate declared that Germany's right to dominate the Poles was "the right of the stronger, the right of conquest." Only a small minority of extreme left-wing deputies held out; the Frankfurt Parliament voted 342 to 31 to support Prussian suppression of the Polish bid for independence.

This was not an isolated episode. Another test of German liberalism developed with respect to the Austrian empire. Because of the large German-speaking population in Bohemia, the Frankfurt Parliament considered its inclusion in the new German state. But the even larger Czech population in Bohemia not unnaturally objected to this proposal and talked of a closer union with other Slavic peoples. Where Czech nationalism conflicted with German nationalist goals, most Frankfurt delegates were willing to sacrifice Czech aspirations.

It is impossible to say what kind of Germany the liberals might have established had the Frankfurt Parliament succeeded. But evidence suggests that in 1848 German liberals were no less nationalistic than other Germans. The fact that in the 1860's many liberals rallied to Bismarck when it became clear that he was achieving the unification of Germany seems to confirm this judgment.

The Austrian Empire

Metternich's attempt to stem the tide of change by insulating Austria from the rest of Europe became increasingly difficult in the 1840's. Though the Habsburg empire lagged behind Prussia and some of the other German states in economic development, its chief cities—Vienna, Prague, and Budapest—did not remain immune to industrialization, with its consequent pattern of social change. In the large cities a growing bourgeois class became restive under the backward economic policies of Metternich's government and impatient with the intrusion of the bureaucracy into its business affairs. The small urban proletariat was subject to the same hardships and uncertainties that plagued the working classes elsewhere. Handicraft workers, resentful of the introduction of machines which deprived them of employment, were particularly discontented. The peasants, the overwhelming mass

Student guards at the old university of Vienna, 1848.

of the population, showed increasing annoyance with one of the few remaining obligations to their landlords, the *robota*, a form of labor rent. When a revolt broke out in Galicia in 1846, the imperial government had to promise to abolish the *robota* in this region, thereby provoking demands during the revolutions of 1848 for its abolition in other parts of the empire.

Subversive political ideas managed to seep into the Austrian empire despite Metternich's strict censorship. Books and pamphlets, smuggled into Bohemia, found their way to universities throughout the empire, which became centers of opposition to the regime. Students exposed to the egalitarian ideas of Rousseau and to the constitutional studies of the German writer Friedrich Dahlmann (1785–1860) envisaged a greater measure of political freedom for Austrians.

Perhaps the greatest threat to the regime, however, lay in the growing nationalist aspirations of the various peoples of the empire. More than one movement which at the outset had been purely cultural, emphasizing the revival of a national language or literature, had by the 1840's become political, its aim being greater autonomy for a particular national group within the empire. The most noteworthy was the Magyar, or Hungarian, national revival. Under the leadership of Louis Kossuth (1802–1894), a dynamic journalist and orator, Hungarian nationalists in the 1840's demanded the complete autonomy of Hungary and the establishment of a

Hungarian national parliament. In 1844 the Hungarian Diet, consisting of representatives of the semifeudal Magyar nobility, abolished Latin as its official language and decreed that Magyar would henceforth be used in all government transactions and in the schools. Similar nationalist revivals occurred among the Czechs of Bohemia, the Croatians on the Adriatic, and the Rumanians of Transylvania, in the eastern region of the empire.

News of the February Revolution in France was the spark dropped into this combustible mass of grievances—social, political, and nationalist. Revolts broke out in the major cities of the empire. In Budapest, Kossuth addressed the Hungarian Diet, denouncing the Metternichian system and calling for a constitution for the empire granting responsible government to Hungary. In Vienna, students drew up a petition to the emperor requesting freedom of speech and the abolition of censorship. When news of Kossuth's speech arrived from Budapest they added, as an afterthought, the demand for a constitution. Despite the relative mildness of their demands the students feared the government's reaction to their petition and therefore enlisted the support of Viennese workers for their demonstrations. On March 13 a clash between the crowd and troops resulted in bloodshed. Fearing further loss of life, Emperor Ferdinand I, like Frederick William IV of Prussia, called off the troops and announced his consent to the demands, including the demand for the convocation of a constituent assembly. On the same day the aged Metternich resigned, after more than half a century of service to the Habsburgs; he left Vienna by common cab and made his way into exile in London. His departure symbolized the end of an era.

From this point on it is difficult to follow events in detail. In Italy, as we shall see, outbreaks in the Austrian territories of Lombardy and Venetia led to an attempt at a war of liberation from the empire. The revolts occurred in several parts of the empire, pursuing a more or less independent course in each. In Budapest the Hungarian Diet moved boldly; it adopted the March Laws, which left Hungary almost independent, joined to the rest of the empire only through allegiance to the emperor. Hungary was to have a regular parliament in place of the Diet, and its own army, budget, and foreign policy. In deference to the peasantry the *robota* was abolished. Though asserting their own autonomy, the Magyars were unwilling to grant it to their subject nationalities. Both Transylvania and Croatia were absorbed into the Hungarian kingdom and their diets were abolished. Ferdinand I, on the defensive throughout the empire, had no alternative for the moment but to accept the new status of his Hungarian possessions.

Prague, the capital of Bohemia and the center of Czech national aspirations, was also the seat of a revolt in March. The initial demands of the revolutionaries were relatively modest; only after the Magyar Diet had passed its March Laws did the Czechs decide to demand their own constitution and virtual autonomy. The imperial government responded with a promise to convoke a constituent assembly and granted the equality of the Czech and German languages in Bohemia. In June the first Pan-Slav Congress assembled in Prague. This body was dominated by Czechs who hoped to demonstrate their solidarity against a proposal of the Frankfurt Parliament to incorporate Bohemia into the new German national state. Though they clearly opposed union with Germany, the Czechs had few specific proposals. They appeared to favor the transformation of the Austrian empire into a federation of nationalities in which the Slavs would have an honorable place along with other national groups. Yet neither the preferences of the Pan-Slav Congress nor the demands of the Czechs for a responsible government of their own received further consideration from the imperial government. A new radical demonstration during June gave General Alfred Windischgrätz (1787–1862), at that time military commander in Prague, a pretext for bringing in reinforcements and ruthlessly suppressing the Czech revolutionary movement. The Pan-Slav Congress was dissolved and Prague was put under a military dictatorship. The seizure of Prague was, in fact, the first victory of the counterrevolutionary forces in the Austrian empire and strengthened the determination of the imperial goverment to proceed against the revolution elsewhere.

In Vienna, despite the revolt in March, there was at first no radical change in the character of the regime. Though the emperor had permitted the establishment there of a national guard composed of civilians and an Academic Legion representing university students, the government remained in the hands of conservative statesmen. Ignoring the emperor's promise to call a constituent assembly, the imperial government in April simply promulgated a new constitution. But this document was not liberal enough to satisfy the radical elements in the capital, and when, in addition, the government attempted to disband the national guard and dissolve the Academic Legion, there was a second uprising, in May, by students, workers and the national guard. The emperor and his family were forced to flee the capital, and took refuge at Innsbruck. The government now agreed to convoke a constituent assembly. This body met in Vienna in July and set to work on a constitution, which turned out to be a far more democratic than the one issued in April. One lasting accomplishment of the assembly, achieved in September, was the abolition of the *robota* in all parts of the empire where this reform had not previously been undertaken. On the surface the revolution seemed to have triumphed in Austria.

But the actual situation was not so clear-cut. From May to October, Vienna remained in the hands of the revolutionaries and the assembly worked at giving constitutional embodiment to the gains of the revolution. But the dynasty had not been overthrown and the army remained loyal to it. While pretending to play along with the constituent assembly, the emperor—or rather the Court party, composed of conservative statesmen and military leaders—encouraged General Windischgrätz to drill his troops in preparation for the recapture of the capital and the suppression of the revolution. In October he had the opportunity to strike. The Viennese radicals, learning that the Court party was moving against the Hungarian revolutionary movement, staged a third insurrection, in the course of which they seized the unpopular minister of war and beat him to death in the streets. This act of violence was used by Windischgrätz as a pretext for treating Vienna as he had treated Prague. He bombarded the city with artillery and by the end of the month had occupied it. Many of the radical leaders were executed on the spot. The constituent assembly was exiled to the Moravian town of Kremsier. To all intents and purposes the revolution in Vienna had been defeated by October, 1848.

Among the adherents to the counterrevolutionary cause in Austria the conviction had grown during 1848 that it was essential to secure the abdication of the feebleminded Emperor Ferdinand I if the power of the Habsburgs was to be restored. After the October revolt, Prince Felix zu Schwarzenberg (1800–1852), the new principal leader of the government, succeeded in convincing the emperor to yield the throne to his eighteen-year-old nephew. Assuming the crown in December, 1848, Francis Joseph I ruled Austria for sixty-eight years, until his death during the First World War. The young emperor was unhampered by the promises Ferdinand had made to the revolutionaries. With Schwarzenberg, who remained as the chief minister, he was determined to restore the power of the imperial house. They did not immediately feel strong enough to dismiss the constituent assembly meeting at Kremsier, but allowed it to complete its deliberations before dissolving it in March, 1849. However, Schwarzenberg rejected the constitution drawn up by this body, which would have established a decentralized, federal government, and instead issued his own. Like Frederick William's constitution in Prussia, this document contained liberal features, such as a diet of elected representatives and a responsible ministry, but having issued it, Schwarzenberg announced that it would come into operation only when the "provisional emergency" confronting Austria had ended. Meanwhile he governed the country autocratically. Schwarzenberg also put an end for the time being to the aspirations of non-German nationalities for greater autonomy by establishing a highly centralized administrative system.

There remained one last smoldering of the outbreaks in the Habsburg empire—the Hungarian revolt. Efforts to suppress this revolt had begun before Francis Joseph came to the throne in December. The way in which the counterrevolutionary Court party handled this problem is particularly complex. At first they merely gave unofficial encouragement to the Croatians, a dissident south Slavic people living under Magyar rule, when they revolted against the new Hungarian regime and sought autonomy from it. But by the end of 1848, the government at Vienna had decided on an all-out effort to suppress the Hungarian revolutionary movement, and ordered an invasion of Hungary by imperial troops. The invaders were no match for the Hungarian defenders, who under Kossuth's leadership, drove them out of the country. Had the suppression of the Magyar revolt been left exclusively to the Austrian armies, Hungary might have emerged an independent state in 1849. In April, the Hungarian parliament proclaimed a Hungarian republic, ending the tie with the Habsburgs and made Kossuth president. At this juncture, however, Tsar Nicholas I of Russia, always the enemy of revolutionary movements and fearful that the success of the Hungarian movement might set off a revolt in Poland, offered military assistance to the Austrian emperor. A joint invasion of Hungary by Austrian troops from the west and 140,000 Russian troops from the north took place in June, 1849. The Hungarians, commanded by General Arthur von Görgey (1818–1916), resisted fiercely, but weakened by further revolts of national minorities at home, they surrendered in August. Despite promises by the Austrian general, Baron Julius von Haynau (1786–1853), of clemency for the defenders, the victors wrought a bloody vengeance, flogging, hanging and shooting their victims. Kossuth managed to escape to Turkey and eventually reached the United States, where he made a prolonged speaking tour in an effort to raise money for Hungary's liberation.

The defeat of the Hungarians marked the end of the revolutions of 1848–1849 in the Austrian empire. Hungary, along with the rest of the empire, lost all semblance of autonomy and was thenceforth controlled absolutely from Vienna. Despite the provisions for a responsible ministry and a representative diet in the constitution promulgated by Schwarzenberg in 1849, Austria was thereafter ruled just as autocratically and a good deal more efficiently than under Metternich. In the end, the revolutions of 1848–1849 brought no improvement in the situation of the various nationalities within the empire, and in fact, sharpened the tensions among them. One of the few lasting results of the revolutions was the abolition of the *robota*; this benefited the peasantry, but it may also be one explanation for the failure of the uprisings. For once the peasants had secured this concession they were no longer interested in the fate of the revolutions, which faltered without the support of the masses, and could ultimately be suppressed by the emperor.

THE REVOLUTIONS OF 1848 IN ITALY

The events of 1848–1849 in Italy fall naturally into three phases: first, the separate revolts that took place in many of the states and in the territories under Austrian rule; second, the war for Italian independence from Austrian domination, led by King Charles Albert of Sardinia; and third, the short-lived attempt by Mazzini and others to establish the Roman Republic. As elsewhere in Europe, all the revolutions in Italy apparently ended in failure; yet in fact they marked a significant step forward in the process of Italian unification, for through them the revolutionaries learned certain important lessons.

The series of revolts began with the January uprising in Sicily. Ferdinand II, king of Naples and Sicily, the first ruler in Europe affected by a revolution in 1848, granted a constitution to his people much like the French Charter of 1830. From the southernmost state in Italy the revolts spread northward. Grand Duke Leopold of Tuscany (1797–1870) was the next to yield to the demands of his people for a constitution. In Sardinia, the Moderates, including Count Cavour, prevailed upon Charles Albert to promulgate the constitution known as the *Statuto*, which a decade later became the basis for the constitution of the unified kingdom of Italy. Pope Pius IX, who had already given some evidence of liberal tendencies, followed suit by granting a constitution to the Papal States, though he took care to reserve to the pope and the College of Cardinals the power to veto the acts of an elective council of deputies. Finally, the revolts spread into Lombardy and Venetia, the regions directly under Austrian rule. In January, the chief city of Lombardy, Milan, had experienced riots directed against an unpopular tax on tobacco. In March, the news of the revolt in Vienna and the flight of Metternich precipitated in Milan what came to be known as the Five Glorious Days (March 18–22), an outbreak of fierce street fighting which forced the Austrian general, Joseph Radetzky (1766–1858), to abandon Lombardy. At about the same time a republic was declared in Venice after a short uprising; its first president was Daniele Manin (1804–1857), a political prisoner released by Austrian authorities upon the outbreak of the revolt there. By the latter part of March, then, each of the major Italian states had experienced a significant political crisis, though only in Milan had serious fighting occurred.

The spirit and courage shown by the Milanese inspired the liberals and moderates of Sardinia to call for an Italian war of liberation from Austrian domination. King Charles Albert, far from enthusiastic about allying himself with the revolutionary cause, was nevertheless persuaded by his advisers to assume leadership and accordingly invaded Lombardy on March 22. At the same time, he appealed for the support of all the other Italian rulers in ridding the peninsula of the hated Austrians. So great was the enthusiasm for the national cause at the outset that even Ferdinand of Naples felt obligated to supply a contingent of troops to the Sardinians, and what was more surprising, a force from the Papal States joined briefly in the war for independence, although it was withdrawn almost immediately in the face of Austrian protests. Despite his enthusiasm for the cause of Italian unity, Pius IX, as spiritual leader of Catholics throughout the world, could hardly undertake a war against Catholic Austria. The Italian forces led by Sardinia fought against heavy odds. Although enthusiastic and patriotic, they suffered from a lack of discipline, and before long dissension developed between the moderate Sardinians, whose goal was a constitutional monarchy under Charles Albert, and the republican forces which had joined them. The newly established Venetian republic had no intention of dissolving itself in order to submit to the rule of Sardinia. By May, the contingent from Naples had been withdrawn; a counterrevolution had restored absolute control there to Ferdinand. Though Charles Albert's armies won some important victories, in the last analysis they were no match for the better-disciplined armies of General Radetzky. By July, 1848, Radetzky had consolidated his forces, and he inflicted an overwhelming defeat on the Sardinians at Custoza. within ten days he had driven them from Austrian territory and imposed an armistice by which Charles Albert agreed to abandon any claim to Lombardy. A brief epilogue occurred the following spring when Charles Albert, charging the Austrians with having violated the terms of the armistice, once again attacked, but he suffered a decisive defeat at the Battle of Novara in March, 1849. The Austrian government was now free to complete the counterrevolution in territories under its control. Last to succumb was the Venetian republic, which yielded in August, 1849, after heroically resisting a five-weeks siege.

The most radical event during the Italian revolutions was unquestionably the establishment of the Roman Republic in February, 1849. Despite Pope Pius IX's initial concessions, radical elements in Rome became increasingly dissatisfied with his regime and particularly with the prime minister, Count Pellegrino Rossi, who was appointed in September, 1848. In November a fanatical democrat assassinated Rossi and Pius fled Rome, taking refuge in Naples. With the pope gone, the Romans elected a constituent assembly, which met in February, 1849, proclaimed the overthrow of the pope as temporal ruler, and established the Roman Republic. Although the revolutionaries controlled only Rome and its immediate environs, the Roman Republic was to be the nucleus of a unified Italian state. Giuseppe Mazzini was summoned to head a triumvirate which would rule the new republic. This was the fulfillment of his lifelong dream; Mazzini issued decrees calling for the confiscation of Church lands for distribution to the peasantry, public housing for the poor, and other humanitarian measures. But from the first the government was beset by serious inflation and appeared unable to solve its economic difficulties. Even if foreign intervention had not ended the Roman Republic, it would probably have collapsed in a matter of months.

Intervention on behalf of the pope came, surprisingly enough, not from a conservative central European state, but from the Second French Republic of Louis Napoleon. Leading the French assembly to believe that the move was being undertaken to forestall Austrian ambitions in Italy, Louis Napoleon secured approval for an expeditionary force. His real motive seems to have been a desire to win the support of French Catholics for his regime. In any case, he underestimated the difficulties of the enterprise and the strength of feeling in Rome for the republic; French forces attacking

Rome met fierce resistance. Defenders of the city had been hastily organized by Giuseppe Garibaldi (1807–1882), whose exploits at this time won him a reputation throughout Europe. Unquestionably the most colorful figure of the *Risorgimento*, Garibaldi had been forced into exile in 1834 for his role in a plot against the government of Sardinia. With a price on his head he fled to South America, where he fought for revolutionary movements in Brazil and Uruguay. Garibaldi, the son of a sailor, consciously identified himself throughout his life with the cause of oppressed peoples everywhere, but his highest dream remained the establishment of a unified Italian republic. When he returned to Italy during the revolutions of 1848, his countrymen found him a striking figure, with his long blond hair, somewhat rough manner, and the distinctive red shirt which he and his followers adopted as part of their uniform. After leading a volunteer legion in Charles Albert's unsuccessful war against Austria, Garibaldi rallied to the Roman Republic. Despite their initial successes, his ill-equipped and ill-trained forces were in the long run no match for the more numerous and better-disciplined French armies. In July, 1849, after an existence of only five months, the Roman Republic capitulated. Garibaldi led his band in a heroic retreat across the Italian peninsula. Most of his followers died or were captured, but he ultimately escaped to the United States, where he remained until he could return to Italy in the 1850's to help complete Italian unification. After the collapse of the Roman Republic the pope returned to Rome under the protection of a French garrison, which Louis Napoleon maintained there until 1870.

By the end of the summer of 1849 the revolutionary movement appeared to have been defeated everywhere in the Italian peninsula. Only in Sardinia a moderate regime remained. There Charles Albert, after his second defeat by the Austrians at Novara in March, 1849, had abdicated in favor of his son Victor Emmanuel II, and retired to a Portuguese monastery. The new young monarch succeeded in winning less harsh terms than had been expected from the Austrian empire, including permission to retain the constitution granted by his father the year before.

Despite the apparent failure of the revolutionaries in most of Italy, the events of 1848–1849 provided at least three valuable lessons for patriots striving for Italian unification. First, this unification could not be accomplished under papal leadership, as those in the Neo-Guelph movement had hoped before 1848. The pope's withdrawal of his troops from the Italian army of liberation just after the initial attack on the Austrian forces discredited him as a potential leader of a unified Italy, though his defenders might argue that he had had no alternative because of his position as spiritual leader of the Catholic world. If the Neo-Guelph cause suffered in 1848, the chances of Sardinian leadership in the unification of Italy certainly improved. Here was the second important lesson of the events of 1848–1849. The Sardinians had resisted Austria, and the new king, Victor Emmanuel

II, in refusing to renounce the liberal constitution of 1848 as Radetzky demanded, further enhanced the prestige of Sardinia among liberals everywhere in Italy. But the final, and perhaps most important, lesson learned in 1848 was this: Italians alone could not eject the Austrians from Italy. Though the Austrian armies had retreated initially in 1848 and the Austrians had made certain concessions, their power in Italy had never been destroyed. Among those who recognized that foreign help would be necessary was Count Cavour, who in 1851 became the prime minister of Sardinia. Convinced that Sardinia alone was not up to the task, he made his principal diplomatic goal in the 1850's the acquisition of allies for the war against Austria which he considered essential for the unification of Italy under Sardinia's rule.

CONSEQUENCES OF THE REVOLUTIONS OF 1848

Not long after the failure of the revolutions of 1848, the French anarchist Pierre Joseph Proudhon (1809–1865) wrote, ". . . we have been beaten and humiliated . . . scattered, imprisoned, disarmed and gagged. The fate of European democracy has slipped from our hands. . . ."[3] Most of the revolutionaries throughout Europe must have reacted in this way. Begun with such high hopes, the uprisings produced results that were indeed disappointing. Almost without exception the rulers who were challenged in 1848 managed to reassert their authority by 1849. Where constitutions had been granted, they were withdrawn or replaced by documents which denied the very principles for which the revolutionaries had struggled. The revolutions appeared to have been fought in vain; yet they were certainly not without their consequences, both immediate and long-range. In the judgment of one historian, the revolutions "crystallized ideas and projected the pattern of things to come."[4]

The long-range impact of the revolutions was to be felt for at least the next fifty years. The experience of 1848–1849 certainly crystallized and focused the urge toward national unity that was already present during the first half of the nineteenth century. Whether the revolutions provided a comparable impetus to the ultimate achievement of *liberal* goals is more debatable. The dissolution of elected assemblies, as in Prussia and Austria, the rejection by the monarchs of the constitutions drafted by these bodies, and the suppression of individual freedoms that characterized the postrevolutionary era suggest that the defeat of liberalism was nearly total. But the revolutionaries set precedents for subsequent generations of European liberals and democrats. And certain institutions managed to survive the conserva-

---

[3] Quoted in *The Opening of an Era: 1848*, ed. by François Fejtö (London, 1948), p. 414.

[4] Lewis B. Namier, *Avenues of History* (London, 1952), p. 55.

Title page of the Communist Manifesto, 1848. *The final words of the Manifesto appear on the title page: "Proletarians of all countries! Unite!"*

tive reaction of 1849—for example, universal manhood suffrage in France. Louis Napoleon came to power in France by means of universal suffrage, and no subsequent regime there has attempted to dispense with it. The principle, once established in France, became the goal of democrats and radicals throughout Europe. Indeed, the trust put in universal suffrage after the mid-century revolutions corresponds to the faith put in constitutions during the first half of the nineteenth century.

Perhaps the most unequivocal consequence of the failure of the revolutions of 1848 was the destruction of working-class hopes and illusions. With their leaders dead, in hiding, or in exile, the workers did indeed appear "beaten and humiliated...scattered, imprisoned, disarmed and gagged." But even here the revolts served an important function: they foreshadowed a significant change in the character of European socialism and the working-class movement by creating a strong sense of class consciousness among the proletariat. Karl Marx, writing of the revolt in France, declared, "The February republic finally brought the rule of the bourgeoisie clearly into prominence, since it struck off the crown behind which Capital kept itself concealed."[5] Perhaps Marx exaggerated, but clearly events such as the June Days in France and the brutal suppression of the Vienna insurrection in October could not help sharpening the class consciousness of European workers. Up to 1848 they had more often than not been allied with the middle class against the old order, and they fought on the same side of the barricades in many places during the initial phases of the uprisings. But as the revolts progressed, the bourgeoisie, increasingly concerned over the extremism of the mob and the alleged threat to private property, tended to line up with the old order or at least with those intent upon suppressing the threat of a thoroughgoing social revolution. In time, the bitterness and class antagonisms created by the events of 1848 declined, but the possibilities for genuine collaboration between capitalist and proletarian, employer and employee, were never quite the same. It is significant that the First International Workingmen's Association, dedicated to the overthrow of the bourgeoisie, came into being in 1864, a mere decade and a half after 1848.

Finally, a less tangible but no less important consequence of the revolts was the change in the climate of opinion in Europe. Such changes of mood are, of course, difficult to define, and even more difficult to substantiate. But the literature of a given era certainly provides a clue to its mood; other forms of art may reflect it as well. And there is general agreement that the era following the revolutions was characterized by a marked change of atmosphere, frequently reflected in the writings of the time. If one word may be singled out to characterize this new atmosphere, it is "realism." The realistic attitude can be seen in politics, in the conduct of international relations, in class relationships, in a new emphasis on science and technology, as well as in literature.

To tie this new attitude directly to the failure of the revolutions of 1848 is, of course, to raise a host of problems concerning historical causation. Yet it is undeniable that the shattering of the romantic hopes of the revolutionaries and the discrediting of pre-1848 utopian illusions resulted in a more sober evaluation by contemporaries of the world in which they found themselves. The goals of Europeans did not change radically after the experience of 1848–1849, but individuals and groups came to view their goals from a different perspective. Instead of envisioning their ends idealistically, they now tended to evaluate more realistically the concrete means for achieving them. And they very often reached the conclusion that abstract ideals and principles were less important in securing their goals than were power and force. A new tough-mindedness characterized the generation of the 1850's and 1860's, and this mood resulted largely from the disillusionment of 1848–1849. For these reasons the revolutions constituted a significant turning point in the history of nineteenth-century Europe.

[5] Karl Marx, *The Class Struggles in France (1848–50)* (New York, 1934), p. 41.

SUGGESTIONS
FOR FURTHER READING

(Books marked * are available in paperback.)

THE FRENCH REVOLUTION AND THE NAPOLEONIC ERA

The volume of historical literature on the French Revolution and the Napoleonic era alone is staggering. For the nonspecialist, English-speaking reader the best annotated bibliography is contained in a new edition of Leo Gershoy, *The French Revolution and Napoleon* (New York, 1964), which, incidentally, remains one of the outstanding surveys of the period. The original edition of this book was published in 1933 (New York). The title of the edition reprinted in 1964 adds "with new annotated bibliography." Other general works available in English are two concise surveys by *Michael J. Sydenham, *The French Revolution* (London and New York, 1965) and *Albert Goodwin, *The French Revolution* (New York, 1954) (Harper Torchbook edition, 1960); *James M. Thompson, *The French Revolution* (Oxford, 1943) (Oxford Galaxy Books); and a volume in the Rise of Modern Europe series edited by William L. Langer, *Crane Brinton, *A Decade of Revolution, 1789–1799*. Original edition published in New York, 1934. Bibliographical essay revised as of November, 1958; supplemented October, 1962. Harper Torchbook edition published in 1963 (New York). See also the pioneering study of R. R. Palmer, *The Age of the Democratic Revolution: A Political History of Europe and America, 1760–1800*, 2 vols. (Princeton, N.J., 1959–1964), which views the French Revolution as part of a broader democratic revolution in the Western world beginning around 1760. Available in a paperback edition, 2 vols. (Princeton University Press). Works by some of the major twentieth-century French historians of the revolution are now available in English; for example, Georges Lefebvre, *La Révolution française*, third edition (Paris, 1951), and revised editions (1963, 1968) in the *Peuples et civilisations* series has been translated in two volumes, *The French Revolution: From Its Origins to 1793* trans. by Elizabeth Moss Evanson (New York, 1962) and *The French Revolution: From 1793 to 1799*, trans. by John Hall Stewart and James Friguglietti (New York, 1964). Available in a paperback edition, 2 vols. (Columbia University Press). See also *Lefebvre's *The Coming of the French Revolution*, trans. by R. R.

Palmer (Princeton, N.J., 1947) (Princeton). Two of Lefebvre's most distinguished predecessors were François V. A. Aulard, who wrote in the last decades of the nineteenth century his strongly republican *The French Revolution, a Political History, 1789–1804*, 4 vols. (New York, 1910), and Albert Mathiez, whose more economically oriented works, published in 1928 and 1931 (New York) have been translated by Catherine Alison Phillips as *The French Revolution* (New York, 1962) (Universal Library) and *After Robespierre, the Thermidorian Reaction* (New York, 1965) (Universal Library).

On the impact of the revolution upon Europe the classic work remains Albert Sorel, *L'Europe et la Révolution française*, 9 vols. (Paris, 1895–1911), the celebrated first chapter of which is available in English in paperback as *Europe under the Old Regime*, trans. by Francis H. Herrick (Harper Torchbook). A more recent work by one of the best contemporary scholars of the revolution is Jacques L. Godechot, *La Grande Nation: l'expansion révolutionnaire de la France dans le monde de 1789 à 1799*, 2 vols. (Paris, 1956). See also by the same author, in the *Nouvelle Clio* series, *Les Révolutions, 1770–1799*, second edition, revised and augmented (Paris, 1965); available in English as *France and the Atlantic Revolution of the Eighteenth Century, 1770–1799*, translated by Herbert H. Rowen (New York, 1965). On another aspect of the revolution Professor Godechot has published *Les Institutions de la France sous la Révolution et l'empire* (Paris, 1951) and second revised edition (1968). Good studies in English of more specialized topics are the following: Crane Brinton, *The Jacobins* (New York, 1930; reprinted, New York, 1961); Donald M. Greer, *The Incidence of the Terror during the French Revolution: A Statistical Interpretation* (Cambridge, Mass., 1935; reprinted, Gloucester, Mass., 1966) and *The Incidence of the Emigration during the French Revolution* (Cambridge, Mass., 1951; reprinted 1966); *R. R. Palmer, *Twelve Who Ruled: The Committee of Public Safety during the Terror* (Princeton, N.J., 1941) (Atheneum); *George Rudé, *The Crowd in the French Revolution* (New York, 1959) (Oxford Galaxy Books); Albert Soboul, *The Parisian Sans-Culottes and the French Revolution, 1793–1794* (Oxford, 1964); and *Alfred Cobban, *The Social Interpretation of the French Revolution* (Cambridge, 1964), which challenges Marxist and neo-Marxist interpretations of the revolution.

On Napoleon and the Napoleonic era as a whole, see *Geoffrey Bruun, *Europe and the French Imperium, 1799–1814*, Rise of Modern Europe series (New York, 1938) (Harper Torchbook, 1963), which contains a bibliographical essay (revised November, 1957) and George Rudé, *Revolutionary Europe, 1783–1815* (New York, 1966). Georges Lefebvre is the author of *Napoléon*, fourth ed. (Paris, 1953) in the *Peuples et civilisations* series. This work is available in English in two volumes: *Napoleon, from Brumaire to Tilsit, 1799–1807*, translated by Henry F. Stockhold (New York, 1969) and *Napoleon, from Tilsit to Waterloo, 1807–1815*, trans. by J. E. Anderson (New York, 1969). In the *Nouvelle Clio* series, see Jacques L. Godechot, *L'Europe et l'Amerique à l'époque napoléonienne (1800–1815)* (Paris, 1967). Older biographies of Napoleon include an authoritative nine-volume study by F. M. Kircheisen, *Napoleon I: sein Leben und seine Zeit* (Munich and Leipzig, 1911–34), which has been abridged and translated into English by Henry St. Lawrence as *Napoleon*

(New York, 1932). See also J. Holland Rose, *Life of Napoleon I*, 2 vols. (New York, 1907). An interesting study of the evolution of the historical interpretation of Napoleon is *Pieter Geyl, *Napoleon: For and Against*, trans. by Olive Renier (New Haven, 1949) (Yale). Some good recent studies of the Napoleonic era include James M. Thompson, *Napoleon Bonaparte: His Rise and Fall* (Oxford, 1952) and *Felix M. H. Markham, *Napoleon and the Awakening of Europe*, (London, 1954) (Collier).

THE RESTORATION, GENERAL

General bibliographies covering the years 1815–1850 are Lowell J. Ragatz, A *Bibliography for the Study of European History, 1815–1939*, second ed. (Washington, D.C., 1946) and Alan L. C. Bullock and A. J. P. Taylor, A *Select List of Books on European History, 1815–1914*, second ed. (Oxford, 1957). General works on this period include the relevant volumes in the *Cambridge Modern History* (London, 1902–1911) and the *New Cambridge Modern History* (Cambridge, Eng., 1957–   ). In the Rise of Modern Europe series are the useful volumes of *Frederick B. Artz, *Reaction and Revolution, 1814–1832* (New York, 1934) (Harper Torchbook) and *William L. Langer, *Political and Social Upheaval, 1832–1852* (New York, 1969) (Harper Torchbook), both with excellent up-to-date bibliographies. The *Peuples et civilisations* series includes a new edition (1960) of Georges Weill, *L'Éveil des nationalités et le mouvement libéral (1815–1848)* (Paris, 1930). See also, in the French series *Clio*, the volume by Jacques Droz and others, *Restaurations et révolutions, 1815–1871* (Paris, 1953). An interesting new Marxist-oriented interpretation of this period is *E. J. Hobsbawm, *The Age of Revolution, 1789–1848* (Cleveland and New York, 1962) (New American Library).

On the history of international relations and diplomacy, there is a brief survey by René Albrecht-Carrié, A *Diplomatic History of Europe Since the Congress of Vienna* (New York, 1958). A more substantial work, included in the series *Histoire des relations internationales*, is Pierre Renouvin, *Le XIXe Siècle*, Vol. 1, *De 1815 à 1871: l'Europe des nationalités et l'éveil de nouveaux mondes* (Paris, 1954). There are numerous studies of the settlement of 1815 and the subsequent development of the alliance system. One of the most readable is *Sir Harold Nicolson, *The Congress of Vienna: A Study in Allied Unity, 1812–1822* (New York, 1946) (Viking Compass Books). See also *Edward Vose Gulick, *Europe's Classical Balance of Power* (Ithaca, 1955) (Norton Library). An older work on the same subject is W. Alison Phillips, *The Confederation of Europe: A Study of the European Alliance, 1813–1823*, second ed. (London and New York, 1920). On the Holy Alliance, the standard work is Jacques H. Pirenne, *La Sainte-Alliance*, 2 vols. (Neuchâtel, 1946–1949). Some of the best works on the diplomatic history of the Restoration era are by Sir Charles K. Webster: *The Congress of Vienna, 1814–1815*, second ed. (London, 1934); *The Foreign Policy of Castlereagh, 1815–1822*, second ed. (London, 1934), the best study of British foreign policy in the post-Napoleonic era; *Palmerston, Metternich and the European System, 1830–1841* (London, 1934); and *The Foreign Policy of Palmerston*, 2 vols. (London, 1951). On the achievement of another British foreign minister in this era, see Harold W. V. Temperley, *The Foreign Policy of Canning, 1822–1827*, second ed. (London, 1966). The standard work on the major continental diplomat of the period is Heinrich, Ritter von Srbik, *Metternich: der Staatsmann und der Mensch*, 3 vols. (Munich, 1925–1954). Two briefer but not entirely satisfactory studies of Metternich in English are A. Cecil, *Metternich, 1773–1859: A Study of His Period and Personality*, third ed. (London, 1947) and H. du Coudray, *Metternich* (London, 1935). On the diplomatic career of Talleyrand, see *Crane Brinton, *The Lives of Talleyrand* (New York, 1936) (Norton Library). On the "Eastern Question" and the involvment of the major powers in it see C. W. Crawley, *The Question of Greek Independence* (Cambridge, Eng., 1930) and C. M. Woodhouse, *The Greek War of Independence* (London, 1952).

THE REVOLUTIONS OF 1848

Studies of the revolutions of 1848 which transcend national boundaries are *Priscilla S. Robertson, *Revolutions of 1848* (Princeton, N. J., 1952) (Princeton), which attempts quite successfully to convey the reactions of individuals and groups to the revolts; *The Opening of an Era: 1848—An Historical Symposium*, ed. by François Fejtö (London, 1948); Arnold Whitridge, *Men in Crisis: The Revolutions of 1848* (New York, 1948); and the stimulating essay of *Sir Lewis B. Namier, *1848: The Revolution of the Intellectuals* (London, 1946) (Doubleday Anchor), which concentrates primarily on the nationalism of German intellectual leaders in the revolts.

NATIONAL HISTORY

On Great Britain during the era 1789-1850, standard works with good bibliographies are two volumes in the Oxford History of England series: J. Steven Watson, *The Reign of George III, 1760–1815* (New York, 1960) and Ernest L. Woodward, *The Age of Reform, 1815–1870* (Oxford, 1938; new ed., 1962). More stimulating in their interpretations are *Asa Briggs, *The Age of Improvement, 1783–1867* (London, 1959) (Harper Torchbook) and *David Thomson, *England in the Nineteenth Century*, the eighth volume in the nine-volume Pelican History of England (Harmondsworth, 1950–1955). On Britain during the revolutionary and Napoleonic eras consult the two works of J. Holland Rose: *William Pitt and the National Revival* (London, 1911) and *William Pitt and the Great War* (London, 1911). Two newer and more popularly written surveys are by Sir Arthur Bryant: *The Years of Endurance, 1793–1802* (London, 1942) and *The Years of Victory, 1802–1812* (London, 1944). The great classic on England in the nineteenth century is the work of a Frenchman: *Elie Halévy, *History of the English People in the Nineteenth Century*, trans. by E. I. Watkin, second revised ed., 6 vols. (London, 1949–1952) (University Paperbacks). The first volume of this work, *England in 1815*, is particularly brilliant. Another stimulating, though brief, essay is *G. M. Young, *Victorian England: Portrait of an Age*, second ed. (Oxford, 1953) (Galaxy Books). Numerous studies of politics and politicians in this period include Arthur Aspinall, *Lord Brougham and the Whig Party* (Manchester, 1927); William R. Brock, *Lord Liverpool and Liberal Toryism, 1820–1827* (Cambridge, Eng., 1941); George M. Trevelyan, *Lord Grey and the Reform Bill* (London, 1920); and the excellent recent works of Norman Gash: *Politics in the Age of Peel* (London and New York, 1953) and *Mr. Secretary Peel: The Life of Sir Robert Peel to 1830* (Cambridge, Mass., 1961). On economic and social developments, a good introduction, despite its bias, remains John L. Hammond and Barbara Hammond, *The Age of the Chartists, 1832–1854* (London, 1930). In addition to works listed on the Industrial Revolution (below), see Steven Marcus, *Engels, Manchester, and the Working Class* (London, 1974); Sir John H. Clapham's classic *An Economic History of Modern Britain, 1820–1929*, second ed., 3 vols. (Cambridge, Eng., 1930–1938); *George D. H. Cole, *A Short History of the British Working-Class Movement, 1789–1947* (London, 1948) (Papermac); George D. H. Cole and Raymond W. Postgate, *The Common People, 1744–1946*, fourth ed. (London, 1949) (University Paperbacks); and *George M. Trevelyan, *English Social History: A Survey of Six Centuries*, third ed. (London, 1946) (Tartan). A more recent study is *E. P. Thompson, *The Making of the English Working Class* (New York, 1964) (Random House Vintage). A good survey of political thought is *Crane Brinton, *English Political Thought in the Nineteenth Century*, second ed. (Cambridge, Mass., 1949) (Harper Torchbook). On the development of Benthamite thought in England, see *Elie Halévy, *The Growth of Philosophical Radicalism*, trans. by Mary Morris, new ed. (London, 1949) (Beacon).

There are still relatively few good general works available in English on France during the Restoration era. See the relevant chapters in the best textbook on modern France, Gordon Wright, *France in Modern Times: 1760 to the Present* (Chicago, 1960). On the period up to 1830, there is the good, topical survey of Frederick B. Artz, *France under the Bourbon Restoration* (Cambridge, Mass., 1931). Much less satisfactory is Jean Lucas-Dubreton, *The Restoration and the July Monarchy* (New York, 1929). A good recent biography providing interesting insights into the July Monarchy is Thomas E. B. Howarth, *Citizen King: Louis-Philippe* (London, 1961). In French, see the volumes IV and V of *Histoire de France contemporaine*, ed. by Ernest Lavisse: these are S. Charléty, *La Restauration* (Paris, 1921) and the same author's *La Monarchie de Juillet* (Paris, 1921). More recent works include Guillaume de Bertier de Sauvigny's excellent study *The Bourbon Restoration*, translated by Lynn M. Case (Philadelphia, 1967); Félix Ponteil, *La Monarchie parlementaire, 1815–1848* (Paris, 1949); Douglas Johnson, *Guizot: Aspects of French History, 1787–1874* (Toronto, 1963); and the very good, new study by David Pinkney, *The Revolution of 1830* (Princeton, 1972). On the Revolution of 1848, consult Donald C. McKay, *The National Workshops: A Study in the French Revolution of 1848* (Cambridge, Mass., 1933) and the more general treatment of John Plamenatz, *The Revolutionary Movement in France, 1815–1871* (London, 1952). Two accounts in French are Félix Ponteil, *1848* (Paris, 1937) and Jean Dautry, *Histoire de la révolution de 1848 en France* (Paris, 1948). On the emergence of Louis Napoleon are two works by Frederick A. Simpson:

The Rise of Louis Napoleon, third ed. (New York and London, 1950) and Louis Napoleon and the Recovery of France, 1848–1856, third ed. (New York and London, 1951). On French economic development in the nineteenth century, see Rondo E. Cameron, France and the Economic Development of Europe, 1800–1914 (Princeton, 1961); Arthur L. Dunham, The Industrial Revolution in France, 1815–1848 (New York, 1955); and Shepard B. Clough, France: A History of National Economics, 1789–1939 (New York, 1939). Standard works in French are Henri Sée, La Vie économique de la France sous la monarchie censitaire (1815–1848) (Paris, 1927) and the same author's Histoire économique de la France, 2 vols. (Paris, 1948–1951). More specialized is Frank A. Haight, A History of French Commercial Policies (Paris, 1941). Two excellent studies of French socialists are *Frank Manuel, The New World of Henri Saint-Simon (Cambridge, Mass., 1956) (Notre Dame Paperback) and Leo A. Loubère, Louis Blanc: His Life and His Contribution to the Rise of French Jacobin-Socialism (Evanston, Ill., 1961). On the working-class movement there is the old classic: Emile Levasseur, Histoire des classes ouvrières et de l'industrie en France de 1789 à 1870, second revised ed., 2 vols. (Paris, 1903–1904) and Louis Chevalier, Laboring Classes and Dangerous Classes in Paris during the First Half of the Nineteenth Century (tr. by Frank Jellinek) (London, 1973). On two other aspects of nineteenth-century France, see Roger Soltau, French Political Thought in the Nineteenth Century (New Haven, 1931; reissued, 1959) and C. S. Phillips, The Church in France: 1789–1848 (London, 1929).

On Germany, two good general surveys are Ralph Flenley, Modern German History (London, 1953), which emphasizes intellectual and social history, and Koppel S. Pinson, Modern Germany, Its History and Civilization, second ed. (New York, 1966), which is relatively brief on the pre-1848 period. In Hajo Holborn's History of Modern Germany (New York, 1959–1968) vol. II (1648–1840) and vol. III (1840–1945) are relevant to this period. Specifically on the nineteenth century are Heinrich von Treitschke, History of Germany in the Nineteenth Century, 7 vols. (New York, 1915–1919), a strongly nationalistic older work, and Franz Schnabel, Deutche Geschichte im neunzehnten Jahrhundert, 4 vols. (Freiburg, 1929–1937), which narrates general developments only to the 1820's. A celebrated work on the development of German nationalism is Friedrich Meinecke, Weltbürgertum und Nationalstaat, seventh ed. (Munich and Berlin, 1928). This work has recently been translated by B. Kimber as Cosmopolitanism and the National State (Princeton, N.J., 1969). On Germany during the era of the French Revolution see George P. Gooch, Germany and the French Revolution (London and New York, 1920) and the more recent Jacques Droz, L'Allemagne et la Révolution française (Paris, 1949). See also Klaus Epstein, The Genesis of German Conservatism (Princeton, N.J., 1966) which deals with the period from 1770 to 1806. On various intellectual developments prior to 1815 see Reinhold Aris, History of Political Thought in Germany from 1789–1815 (London, 1936); Robert R. Ergang, Herder and the Foundations of German Nationalism (New York, 1931); and Koppel S. Pinson, Pietism as a Factor in the Rise of German Nationalism (New York, 1934). On the Prussian reform movement, in addition to the older introduction of Guy

Stanton Ford, *Stein and the Era of Reform in Prussia, 1807–1815* (Princeton, N.J., 1922), see Walter M. Simon, *The Failure of the Prussian Reform Movement, 1807–1819* (Ithaca, N.Y., 1955) and Peter Paret, *Yorck and the Era of Prussian Reform, 1807–1815* (Princeton, N.J., 1966). On problems of Germany's intellectual development during the nineteenth century there is the extremely perceptive analysis of Leonard Krieger, *The German Idea of Freedom* (Boston, 1957), which traces this conception from the eighteenth to the twentieth centuries. See also the more controversial *Peter Viereck, *Metapolitics: Roots of the Nazi Mind* (New York, 1941) (Capricorn), which finds some quite specific antecedents of Nazism in the early nineteenth century. Also, Richard H. Thomas, *Liberalism, Nationalism, and the German Intellectuals (1822–1847)* (Cambridge, Eng., 1952). An excellent study of certain economic and social transformations occurring during the Restoration is contained in *Theodore Hamerow, *Restoration, Revolution, Reaction: Economics and Politics in Germany, 1815–1871* (Princeton, N.J., 1958) (Princeton). The best study of the German customs union is William O. Henderson, *The Zollverein* (Cambridge, Eng., 1939; reissued, Chicago, 1959). On the revolutions of 1848 in Germany, see in addition to the work of Sir Lewis B. Namier, cited earlier, Veit Valentin, *1848: Chapters of German History* (London, 1940); Jacques Droz, *Les Révolutions allemandes de 1848* (Paris, 1957); Frank Eyck, *The Frankfurt Parliament 1848–49* (London, 1968); and P.H. Noyes, *Organization and Revolution: Working-Class Associations in the German Revolutions of 1848–49* (Princeton, N.J., 1966). On the Austrian Empire, in addition to works on Metternich mentioned earlier, see C. A. Macartney, *The Hapsburg Empire, 1790–1918* (London, 1968); *A. J. P. Taylor, *The Habsburg Monarchy, 1809–1918* (London, 1948) (Harper Torchbook); and Robert A. Kann, *A Study in Austrian Intellectual History* (New York, 1960).

An outline of the history of Italy from the eighteenth to the twentieth centuries is provided by *Arthur J. Whyte, *The Evolution of Modern Italy* (Oxford, 1944) (Norton Library). The most comprehensive survey in English of the *Risorgimento* is still Bolton King, *A History of Italian Unity, Being a Political History of Italy From 1814 to 1871*, 2 vols. (London, 1912). A work with Catholic sympathies is George F. Berkeley and Joan Berkeley, *Italy in the Making, 1815–1848*, 3 vols. (Cambridge, Eng., 1932–1940). See also Kent R. Greenfield, *Economics and Liberalism in the Risorgimento: A Study of Nationalism in Lombardy, 1814–1848* (Baltimore, 1934), which challenges older political interpretations of the movement for national unification. For discussions of the most prominent leaders of the *Risorgimento* consult Gwilym O. Griffith, *Mazzini: Prophet of Modern Europe* (London, 1932) and *Gaetano Salvemini, *Mazzini* (London, 1956) (Collier), which includes selections from Mazzini's writings. The best biography of Cavour remains William R. Thayer, *The Life and Times of Cavour*, 2 vols. (Boston, 1911). A good recent study of Garibaldi is Denis Mack Smith, *Garibaldi: A Great Life in Brief* (New York, 1956). An account of another important figure in nineteenth-century Italian history is Edward E. Y. Hales, *Pio Nono: A Study in European Politics and Religion in the Nineteenth Century* (New York, 1954). On the revolutions of 1848, see the classic work of George M. Trevelyan, *Manin and the Venetian*

Revolution of 1848 (London, 1923) as well as his *Garibaldi's Defence of the Roman Republic* (London and New York, 1907).

For the history of Russia, there are three good, general surveys: *Sir Bernard Pares, A History of Russia*, fifth ed., revised and enlarged (New York, 1947) (Random House Vintage), definitive ed. (New York, 1960) (Random House Vintage); *George Vernadsky, A History of Russia*, fourth ed. (New Haven, 1954) (Yale), fifth revised edition (New Haven, 1961) (Yale); and *Benedict Sumner, A Short History of Russia*, revised ed. (New York, 1949) (Harvest Books). An excellent recent text is Nicholas V. Riasanovsky, *A History of Russia* (New York, 1963); second edition (New York, 1969). Concerning a more limited period in Russia's relations with Europe, see Andrei A. Lobanov-Rostovsky, *Russia and Europe, 1789-1825* (Durham, N.C., 1947). An excellent study of the Decembrist Revolt is *Anatole G. Mazour, The First Russian Revolution, 1825: The Decembrist Movement, Its Origins, Development and Significance* (Berkeley, Calif., 1937) (Stanford). One of the leading statesmen of the first half of the century is treated in Marc Raeff, *Michael Speransky, Statesman of Imperial Russia, 1772-1839* (The Hague, 1957). On the reign of Nicholas I, there are several good studies in English: Sidney Monas, *The Third Section: Police and Society in Russia under Nicholas I* (Cambridge, Mass., 1961), not quite as specialized as the title might suggest; *Nicholas V. Riasanovsky, Nicholas I and Official Nationality in Russia, 1825-1855* (Berkeley, Calif., 1959) (University of California); and the same author's *Russia and the West in the Teaching of the Slavophiles: A Study of Romantic Ideology* (Cambridge, Mass., 1952). For Russian economic development, see J. Mavor, *Economic History of Russia*, second ed., rev. and enl. (New York, 1965) and a Soviet historian's treatment, Petr I. Liashchenko, *History of the National Economy of Russia to the 1917 Revolution* (New York, 1949). Finally, good studies of special topics include Philip E. Mosely, *Russian Diplomacy and the Opening of the Eastern Question in 1838 and 1839* (Cambridge, Mass., 1934); *Hans Kohn, Pan-Slavism, Its History and Ideology* (Notre Dame, Ind., 1953) (Random House Vintage); and Avrahm Yarmolinsky, *Road to Revolution: A Century of Russian Radicalism* (New York, 1959).

POLITICAL AND SOCIAL THEORY

For political movements and ideologies, one of the best introductory works is *John Bowle, *Politics and Opinion in the Nineteenth Century* (London, 1954) (Galaxy Books). On conservatism there is no good single work. Ernest L. Woodward, *Three Studies in European Conservatism* (London, 1929) contains excellent studies of Metternich's views on international relations and of Guizot's political ideas, and an essay on the Catholic Church in the nineteenth century. See also Alfred Cobban, *Edmund Burke and the Revolt against the Eighteenth Century* (London, 1929) and *Herbert Marcuse, *Reason and Revolution: Hegel and the Rise of Social Theory* (New York, 1941) (Beacon). For discussion of nineteenth-century nationalism see Carlton J. H. Hayes, *The Historical Evolution of Modern Nationalism* (New York, 1931) and *Boyd C. Shafer, *Nationalism, Myth and Reality* (New York, 1955) (Harvest Books). General studies of liberalism include Guido de Ruggiero, *The History of European Liberalism* (London, 1927), available in a paperback edition (Beacon Press); and a provocative work by Jacob S. Schapiro, *Liberalism and the Challenge of Fascism: Social Forces in England and France, 1815–1870* (New York, 1949). On socialism, see George Lichtheim, *The Origins of Socialism* (New York, 1969) and *Alexander Gray, *The Socialist Tradition: From Moses to Lenin* (London, 1946) (Harper Torchbook). Illuminating discussions of some of the Utopian Socialists are contained in *Edmund Wilson, *To the Finland Station: A Study in the Writing and Acting of History* (New York, 1940) (Doubleday Anchor).

ECONOMIC HISTORY

Standard economic histories include Shepard B. Clough and Charles W. Cole, *Economic History of Europe*, third ed. (New York, 1952); Herbert Heaton, *Economic History of Europe*, revised ed. (New York, 1948); and Witt Bowden, Michael Karpovich, and Abbot Payson Usher, *Economic History of Europe since 1750* (New York, 1937). On the Industrial Revolution, see the important recent study by *David S. Landes, *The Unbound Prometheus: Technological Change and Industrial Development in Western Europe from 1750 to the Present* (Cambridge, 1969), an expanded and somewhat revised version of Chapter V in volume 6 of the *Cambridge Economic History of Europe*, edited by H. J. Habakkuk and M. Postan (Cambridge, 1965). Landes's extensive bibliography on the Industrial Revolution can be found at the end of volume 6, part II, of the *Cambridge Economic History of Europe*. For a brief introduction to the Industrial Revolution, especially in Great Britain, *Thomas S. Ashton, *The Industrial Revolution, 1760–1830* (London and New York, 1948) (Galaxy Books). See also Ashton's *Economic History of England: The Eighteenth Century* (London, 1955) and the older study by *Paul J. Mantoux, *The Industrial Revolution in the Eighteenth Century: An Outline of the Beginnings of the Modern Factory System in England* (New York, 1928) (Harper Torchbook). On the economic ties between Britain and the Continent there is William O. Henderson, *Britain and Industrial Europe, 1750–1870* (Liverpool, 1954), and specifically on the two most important continental countries is *John H. Clapham, *The Economic Development of France and Germany, 1815–1914*, fourth ed. (Cambridge, Eng., 1936) (Cambridge). See also the title cited earlier among the works on French economic development, in the section on National History, Rondo E. Cameron, *France and the Economic Development of Europe, 1800–1914* (Princeton, 1961), which deals with the role played by Frenchmen in transmitting to the rest of Europe the fundamental elements of Britain's economic revolution. For a general introduction to European social history in the nineteenth century with bibliography, see *Peter N. Stearns, *European Society in Upheaval: Social History since 1800* (New York, 1967) and a recent collection of essays edited by *Robert J. Bezucha, *Modern European Social History* (Lexington, Mass., 1972).

CULTURAL HISTORY

On literature and the arts, a standard older work is Georg M. C. Brandes, *Main Currents in Nineteenth Century Literature*, 6 vols. (New York, 1901–

1905). Two good works on romanticism are *Jacques Barzun, *Romanticism and the Modern Ego* (Boston, 1943) (Doubleday Anchor) , which has been retitled in a new edition: *Classic, Romantic and Modern*, second revised edition (Boston, 1961) (Anchor Doubleday) and P. Van Tieghem, *Le Romantisme dans la littérature européenne* (Paris, 1948). For the art of the period consult Edgar P. Richardson, *The Way of Western Art, 1776–1914* (Cambridge, Mass., 1939) and the standard works of Thomas Craven, *Modern Art* (New York, 1934); Lionello Venturi, *Modern Painters*, 2 vols. (New York, 1947–1950); Henri Focillon, *La Peinture au XIXe et XXe siècles* (Paris, 1928); and Marcel Brion, *Romantic Art* (London, 1960). This work is now available in paperback as *Art of the Romantic Era: Classicism, Romanticism, Realism* (Praeger). See also the appropriate chapters in *Arnold Hauser, *The Social History of Art*, translated in collaboration with the author by Stanley Godman, 2 vols. (New York, 1951) (Random House Vintage). On music, the best works are Alfred Einstein, *Music in the Romantic Era* (New York, 1947) and the outstanding book by Paul H. Lang, *Music in Western Civilization* (New York, 1941). See also Donald J. Grout, *A History of Western Music* (New York, 1960).

Index

Abdul-Medjid (Sultan of Turkey), 151, 152
Abukir Bay, Battle of (1798), 56
Academic Legion (Austrian organization), 270
Addington, Henry, 80
Addresses to the German Nation (Fichte), 99, 194
Adrianople, Treaty of (1829), 145–46
Aide-toi, et le ciel t'aidera (French organization), 219
Aiguillon, Duke of (Emmanuel Vignerot du Plessis de Richelieu), 14
Aix-la-Chapelle, Congress of (1818), 137–38
Alber, Charles, 140
Albert (mechanic), 257
Alexander I (Tsar of Russia), 105, 150, 250, 251
  biography and characteristics of, 89–90, 188, 244
  Concert of Europe and
    Aix-la-Chapelle Congress and, 137–38
    Greek revolt and, 143
    southern European revolts and, 138–40
  in Congress of Vienna, 123, 127–29, 134
    goals of Alexander, 125, 127
    and Polish-Saxon settlement, 128, 129
  death of, 246, 247
  and Holy Alliance, 134, 181
  in Napoleonic era, 93–95, 103, 109–12
    and Russian campaign, 110–12
    in war of liberation (1814), 114
  in Restoration era, 245–49
    Decembrist Revolt, 243–47
    first and second periods of reforms under, 244–45
Alexander the Great, 56, 68
Alliance Solidaire, 137–38
Alsace-Lorraine, 30, 133
American Revolution (1776), 1, 2, 25

Amiens, Treaty of (1802), 80–82, 86, 88
Anatomy of Revolution (Brinton), 4
Angoulême, Duke of (Louis Antoine de Bourbon), 217
Arago, François, 257
Aristocracy
  French
    émigrés, 25, 30, 31, 82, 132
    in prerevolutionary era, 2, 5, 6
    during Revolution, 14
    as Second Estate, 5, 9
    see also France—in Restoration era
  German, in 1848, 236
Arkwright, Richard, 161
Army officers in opposition to Restoration, 187
Arndt, Ernst Moritz, 231
Artisans
  French Revolution and, 18
  German, 235–36
  Industrial Revolution and, 165, 172–73
Artois, Counts of
  Charles X, 25, 218–21
  Charles Philippe, 115
Ashley, first Baron (Anthony Ashley Cooper, later Earl of Shaftesbury), 214
Ashton, T. S., 155
Atlantic revolution, argument supporting concept of, 1–2
Attwood, Thomas, 215
Auber, Daniel, 148
Auerstedt, Battle of (1806), 93
Augsburg (free city), 81
Austerlitz, Battle of (1805), 91, 95, 96, 103, 104, 113
Austria, 55–56, 99
  in Concert of Europe, 136
    Belgian revolt and, 148, 149
    Eastern Question and, 152
  in Congress of Vienna, 126–31
    Polish-Saxon settlement and, 128–30
    receives territorial restorations, 131, 135

Austria *(continued)*
  first Treaty of Paris and, 122, 123
  in Holy Alliance, 134; *see also* Holy Alliance
  in Napoleonic era
    and 1806–1807 war with Prussia, 93
    reactions to Hundred Days, 117
    and reorganization of Germany, 81–82
    and Russian campaign, 110
    in Second Coalition war, 56–60, 79
    in Third Coalition war, 88–91
    and Treaty of Tilsit, 95
    in war of 1809, 103–5
    in war of liberation, 113
  in Restoration era, 229, 235–39
    1848 revolutions in, 252–54, 262, 267–72, 276, 278
    and 1848 revolutions in Italy, 275–76
    Frankfurt Parliament and, 264–66
  and revolutionary France
    in First Coalition war, 30–31, 36–37
    reactions to French Revolution, 29–30, 62–63
Austrian Netherlands, 30, 37, 55, 58, 61, 122
  Holland annexes, 130, 135
  see also Belgium

Babeuf, François Émile, 52
Baden, 81–83, 90, 91, 229
Balzac, Honoré de, 222–23
Barbès, Armand, 258
Barras, Viscount (Paul François de Barras), 53, 54, 65
Barthélemy, François de, 53
Basel, Treaty of (1795), 81
Bastille, stormed (July 14, 1789), 10–13, 18
Batavian Republic, 56, 58, 79, 80, 86, 90, 96; *see also* Holland
Bavaria, 56, 91, 103, 113, 229
  in Confederation of the Rhine, 92
  and reorganization of Germany, 81, 82
Beauharnais, Eugène de, 96
Beauharnais, Joséphine de (later Empress Joséphine), 66, 75, 104–5
Beethoven, Ludwig van, 199
Belgium, 30, 80, 130
  Industrial Revolution in, 233
  in Restoration era, 251
  revolt in (1830–1831), 146–50
  see also Austrian Netherlands
Bentham, Jeremy, 189
Beresford, Marshal William Carr, 139
Berg, duchy of, 92, 97

Berlin Decree (November, 1806), 100
Berlin demonstrations (1848), 261
Berlioz, Hector, 199
Bernadotte, Crown Prince (Sweden), 91, 110, 113
Berry, Duke of (Charles Ferdinand de Bourbon), 218
Bill of Rights (U.S.), 14–15
Birmingham Political Union (British organization), 215
Bismarck, Otto von, 121, 266, 267
Blanc, Louis, 177–78, 257–58
Blanqui, Auguste, 258
Blücher, Gebhard von, 114, 117–18
Bohemia, kingdom of, 30, 238, 267–70
Bologna, legation of, 55, 78
Bonald, Viscount (Louis Gabriel de Bonald), 182, 189
Bonaparte, Jerome, 95, 97
Bonaparte, Joseph, 96, 102, 114
Bonaparte, Louis, 96–98, 104
Bonaparte, Louis Napoleon, 224
  election of, 254, 259–60, 277
  intervenes in Italy (1849), 274–75
Bonaparte, Lucien, 54, 82
Bonaparte, Napoleon, *see* Napoleon I
Bonapartists (French political group), 223–24
Borodino, Battle of (1812), 111, 117*n*
Bosporus Straits, 152
Boulton, Matthew, 162
Bourbon Restoration, 107, 115–18, 150, 216–21
Bourgeoisie, 185, 187
  French
    Bourbon Restoration and, 218
    effects of February Revolution on, 278
    July Monarchy and, 222–23
    Napoleonic reforms and, 119
    prerevolutionary, 5–6
    in revolutionary France, 18; *see also* Third Estate
    Industrial Revolution and, 163, 170–73
    in opposition to Restoration, 185, 187
Bremen, 81, 235
Bright, John, 212
Brinton, Crane, 4, 17, 47
Brissotins (Girondins), 28, 30, 34–36, 39, 40, 45
Brunswick, 232
Brunswick, Ferdinand, Duke of, 31
Bruun, Geoffrey, 58
Burke, Edmund, 29, 182, 183, 206
Burschenschaften (German student societies), 231–32

Byron, George Gordon Lord, 144, 198, 202

Cadoudal, Georges, 83
Cadoudal conspiracy (1804), 83
Cambacérès, Jean Jacques Régis de, 69
Campoformio, Treaty of (1797), 57–58, 79, 81
Canals, development of, 163
Canning, George, 141–42, 145, 208–9
Cape Colony, 131
Capitalism, *see* Economy; Industrial Revolution
Capodistrias, Count Johannes Antonius, 143
Carbonari (Italian organization), 97, 139, 187, 240
Carlsbad Decrees (German, 1819), 232
Carnot, Lazare, 53
Caroline (Queen to George IV of England), 205
Castlereagh, Viscount (Robert Stewart, second Marquis of Londonderry), 122
    and *Alliance Solidaire*, 137
    in Congress of Vienna, 123, 127, 128, 133, 135
    death of, 208
    and Greek revolt, 143
    on Holy Alliance, 134
    and Quadruple Alliance, 135
    and southern European revolts (1820–1823), 138–41
Catherine the Great (Tsarina of Russia), 30–31, 59, 62, 90, 243, 244, 246
Catholic Emancipation Act (British, 1829), 209
Catholics, *see* Roman Catholic Church
Cato Street Conspiracy (1819), 207–8
Cavaignac, Gen. Louis, 259
Cavour, Count Camillo Benso di, 242, 273, 276
Ceylon, 80, 131
Chadwick, Edwin, 167–68
Chaptal, Jean, 67
Charlemagne (Frankish emperor), 68, 85, 100
Charles IV (King of Spain), 102
Charles X (King of France, earlier Count of Artois), 25, 218–21
Charles Albert (King of Sardinia), 243, 272–75
Charles Louis, Archduke (Austria), 55, 103–4
Charles Philippe (Count of Artois), 115
Charlotte, Princess (British), 149

Charter of 1814 (French), 115, 216–17, 218–22, 229
Charter of 1830 (French), 272
Charterhouse of Parma, The (Stendhal), 224
Chartism (British political movement), 187, 210–16
Chateaubriand, François René de, 201
Chaumont, Treaty of (1814), 122–23
Church, the, *see* Roman Catholic Church
Cisalpine Republic (Republic of Italy), 58, 79, 86, 90
Civil Constitution of the Clergy (French, 1791), 19, 22, 78, 107
Civil and Moral Primacy of the Italians, The (Gioberti), 242
Clergy, *see* Roman Catholic Church; Second Estate
Clericals (Belgian political group), 147
Coal-mining shafts, 162, 234
Cobbett, William, 206
Cobden, Richard, 212
Code Napoléon, 73, 97–98, 118, 190
Coleridge, Samuel Taylor, 202
Combination Acts (British, 1824), 208
Comédie Humaine (Balzac), 223
Concert of Europe, 120–54
    Belgian revolt and, 146–50
    conference system of, 136–46
        Congress of Aix-la-Chapelle in, 137–38
        revolutions in southern Europe and, 138–42
    and Congress of Vienna, *see* Congress of Vienna
    Eastern Question and, 150–54
    Greek revolt and, 141–46
    Treaty of Chaumont and first Treaty of Paris and, 122–23
Concordat (1801), 23, 76–79, 82, 105, 119, 216
Condorcet, Marquis de (Marie Jean de Caritat), 5
Confederation of the Rhine, 92, 95, 99, 110, 113, 114; *see also* Rhineland
Congress of Vienna (1814–1815), 107, 123–31, 205, 228, 239
    appraised, 135–36, 192
    final settlement at, 129–31
    Germanic Confederation created by, 131, 229–33; *see also* Deutscher Bund
    organization and leadership of, 123–28
    Polish-Saxon settlement at, 128–30, 245, 250
    principle of legitimacy at, 129, 180–81

Congress of Vienna (*continued*)
  second Treaty of Paris and Holy Alliance and, 131–35
Conservatism
  in Restoration, 180–96
    early 19th-century liberalism and, 188–91
    early 19th-century nationalism and, 191–96
    opposition to Restoration and, 185–88
  view of French Revolution, 64
  see also Reaction
Conspiracy of the Equals (1795–1796), 52
Constantine, Grand Duke (Russia), 247, 250
Constituent Assembly, *see* National Assembly
Constitution (U.S.), 14–15
Constitution of 1791 (French), 9, 15–16, 18–19, 27, 41, 72, 91, 115
Constitution of 1793 (French), 16, 41, 52
Constitution of 1795 (French), 16, 50–51
Constitution of 1812 (Spanish), 138, 139
Constitution of 1818 (Polish), 245
Constitution of the Year VIII (1799, French), 69
Constitution of the Year XII (1804, French), 84
Constitutional monarchy
  Belgium becomes (1830), 148
  French (1789–1792), 16, 18–28
    achievements of, 18–23
    decline of, 23–28
    Directory compared with, 51–52
    see also July Monarchy
Constitutionnel (French newspaper), 219
Constitutions granted in 1848 and 1849, 259
  in Austria-Hungary, 265–66, 272
  in Kingdom of Two Sicilies, 273
  to Papal States, 273
  in Prussia, 262
  in Sardinia, 273, 275, 276
  in Tuscany, 273
Consulate (French, 1799–1804), 67–82
  codes written under, 73–74, 97–98, 118, 190
  Concordat signed, 23, 74–79, 82, 105, 119, 216
  international developments during, 79–82
  police state under, 74–76
  public education under, 72–73

  structure of, 69–70
  taxation and economy under, 71–72
Continental System, 87, 98, 101–2, 104, 105, 110
Convention, *see* National Convention
Corn Law (British, 1815), 174, 206, 212
Corneille, Pierre, 200
Corresponding Society (British), 62
Corsican independence movement, 65
Cort, Henry, 162–63
Cousine Bette (Balzac), 223
Craig, Gordon, 153
Crimean War (1854–1856), 121, 249
Croatia, 269
Cuba, 142
Custine, Gen. Adam Philippe de, 37
Custoza, Battle of (1848), 274
Czartoryski, Prince Adam, 123, 244

Dahlmann, Friedrich, 268
Danton, Jacques, 33, 34, 48, 49
Dantonists (French political group), 48
Darby, Abraham, 162
Dardanelles, Straits of, 150, 152
Daumier, Honoré, 224, 226
Davout, Marshal Louis Nicolas, 76
Decazes, Duke Élie, 218
Decembrist Revolt (Russian, 1825), 243–47
Declaration of Independence (U.S., 1776), 265
Declaration of Pillnitz (1791), 30
Declaration of the Rights of Man and the Citizen (French, 1789), 21, 74, 75, 115, 119, 191
  drafted, 9
  influence of, 64, 265
  issued, 14–16, 19
Deism, 200
Delacroix, Eugène, 145, 197–99
De Launay, Bernard, 12
De Maistre, Joseph, 182, 184, 189
Demerara (Guiana), 131
Denmark, 59, 110, 264
Desaix, Gen. Louis, 79
Desmoulins, Camille, 11
Deutscher Bund (Germanic Confederation)
  1848 revolutions in, 252, 257, 260–72
    in Austria, 267–72
    Frankfurt Parliament and, 262–67
    Prussia, 260–62
  established (1815), 131, 229–33
  in Restoration era, 180, 242, 251
    early 19th-century nationalism in, 192–95

liberalism in, 188–90
opposition to Metternich's repressive
policies in, 229–33
romanticism in, 196, 197, 199–203
Vormärz era in, 233–36
see also Austria; Prussia
Dickens, Charles, 166, 169
Diderot, Denis, 5
Directory (French, 1795–1799), 16, 51–57, 68
economy under, 54–55
18 Brumaire ends, 9, 16, 53–54, 57, 67, 69, 107
internal threats to, 52–53
power distribution in, 51–52
Second Coalition and, 58
Dostoevski, Fëdor, 249
Dresden, Battle of (1813), 113
Ducos, Roger, 53, 54, 57, 69
Dumouriez, Charles François, 30, 36–38, 61
Düsseldorfer Zeitung (German newspaper), 236
Dutch Republic, *see* Holland
Duties of Man, The (Mazzini), 241

Eastern Question, 150–54
Ecclesiastical states, 81–82; *see also* Papal States
Economic liberalism (*laissez-faire*), 173–75, 212–14, 225
Economy (and economic conditions)
Belgian, 146
British, 206–16
Continental System to restrict British trade, 87, 95, 101–2, 104, 105, 110
free trade and, 210–16
under Tory rule, 206–10
French
under Consulate, 71–72
1810, 105
1814–1815, 115–16
February Revolution and, 252–53, 255, 257–58
in prerevolutionary France, 2–3
in revolutionary France, 21, 39–40, 44, 50, 54–55
state of, preceding February Revolution, 170, 178
of Germanic Confederation (prior to 1848), 233–36
Sardinian, 243
see also Industrial Revolution
Egypt
Eastern Question and, 150–52

expedition into (1798–1799), 53, 56–57, 66
England expels French from Egypt, 79
Napoleon considers recapture of, 87
Greek revolt and, 145
18 Brumaire (1799), 9, 16, 17, 53–54, 57, 67, 69, 107
1809, war of, 103–5
Elba, Napoleon I exiled at, 115, 116
Émigrés (French), 25, 30, 31, 82, 182
Engels, Frederick, 178
Enghien, Duke of (Louis Antoine de Bourbon-Condé), 83–84, 90
England, *see* Great Britain
England, Bank of, 207
Enlightenment, the, 184, 188, 191; *see also Philosophes*
Enragés (French political group), 39–40
Estates-General, 3, 5, 7, 9, 11, 16
Eugénie Grandet (Balzac), 223
Europe, Concert of, *see* Concert of Europe
Europe and the French Imperium (Bruun), 58
Eylau, Battle of (1807), 93

Factory Act (British, 1833), 170, 213
February Revolution (French, 1848), 170, 178, 223, 227, 228, 252–60, 269
Ferdinand (Duke of Brunswick), 31
Ferdinand I (Emperor of Austria), 239, 269, 271
Ferdinand I (King of Two Sicilies), 131, 139, 140, 240
Ferdinand II (King of Two Sicilies), 252, 273, 274
Ferdinand VII (King of Spain), 102, 131, 138–39, 188
Ferrara, legation of, 55, 78
Fersen, Count Hans Axel von, 26
Fichte, Johann Gottlieb, 99, 182–83, 193–95
Final Act (1815), 129–31, 133
Finland, 131
First Coalition (1793–1795), 37–38, 50, 60, 62
First Estate, 5, 9
First International Workingmen's Association, 278
First Republic (French, 1792–1799)
established, 31–36
see also Directory; National Convention; Terror, Reign of; Thermidorean reaction
First World War (1914–1918), 136, 237

Five Glorious Days (Milan, March 18–22, 1848), 273
Fouché, Joseph, 49, 75
Fourier, Charles, 175–77
Fox, Charles James, 28–29, 63
France
  and Concert of Europe, 137, 154
    Belgian revolt and, 148–50
    Eastern Question and, 150–53
    Greek revolt and, 143, 145, 146
    reactions to revolutions in southern Europe, 138, 140–42
  Congress of Vienna and, 125, 127–31, 136
    French borders redefined at, 130–31
    Polish-Saxon settlement and, 138
    second Treaty of Paris and, 131, 133
  in Crimean War, 249
  first Treaty of Paris and, 122
  French Empire, *see* Napoleon I—as Emperor
  Industrial Revolution in, 160, 233, 234
    economic liberalism in, 174
    emergence of socialism, 175–78
    expansion of middle class, 171, 173
    population growth and, 156
    urbanization and, 167
  prerevolutionary, 2–6
    economy of, 2–3
    intellectuals as critics of, 4–5
    political weaknesses of, 3–4
  in Restoration era, 181, 205, 251
    Bourbon Restoration, 216–21
    February Revolution in, 170, 178, 223, 227, 228, 252–60, 269
    intervenes in Italian revolutions (1848), 274–75
    July Monarchy in, 221–28
    liberalism in, 189, 190
    opposition to, 185
    romanticism in, 196–203
  revolutionary, *see* French Revolution
  see also Napoleon I
France, Bank of, 71
Francis I (Emperor of Austria, earlier Francis II, Holy Roman Emperor), 92, 96, 103, 237, 239
  Congress of Vienna and, 124–26
  and Holy Alliance, 134
  as Holy Roman Emperor, 30, 62, 90
Francis II (Holy Roman Emperor), *see* Francis I
Francis Joseph I (Emperor of Austria), 265–66, 271
Franco-Prussian alliance (1806), 91–92
Frankfurt (free city), 81

Frankfurt Parliament, 262–67, 270
Frederick Augustus I (Ruler of Saxony), 123
Frederick the Great (King of Prussia), 29, 69, 92
Frederick William II (King of Prussia), 29, 30
Frederick William III (King of Prussia), 114, 127, 148
  and Holy Alliance, 134
  in Napoleonic wars, 92–94, 119
  reign of, 230
  and repression in Germanic Confederation, 232
Frederick William IV (King of Prussia), 260–62, 266, 269, 271
French Empire, *see* Napoleon I—as Emperor
French Revolution (1789), 1–15, 155, 176, 187
  appraised, 63–64
  conservatives of Restoration era and, 182, 183
  Europe and, 28–31
  influence of, 191, 241, 251
  liberalism and, 188
  Metternich's view of, 126
  outbreak of, 7–15
  prospects opened to Napoleon by, 65
  role of Parisians in, 18
  see also Constitutional monarchy; Directory; Legislative Assembly; National Assembly; National Convention; Terror, Reign of; Thermidorean reaction
Friedland, Battle of (1807), 93, 117n
Friedrich, Caspar David, 197
Fructidor *coup d'état* (1797), 53
"Fundamental Rights of the German People," 265

Galicia, 104, 109, 129, 268
Garibaldi, Giuseppe, 275
Geneva (city-state), 1, 2
Genoa, Republic of (Ligurian Republic), 58, 79
Gentz, Friedrich von, 127, 182
George III (King of England), 205
George IV (King of England), 134, 205, 209, 210
German History in the Era of the Reformation (Ranke), 203
Germanic Confederation, *see Deutscher Bund*
Germany
  Industrial Revolution in, 155

artisan revolt in (1844), 173
and population growth, 156
urbanization and, 167
in Napoleonic era, 90, 95
Continental System and, 101
reorganization of (1803), 80–82, 86, 98–99
reactions of, to French Revolution, 29, 62
Germany in Her Deepest Humiliation (pamphlet), 93
Gioberti, Vincenzo, 242
Girondins (Brissotins), 28, .30, 34–36, 39, 40, 45
Glorious Revolution (British, 1688), 29
Gneisenau, Neithardt von, 44, 230
Goderich, Viscount (Frederick John Robinson), 209
Godoy, Manuel de, 102
Goethe, Johann Wolfgang von, 196, 201
Gogol, Nikolai, 249
Gohier, Louis Jérome, 53
Gordon Riots (British, 1780), 2
Görgey, Gen. Arthur von, 272
Görres, Joseph von, 231
Government decrees of 1803 (Russian), 244–45
Great Britain
   in Concert of Europe, 136
      Belgian revolt and, 148–50
      and Congress of Aix-la-Chapelle, 137
      and Eastern Question, 150–53
      Greek revolt and, 142, 143, 145, 146
      reactions to southern European revolutions, 138–42
   Congress of Vienna and, 127–29, 131
   in Crimean War, 249
   first Treaty of Paris and, 123
   Glorious Revolution in, 29
   Gordon riots in, 2
   Industrial Revolution in, 155, 156, 187, 233
      conditions favoring development of, 158–63
      conditions of working class in, 168–70; *see also* Proletariat—British
      economic liberalism and, 173–75
      emergence of socialism and, 175–77
      expansion of middle-class in, 171, 173
      population growth and, 156, 158
      social impact of, 163–68
   in Napoleonic era, 109, 110
      Continental System against, 87, 98, 100–2, 104, 105, 110
      1806–1807 war with Prussia and, 93

Egyptian expedition and, *see* Egypt—expedition into
   reactions of, to Hundred Days, 117
   Russian campaign and, 110, 112
   and Second Coalition, 56, 57, 59, 60, 79–80
   and Third Coalition, 86–91
   Treaty of Tilsit and, 95
   in war of liberation, 113
   in Restoration era, 181, 183–85, 251
   1848 revolutions and, 252
   liberalism in, 188, 189
   opposition to, 185, 187
   reform, free trade, and Chartism in, 187, 210–16
   romanticism in, 196–98, 200–3
   Tory rule in, 205–10
   unrest in (1815–1820), 207
   revolutionary France and, 37
   Directory and, 55, 56
   First Coalition war and, 37–38
   reactions to, 28, 29, 62–63
   1780 unrest in, 1, 2
Great Fear (1789), 13
Great Powers, 121; *see also* Austria; France; Great Britain; Prussia; Russia
Greek revolt (1821–1832, Greco-Turkish war), 141–46, 150, 195, 199, 251
Grey, second Earl (Charles Grey), 148, 210
Grimm, Jacob, 193
Grimm, Wilhelm, 193
Guizot, François, 223, 227, 228, 252, 255

Habeas Corpus Act (British), 206
Haitian campaign (1803), 87
Hamburg, 81, 235
Handloom weavers' revolt (Silesia, 1844), 173
Hanover, 92, 129, 235
Hapsburg Empire, 29, 156; *see also* Austria; Hungary
Hardenberg, Friedrich von (Novalis), 201
Hardenberg, Baron (later Prince) Karl August von, 127, 128, 133, 230, 231
Hargreaves, James, 161
Hard Times (Dickens), 166, 169
Hauptmann, Gerhard, 173
Haydn, Franz Josef, 199
Haynau, Gen. Baron Julius von, 272
Hébert, Jacques, 48, 49
Hébertists (French political group), 48–49
Hegel, G. W. F., 182–83, 194–95
Heine, Heinrich, 202

Helvetic Republic (later Swiss Confederation), 58, 79, 80, 86
Henry IV (King of France), 4
Herder, Johann Gottfried von, 29, 192–95
Hesse-Cassel, revolution in (1830), 232
Hesse-Darmstadt, 92
Hetaíria Philiké (Society of Friends, Greek), 143
History of England (Macaulay), 203
History of France (Michelet), 202
History of the Popes (Ranke), 203
Hitler, Adolph, 109, 120
Holland, 30, 95, 97, 104
  annexes Austrian Netherlands, 130, 135
  as Batavian Republic, 56, 58, 79, 80, 86, 90, 96
  Belgian revolt and, 146–49
  Continental System and, 101
  first Treaty of Paris and, 122
  Orange rule restored in, 114
  in Restoration era, 187
  unrest in (1780's), 1
  in war of First Coalition, 37–38
Holy Alliance (1815), 131–35, 141, 150, 181, 232
  opposition to, 188, 192, 233
  Troppau Protocol and, 140
Holy Roman Empire, 56, 96, 131, 180
  dissolved, 92, 99, 237
Humboldt, Wilhelm von, 230
Hundred Days (1815), 115–18, 131, 133, 180, 217
Hungary, 29–30, 195, 237
  1848 revolution in, 254, 268–69, 271–72
  Frankfurt Parliament and, 265
  reactions of, to French Revolution, 62
Hunt, Henry, 207
Huskisson, William, 208

Ibrahim Pasha, 145, 150, 151
Illyrian Provinces, 105, 131
Imperial Recess (1803), 81
Indemnity, Law of (French, 1825), 218
India, 56, 57
Industrial Revolution, 251
  emergence of socialism in, 175–79
  population growth and, 156–60
  see also Great Britain—Industrial Revolution in
Ionian Islands, 80, 90, 95
Ireland, 1, 209, 212, 252
Italian campaign (1796), 55, 56
Italian Peninsula, 59. 79, 91, 96, 154, 228
  Congress of Vienna and, 131

1848 revolutions in, 218, 240, 252, 253, 269, 272–76
  opposition, 187
  Risorgimento in, 238–43, 275
  Industrial Revolution in, 155
  liberalism in, 190
  in Restoration era, 195–96, 251
  1830 revolts in, 143, 148–50, 240
Italy, Kingdom of, 90–91, 96, 99
Italy, Republic of (Cisalpine Republic), 58, 79, 86, 90

Jacobins (Mountain), 18, 26, 31, 62, 246
  Babeuf compared with, 52
  British, 62
  Directory and, 53–54
  Girondins compared with, 34–35
  and Louis XVI's death, 36
  Napoleon exiles, 82
  see also Terror, Reign of
Jahn, Friedrich Ludwig, 231–32
Jemappes, Battle of (1792), 37
Jena, Battle of (1806), 44, 93, 113, 230
Jews
  in Napoleonic era, 78–79
  in Ottoman Empire, 143
John VI (King of Portugal), 139
Joseph II (Emperor of Austria), 69
Joseph II (Holy Roman Emperor), 29
Joséphine (Empress to Napoleon I, earlier Joséphine de Beauharnais), 66, 75, 104–5
Journal (Delacroix), 198
Journal des Débats (French newspaper), 219
Julius Caesar (Roman Emperor), 68
July Monarchy (1830–1848), 177, 221–28, 255, 258
July Ordinances (French, 1830), 219, 220
July Revolution (French, 1830), 147, 209, 220–23, 227, 232, 240, 259
June Days (French, 1848), 258–59, 278

Kellerman, Gen. François Christophe, 36
Kossuth, Louis, 268–69, 272
Kotzebue, August von, 232
Krüdener, Baroness Barbara von, 134
Kutuzov, Gen. Mikhail, 111, 112

Lafayette, Marquis de (Marie Joseph du Motier), 25–26, 221, 233
La Harpe, Frédéric César de, 90, 244
Laissez-faire (economic liberalism), 173–75, 212–14, 225
Lamartine, Alphonse de, 256, 258, 259
Landes, David, 168–69

La Réveillière-Lépeaux, Louis Marie, 53
League of Armed Neutrality (1800), 59
League of Nations, 242
Lebrun, Charles François, 69
Ledru-Rollin, Alexandre Auguste, 259
Lefebvre, Georges, 59, 68
Left, the, origin of term, 17
Legislative Assembly (French, 1791–1792), 19
  accomplishments of, 68
  Paris Commune and, 32–33
Legitimists (French political group), 223
Leipzig, Battle of (1813), 113–14, 232
Leopold (Grand Duke of Tuscany), 273
Leopold (of Saxe-Coburg), 149
Leopold II (Holy Roman Emperor), 25, 26, 29–30
Lermontov, Mikhail, 249
Liberalism
  Bourbon Restoration and, 218–19
  early 19th-century, 188–91
  early 19th-century nationalism and, 191–96
  economic, 212–14, 225
  German, 266–67
  see also Reforms; Revolutions—of 1848
Liberals (Belgian political group), 147
Liberation, war of (1813–1814), 113–15, 122
"Liberty Leading the People" (Delacroix), 199
Lieder (Schubert), 199
Ligurian Republic (Republic of Genoa), 58, 79
Literature
  romantic, 199–203
  Russian, 249
Liverpool, second Earl (Robert Banks Jenkinson), 141, 206, 208
Locke, John, 184
Lombardy, 131, 135, 239, 240, 242
  1848 revolution in, 269, 273
London, Treaty of (1827), 145
London, Treaty of (1840), 152
London Workingmen's Association, 214
Looms, invention of hand and power, 161
Louis XIV (King of France), 3, 4
Louis XVI (King of France), 19, 21, 30–32, 52, 115
  attempts to flee, 26–27
  attempts reconciliation, 13
  downfall of, 23–33
  execution of, 9, 35–37, 107
  and outbreak of revolution, 8
  and storming of the Bastille, 13
  Third Estate and, 9–11

Louis XVIII (King of France, earlier Count of Provence), 117n
  and Congress of Vienna, 127–29
  dissolves Chamber of Deputies (1816), 218
  and first Treaty of Paris, 122
  flees (1815), 116
  Restoration of, 107, 115, 133, 216
Louis Philippe (King of France), 107, 147, 149, 266
  Italian revolutionaries of 1830–1831 and aid from, 240
  as monarch, 150
  Napoleonic policy compared with that of, 260
  and Near East problem (1840, 1841), 152
  overthrown, 253, 255
  reign of, as "the bourgeois monarchy," 221–28
Louis Philippe Joseph (Duke of Orléans), 11
Louis Xavier Stanislas (Count of Provence), 25, 52; *see also* Louis XVIII
Louisiana Territory, 87
Lovett, William, 214
Low Countries
  Industrial Revolution in, 171
  Restoration in, 185, 187, 205
  see also Belgium; Holland
Lübeck, 81, 235
Lucien Leuwen (Stendhal), 224
Luddites (British group), 173
Ludwig I (King of Bavaria), 146
Lunéville, Treaty of (1801), 79, 81
Luther, Martin, 232
Lyons insurrections (French, 1831, 1834), 226

Macaulay, Thomas Babington, 202–3
Mack, General (Baron Karl Mack von Leiberich), 91
Mahmud II (Sultan of Turkey), 145, 150–51
Mainz (ecclesiastical state), 81
Malta, island of, 56, 77, 80, 88, 122
Manin, Daniele, 273
Manufacturers, *see* Bourgeoisie
March Laws (Hungarian, 1848), 269
Marengo, Battle of (1800), 79, 82
Marie, Alexandre, 257
Marie Antoinette (Queen of France), 24, 26, 29, 45
Marie Louise (Empress to Napoleon I), 105
Martignac, Jean Baptiste Viscount de, 219

Marx, Karl
philosophical influences on, 195
on productive forces released by Industrial Revolution, 171
on revolt in France (1848), 277–78
theory of social evolution, 185
Utopian Socialists compared with, 175, 178
"Massacre at Chios" (Delacroix), 199
"Massacre in the Rue Transnonain, The" (Daumier), 226
Masséna, Marshal André, 76
Mauritius, 122
Maximum, Law of the (September, 1793, French), 40, 44
Mazzini, Giuseppe, 191–92, 240–43, 272, 274
Mehemet Ali (Pasha of Egypt), 145, 150–52
Melito, Count André François Miot de, 66–67
Mendelssohn, Felix, 199
Merchants, *see* Bourgeoisie
Methodism (British), 199
Metternich, Prince Klemens von, 192, 272
biography and characteristics of, 126–27
conceit and pompousness, 126
conservatism, 181, 182, 188
on his relationship to Europe, 136
Concert of Europe and
Belgian revolt and, 148
on Congress of Aix-la-Chapelle, 137
and Greek revolt, 143
and Near East crisis, 153
and revolts in 1820–1823, 138–40
at Congress of Vienna, 123, 126
appraisal of his role, 135
final settlement, 131
and Holy Alliance, 134
Polish-Saxon settlement, 128, 129
1848 revolutions and, 253, 267, 269, 273
Louis Philippe and, 150
in Napoleonic era, 113, 114
Hundred Days and, 116–17
and marriage of Napoleon and Marie Louise, 105
repressive policies of (1830's–1840's), 228–39
Talleyrand and, 107
view of Italy, 240
Michelet, Jules, 202
Mill, John Stuart, 185
Mirabeau, Count de (Honoré Gabriel Riqueti), 8, 25
Modena, duchy of, 131

revolt in (1830), 240
Moderates (Italian political group), 242, 243, 273
Moldavia, 94, 95, 143, 145
Molé, Count Louis, 255
Moniteur (French newspaper), 87
Monroe, James, 142
Monroe Doctrine (1823), 142
Morea revolt, 144
Moreau, Gen. Jean Victor, 83
Moscow, capture and retreat from (1812), 111, 112
Moulin, Gen. Jean François, 53
Movement, Party of (French), 223
Mozart, Wolfgang Amadeus, 199
Municipal Ordinance (Prussian, 1808), 230
Murat, Caroline Bonaparte, 76
Murat, Marshal Joachim, 76, 96, 97, 131, 180
Music, romantic, 199

Namier, Sir Louis, 253
Naples in First Coalition war (1793), 37–38
Naples, Kingdom of, 80, 95, 96, 98–100; *see also* Two Sicilies, Kingdom of
Napoleon I (Emperor of the French), 21, 51, 123, 135, 160, 219, 224, 230, 237
biography and characteristics of, 65–69
compulsion to military exploits, 86
crowns himself, 85
lack of religion, 76
order, 73
the Church and, *see* Roman Catholic Church—Napoleon and
coup d'état by, 9, 16, 17, 53–54, 57, 67, 69, 107
as Emperor, 58–59, 63, 82–118, 160
achievement and legacy of, 118–20
Continental System and, 87, 98, 101–2, 104, 105, 110
defeats Prussia and Russia, 91–95
Empire proclaimed, 82–86
final exile of, 118
Grand Empire design of, 95–100
the Hundred Days, 115–18, 131, 133, 180, 217
in Peninsular War, 101–5, 131
Russian campaign of, 93, 109–12, 244, 245
in short war with Austria, 103–4
state of the Empire in 1810 and, 104–7
war with Great Britain and Third

Coalition, 86–91
  war of liberation against, 113–15, 127
  fascination for, in post-Napoleonic generation, 224, 260
  as First Consul, 69–82
    end of Second Coalition and, 79–80
    financial, administrative, and legal reforms made, 70–73
    makes peace with the Church, 23, 76–79, 82, 105, 119, 216
    police-state character of regime, 74–76
    reorganizes Germany, 80–82, 86, 98–99
  during Revolution, 55–59
    defends Convention (1795), 51, 53
    Egyptian campaign, *see* Egypt—expedition into
    Italian campaign, 55, 66
    recaptures Toulon (1793), 44, 65
    in Second Coalition war, 57–59
National, Le (French newspaper), 256
National Assembly (Constituent Assembly, French)
  accomplishments of, 68
  Bastille stormed to protect, 10–13, 18
  Declaration of the Rights of Man by, 14–16, 19; *see also* Declaration of the Rights of Man and the Citizen
  proclaimed, 10, 16
  and widespread violence in France, 13–14
  see also Constitutional monarchy
National Chartist Association (British), 216
National Convention (French), 16, 28
  elections for, 32–34
  purpose of war as viewed by, 60–61
  system of public education reaffirmed under, 72
  see also Jacobins; Terror, Reign of
National Workshops, 178, 257–58
Nationalism
  aroused by Napoleon, 98–100, 135
  early 19th-century, 191–96
  Polish, 98, 99, 154, 239
  Risorgimento as, 239–43, 275
  see also Revolutions—of 1848
Nations, Battle of (1813), 113–14
Navarino, Battle of (1827), 145
Necker, Jacques, 10, 11, 13
Nelson, Adm. Horatio, 56, 88, 89
Nemours, Duke of (Louis Charles d'Orléans), 149, 256
Neo-Guelph movement (Italian), 242, 275

Netherlands, *see* Austrian Netherlands; Holland
New Harmony (community), 177
New Lanark (community), 176–77
Newcomen, Thomas, 162
Ney, Marshal (Duke of Elchingen), 76, 117–18
Nice, 37, 55, 61
Nicholas I (Tsar of Russia)
  accession of, 247
  and Belgian revolt, 148
  declares war on Turkey (1828), 145
  and Eastern Question, 152
  invades Hungary (1849), 272
  reign of, 248–51
  and revolutions of 1848, 252
Nicolson, Sir Harold, 124–25
Noailles, Viscount de (Louis Marie), 14
Nobility, *see* Aristocracy
Northern Union (Russian), 246
Norway, 110, 131
Novalis (Friedrich von Hardenberg), 201
Navara, Battle of (1849), 274, 275
Nuremberg (free city), 81

O'Connell, Daniel, 209
O'Connor, Feargus, 215, 216
October Days (France, 1789), 18, 24, 26
Oldenburg, 235
Orange, Prince of, *see* William I
"Organization of Labor, The" (Blanc), 177, 178, 257
Orléans, Duchess of (Marie Amelia), 255–56
Orléans, Dukes of
  Louis Philippe, *see* Louis Philippe
  Louis Philippe Joseph, 11
Orléans, Louis Philippe Albert d' (Count of Paris), 255, 256
Otto I (King of Greece), 146
Ottoman Empire, 56, 58, 59
  Eastern Question and, 150–51
  Greek revolt against, 141–46, 150, 195, 199, 251
  Holy Alliance and, 134
  Russo-Turkish war, 95, 109, 110
  Serbian revolt against, 195
Owen, Robert, 175–76

Painters, romantic, 197–99
Palermo, revolt in (1848), 252, 253
Palm, Johann Philipp, 93
Palmer, Robert R., 1
Palmerston, third Viscount (Henry John Temple), 148, 149, 151, 152
Pan-Slav Congress (1848), 270

Paoli, Pasquale di, 65
Papal States, 55, 78, 80, 105, 131, 242, 273
  1830 revolt in, 240
  1848 revolution in, 253
Paris, Count of (Louis Philippe Albert d'Orléans), 255, 256
Paris, first Treaty of (1814), 115, 122–23
Paris, Peace of (Treaty of Versailles, 1919), 121, 136
Paris, second Treaty of (1815), 131, 133–35, 137
Paris Commune (1792), 32–34, 40, 49
Paris Peace Conference (1919), 136
Parma, duchy of, 131
  revolt in (1830), 240
Patriots, the (French group), 8
Paul I (Tsar of Russia), 57, 62, 90
  assassination of, 59–60
  isolation of Russia under, 244
  reign of, 243
  in war of Second Coalition, 59
Peasantry, 187
  Austrian, 267–69
  French
    Napoleonic reforms and, 120
    prerevolutionary, 2–3, 5–6
    of revolutionary France, 14
    in Vendée rebellion, 45
    see also Third Estate
  Russian, 244, 246
Peel, Sir Robert, 208, 209, 212
Peninsular War (1808–1813), 101–5, 131
People's Charter (British, 1815), 215
People's Republic of China, 173
Père Goriot, Le (Balzac), 223
Pestel, Col. Paul, 246
Peterloo Massacre (1819), 206–7
Philhellenism, 144
Philosophes, 5, 19, 46, 74
  conservatism and, 183
  influence of, on German intellectuals, 193
  romanticism as reaction to, 196, 199, 201, 202
  Utopian Socialists and, 178, 203
Philosophy, 19th-century German, 192–95
Pichegru, Gen. Charles, 83
Piedmont, see Sardinia, Kingdom of
Pitt, William (Earl of Chatham), 58, 62–63, 79–80
Pitt, William (the Younger), 37, 174
Pius VI (Pope), 22
Pius VII (Pope), 240
  on Holy Alliance, 134
  Napoleon and

Concordat signed, 23, 76–79, 82, 105, 118, 216
  coronation of Napoleon and, 85
  Napoleon moves against, 105, 181–82
Pius IX (Pope), 242, 273–75
Poland, 31, 93, 242
  effects of Treaty of Tilsit on, 95
  1818 constitution of, 245
  fate of, at Congress of Vienna, 123, 125, 127–29, 135
  Frankfurt Parliament and, 266–67
  liberalism in, 190
  nationalism in, 98, 99, 154, 239
  revolt in (1831), 148–50, 250–51
Polignac, Prince of (Auguste Jules Marie), 219
Polish-Saxon crisis, 128–30, 245, 250
Portland, third Duke of (William Henry Cavendish Bentinck), 63
Portugal, 56, 142
  in Peninsular War, 101–2
  in Restoration era, 187, 251
  revolution in (1820), 139, 218
  Treaty of Tilsit and, 95
Prague, revolt in (1848), 269–70
Pressburg, Treaty of (1805), 91
Proletariat, 31, 187
  Austrian, in 1848 revolution, 267, 268
  British, 168–70, 208, 213
    Chartist movement and, 187, 210–16
    effects of 1848 revolutions on, 277–78
  French, 253–59
    1830's–1840's, 224–27
    February Revolution and, 257–59
    July Revolution and, 223
  German, 236
  in Industrial Revolution, 161, 163–70
  Napoleon and, 78
Proudhon, Pierre Joseph, 276
Provence, Count of (Louis Xavier Stanislas, later Louis XVIII), 25, 52
Prussia
  in Concert of Europe, 131, 136
  Belgian revolt and, 148
  Eastern Question and, 152
  southern European revolutions and, 138, 140
  Congress of Vienna and, 127–30
  first Treaty of Paris and, 122
  in Holy Alliance, 134; *see also* Holy Alliance
  in League of Armed Neutrality, 59
  in Napoleonic era, 90, 91, 118, 119
    Prussian defeats (1806–1807), 91–95
    reactions of, to Hundred Days, 117

and reorganization of Germany, 81
Russian campaign and, 110
in war of liberation, 113
in war of Second Coalition, 58
in Restoration era, 230–31, 234–35
1848 revolution in, 252, 253, 260–62, 276
Frankfurt Parliament and, 264–67
and revolutionary France, 30–31
reactions to revolution, 29, 30, 62, 63
in war of First Coalition, 36–38, 50
Public Safety, Committee of (French), 16, 41–42, 46, 48, 49
Pushkin, Alexander, 249
Pyramids, Battle of (1798), 56

Quadruple Alliance, 133–46
British purpose in, 137–38
collapse of, 136–37
fate of conference system of, 136–46
important decisions of Congress of Vienna under, 123–25
as instrument of repression, 134–35
reaffirmed, 133–34
and revolts of 1820–1823, 138–39
Troppau Protocol and, 140
see also Austria; Great Britain; Prussia; Russia

Racine, Jean, 200
Radetzky, Gen. Joseph, 273, 274, 276
Railroads, development of, 163, 227–28, 234
Ranke, Leopold von, 203
Raspail, François, 259
Reaction
in Austria, 270–72
in Great Britain, under Tory rule, 205–10
Metternich's repressive policies as, 228–29
in Russia, 245–49
Thermidorean, 49–50, 55
see also Conservatism
Rebecque, Benjamin Constant de, 189
Red and the Black, The (Stendhal), 224
Reflections on the French Revolution (Burke), 182, 206
Reform Bill (British, 1832), 209–14
Réforme, La (French newspaper), 256
Reforms
British, 210–16
Napoleonic, 70–74, 118–20
by National Assembly, 19–22
Prussian, 230–31
Russian, 244–46

Sardinian, 243
see also Liberalism
Reichstadt, Duke of (François Charles Joseph Bonaparte), 224
Report on the Sanitary Condition of the Labouring Population (Chadwick), 167
Resistance, Party of (French), 223
Restoration, 107, 122, 180–204
Bourbon, 115, 181–82, 184, 218–19
conservatism in, 180–96
early 19th-century liberalism and, 188–91
early 19th-century nationalism and, 191–96
opposition to Restoration and, 185–88
romanticism in, 196–204
see also Restoration under specific countries
Revolutions (and revolts)
American, 1, 2, 25
Decembrist revolt (1825), 243–48
of 1830
in Italy, 143, 148–50, 240
July Revolution, 147, 209, 220–23, 227, 232, 240, 259
Polish, 148–50, 250–51
in Saxony, 232, 233
of 1848, 252–78
consequences of, 276–78
February Revolution, 170, 178, 223, 227, 228, 252–60, 264
in German states, *see Deutscher Bund*—1848 revolutions in
in Italy, 218, 240, 252, 253, 259, 272–76
German artisan revolt (1844), 173
Glorious Revolution, 29
Lyons insurrections (1831, 1834), 226
in Portugal (1820), 139, 218
in Serbia (1804), 195
Silesian weavers' riot (1844), 235–36
in southern Europe (1820–1823), 138–43, 218, 240
13 Vendémiaire insurrection (1795), 51
of Tipu Sahib, 56
Vendée (1793), 38–41, 44, 45, 49
see also French Revolution
Rewbell, Jean François, 53
Rheinische Merkur, Der (German newspaper), 231
Rhineland, 37, 43, 79–81, 130
industrialization of, 43, 228, 233
in Polish-Saxon settlement, 129
Ricardo, David, 213

Richelieu, Duke of (Louis Armand du Plessis), 218
Right, the, origin of term, 17
Risorgimento, 239–43, 275
Robespierre, Maximilien, 42, 46–50, 65
Robespierrists (French political group), 49
Rolling (or puddling) process, developed, 162–63
Romagna, 55, 78
Roman Catholic Church
  in Austrian Netherlands, 61
  Directory and, 58
  in Italy, 1848 revolutions and, 274
  Napoleon and
    Concordat signed, 23, 76–79, 82, 105, 119, 216
    in Grand Empire, 97
    moves against Pius VII, 105, 181–82
    in Spain, 103
  National Assembly and, 19, 21–23, 25
  in Restoration era, 115, 181–82, 184, 218–19
Roman Republic, 58, 274–75
Romania (formerly Moldavia and Walachia), 78, 94, 95, 143, 145
Romanticism, 196–204
Rossi, Count Pellegrino, 274
Rousseau, Jean Jacques, 5, 15, 185, 200, 241, 268
Roux, Jacques, 39–40
Russia, 31, 62, 63, 80
  in Concert of Europe, 136
    Belgian revolt and, 148, 149
    and Congress of Aix-la-Chapelle, 137
    Eastern Question and, 150–53
    Greek revolt and, 142, 143, 145, 146
    and southern European revolutions, 138–40
  Congress of Vienna and, 125, 128, 129
  Finland and, 131
  first Treaty of Paris and, 122–23
  in Holy Alliance, 134; *see also* Holy Alliance
  in Napoleonic era
    reactions to Hundred Days, 117
    Russian campaign, 93, 109–13, 244, 245
    Russian defeats (1806–1807), 91–95
    in Second Coalition, 56–59
    in Third Coalition, 89
    and war of 1809, 103
    in war of liberation, 113
  in Restoration era, 187, 243–51
    Decembrist Revolt (1825), 243–48
    1848 revolutions and, 252
    liberalism in, 188

Nicholas I and, 248–51
  reaction, 245–49
  romanticism in, 196
Russo-Turkish war (1806), 95, 109, 110

Saar Valley, 133
Sacrilege, Law of (French, 1825), 218–19
Sadler, Michael, 214
Saint Helena, Napoleon exiled in, 118
Saint Lucia, 122
Saint-Simon, Henri de, 175–78
Salzburg (ecclesiastical state), 56, 81, 131
Sand, Karl, 232
Sardinia, Kingdom of (Piedmont), 58, 90, 131, 243
  1820 revolution in, 140, 240
  1848 revolution in, 253, 254, 272–76
  in Restoration era, 242, 243
  Vienna settlement and, 133
  in war of First Coalition, 37, 38
Savoy, 55, 58, 90, 133
  first Treaty of Paris and, 122
  France annexes, 36, 61
Saxony, Kingdom of, 123, 129, 232, 233
Scharnhorst, Gerhard von, 230
Schönbrunn, Treaty of (1809), 104
Schubert, Franz, 199
Schumann, Robert, 199
Schwarzenberg, Prince Felix zu, 271, 272
Schwarzenberg, Prince Karl Philipp zu, 114
Scientific (professional) history, 203
Scotch Symphony (Mendelssohn), 199
Scott, Sir Walter, 198, 201
Scribe, Eugène, 148
Sébastiani, Col. Horace, 87
Second Coalition (1799–1802), 56–60, 79–80, 90
Second Estate, 5, 9; *see also* Aristocracy—French
Second Republic (1848–1871, French), 257, 274
Second Treaty of Paris (1815), 131–35
September Laws (French, 1835), 227
September Massacres (1792), 33, 34, 37, 62
Serbia, revolt in (1804), 195
Seven Years' War (1756–1763), 29
Shakespeare, William, 198
Shelley, Percy Bysshe, 114, 202
Short war (Franco-Austrian, 1809), 103–4
Sicily, kingdom of, 92, 99; *see also* Two Sicilies, Kingdom of
Sieyès, Emmanuel Joseph Abbé, 8
  in Consulate, 69

in 18 Brumaire coup, 53, 54, 57
as representative of Third Estate, 8–9
Silesia, weavers' riot in (1844), 235–36
Six Acts (British, 1819), 207
Smelting system, 162
Smith, Adam, 174, 213
Social classes, *see* Aristocracy; Artisans; Bourgeoisie; Peasantry; Proletariat
Social Contract (Rousseau), 5
Socialism
of Babeuf, 52
emergence of, 175–79
influence of French Revolution on, 64
Society for Promoting Constitutional Information (British), 62
Society for the Rights of Man. (French), 187
Society of Friends of the Constitution (French), 26; *see also* Jacobins
Sorrows of Young Werther, The (Goethe), 201
Spain, 79, 80
after Congress of Vienna, 131
in Napoleonic era
Peninsular War in, 101–5, 131
in Third Coalition, 88
population growth in (18th century), 156
in Restoration era, 187, 188, 190, 251
revolutions in (1820), 138–43, 218
in war of First Coalition, 37, 50
Speranski, Count Mikhail, 245
Spinning jenny, invented, 161
Stalin, Joseph, 54
Steam engine, invented, 162
Stein, Baron Heinrich vom und zum, 230, 231
Stendhal (Henri Beyle), 224
Stephenson, George, 163
Straits Convention (1841), 152
Students
Austrian, 268–70
Burschenschaften, 231–32
in 1830 Belgian revolt, 148
in opposition to Restoration, 187–88
in *Risorgimento*, 241
Sturm und Drang ("storm and stress," literary movement), 200
Suez Isthmus, 56
Supreme Being, Cult of, 46–47
Suvorov, General, 59
Sweden, 59, 110, 113, 131
Swedish Pomerania, 129
Switzerland, 59, 130, 242
as Helvetic Republic, 58, 79, 80, 86
Syria, 57, 150–52

Talleyrand, Charles Maurice de (Prince of Benevento), 56, 81
and Belgian revolt, 148
at Congress of Vienna, 127–29
Polish-Saxon settlement and, 128–29
and fall of Napoleon, 114
and Restoration, 115
Taxation, *see* Economy
Ten Hours Act (British, 1847), 213, 214
Tennis Court Oath (1789), 10
Terror, Reign of (1793–1794), 9, 16, 17, 41–51, 66
Dantonists and Hébertists executed in, 49
as dictatorship, 41–42
European reactions to, 29
messianic character of, 46
national emergencies as basis for success of, 47
number of death sentences carried out in, 45
prelude to, 36–41
September Massacres, 33, 34, 37, 62
universal conscription plan under, 42–43
White Terror compared with, 217
Thermidorean reaction (1795), 49–50, 55
Thiers, Adolphe, 152, 223, 255
Third Coalition (1804–1805), 86–91
Third Estate, 3
composition and size of, 5–6
representatives of, 7–9
grievances of, 7
proclaims itself National Assembly, 10; *see also* National Assembly
Thistlewood, Arthur, 207–8
Tilsit, Treaty of (1807), 91–95, 97, 103, 109
Tipu Sahib, 56
Tobago, 122
Tocqueville, Alexis de, 254–55
Tory rule in Great Britain, 205–10
Toulon (French port), recaptured (1793), 44, 65
Toussaint L'Ouverture, Pierre Dominique, 87
Trade, *see* Economy
Trafalgar, Battle of (1805), 89, 91
Transylvania, 269
Trinidad, 88, 122
Troppau, Congress of (1820), 140, 141
Troppau Protocol (1820), 140–42
Turgenev, Ivan, 249
Turkey, *see* Ottoman Empire
Turner, Joseph Mallord William, 197–98
Tuscany, duchy of, 131, 240

Tuscany, duchy of *(continued)*
  1848 revolution in, 253, 273
Two Acts (British, 1795–1796), 62–63
Two Sicilies, Kingdom of, 131, 240
  1820 revolution in, 138–40
  1848 revolution in, 252, 253, 273
Tyrol, 131

Ulm, Battle of (1805), 89, 91
Ultraroyalists (French political group), 115, 217, 218
Union of Soviet Socialist Republics (U.S.S.R.), 173
United States, 142, 188
  acquires Louisiana Territory, 87
Unkiar-Skelessi, Treaty of (1833), 151, 152
Utrecht, Peace of (1713), 121
Utopian Socialism, 175–76, 178–79, 203
Uvarov, S. S., 248

Valmy, Battle of (1792), 36
Varlet, 39–40
Vendée revolt (1793), 38–41, 44, 45, 49
Venetia, 55
  1848 revolution in, 260, 273, 274
  Risorgimento in, 240, 242
  settlement of 1815 and, 131, 135, 239
  in war of Second Coalition, 79
Verona, Congress of (1822), 141–42
Versailles, Treaty of (Peace of Paris, 1919), 121, 136
Victor Emmanuel I (King of Sardinia), 140, 240
Victor Emmanuel II (King of Sardinia), 275–76
Victoria (Queen of England), 149, 252
Vienna, revolt in (1848), 269–71, 278
Vienna, Congress of, *see* Congress of Vienna
Villèle, Count of, 218, 219
Villeneuve, Adm. Pierre, 88–89

Voltaire, 5, 184, 201

Wagram, Battle of (1809), 76, 104
Walachia, 94, 95, 145
Warsaw, duchy of, 95, 99, 104, 109, 123, 129
Warville, Jacques Pierre Brissot de, 28
Water frame, invented, 161
Waterloo, Battle of (1815), 116, 133
Watt, James, 162
Wealth of Nations (Smith), 174
Weavers (Hauptmann), 173
Wellington, first Duke of (Sir Arthur Wellesley), 102, 114
  and Belgian revolt, 148
  Congress of Verona and, 127, 141–42
  and Greek revolt, 145
  as prime minister, 209, 210
  at Waterloo, 117–18
Westphalia, kingdom of, 95, 97, 129
Westphalia, Peace of (1648), 121, 130
What Is the Third Estate? (Sieyès), 8
White Terror (1815), 217–18
William I (King of the Netherlands, earlier Prince of Orange), 114, 131
  and Belgian revolt, 146, 148, 149
William IV (King of England), 209, 210
Wilson, Woodrow, 242
Windischgrätz, Gen. Alfred, 270–71
Wordsworth, William, 28, 202
Working class, *see* Proletariat
Württemberg, 81, 82, 91, 92, 229

York, Duke of (Frederick Augustus), 59
Young Europe movement, 241–42
Young Ireland, 188
Young Italy, 188, 241
Young Poland, 188
Ypsilanti, Prince Alexander, 143

Zollverein (customs union), 234–36